# GLOBAL CITIZENSHIP

S42917

## University Centre Barnsley

*University of*
**HUDDERSFIELD**

Telephone: 01226 644281

**University**Centre
Barnsley

# GLOBAL CITIZENSHIP

## A Critical Reader

Edited by

Nigel Dower & John Williams

EDINBURGH UNIVERSITY PRESS

Edinburgh University Press Ltd
22 George Square, Edinburgh

Typeset in Sabon by
Hewer Text Ltd, Edinburgh, and
printed and bound in Great Britain by
MPG Books Ltd, Bodmin, Cornwall

A CIP Record for this book is
available from the British Library

ISBN 0 7486 1546 6 (hardback)
ISBN 0 7486 1547 4 (paperback)

# CONTENTS

# FOREWORD

The ethical and political norms and principles that we constantly use and discuss are marked by the world of states in which they arose. Ethical thought was designed for personal and face-to-face contexts; discussions of justice and democracy were designed for use within states. States were indeed seen as composing a system of states; but since each was sovereign they lacked common institutions and shared ways of reaching decisions. There was therefore no context for thinking about global justice, about global democracy or about global citizenship.

Normative questions about activities whose effects cross state borders had to be dealt with by supplementing state-centred views of justice and democracy. They were variously seen as questions for the foreign policy of individual states, or as covered by a rather limited body of accepted international (more accurately *inter-statal*) law, or as matters to be dealt with by explicit inter-governmental agreements and treaties. Despite the resonant cosmopolitan rhetoric of earlier periods, citizenship in a world of states was seen simply as citizenship in one or another state. The idea of global citizenship was viewed by many as incoherent, and even as a questionable aspiration because it could be institutionally realised only in a world state that centralised excessive power, and might lack all democratic legitimation.

These certainties have been shaken in recent decades. What is new is not the thought that some ethical and political norms may be relevant for all people at all times and places. Cosmopolitan ideals have been put forward since antiquity. In the last fifty years the aspirations of the human rights movement have been resolutely cosmopolitan: human rights are always seen as universal, as owed to all people at all times. However the *Universal Declaration of Human Rights* of

1948 proclaims these rights and then assigns the major responsibility for securing them to states. For this reason many discussions about the obligations that are need to make a reality of human rights remain largely statist. The *Declaration's* limited account of obligations that go beyond borders has focussed mainly on state obligations in dealing with aliens and refugees, and state obligations to intervene to halt extreme violations of rights in other states. Other state obligations have been created by treaty and agreement between states, and typically deal with matters such as arms control and the prevention of terrorism, the regulation of trade and environmental protection.

Global citizenship has no place in a purely statist view of justice and democracy, where each of us is seen as a citizen only of his or her 'own' state. But the countless institutional changes that we group under the label 'globalisation' may have altered the very context of political action, and created the space for something that we could well call 'global citizenship'. If this is the case, the *moral cosmopolitanism* that has been articulated and praised since antiquity may perhaps from now on be increasingly realised through forms of *institutional cosmopolitanism*, in which actions whose effects go beyond borders will be judged in a new and more demanding light.

The excitement of this book is that there is no agreement yet about the direction in which we are heading. Some contributors think of global citizenship as a new term for the citizenship of those states that act to foster the universal norms of the human rights movement. Others think that new structures may allow, or require, individuals to see themselves not only as citizens of their 'own' state, but as global citizens whose obligations stretch to all fellow human beings.

The idea of individuals as global citizens poses many challenges. Do all (or perhaps only some) individuals have obligations to support others, including the poorest of the poor, beyond borders and to secure human rights for all? What is the basis of these massive obligations? Is global democracy required if we are to have global citizens with global obligations? And how could we move towards global democracy? Is the United Nations a prototype for or an obstacle to global democracy? Do current international economic institutions provide a prototype or an obstacle to international economic justice? Or is global citizenship better thought of as the moral aspiration of a few, anchored mainly in the thinking of a range of border-crossing institutions including churches, international non-governmental organisations and (more controversially) some transnational corporations?

There is still no settled answer to these and many other questions about global citizenship. But there is already much to be learnt. The conclusions we reach – whatever they may be – are unlikely to leave our views about ethics or about politics unchanged.

Onora O'Neill
Newnham College, Cambridge
July 2001

# PREFACE

The deliberate crashing of commercial airliners into the World Trade Center and the Pentagon on 11 September 2001 took place after the chapters of this reader had been finalised. Thus none directly address what may yet prove to be world-changing events. Neither do they consider the aftermath. This saw global revulsion and, occasionally, celebration; the assembling of a broad-based, diplomatic coalition of states agreeing to support, or at least not hinder, efforts to tackle global terrorism; and ultimately a military assault upon Afghanistan, charged with harbouring the Al-Qaida network believed to be responsible for the attacks.

That on 11 September the world changed is almost universally accepted. How it has changed and will change is less clear. What impact does it have for the idea and ideals of global citizenship? Are they rendered irrelevant as countries and regions at best retreat into preoccupations with security, reduce their commitment to tackle global problems or at worst settle into the 'posture of war' and increasing global conflict? Or do they become even more important, as we seek to find global solutions to the worldwide threat of terrorism, collectively tackle the root causes of terrorism and cooperate to promote and strengthen peace between people of good will from all faiths and nations? The 'events' of 11 September symbolise and, in the days after, operationalise, a sense of common humanity, the great majority of which was touched by what occurred, even if we may not have had any direct connection to the individuals involved. Most of us felt that we were global citizens for perhaps just a few moments or days as a result of what took place in New York and Washington. Though whether that feeling grows or recedes depends on many factors.

We ask the above questions as matters for *decision* rather than as matters of *prediction*. No doubt we are all on a sliding scale running from optimism to pessimism about what we think will happen but the key premise of this reader is: we are not *passive observers* of world events but potentially *agents of change*. How events in the world will unfold depends on us. What values do we promote, in attitude, advocacy and commitment? Nothing has changed the fundamental values that should be accepted. That peace, justice, care for the environment and respect for human rights are core global values is not changed by any event, however tragic. What is to be done to promote these, of course, has changed.

Almost all will support increased security against all manner of terrorist attack, vigorous moves to disable terrorist networks (for example, by freezing accounts), the robust pursuit of terrorists to be brought to international justice. All these measures nevertheless mean more effort and resources put into pursuing them and hence, in all likelihood, less attention to other global agendas. Some will see the pursuit of war, as currently in Afghanistan, as the right way from a global point of view to combat terrorism, whilst others will think this is wrong or counter-productive in various ways. Some will favour a far-reaching assessment of the wider root causes such as Middle East policies, global inequality, perceived Western dominance and hegemony in the world, the perversion of the Islamic faith or the sheer militarisation of the world – issues which seem irrelevant or inappropriate to others.

Anyone interested in global citizenship will see these issues as central ones to be addressed in some way or another within a global perspective rather than from the perspective of what is good for some countries. It must not be assumed that all global citizens will agree on the right way forward. Some may approve of the current war, for instance, while others oppose it. What all global citizens will agree is that this is not a matter to be left to professional politicians or the technically expert. We need to engage in public debate and deliberation. Global responsibility requires nothing less. How we seek to find global responses to the issue of terrorism is a microcosm of how we seek to find responses to other global issues, such as peace, environmental degradation, poverty, human rights and the implications of technological and economic transformation.

Global citizenship is, as many of the chapters in the reader bring out, involved in an important aspect of globalisation, namely the development of global civil society. How will this be affected? The so-called 'anti-globalisation' movement (supported by many global citizens, though not all), which is really a manifestation of one form of globalisation in response to the dominant free-market capitalist aspects of globalisation, may suffer set-backs, in so far as it is perceived, erroneously, as implicitly supporting Bin Laden because of partial similarities in what they are opposed to. But in the long run it may be strengthened in so far as people will see that the current working of the international economic system may well be part of our global problematique. More generally there is no reason to suppose that the engagement of individuals through non-governmental organisations, the Internet or other networks will diminish and every reason to think they will increase.

Indeed the best hope for the world if it is to learn from such appalling tragedy and move forward and not compound evil with evil is precisely the involvement of concerned individuals in dialogue, including global dialogue. The agenda and global perspective of this reader is therefore more important than ever.

Nigel Dower
John Williams
July 2001

# NOTES ON THE CONTRIBUTORS

Sabina Alkire completed her PhD in 1999 in the field of development ethics, where her focus has been on the work of John Finnis and the 'capabilities' approach of Amartya Sen and Martha Nussbaum. To date she has worked as a consultant with the Poverty Program of the World Bank and now works for the Commission on Human Security.

Robin Attfield is Professor of Philosophy at Cardiff University, where he has taught since 1968. He has also taught in Nigeria and Kenya. His books include *The Ethics of Environmental Concern* (1983) and *The Ethics of the Global Environment* (1999).

Roland Axtmann is Reader in the Department of Politics and International Relations at the University of Aberdeen and teaches political theory and political sociology. He has published widely on state formation in Europe and on globalisation, and recently edited *Globalisation and Europe* (1998).

Chris Blackmore is a lecturer in Environment and Development in the UK Open University's (OU) Systems Discipline where she works on developing and presenting open learning courses in Environmental Decision Making and Systems. She previously managed the OU's community-based Farm Interpretation Project and has focused on education and learning systems for sustainable development since around 1990, from an OU base but with other agencies such as UNED-UK. Chris has also worked in rural development and teaching in Nigeria, Lesotho, Sierra Leone and the UK.

Nigel Dower is Senior Lecturer in Philosophy at the University of Aberdeen and Director of the Centre for Philosophy, Technology & Society. He has also taught in Zimbabwe and the USA. His research interests focus on the ethics of international relations, development and the environment. Apart from numerous articles and chapters, he has written *World Poverty – Challenge and Response* (1983) and *World Ethics – the New Agenda* (1998), and edited *Ethics and Environmental Responsibility* (1989). He is vice-president of the International Development Ethics Association.

Richard Falk retired from Princeton in 2001 after being on its faculty for forty years, being the Albert G. Millbank Professor of International Law and Practice since 1965. His most recent books are *Human Rights Horizons* (2000) and *Religion and Humane Global Governance* (2001).

Andreas Follesdal is Professor at the Department of Philosophy and at the Institute of Human Rights, University of Oslo, and Research Professor at ARENA – Advanced Research on the Europeanisation of the Nation-State – at the Research Council of Norway. Andreas Follesdal publishes in the field of political philosophy, with a focus on issues of international political theory as they arise in the wake of changes in Europe.

David Held is Graham Wallas Professor of Political Science at the London School of Economics. Among his recent books are (as co-author) *Global Transformations: Politics, Economics and Culture* (1999) and (as co-editor) *The Global Transformations Reader* (2000). He is currently working on a book on cosmopolitanism.

Kimberly Hutchings is Senior Lecturer in political theory at the Department of Politics, Edinburgh University. Her interests include the philosophies of Kant and Hegel, international and feminist ethics. She is the author of *Kant, Critique and Politics* (1996); *International Political Theory* (1999) and co-editor (with Roland Dannreuther) of *Cosmopolitan Citizenship* (1999). Her book *Hegel and Feminist Philosophy* is forthcoming in 2002.

Mark Imber is a senior lecturer in International Relations at the University of St Andrews. His research and publications range over the UN system, US–UN relations and environmental politics.

Hans Küng is a theologian who has held various positions including Professor of Dogmatic and Ecumenical Theology at the Faculty of Catholic Theology (1963–80) and Director of the Institute for Ecumenical Research at the University of Tübingen. In 1996 he became President of the Foundation for a Global Ethic (*Weltethos*). Küng is co-editor of several journals and has written many books, including *On Being a Christian* (1977) and *Global*

*Responsibility* (1991). He co-edited *A Global Ethic – The Declaration of the Parliament of the World's Religions* (1993).

David Miller is a fellow of Nuffield College, Oxford, where his principal research interests are theories of justice and equality; multiculturalism and justice; nationality, citizenship and deliberative justice; and responsibilities between and within nations. He has published very widely on issues of nationality, citizenship and justice including two recent books *Citizenship and National Identity* (2000) and *On Nationality* (1997).

David Newlands is Senior Lecturer in Economics at the University of Aberdeen. He has also taught at universities in Poland and Australia. His research interests and publications relate to economic globalisation and the effects of the global economy on Third World countries, and on regional and urban economics in Scotland.

Valeria Ottonelli is a lecturer in Philosophy in the University of Genova, Italy. She graduated in Philosophy in Genova and got her PhD in Milan in General Theory of Law. She has written a book on F. A. Hayek and published various articles on libertarianism, procedural justice and theories of social justice.

John Smyth is Emeritus Professor of Biology at the University of Paisley and an Honorary Professor at the University of Stirling. He was President of the Scottish Environmental Education Council and chaired the Secretary of State for Scotland's Working Group on Environmental Education 1991–3. He has been active with IUCN and UNESCO.

Sytse Strijbos received training in technical physics and philosophy. He teaches in Amsterdam in the Philosophy Faculty of the Vrije Universiteit and is also associated with the Centre for Faith and Science at Potchefstroom University for Christian Higher Education in South Africa. His publications and research cover a range of issues in the philosophy of technology and culture.

Christien van den Anker is Senior Lecturer in Global Ethics in the Centre for Global Ethics at the University of Birmingham. She publishes on theories of global justice and their relevance to contemporary issues of global politics.

John Williams, Lecturer in International Relations in the Department of Politics at the University of Durham, was previously Lecturer in the Department of Politics and International Relations at the University of Aberdeen. His research interests are concentrated in normative international political theory, where he has written extensively on legitimacy in international relations, the ethics of territorial borders, ethics and the UN Security Council's response to Yugoslavia's collapse and the 'English School' of international relations theory.

# GLOSSARY

The purpose of this glossary is not to provide dictionary definitions, but brief accounts of what some of the key words and phrases refer to and how they relate to the issues in this reader.

*Citizenship*: membership, determined by formal factors such as place of birth, parentage or act of naturalisation, of a political community (generally a nation-state) by virtue of which one has legally defined rights (including political rights not necessarily accorded to other residents) and duties, and moral responsibilities to participate in the public life of one's political community. In so far as the idea of global citizenship builds on the back of citizenship itself, the question is: what element or elements above are the important ones?

*Communitarianism*: a position in social and political philosophy popular in the late twentieth century according to which moral, social and political values are constituted by the social relations within an established society or community with a shared tradition. Whilst it is primarily a response to liberalism, it is also often seen as a contrast to cosmopolitanism, on the grounds that the relevant conditions of society do not exist on a global scale for us to talk meaningfully of a global morality. Others may argue that global society/community does indeed exist albeit in embryonic form.

*Cosmopolitan/global democracy*: a set of political arrangements whereby individuals can participate through appropriate institutions in making decisions about global affairs which significantly affect them, and corporate actors acting beyond the control of nation-states are made accountable to individuals whose lives they affect. Advocates stress that there is this 'democratic deficit' to be made up, that there are already institutions in place through which we can act as democratic citizens and that we ought to strengthen and formalise them; but critics stress the impracticality and/or undesirability of such developments.

*Cosmopolitanism*: an ethical theory according to which all human beings belong to one moral realm or domain and in principle have obligations towards one another across that domain. Although some still note the etymological meaning of cosmopolitanism as being the idea that we are citizens (polites) of the universe/world (cosmos), it is generally taken to be a robust form of a global ethic. For global citizens and others interested in international relations, it provides a critical framework for assessing the foreign policy of states and is in contrast to internationalism which stresses the norms of respecting sovereignty and observing established international law, and sceptical realism which questions the relevance of ethics to international relations.

*Environmentalism*: active engagement in protecting the environment. Much of the concern of global citizenship centres on this. Two kinds of approach underlie it. Anthropocentrism: the natural world or the environment and non-human life do not have intrinsic value independent of us and are there for human beings to use. (Such activists reject the common exploitative approach, however, since there are good reasons to protect nature for future humans and/or to appreciate nature now for aesthetic reasons.) Biocentrism: the natural world or the environment is not simply there for humans to use, non-human life has an intrinsic value independent of human interests, and therefore humans ought to respect nature. (Advocacy of animal welfare occupies a halfway house between anthropocentrism and biocentrism.)

*Ethic*: a set of norms (or single norm) answering the question 'how ought one to act?' which guides the decisions of an individual or social group whose ethic it is, plus (generally, though not always) lying behind such a set of norms an ethical theory, story or worldview which both justifies the norms and gives meaning to them. An ethic may take many forms – an ethic based on the primacy of care, Utilitarianism, Kantianism and so on. The ethic of a social group is generally expressed in or embedded in publicly shared rules and practices. A global ethic either refers to the global norms accepted by an individual or group, or it refers to values which are shared by people throughout the world and expressed in public practices, declarations and the like.

*Ethics*: sustained and systematic reflection on the nature and justification of an ethic or morality. Such reflection, generally conducted by philosophers and other academic theorists, takes further the more informal reflections anyone can have about their moral values and principles. In addition to understanding the nature of morality (for example, are moral judgements objective or subjective?) and answering the question 'why do I have the values I have?' (often by comparing alternative views), ethics deals with particular ethical issues and problems (for example, punishment; abortion) and in this respect is sometimes called 'applied ethics'. Global ethics is enquiry into the nature and justification of ethical norms as they apply globally and into issues which are global in character (such as the environment, immigration, poverty). Many of the chapters in this book are in part exercises in global ethics.

*Global civil society*: the sense of civil society presupposed here is that of the matrix of social relationships and organisations in a society, other than political institutions and economic institutions involving commerce, through which shared or public goods are pursued (schools, churches, charities, neighbourhood watch groups). At the global level, the existence of NGOs and networks of communications (for example, through the Internet) constitute instances of civil society at the global level.

*Global economy*: the matrix of economic relationships in the world today in which extensive economic activity is conducted across national borders in the form of investment and trading in goods and services, in which much of this activity is conducted by very large transnational companies, and in which it is assumed that the norms governing economic transactions are those of the liberal free market.

*Global environment*: the environment seen as coextensive with the planet in which the activities of human beings anywhere on the planet are seen as having significant cumulative impacts on the general state of the planet's ecosystems. Whilst many impacts on environments were in the past (and continue to be in the present) primarily local, it was problems on a global scale (resource depletion, pollution, global warming, habitat and species destruction) which came to define the 'environmental crisis' in the last three decades of the twentieth century. Since global problems require coordinated global responses, the need to accept a global dimension to responsibility became dominant. For many concerned individuals it is this recognition that is central to their seeing themselves as citizens of the world.

*Global governance*: the patterns of decision-making and the institutions which facilitate them whereby human beings order their public affairs at a global level, or cooperate in respect to common global problems (such as the maintenance of peace, environmental challenges, alleviating world poverty). Governance is distinct from government (which is reliant on regulation by coercion) which is the most conspicuous form of governance. There are many forms of global governance, in some of which global citizenship has a significant role to play.

*Globalisation*: the economic, political and cultural process whereby individuals and corporate bodies increasingly perform actions which have impacts across/throughout the world, and perceive themselves as having identities, concerns and impacts which are global. The process has been going on over centuries but it was only in the 1990s that the phenomenon of globalisation came to dominate public consciousness. Though the development of the global economy and especially the role of large financial and business corporations has been the main focus of attention, the process of cultural globalisation and the development of networks of communication is also significant, especially to the development of global citizenship identities.

*Human rights*: rights held by all human beings in virtue of their common humanity: they may be thought of as fundamental moral rights or as legal rights established by international law – either way they are contrasted with legal and moral rights which exist by virtue of a particular legal system or the conventions of a particular society. If global citizenship is in part constituted by the possession of rights, the rights in question are human rights.

*Institutions*: organisations or associations which are set up or maintained for a particular purpose or set of purposes – they may be economic, political, social, religious and so on. Global citizenship is generally said to involve an institutional element, but just what the institutions are that are involved is a matter of dispute. (A second sense of 'institution' relevant to global citizenship is that of an established rule or practice; in this sense morality is itself an institution and such institutions are relevant to global citizenship.)

*International society*: the society of nation-states, which as a society is governed by moral norms such as respect for sovereignty and rules against aggression. Such a conception of international relations (often referred to as internationalism or the internationalist tradition) is contrasted to both realism (which is sceptical about the relevance of ethical norms in international relations), and cosmopolitanism (which favours a more extensive international ethic). If states can be viewed as citizens of the society of states, then international citizenship may be seen as one form of global citizenship.

*Justice*: that domain of morality which is concerned with giving each person his or her due. Theories of justice differ considerably on how to interpret this, some stressing liberty, some equality and some the respect for rights. In practice, most thinkers who accept that justice applies globally (though not all would accept it should apply globally) see the requirement of global justice as including measures to protect human rights and oppose their violation, measures to ensure the liberty of all to lead the life of their choosing, and measures to (re)distribute wealth and resources so as to enable the very poor to escape from their poverty. The positions of global citizens are often expressed in terms of global justice.

*Kantianism*: the ethical approach, based on the philosophy of Immanuel Kant, which founds morality on respect for all human beings as people; respect for persons is based on the fact that human beings are rational agents. Kant was a self-confessed cosmopolitan who was clear that morally human beings all belong to one moral realm which he called the 'kingdom of ends'. Kantianism, though similar to Utilitarianism in being a global ethic, stands in sharp contrast to it in stressing that moral duty is not based on (anticipated) best consequences but on the principle of universalisability: 'so act that you will the maxim of your action to be universal law'.

*Libertarianism*: a social and political philosophy according to which the basic value which morality should defend is liberty – individuals should allow one another as much liberty as possible and the state should not interfere in people's lives beyond what is minimally necessary to maintain liberty and public order. An important dimension of liberty is economic liberty. Thus libertarianism underpins the free market including the global free market. What makes it controversial is its denial of the importance of other values such as the need for redistribution in favour of those who are least well off. Many global citizens see themselves opposed to the global ethic implicit in libertarianism and expressed in the processes of economic globalisation.

*NGO*: a non-governmental organisation, in the present context, is an organisation made up of individuals working for a global goal (like combating poverty, saving the whale, resisting the death penalty) and supported largely by voluntary contributions of money and time from individuals. Although in some contexts any organisation including a local business or a large transnational company or bank would count as an NGO, in the present context NGOs are contrasted to both economic actors and governments, and include institutions like Amnesty International, Greenpeace and Oxfam as well as bodies like churches or educational establishments. International NGOs are called INGOs. Working in or supporting NGOs is one of the most effective ways in which individuals concerned about the world can express their concerns. Active global citizenship finds much of its practical expression in this area.

*Patriotism*: an attitude of loyalty on the part of a citizen towards his or her own country. Since global citizenship can be seen as an attitude of loyalty towards the world as a whole or towards all of humanity, these two attitudes may seem to be in conflict and sometimes are. But there is no reason why they have to be. Patriotism (as contrasted to a narrow-minded nationalism) may well be a value which can be supported from a universal point of view; and multiple loyalties and identities are possible so long as none claims exclusivity. A global citizen need not be unpatriotic though his or her patriotism will have to be a critical patriotism.

*Peace*: the absence of war or violent conflict in the relations of individuals and groups with one another. A community which fully enjoys peace has to have this relationship with all the groups it interacts with at the time and into the foreseeable future. Peace is an important value because it is the prerequisite for the meaningful performance of most other human activities. Peace can also be defined less negatively as the presence of harmonious relationship (shalom). Concern for peace and disarmament was the area in which global citizenship first manifested itself early on in the twentieth century.

*Realism*: A theory of international relations that stresses the difficult and dangerous nature of politics amongst sovereign states where power and security are the prime goals of all states. Realists usually emphasise that this condition is caused or exacerbated by the absence of any effective world government able to provide for and protect states, thus requiring them to safeguard their own interests by their own efforts, or face being conquered or defeated by others. Realists are thus often sceptical about the possibility and/ or the applicability of ethical principles and ideas, arguing that the need for power and security overrides such restraints or limitations on policy. Indeed, some Realists suggest attempting to act ethically in international politics is foolhardy as it will be exploited by others not so constrained and who cannot be coerced into abiding by ethical principles by a world government. Realism thus stresses states as by far the most significant actors in international politics, seeing individuals, NGOs, corporations and international organisations as playing a far less important part in shaping the world in which we live.

*Relativism*: the view that moral values vary from culture to culture. As a robust thesis, it challenges the thesis of global ethics that there are universal values or that there is one global domain of moral values (and hence challenges the normal ethical assumption lying behind global citizenship); as a weaker thesis, it serves as a reminder that a global ethic must recognise the legitimate variations in the values of different societies.

*Responsibility*: the ethical norm, generally accepted and advocated by global citizens, according to which individuals have duties to further human well-being and combat what impedes it, such as injustices; these duties go beyond the duties of ordinary morality in day-to-day interactions. (Accepting responsibility is this sense does not entail accepting that one is responsible for – that is, part of the cause of – the evils and problems in the world, though this is often also accepted.)

*Rights*: a claim that an agent can make (or that can be made by an agent on behalf of some being who is not an agent) to some benefit such as liberty, privacy, security, food or medical care, corresponding to which agents – either specific agents or agents in general – have duties to respect, protect, promote or provide. A right may be a moral right (by virtue of a moral practice or theory) or a legal right (by virtue of a legal system, national or international). Rights are important to citizenship and, in so far as global citizenship is analogous, global citizenship.

*United Nations*: the international organisation set up in 1945 after the Second World War with the primary objective of providing international security but with other aims such as economic advancement for all countries and the protection of human rights. All countries are members of the United Nations (currently about 190). It is important to many global citizens as it is seen as the embodiment – albeit imperfect – of global ideals of peace, justice and well-being for all, and as a symbol of a perspective lying beyond that of particular countries and nation-states. But for others it remains primarily an inter-state organisation which mediates between the interests of competing states.

*Universalism*: the ethical idea that there are universal values which are accepted or ought to be accepted by people in all parts of the world. Universalism is often regarded with suspicion, either by relativists or by those who regard what is presented as universal values as really being a projection of Western or Enlightenment values onto the rest of the world. However most ethical theories and certainly those that can be seen as global ethics have *some* universal elements, for instance the universal value of respecting diversity in beliefs and practices, and of certain elements of well-being such as freedom from starvation and disease.

*Utilitarianism*: the ethical theory that says that an action is right if it promotes the best balance of good over evil; classically this was seen by Mill and Bentham as the greatest happiness principle, but more recent Utilitarians prefer to talk about maximising interests or the satisfaction of preferences. Whilst the theory is controversial because it is not clear whether producing good consequences is the only ethical requirement, much ethical reasoning does rest on determining the overall effects of actions and this is true of much proposed action to combat evils on a global scale.

*Value*: that which is regarded as good, right or otherwise desirable by an agent. It is a matter of controversy whether values depend on agents who value certain states of affairs (objects, properties, actions and so on) or constitute properties such as goodness or rightness which are discovered by an agent. Values may be non-moral such as those things which constitute an individual human being's flourishing or well-being, or they may be moral, such as the virtue of honesty or the duty not to steal. Sometimes values are contrasted with norms, where values refer to what is good and norms refer to principles of conduct such as rules, duties or obligations, but in other contexts values embrace moral norms as well.

*Westphalian system*: the system of international relations based upon territorially defined states each of which claims sovereignty. This system, which has provided the basic framing arrangement for international relations until the present day, was symbolically instigated by the Peace of Westphalia signed in October 1648, bringing to an end the Thirty Years War. The Treaty helped end non-territorial claims to political authority, such as those of the Pope and the Holy Roman Emperor, thus establishing the territorial state as the highest form of political authority. The absence of any recognised authority above the states often results in the Westphalian system being described as 'anarchic'. This does not mean that it is necessarily chaotic, although it sometimes is, but that there is no overarching power above the states. Relations amongst these states emphasise principles such as the sanctity of borders, non-intervention in the domestic affairs of other states, respect for treaties and the customary norms of diplomacy, although these are, of course, sometimes broken; and recognises the balance of power, the national interest and national security as important policy goals. Whether we are currently living through the end of the Westphalian system is an issue of considerable academic controversy.

*World government*: a form of political rule (sometimes referred to as world federalism) in which the whole world would be under the government of one central authority, and nation-states would no longer exist as separate sovereign states but rather, if at all, as regional governments. Advocates hope that it would be democratic, critics fear it would be global tyranny. Although many of those who have called themselves global citizens have advocated world government, there is no necessary connection between the two and nowadays most global citizens would favour alternative forms of global governance.

*World poverty*: a condition of absolute poverty characterised by malnutrition, hunger, extensive disease and short life expectancy experienced by over a billion of the world population (one sixth) mainly in the so-called developing countries of the world. Internationally coordinated measures to tackle world poverty, in the form of aid programmes and regulating the international trading system, have been taken by governments, especially in the second half of the twentieth century, and much effort has been devoted by concerned individuals, working through NGOs and in other ways, to supporting and urging enlightened trade and aid policies in governments. Since, if global obligations are accepted, the obligation to give aid is an obvious because effective dimension to it, much commitment to global citizenship centres on this area of global concern.

# INTRODUCTION

The idea of global citizenship or world citizenship is the idea that human beings are 'citizens of the world'. What exactly this means and whether we are global citizens or not are questions which are much disputed as we shall see. But there is at least an important core feature which anyone using the term will accept, even if in accepting it they then go on to say that we are not global citizens. It is that a global citizen is a member of the wider community of all humanity, the world or a similar whole that is wider than that of a nation-state or other political community of which we are normally thought to be citizens. This membership is important in the sense that it involves (or would involve if people accept that they are global citizens) a significant identity, loyalty or commitment beyond the nation-state.

The reasons for this identity, loyalty or commitment, and some hints about the forms that it may take, can be gained from a very brief history of the idea of global citizenship. This core element of recognition of membership of a wider, global, universal or cosmopolitan whole goes a long way back in history. It was a leading idea in the thought of the Stoics in the ancient world of the Greeks and the Romans (Heater 1996). During the period from approximately the third century BC to the second century AD many people of all classes – from slaves to emperors – were attracted to a philosophy of life in which virtue was seen as the highest good, including the virtues of moderation in the passions and endurance of pain and adversity. Characteristically they described themselves as 'cosmo-polites' or 'citizens of the cosmos'. For them the 'cosmos' was indeed larger than or different from 'the world', if the latter is seen as the planet earth or the total human population on it. The cosmos or universe was seen as a divine order governed by Reason and as rational beings they participated in it. They were global citizens because they understood themselves as existing meaningfully only within this ordered, reasoned whole. One could choose to be a Stoic, perhaps, but once a Stoic one could not be anything but a global citizen. Global citizenship was thus a response to how one understood one's position on life and the cosmos, rather than being a response to particular events, issues or problems. For modern world citizens the world is seen as the world of all human beings on the planet (though some will include future generations of humans and/or non-human life as well), rather than being all members of a cosmos ordered according to some grand principle, such as Reason.

But this much is in common: what is being asserted is that humans are in some fundamental sense members of a wider body as contrasted to the membership of a particular political community such as a city-state, nation-state or even an empire. All the latter are accidents of one's birth or circumstance. That one is a global citizen points to a more fundamental fact about who one is, one's being, for instance, a human being sharing the essential characteristics of humanity – for example, rationality – with all other human beings. There is something – exactly what, as the following chapters make clear, is disputed – that ties us together in terms of identity, loyalty or commitment. Global citizenship attests, then, to a certain view of the world that is holistic in the sense that there are no essential reasons why barriers, borders, diversity and the disparateness of the human condition render one person and their conditions and actions irrelevant to any other. Many of the chapters advocating global citizenship attempt to establish the bases, reasons and consequences for adopting such a view of the world. Other chapters attempt to refute it, or at least to refute it as being in any practical sense important in the world today.

However, this move from a conception of global citizenship based on a belief in a divinely ordered and reasoned cosmos to a more humanistic, and often straightforwardly secular, conception stressing interconnectedness through human, rather than divine agency, is not solely a recent development. Important intellectual and practical developments have shaped the way an idea rooted in the very different world of ancient Greece and Rome has been transmitted to us. Interest in the idea of 'cosmopolitanism' revived significantly in the seventeenth and eighteenth centuries. This was partly a response to the development of the European nation-state system in which sovereign states exercise complete legitimate power over clearly defined territories. Although one of the premises of the international system was that it would regulate and limit wars and thus promote order and peace amongst peoples, the frequency of wars prompted some thinkers to propose better ways to achieve more permanent peace or what was sometimes called 'perpetual peace'. Some advocated world government, others more solid commitment to universal moral principles. Immanuel Kant, the great German philosopher of the Enlightenment, was prominent is his advocacy of cosmopolitanism. He did not advocate world government but an international system based on principles of mutual respect (his 'articles of peace') (Kant 1949). He urged the creation of a system where mutual respect was protected within states through the adoption of what he called 'republican' constitutional principles, broadly similar to what we would recognise as liberal democratic political practices. A loose international confederation of such republics would enable, slowly and not without mishap and mistake, international disputes to be resolved peacefully to the extent that war would eventually become unthinkable. This plan was partly a reflection of his understanding of human beings as rational beings capable of using their reason to identify the morally right thing to do. This capacity for reason made them all members of a potential 'kingdom of ends', where reason and morality would ensure all were treated as ends in themselves, and not as means to someone else's ends. Properly moral behaviour involved acting to bring about such a situation, even though present circumstances may be very different. The plan was also partly a recognition that with increasing international travel, commerce and exploration, there was a need to accord strangers or foreigners respect – what he called the 'cosmopolitan duty' of hospitality: foreigners should be treated with respect and their humanity recognised, even if they did not have to be made citizens or granted equal rights as existing full members of the community.

The Enlightenment legacy, exemplified by Kant, is important in generating the kind of worldview adopted by many modern advocates of global citizenship. During the first half of the twentieth century there was significant minority interest both in world government and in world citizenship. In a variety of ways individuals were beginning to think of themselves as capable of playing a part in world affairs and getting organised into international movements. They were adopting what one prominent cosmopolitan, H. G. Wells, called a 'mental cosmopolis' in which one thinks of oneself as a citizen of the world even if the reality of the world does not conform to one's conception (Heater 1996: 129). The world federalist movement brought together many individuals who saw themselves as world citizens and who committed themselves to trying to create a new world order based on federation as an alternative to lots of separate sovereign states constantly in conflict with each other. Events of the twentieth century persuaded many others of the need for radical reform of the prevailing international system, often in cosmopolitan directions. The First World War was, with its hitherto unparalleled levels of destruction, a catalyst to much thinking about how to create alternatives to war. Pacifism was for the first time attracting sufficient adherents so as to lead to international movements challenging the assumptions of the international system. Others wanted a new world order that, rather than rely on the consciences of individuals, would generate peace by instituting one overarching power to command and, if necessary, compel compliance to the basic rules of social order.

Of course, as we all know, wars continued, most notably the even more destructive Second World War, and have continued ever since. The United Nations, founded in 1945 on more sober and less idealistic expectations than the ill-fated League of Nations, was set up primarily to save succeeding generations from the scourge of war. Although at the UN's conception there was already the possibility that it might become eventually a world government, the onset of the Cold War quickly confirmed its function as an inter-state organisation and as one moderating but not replacing states. Many who saw themselves as world citizens in the mid-century were keen supporters of the United Nations through organisations like the United Nations Associations of many countries or, for instance, the Council for Education in World Citizenship (CEWC) in the UK. Many others poured their energies into the peace movement through organisations such as the Campaign for Nuclear Disarmament (CND), in response to the threat of nuclear annihilation during the Cold War that cast a shadow over world affairs from the 1950s to the 1980s.

But by the 1970s several major factors were altering the way global problems were being perceived and the way concerned individuals were thinking about the world and what should be done. The traditional focus on peace and the problem of war was giving way to concerns about world poverty and what needed to be done to alleviate it through aid programmes and reforming the way international trade occurred. Emerging evidence about the global environment – both about resource depletion and about damage to and pollution of the environment – provided inspiration and motivation for a new group of environmentalist cosmopolitans. Ongoing, and historically deep-rooted, concern about the violation of human rights in other parts of the world received increasing attention. This was partly because of the impact of technology on news-gathering which made hiding such practices harder and harder and partly because of the emergence of some appalling regimes, such as the Khmer Rouge in Cambodia and Idi Amin in Uganda, whose practices recalled the Holocaust. Alongside these issues and events there has been a process, initially gradual but accelerating rapidly since the early 1970s, called 'globalisation' – of communication, transportation and transnational economic activity. Although the term 'globalisation' only caught on in the 1990s, the process has been going on over a very long period. The process can be seen both as a major cause of many of the global problems we face but at the same time as the context in which individuals increasingly see themselves as involved in the wider world and are thus more likely to see themselves as 'world citizens'.

Many who would regard themselves as global citizens have thus been inspired and motivated not by a general philosophical worldview, such as Stoicism, Kantianism or Wells' 'mental cosmopolis', but by their response to social, political and economic problems in areas like development, the environment, human rights and globalisation. What is striking is that this modern revival of interest in global citizenship has much less to do with the desire for world government and is less preoccupied with peace than was the case earlier in the twentieth century. This expansion and diversification of the agenda of global citizenship has been vital to the current prominence of the idea, but with expansion and diversity come new intellectual problems of maintaining coherence and focus. Globalisation, as many chapters in the book demonstrate, is very important to contemporary discussions of global citizenship, but it is a term often castigated for having become meaningless, so much is it supposed to cover. Global citizenship needs to avoid this fate and one of the hopes of this book is to contribute to bringing more people into a debate on the idea of global citizenship. The philosophical inspiration for global citizenship must not be lost sight of in the face of the maelstrom of events and issues that seem to demand a global response and that may cause us to press for a renewed sense of global citizenship. Several of the chapters take on this task, either directly or indirectly, but some initial observations are worth making right at the outset. Both the factors mentioned above – new global problems and the process of globalisation – make pressing a consideration of global citizenship. The first relates to what may be called the 'ethical' component of global citizenship, the second to the 'citizenship' component. (The alignment is not as simple as this and can be disputed but it provides a useful way into the issue.) These two axes of debate about global citizenship seem to us to be where the main intellectual controversies lie, and thus a brief account of them here will help set the scene for some of the more detailed considerations that follow.

The ethical component is concerned with what values and norms are being advocated by someone who says he is a world citizen (or says that we are all world citizens). As will be apparent from the later chapters, there is by no means agreement about what these should be, or how they should be justified. Is what is important to global citizenship the idea of rights, perhaps best thought of as human rights, which all have (and should enjoy even if they don't)? Should the emphasis be upon duties and obligations? If so, should these be seen as the ordinary duties we have to respect all fellow human beings in our ordinary transactions with them, or does it include the idea of active responsibility to play one's part in creating a better world? What should the core norms be? Impartial justice or the ethics of caring? Many of the contributions in the reader deal with these central questions of ethics. Many others in the reader look at particular areas in which ethical issues and challenges arise, such as the environment, economic globalisation and immigration.

The 'citizenship' component is concerned with the question: in what sense is a global citizen a 'citizen'? Whilst many who call themselves world citizens are quite content to think of themselves as agents who accept global responsibility (and thus give the word 'citizen' no real conceptual work to do at all), it is an important question to face: is there a plausible and substantive sense of 'citizen' in which it makes sense to say that we are global citizens? There is considerable disagreement about this. Many would agree that as the world is at the moment being a world citizen in the sense of being a citizen of a world state is an unrealistic idea (attractive and a matter of aspiration for some, unattractive to others including other self-described global citizens). However, it remains plausible to argue that various kinds of institutions like NGOs, processes like the spread of Internet networking, events such as public declarations, and practices like the observance of human rights are in existence and do give substance to the claim that we are 'citizens' beyond the confines of our nation-states. Moreover, apart from what is already in place, there are demands for the strengthening of global civil society and global democracy in order to meet what is often called the 'democratic deficit' – the fact that increasingly the forces that determine the life-prospects of people within countries lie beyond what domestic governments can, however democratic they are, really control. In the eyes of many, globalisation, especially in its economic aspects, challenges the existing structure of citizenship and political control. Thus, global citizenship that takes on some institutionalised form may be a necessary response to the need to regain or re-assert popular political authority over de-territorialised capital and the expanding reach of transnational corporations on the one hand and global institutions, like the World Trade Organisation, on the other that often seem to be outside oversight and control.

Processes by which individuals can become involved in deliberative outcomes beyond their own states are, of course, themselves part of the processes of globalisation. And although globalisation is not itself as such concerned with ethics in the sense of ethical justification – since it is a social, cultural and economic process which is unfolding as a matter of fact – it provides the matrix within which realistic ethical choices have to be made. Its processes are vital to the effective expression of ethical responsibilities (for those who wish to use it in this way) and for some thinkers it is a necessary condition for the very reality of global ethics itself. A number of the chapters deal with the 'citizenship' component, just what it might mean and whether it is something to be developed or not. Thus even the more 'practical' or 'applied' chapters contribute to the discussion of how far we need a particular worldview in order to make the idea of global citizenship meaningful.

This reader therefore deals with some of the central issues of our time – global challenges and our responsibilities to address them and the changing political structures of the world in which continuing to think of oneself as simply a member of a largely self-contained unit called the nation-state simply is inadequate. The reader is thoroughly interdisciplinary, involving philosophy, political theory, sociology and economics amongst other disciplines. It does not claim to cover all the areas that could be covered but it is sufficient to enable the student to see what a wide-ranging and important topic it is. Two omissions are worth noting. First, the reader takes as its main focus of attention the ordinary individual who might think of him- or herself as a global citizen. It does not deal with what may be recognised as an important and growing area of interest, namely corporate global citizenship. This often takes two forms: the first is of corporations portraying or regarding themselves as global citizens; the second the idea that a business elite of senior executives within globally operating firms are now global citizens, having lost, at least in their working lives, any sense of loyalty to a particular state. That big companies in the business world are interested in the ethical dimensions of their activities is to be welcomed, although it is notable that many seem more eager to assert their global 'rights' to invest wherever they choose and to access raw material and labour markets with minimal restrictions, rather than to recognise their global responsibilities to the environment, human rights and a more just distribution of wealth. It is also to be recognised that the globe-trotting executive has as much of a global identity as anyone and his or her perceptions are important. But we simply have not dealt with this aspect in detail because our concern has been to consider the idea more generally and in ways likely to appeal to and engage a wider readership.

Second, and paradoxically given the immense importance many involved in this project attach to the subject, there is no chapter precisely on the ethics of aid and on that aspect of global citizenship which is important to many, namely the responsibility which the affluent have in relation to the poor of the world. It is not that we do not think this to be an important dimension of global citizenship, and indeed a number of the chapters do deal with the issue, albeit from different starting points. The discussions of global distributive justice, economic globalisation and immigration all have a bearing on the challenge of world poverty; the role of the UN's Specialised Agencies dealing with aid and development is also considered, and running through a number of pieces is the theme of human rights including the socio-economic rights which the world's poor are not able to exercise.

There are four sections on major aspects of global citizenship ('The Idea of Global Citizenship'; 'Institutional Issues and the Bases of Scepticism'; 'Ethical Bases'; and 'Specific Areas: Environment, Economic Globalisation, Technology, Immigration and Peace') each of which contains a separate section introduction. These introductions contain summaries of all the chapters as well as taking a synoptic view of the section and adding critical comments on some of the issues discussed. Each chapter also contains at the end several questions for use in private study or group work. A glossary of some of the key ideas precedes this introduction, and at the end there is a combined bibliography, mainly of books, articles and chapters, but also of some more useful websites. Most of the bibliographical materials are referred to in the chapters, though some extra items have been added.

The idea of the reader arose in the course of a Project on Global Citizenship which ran in Aberdeen from 1997 to 1999. The Gordon Cook Foundation which funds 'values education' financed this project which looked at ways of promoting the teaching of global citizenship at university level. We had a number of seminar meetings over the two years and arranged a small conference to round the Project off. Most of the papers from that conference went into (and were written with a view to going into) this reader, and to them were added a number of other invited papers. Some of the latter were specially written (Axtmann, Falk, Follesdal, Imber) whilst others were already in print elsewhere (Held, Küng, Miller). We wish to record acknowledgment to the CUP, Küng and *Dissent* respectively for permission to reproduce the latter three chapters. Since the Gordon Cook Foundation holds the copyright on all the materials which appeared in the *Global Citizenship Report* (1999), we both acknowledge that the GCF holds the copyright for all the remaining pieces (Alkire, Attfield, Dower (3), Hutchings, Newlands, Ottonelli, Smyth and Blackmore, Strijbos, van den Anker, Williams), and record our thanks to them for allowing us to disseminate all this material free of copyright charge. We also thank Peter McCaffery for his assistance in preparing additional bibliography and website materials.

# SECTION I

# THE IDEA OF GLOBAL CITIZENSHIP

# SECTION INTRODUCTION

## John Williams

The idea of global citizenship is far from straightforward. As discussed in the introduction, it is an idea with a long, if somewhat chequered, past. It is an idea that has never entirely gone away, whilst rarely commanding general support, and yet an idea that cannot really claim to have a single, cohesive shape and form throughout its history.

Thus in introducing this section of the reader it is necessary to issue an initial caveat. Talking about *the* idea of global citizenship is very difficult, indeed impossible. It is not a singular thing, arguably never has been and certainly is not in contemporary debate. Instead, this section aims to offer four alternative takes on how we might think about the idea of global citizenship, particularly in the circumstances of contemporary politics, both national and international. However, it would also be wrong to suggest that these four readings are either exclusive of one another or exhaustive in their coverage of possible ways of thinking coherently and constructively about global citizenship.

Indeed the metaphor of a 'take', familiar from the film set, is an apt one. All four readings offer different ways in which the same basic material – the idea of global citizenship – can produce different emphases, nuances, understandings and moods depending on how the material is interpreted, how it is presented and how it is understood in relation to the bigger picture of contemporary politics. Other interpretations are undoubtedly possible, as the material of global citizenship is extensive and varied. Those searching for a clear and definitive statement of what global citizenship is are therefore going to be disappointed. The interpretations and ideas presented in this section differ strongly from one another. Arguably this is one of the strengths of the idea of global citizenship: it is amenable to different readings and interpretations that enable it to be malleable enough to allow its advocates to search for evidence of its influence or applicability in a very divergent range of situations and circumstances. We can be global citizens in various ways. For others, this lack of a clear definition is seriously problematic. It renders the idea of global citizenship too vague and woolly, too accommodative of difference to fulfil functions we might expect. They argue it cannot offer prescriptive advice to policy-makers, an ethical yardstick against which we can judge actions and actors or a handbook of conduct for individuals keen to adopt the identity of 'global citizen' and wanting to be told how they should act and think as a result.

These varieties of dissatisfaction are evident elsewhere in the reader. In this section, though, the idea of global citizenship takes a more heterogeneous form but it retains a common core, and one associated with the origins of the idea in Stoic thought. This is to view global citizenship as recognising that individuals can be citizens of the world in the sense that the idea of a universal community of humanity is an idea, and ideal, that has purchase upon the situations and circumstances within which we live our lives. This element of global citizenship being an idea and an ideal is important. It highlights both an empirical claim – it makes some sense (exactly how much is open to debate) to talk of individuals as members of an existing universal community – and an ethical one that this sense is desirable and ought to be promoted.

Global citizenship has an agenda, then, and a belief that the ideas we hold shape the practice we undertake. It is not a purely descriptive or analytical category, as the contributions to this section make clear, with all asserting that the adoption of ideas of global citizenship would help to make the world a better place in which to live. This also means that the idea of global citizenship may be malleable but it is not shatter-proof. It cannot contain everything and thus this section hopefully not only offers different 'takes' on the how the idea may be thought about in relation to contemporary theory and practice but also some sense of where the boundaries of global citizenship lie.

Falk discusses the idea of a 'matrix of citizenship' made up of dominant notions of citizenship of the state; emergent notions of citizenship of regions of the world, principally Europe; and the need for activists for a global citizenship that he sees as only hazily in prospect at present. Falk's argument stresses the strength and durability of citizenship within states but that the ability of the state to fulfil the expectations of citizens is under growing pressure. Some of this pressure is, in Falk's view, undesirable: economic globalisation of a neo-liberal kind is undermining the state's welfare and labour protection functions, for example. Other developments are desirable: changing international legal and political practice gives greater prominence to human rights and the punishment of gross crimes, whether committed in war or by authoritarian rulers. What he calls 'Westphalian citizenship' – the idea of individuals as citizens of sovereign states that claim autonomy in relations with other states and supreme authority within their specified territorial borders, a conception of statehood associated with the Peace of Westphalia of 1648 – is facing challenges it cannot meet.

Regional citizenships are one potential way of addressing this, although Falk is doubtful about their potential success in addressing global phenomena. However, they may be complementary to national citizenship and thus have practical value. His idea of global citizenship is principally aspirational, rather than pointing to existing structures and systems. He argues for what he calls 'citizen pilgrims' to lead a visionary and evangelical movement that seeks to seize on the opportunities presented by the changing circumstances of global politics, economics and society. There is a need to think into the future and to begin to address emerging ethical challenges, such as those deriving from technology, and the needs for global accountability for global firms and markets. Citizen pilgrims are necessary to try and ensure that we are equipped to shape a future in which citizenship remains a meaningful idea linked to the protection of rights, a sense of community and duty, and respect for the value of human life and dignity everywhere.

Dower's 'Global Citizenship: Yes or No?' speaks most explicitly to the idea of global citizenship as a malleable concept, sensitive to political and other realities, but one with a commitment to universality and responsibility in practice and in principle. It schematically summarises several of the most common questions that come to many people's minds when confronted with the idea of global citizenship. These include its institutional or ethical character, the meaningfulness of its use of citizenship in a non-state context, its relationship to world government and its ability to handle ethical diversity. Dower points out the most usual topics in discussions on these and other key issues and tries to generate a defence of global citizenship. He does not deny the force of some of the arguments but suggests that even taken together they do not demolish either the utility or desirability of adopting an idea of global citizenship as, at the very least, a useful additional perspective upon key contemporary issues.

Williams follows Falk's recognition of the state's dominant role in debates about citizenship but analyses an alternative mechanism for addressing some of the same challenges Falk points to, such as protecting human rights and responding to environmental change. He discusses global citizenship in relation to an idea labelled 'good international citizenship'. This suggests that the international political system remains very hostile to the idea of individuals as global citizens. However, issues associated with global citizenship may be more effectively addressed if states, or rather those who govern them, conceive of themselves as international citizens of the states system, taking on the sense of rights and, above all, responsibilities to other states that we associate with individuals within a state. Advocates suggest there are good reasons for arguing that some progress has been made here and that it makes good pragmatic sense to try and further human rights, for example, via states rather than via individual action. Being a global citizen may thus be about working primarily within your state to try and make government face up to responsibilities owed not to individuals the world over but to other states.

Williams is somewhat sceptical about the idea of good international citizenship, whilst recognising that its practicality and realistic assessment of the state of international politics make it a valuable, if ultimately unsatisfactory, contribution to the idea of global citizenship.

Hutchings offers a view of global citizenship that raises a question that may not be immediately obvious to many. The term 'global citizen' would appear to be gender neutral and many may instinctively respond to the question 'Are men and women global citizens in the same way?' with an immediate and straightforward 'Yes, of course.' Hutchings demonstrates the need for deeper reflection on this and that feminist thought and experience has important implications for global citizenship. At one level, she argues that women's struggle to improve their lot in the world offers an example that global citizenship can learn from and one that has made gender an inescapable issue. On the idea of global citizenship, Hutchings surveys a range of feminist thought useful to global citizenship and explores in more detail the example of a feminist 'ethic of care'. This is rooted in practical relationships of responsibility for others, such as those associated with motherhood, to suggest resources of experience and ideas that enable us to think about responsibilities in a global citizenship context.

These four chapters, then, are disparate in approach and focus but linked by their concern to discuss the idea of global citizenship in important contemporary contexts and in response to practical questions and issues. They are not works of abstract philosophy. Instead they hopefully show how the idea of global citizenship is responsive to and draws on diverse issues and a multiplicity of approaches, and that this is, generally, a strength. Nevertheless, for all their apparent diversity, they do share the common core of the idea of global citizenship – a universal community of responsibility.

# I. AN EMERGENT MATRIX OF CITIZENSHIP: COMPLEX, UNEVEN, AND FLUID

## Richard Falk

### INTRODUCTORY REFLECTIONS

A surge of interest in the theory and parameters of citizenship reflects the impact of a series of recent trends: globalisation, migration, identity politics, regionalism, humanitarian intervention, and human rights. The relative clarity of a statist framing of world order focused inquiries about citizenship mainly on the evolution of state/society relations within the Euro/American context of liberal democracy and particularly on the gradual expansion of the identities and rights of individuals who could claim the status of citizen within a particular nation-state. In general terms, most influentially specified by T. H. Marshall, this evolutionary path led from elemental civil rights (in the sense of restraints on governmental abuse) to political rights (of a participatory character in the collective life of a society) and on to social rights (of a character that ensured basic human needs would be addressed by safety nets and state subsidies to the extent necessary).

What gives the question of citizenship its current salience relates to the tensions generated by increased normativity of international life; a neo-liberal ideological climate; the erosion of statist responsibility, creativity, capacity, and autonomy; and the general technological and economistic embrace of corporate or neo-liberal globalisation. This latter point can also be made inversely. The state is more accountable internally and externally for its undertakings, breaking down the inside/outside dichotomy between unconditional sovereignty within territorial space and realist power politics in the relations among states. That is, the expectation of individuals is for an extension of rights in various directions, and with respect to overlapping frameworks of authority, while the state is losing much of its grip as the main arena of decision bearing on identity, well-being and security. An aspect of this loss of control arises from the success of transnational market forces in inducing almost every state in the world to adhere to a neo-liberal policy framework that includes minimising social roles and subordinating the provision of public goods, while endorsing ideals of liberalisation and privatisation as enhancing the efficiency of capital and global competitiveness. As a result, individuals cannot look as confidently to the state for the fulfilment of basic aspirations, making traditional forms of citizenship less organically connected to an individual's search for security and meaning in life. Put differently, to the extent that the state has been instrumentalised by a combination of global market forces and a general antipathy toward bureau-cracies and regulation, the sphere of governmental autonomy with respect to promoting the well-being of the territorial citizenry is diminished.

Such a dynamic is reinforced by other influential developments, none more consequential than the rise of information technology (IT) as a basic re-structuring and wealth-creating influence in business, politics, military affairs, human relations and worldview. The shift from hierarchy to network as an organisational mode also has an overall psycho-political effect of de-centring authority, lessening the significance of territorial boundaries and creating a multitude of systems of interaction beyond the control of the state (Castells 1996; 1997; 1998). The mentality associated with this technology merges with market-driven ideologies to highlight the virtues of self-organising modes of social action, to marginalise the regulative role of the state, and especially to resist its social intervention to alleviate unemployment and poverty. The impact of IT is great on political consciousness, fashioning a quasi-libertarian ethos and even an emergent specific identity called 'netizen', that challenges the idea of a state-centric world, thereby rendering a traditional citizen obsolete. Such an identity is potential and partial, of relevance to that small minority who are pioneering the various electronic frontiers and 'virtual communities' of cyberspace, but also relevant to an assessment of new configurations of belief and allegiance.

The essence of this new configuration is to supersede and challenge the traditional bonding between state and individual, and more generally the bonding between the territory/nationality of sovereign space as delimited on a world map and citizenship. In contrast, the full-fledged netizen bonds primarily through association by Internet, establishing identities on the basis of shared interests and affinities among individuals and groups that may be geographically isolated and disparate, that are unmoved by the patriotism of nation-states and that do not regard themselves as subject to the authority of laws and government. There are, of course, weaker moves toward netizenship that combine a fascination with Internet communities with an everyday experience in the territorial space of a sovereign state, and thus produce more hybrid varieties of citizenship. This hybridity combines a non-territorial netizenship that animates the imagination of individuals with a practical orientation toward citizenship that acknowledges the habitual territorial loyalties and beliefs of a state-centric world order.

These developments interact with others that complicate the picture still further. The partial and uneven breakdown of state authority, as well as migration patterns and increased labour mobility, contributes to multicultur-alism within states and to the embrace of intense forms of separatist politics by abused minorities who increasingly conceive of themselves as 'captive nationalities,' or alienated ethnic enclaves. These centrifugal tendencies are strengthened by the legal, moral, and political promise of a right of self-determination to all 'peoples', a right initially subordinated to Westphalian categories of statist unity but endorsed in state-shattering forms in relation to the former Yugoslavia during the 1990s.[1] The rise of numerous micro-nationalisms seeking varying degrees of autonomy, if not full independence, also appears to represent a search for identity and resistance to globalisation in a world order where the state is outwardly oriented toward the world economy and less capable of generating allegiance on the part of its citizens.

The claims of indigenous peoples to a right of self-determination, at the very least, further dilutes the notion of territorial sovereignty, establishing zones of self-government and autonomy within the boundaries of existing states (Danspeckgruber with Watts 1997; Lam 2000). These developments threaten the modernist idea that the secular state incorporates ethnic and cultural differences into an integral whole that is administered by a governmental centre on the basis of a single overarching legal framework. Even the federalist notion of the state was based on an ideal of nationalist solidarity, as well as on a shared framework of socio-economic values premised on rationality and modernity, that is, negating the relevance of religious, ethnic, and cultural difference. To the extent that indigenous peoples win a genuine exemption from such a consensus on values and allegiance, rather than receive only offers of assimilation and non-discrimination, there is a reduction in the overall weight of sovereign authority.

As significant is the rise of normative claims based on international law that are binding on the state and recognise that the rights and duties of individuals no longer begin and end with the discretion and authority of the state. Of course, conceptually the state can absorb these wider normative imperatives within its domestic legal structure by adopting the global norms as its own. Yet such adjustments do not hide the remarkable trend toward the rise of various types of external accountability along with moves toward procedures and institutions with a mandate to implement these global norms internally. These moves toward global normative governance seem like a dramatic encroachment on the sort of sovereignty that allowed the state to dominate the political and moral imagination of individuals and their political communities, lending such powerful credibility to the Westphalian architecture of a statist system of world order. For centuries individuals had no direct status under international law but were dependent for the protection of their international legal interests upon support from their national government. In this sense, individuals were treated as *objects* of international law, and states were its exclusive *subjects*, with the authority to represent claims on behalf of their citizens. With the development of international human rights, the decline of diplomatic protection of aliens abroad and the spread of the democratic ethos there is a growing sense that individuals are becoming for many purposes subjects alongside states, capable of acting on their own to uphold their legal rights. Complementary to this development is the effort of the last half-century to extend individual responsibility to those who act on behalf of the state, thereby qualifying, and in some instances nullifying, the idea of 'sovereign immunity' that was such a hallmark of the Westphalian ethos. Such immunity had shielded political and military officials from any type of legal accountability for their human wrongs and state crimes.

One dimension of such accountability was illustrated by the Pinochet litigation, suggesting that individuals, including even heads of state, could be held criminally liable anywhere for conduct performed within their own country in accordance with the prevailing governmental structure, including accountability for previous official actions (Brody and Ratner 2000). A related dimension was the revival of the Nuremberg imposition of criminal responsibility through the establishment of the International Criminal Tribunal for the former Yugoslavia located at The Hague. This initiative led in turn to the 1998 Rome Treaty that proposes to establish a permanent international criminal tribunal available to handle all credible accusations of extreme criminality at the level of the state that are not addressed by national courts. Whatever else, the emergence of external criteria and procedures of accountability as responding to demands for redress of grievances weakens the statist character of world order in a decisive way (Barkan 2000). Transnational redress radically reconfigures our conception of the state, as in Andrew Linklater's influential formulations arguing in favour of the emergence of 'the post-Westphalian state'. Such a state is stripped of its sovereign pretension to be above the law and of its insistence that an individual had neither rights nor duties on the international level since all authority derived from the nation-state (Linklater 1998b; Linklater 1998c).

A related development involves an alleged 'legal entitlement' to democratic governance by which is meant at the very least a fair procedure to enable citizens to give their consent periodically through the vehicle of multi-party free elections (Franck 1992). This legal entitlement has a range of uncertain and controversial implications, including whether there exists a legal right on the part of democratic governments or the community of states to intervene to safeguard or restore political democracy (Marks 2000; Fox and Roth 2000). In an important sense the renewed emphasis on this democratic entitlement represents a series of moves to take seriously the right of political participation already conferred in Articles 19–21 of the *Universal Declaration of Human Rights* adopted by the UN General Assembly in 1948, and given somewhat greater specificity in Articles 19, 21, and 22 of the *International Covenant of Civil and Political Rights* that was finalised in 1966. As long as the Cold War persisted, the idea of coexistence was seen as paramount and there was no attempt to link adherence by a government to constitutional democracy as a precondition for the legitimacy of the state under international law. Since the end of the Cold War such linkage has been widely proposed as a project to be realised by international law, thereby both empowering citizens to enjoy the benefits of constitutionalism and potentially disempowering those citizens who continue to reside in states whose governing process does not qualify as democratic.

There are complications that must be noted. A hegemonic dimension of global politics gives particular, and quite possibly undue, influence to the actions, attitudes, and values professed by the United States. In the present period, the United States seems embarked on a project to consolidate its global power by reliance on space-based weapons systems, a missile defence shield and deployments of offensive weapons in space. Such an undertaking to provide global leadership can be viewed as a benevolent dimension of global governance that provides the best hope for minimum order in the decades ahead. However, it is ambiguous in content and perception, and such hegemonic roles can also be regarded as unacceptable moves to achieve global dominance that is designed to impose values and control, as well as to freeze the inequities of the present world by shutting down the avenues of change and resistance. In this regard the war-making ethos and interventionary capabilities of hegemonic states remains central to an interpretation of world order. Equally sobering is the current unwillingness of the United States to comply with emergent international legal standards governing the emission of greenhouse gases. Washington argues that the implementation of agreed standards would impinge upon American lifestyle and growth prospects, while ignoring the impact of its non-implementation on climate change, and the well-being of future generations of peoples throughout the world. The revolutionary extension of citizenship beyond the state, and the internal impact of global norms, needs to be qualified to the extent that hegemonic structures of power and authority are able to avoid the impact of international legal claims. Hegemonic states and their closest allies can exempt themselves from implementing procedures that are becoming more available. Take the most visible instance of this unevenness in the application of post-Westphalian international law, the accountability of heads of state. Pinochet and Milošević are indicted for crimes against humanity, while the crimes of equally indictable heads of state are overlooked. The same pattern affects other spheres of international activity: the unevenness of implementation with respect to international standards of human rights or patterns of diplomacy associated with humanitarian intervention. In effect, we need to assess the impacts and strategic interests of the strong state on the character of citizenship in this era of globalisation, especially the disempowering effects of unilateralism on the rights and security of the peoples resident in weak states. Also at stake is the way in which responses to world risks are organised given this hegemonic power/policy structure (Beck 1999). In effect, this hegemonic structure dilutes international efforts to base global governance on the Rule of Law, which presupposes that equals are treated equally. As a result of a hegemonic form of world order it is inevitable that in vital matters the burdens of the law fall unequally, exempting the strong while constraining the weak. Arguably, such inequality affects all legal systems, including those of leading constitutional democracies. In the United States, for instance, 'racial profiling' by the police, the greater imposition of capital punishment on ethnic minorities and the relative leniency accorded white-collar crime are illustrative.

Similarly, it is important to take the measure of the weak state, unable to maintain order or minimal adherence to global norms within its territorial space. Sub-Saharan Africa has become the scene of the breakdown of Westphalian structures in the most devastating forms, producing genocide, massive atrocities, persistent warfare, lethal epidemics, collective destitution, and pervasive criminality and corruption (Jackson 1990). This challenge of the pathologically weak state raises difficult issues about intervention, trustee-ship and human solidarity. Citizenship in such nominal states provides none of the Westphalian benefits aside from symbolic matters of status. Beyond this, in the era of globalisation the international community tends increasingly to be unwilling to assume the economic burdens and political risks and costs of humanitarian diplomacy that would compensate for the failures of terri-torial governments to provide for the minimum physical and material needs of their citizens. In weak states, the benefits of citizenship are not present unless significantly reinforced by action undertaken by the organised international community.

What constitutes political community is drawn into question by these developments, and with it either the erosion of traditional citizenship as the foundation of community and identity or the refashioning of citizenship to take account of multiple identities, centres of authority and responsibility, and diverse notions of community. As such, the capacity of the state to function as the centre of loyalty and aspiration is thrown into doubt, particularly in advanced, affluent states where dying on behalf of one's country is being increasingly questioned.[2] Of course, the persisting unevenness of international society creates wildly different attitudes toward the linkage between state and identity. For peoples denied statehood and enduring oppressive circum-stances, the acquisition of a state of their own is likely to function as the highest political goal, the attainment of which is worthy of dying and killing. Nevertheless, the leading states establish and bear witness to systemic trends toward a more complex ethos of citizenship than had prevailed prior to this advent of globalisation and regionalisation of authority structures. These trends are accentuated by rising normative expectations relating to human rights and criminal accountability. Superimposing global standards of accountability renders uncertain under what conditions the state provides a safe haven for someone accused of criminality in relation to action that was permissible at its territorial point of origin.

There is an ambiguity in the way the term 'citizenship' is used. It can refer to the formal linkages established by law but it can also refer to the psycho-political linkages arising from patterns of aspiration and belief. In these respects it parallels the ambiguity in the idea of the 'nation-state', which is a technical recognition that the state confers nationality by its juridical authority but also an ethical/political claim that the state embodies a specific national identity. This claim may be psycho-politically untrue to varying extents depending on what minority inhabitants of the territorial community 'feel' with respect to identity and community.

Against this background, it seems most useful to consider the new matrix of citizenship in relation to several crucial frames of reference: the resilience of the sovereign state and the persistence of Westphalian citizenship; the case for regional citizenship; the role of the citizen pilgrim. Such emphases pick up selected aspects of an overall assessment of a confused, confusing, and exceedingly complicated pattern of shifting, inconsistent and overlapping allegiances that continue to inform the overall theme of citizenship.

## 1. WESTPHALIAN CITIZENSHIP: A RESILIENT REALITY

Despite globalisation in its various impacts, the individual overwhelmingly continues to be caught in a statist web of rights, duties and identities. At one level the right to travel depends on passports issued by states to their citizens and to none others (with trivial exceptions); borders are exclusively managed by governmental authority, and an abuse of rights in a foreign country is almost always dealt with by seeking help from one's country of citizenship. By controlling the conditions of access to sovereign territory, states control mobility in the world, including the possibility of entry into labour markets of foreign countries. Migration, to the extent that it is 'legal', rests on Westphalian notions of territorial sovereignty. To the extent that migration is 'illegal', it puts strains on Westphalian patterns of control but it also discloses their persistence as the illegal migrant is a figure of acute vulnerability, exposed to risks of deportation and exploitation, as well as being denied many of the benefits of legal residence and citizenship.

At another level, the duty to defend a country is related to the reciprocal privilege of being a citizen, although there are mercenaries and those impressed into military service whose role is not based on citizenship. Citizenship also engages most individuals in their most meaningful form of political action, voting for political leaders, giving freely in an electoral process consent to be governed. Even in non-democratic states where power is exercised without constitutional constraint, those who are treated as citizens are beneficiaries of certain rights of movement, travel and eligibility for government and military service that are generally denied to non-citizens. In contrast, those who cannot claim citizenship may be unable to cross borders freely unless they become recipients of a special status in recognition of their vulnerability. Refugees are protected by the UN High Commissioner of Refugees, who can issue travel documents, which may or may not be widely recognised. 'Statelessness' remains a status of severe deprivation, the very term implying the persistence of statism.

Beyond this, those 'citizens' who are victims of persecution or discrimination due to their specific ethnic or religious identity remain vulnerable to state power. That is, the failure of citizenship to secure basic human rights has not yet been addressed in a systematic manner by the international community. The state remains empowered in most instances to engage in 'human wrongs' directed at those present within a given territorial community, including citizens (Booth 1995; Dunne and Wheeler 1999). In effect, despite some instances of 'humanitarian intervention', non-Westphalian modalities of citizenship have not demonstrated any efficacy in providing protection to those abused by the state or as victims of discriminatory cultural and societal practices (Wheeler 2000). Ethnic cleansing and genocide, despite being criminalised on an international level, are not regularly or effectively challenged in most instances.[3] The only reliable protection for individuals and groups arises from the structures of constitutional authority operative at the level of the state, and in subordinate institutions under its control. The most important opportunities for reform bearing on human well-being also remain related to changes in domestic laws, administrative practices and political climate.

In this respect, the citizen who lives under the authority of a well-governed democratic state is generally secure, but not equally, whereas citizens who are subject to the vagaries of a gangster, corrupt or inept state are daily confronted by dangerous and troublesome forms of insecurity. Even in democratic states with strong traditions of constitutionalism there are important, even decisive, gaps in citizen protection. The circumstances of racial and religious minorities, the homeless, the non-heterosexual (homosexual, transsexual), the cult member and the political extremist are illustrative of categories of individuals who may find themselves targets of abuse in those Westphalian states that receive the highest ratings from Freedom House or the Human Development Report.[4] In this regard, the key indicator of the quality of citizenship remains the internal governing process of the Westphalian state, which is itself subject only to the most minimal forms of global regulation, and these are not consistently implemented. And it is not only a matter of governmental policy. Education and culture are of fundamental importance in determining the extent to which global norms are internalised in societal patterns, especially in relation to tolerance and respect for difference. With the exception of Western Europe, the citizen cannot gain substantive relief from internal denials of rights by invoking external norms and procedures. Because such norms and procedures exist to varying degrees in different parts of the world, it is possible under some circumstances to obtain *symbolic* relief, and even *substantive* reform, by way of media exposure, people's tribunals, censure moves in the UN, consumer boycott and conditionalities imposed by international financial institutions.

In the end, it is impossible to deny the centrality of Westphalian citizenship, which means that the state is the core actor in determining its quality within the life-world of individuals and groups. It is true that globalisation, the spread of electoral democracy and human rights, and a worldwide media challenge the state to uphold certain standards of behaviour in dealing with their citizens (and with foreigners, especially from leading countries). But contradictory developments accentuate unevenness, including the independence of the peoples of non-Western civilisations, the spread of transnational crime and corruption, the prevalence of failed states of various kinds, the neo-liberal antipathy to the implementation of economic and social rights, and the perceived failures of humanitarian intervention under UN auspices.[5]

## 2. The Case for Regional Citizenship

Regional citizenship is both competitive with and complementary to Westphalian citizenship. It is competitive in the fundamental sense of challenging the unitary and primary ideal of citizenship associated with the juridical/political construct of the nation-state, the backbone of the modern system of world order. There is an inevitable zero sum attribute to citizenship that arises as soon as what was once unquestionably situated, if at all, at the level of the state is transferred to other levels of authority and loyalty. In this respect, not surprisingly, ultra-nationalists are instinctively and intensely opposed to any deepening of regional attachments.

Viewed differently, regionalism complements Westphalian citizenship in a manner that is mutually beneficial. The emergence of regional community helps overcome attitudes of disillusionment with respect to the declining capacity of the territorial state to uphold the interests of its population. Also, the regional reality, to the extent that it is a functional success, helps to raise material standards, protect against environmental challenges and cooperate against transnational criminality. Furthermore, regional levels of identity potentially allow micro-nationalisms to participate in larger collective frameworks without the bitterness associated with subordination to a dominant territorial nationalism. At the same time, common bonds of culture, religion, language and history give psychological strength to regional identity, allowing it to be set off against 'others' in either defensive or assertive modes. In this regard, it is possible to view some regional frameworks as counter-hegemonic projects, which in the present historical period are designed to restrict the influence or dominance of the United States or the West. But it is also the case, especially with European regionalism, that it is partly counter-hegemonic but that it is also assertive, facilitating the projection of European influence and interests in a manner that is more effective than their pursuit via the disaggregated activity of separate European states.

There is considerable regional variation with respect to function, purpose and psycho-political role. Some regional frameworks, as is the case for such purely economic groupings as the North American Free Trade Area or MERCOSUR (the economic grouping of southern Latin American states), have no ambition to alter loyalty patterns in any way that bears significantly on citizenship. Others operate as vehicles for hegemonic domination on a regional level and again serve mainly as instruments of policy within a Westphalian setting, as was the case for the Organisation of American States (OAS), especially during the Cold War.

It could be contended that raising the issue of regional citizenship is premature, except possibly in the setting of the European Union. Vague ideas of African or Latin American consciousness or assertions of 'Asian values', although widely shared, fall far short of establishing the sort of bonds of loyalty and allegiance associated with Westphalian citizenship. In these post-colonial regions, even where state formation lags or is artificial, there is an attachment to political community defined by the boundaries of the sovereign state, if only as a contrast to the sort of subjugation of the colonial era. But patterns of ethnic nationalism in Asia and Africa are subverting the idea of citizenship altogether, except in the aspirational sense of a secessionist move-ment seeking to create a Westphalian state of its own.

Even EU regional citizenship has yet to be tested as a viable complement to Westphalian citizenship. The existence of the Euro, labour mobility and the growing influence of the directly elected European Parliament provide strong possibilities for building a genuine European identity and bondedness based on shared values and memories that goes beyond the functional advantages and geopolitical benefits of regional cooperation. Part of the complexity of the European experiment arises from its double hegemonic dimension, as further complicated by the security dimension. European regionalism is widely interpreted as containing US (external) and German (internal) domination but as also facilitating the implementation of hegemonic influence in mod-alities that are made to appear 'legitimate'. The interplay of European security concerns with these hegemonic preoccupations is also rather convoluted, combining views that the peace of Europe depends on continuing American engagement with the idea that with the collapse of the Soviet Union there is no longer any need or justification for accepting the primacy of the United States in the European security sphere. Such factors, along with the dilution of European identity that will accompany enlargement, work against the construction of comparable sentiments of allegiance to those associated with robust instances of Westphalian citizenship.

To the extent that Europeans perceive European regionalism as vehicles for American or German hegemony it obstructs the formation of even weak attitudes of loyalty and allegiance. At the same time it is impressive that in the EU setting there has been a juridical willingness by the constituent states in the Maastricht Treaty to agree formally to the conferral of European citizenship. Such a move expresses some willingness by sovereign governments to relinquish their exclusive claims of allegiance and in this sense participate in the transformation of the Westphalian structure. Just how much of a relinquishment is unclear and will not become evident for some decades. Form does not necessarily entail substantive changes. The experience of federal states underlines the extent to which juridical statehood cannot itself establish Westphalian citizenship in a stable form. Where subnationalisms remain dissatisfied, or where the federal entity encompasses cleavages on values and identities, feelings of unity and of belonging to the whole will not be forthcoming. The parts generate stronger feelings of solidarity than the whole and when crises occur the whole tends to fragment. The recent experiences of the Soviet Union, Indonesia and especially the former Yugoslavia illustrate some facets of weak citizenship within the Westphalian framework. In this regard, a European polity is likely, at best, to be a exceedingly fragile form of regional federalism, where allegiance to the parts overshadows allegiance to the whole for the foreseeable future. Such a pattern means that the regional entity is sustained by the perceived benefits of cooperation (as unlike failed federal experiments, European institutions of governance are not likely to have the mandate or the capability to prevent withdrawal of members). Many civil wars are about secessionist claims, including the American Civil War. In this regard, the prospects for robust European citizenship need to be viewed sceptically.

At the same time, the Westphalian prism may not determine the quality of European or regional citizenship. If functional and normative factors convince Europeans that their life is greatly enhanced by its regional character, and if cultural formations take hold, then there may arise a psycho-political process of confidence-building that is more comparable to what has occurred in strong federal states. The United States since the American Civil War is exemplary. Canada, Australia and India, despite strong sub-nationalisms, also have managed to produce Westphalian states where the whole dominates the parts. Europe has this possibility, although likely along the more economistic lines of regional nationalism understood as a response to the challenges of globalisation.

In any event, it is to be expected that other regions, especially in Asia, will closely watch this European experiment with regionalism, including its conferral of citizenship, and will either be drawn toward or away from imitation. There is no question, as Jacques Delors made so clear, that economic integration cannot advance beyond a certain point without parallel political integration and that the latter presupposes the formation of complementary allegiance patterns of the sort associated with at least weak or thin forms of citizenship. Whether this makes the emergent European polity stable and sustainable over time is a matter of conjecture at this point.

### 3. VISIONARY PERSPECTIVES: THE ROLE OF THE CITIZEN PILGRIM

The contemporary predicament of citizenship is associated with the resilience of the Westphalian state in a global setting that bypasses and penetrates the state but does not generate alternative political frameworks that can become new focal points of identity and loyalty. The European regional response is an experiment in supplemental citizenship but it remains at such an early and rudimentary stage that its impact cannot be assessed. Another approach to this diffusion of authority and the porousness of borders has been to invoke the image of the medieval precursor to the Westphalian era of states, arguing that the new reality can be best understood on the basis of multiple centres of authority and allegiance. The neo-medieval contention rests on the globality of the normative: human rights, the religious revival and international law; and the functional: world economy and global climate change. It also rests on a variety of developments that challenge the territorial primacy of the state, including the rise of ethnic politics, the claims of indigenous peoples and the emphasis on local sites of struggle. The combination of global, statist, transnational, regional and local is what gives plausibility to the neo-medieval hypothesis. But such a plausibility is mainly a conceptual construct to explain the complexity of the post-modern circumstance of politics, and does not seem to be fashioning the sorts of identities that can be associated with 'citizenship'. True, social movements create strong gender, religious and civilisational identities that to some extent have displaced Westphalian identities. But the sense of belonging is not comparable to the idea of being a member of a comprehensive political community, which is the core meaning of 'citizenship'.

When world citizenship is claimed by idealists, who are usually proponents of world governments, most eyes glaze over. The cosmopolitan sentiment is detached from any viable political project or emergent political community. It is dismissed as utopian foolishness. Similarly, when more recently members of the global corporate or banking elite describe themselves as world citizens, it exhibits confusion about the nature of citizenship, associating it with a global lifestyle and modes of business that do not restrict their operations by reference to territorial boundaries. The extreme thinness of such 'citizenship', if it can even be so denominated, is exhibited by the lack of commitment to global public goods, by the absence of concern about the well-being of all persons on the planet, and by the lack of support for effective forms of global governance.

My point here is that the only kind of visionary citizenship that can be taken seriously will have to be grounded in what is occurring on the level of fact, norm and value as both trend and potentiality. It must be rooted in the future, the not-yet, rather than unconvincingly affirm as 'real' such a reconfiguring of political allegiance as is so unconvincingly claimed by secular-minded 'world citizens'. I have used the metaphor of 'citizen pilgrim' to describe the spirit of a sojourner, committed to transformation that is spiritual as well as material, that is premised on the wholeness and equality of the human family, and that is disinterested in devising technical fixes that will enable global governance to succeed as a functional project.[6]

It is difficult to specify too concretely at this point what will follow from the perspectives of citizen pilgrims. They are a diverse lot, although oriented toward the achievement of 'humane governance' locally and globally for all peoples in the world, as well as toward promoting sustainable development that is protective of future generations while appreciating the importance of improving the material conditions of those now alive. The citizen pilgrim recognises that these goals cannot be fulfilled by relying only on the agency of the sovereign state. The impact of globalisation is such that the ideals of humane governance must infuse the undertakings of local, regional and global arenas, implying participation, accountability, transparency and legality wherever policy is being shaped and implemented. As such, the citizen pilgrim is dedicated to establishing the global conditions across and beyond Westphalian borders, which in turn will deepen and enrich the prospects within sovereign states. Part of this outlook is encompassed by wider and distant horizons of aspiration and by the imagery of 'cosmopolitan democracy'. Globalising democracy underscores the extent to which the fulfilment of the goals of citizenship in the future depends on allegiance to *values* and not to *states*, especially the extent to which states are being subordinated to the priorities of market forces and to which the quality of citizenship within states will increasingly depend on extending democracy to arenas of authority and decision *beyond* the control of states.

The citizen pilgrim rejects the premises of materialism and believes that a sustainable world community can only result from a combination of secular and spiritual energies. It is from such a perspective that the religious resurgence must be understood as providing an indispensable source of hope, as well as a dangerous challenge to the achievements of modernity (Falk 2001). So conceived, the many initiatives associated with inter-civilisational dialogue can be seen as a crucial part of this world cultural preparation for the next stage in world order centred on human solidarity, sustainable development, global civil society and multi-level arrangements of global governance. So comprehended, the negative energies of resistance to such transformative possibilities arouse intense emotions, as was evident in the global resonance to Samuel Huntington's depiction of the coming clash of civilisations (Huntington 1996). The clash hypothesis is the shadow side of post-Westphalian struggle, a darkness that lacks any impulse toward transcendence. The silver lining of dialogic interaction is not merely an exchange of views to avoid perverse misunderstandings and recriminations, it is an endeavour to collaborate in the hard work of political and moral imagination that must be done on a global scale if the outcome is to be eventually welcomed.

The citizen pilgrim is engaged as a militant in this process. The religious factor need not be explicit or direct. Reliance on 'human rights' as a universal political language is a secular alternative for engaging in dialogue, despite some serious drawbacks arising from perceived Western biases and the marginal role of non-Western civilisations in the norm-generating experience. By accepting the challenge of dialogue, as in the work of such seminal non-Western thinkers as Chandra Muzaffar, Tu Weiming and Ahmet Davutoglu, there arises a real possibility that a shared understanding of what needs to be done to safeguard the human future can begin to take shape.

The moves in this direction remain at the margins of entrenched power, both the residual power of the state and the new constellation of forces associated with globalisation (and regionalisation). But there are signs on the horizons that such a dialogic civilisational/religious challenge will become inevitably more credible. As yet, little has been done to prepare humanity for the advent of radical technologies likely to emerge in the course of the next several decades. The ethical/political problems associated with biogenetics (including human cloning), advanced robotics (including sophisticated robot armies) and super-computers (with problem-solving and decision-making capabilities far exceeding what humans can achieve) present a series of challenges to the meaning and nature of life that cannot be confined in space without risking catastrophic developments that could imperil human survival (Joy 2000). It is not relevant to interpret the controversy unleashed as to whether the technological innovations on the horizons are as a big a menace as Joy supposes. What seems inevitable is that human consciousness will be profoundly challenged throughout the world to respond in a manner that allows for a global democratic process of assessment and regulation.

It is within such a future that the citizen pilgrim will have prefigured a community of believers in the collective destiny of the human species. When such attitudes intersect with tendencies toward transnational networking and institutional innovation, the foundations for new varieties of citizenship will begin to emerge, with appropriate patterns of allegiance, participation and accountability. Such varieties remain over the horizon, beyond our imagining capacities, but their preconditions are beginning to become clear, expressive of an ethos of non-violence, sustainability, compassion and solidarity. Such an ethos is the clay out of which the citizen pilgrim is beginning to mould the political sculptures of a benevolent human future.

QUESTIONS

1. Why, according to Falk, does the nation-state so dominate the lives of individuals as citizens?
2. What are the main developments challenging the statist view and associated ideas of citizenship?
3. How realistic are hopes for the emergence of 'European citizenship' as either a complement or rival to existing national citizenships?
4. To what extent do conceptions of 'netizen' and 'citizen pilgrim' reflect a different approach to the basis and nature of citizenship, as compared to 'Westphalian citizenship'?

NOTES

1. The right of self-determination was supposed to be exercised in a manner that did not result in the dismemberment of existing states (see standard formulation in Declaration of Principles Concerning Friendly Relations and Co-operation Among States, United Nations General Assembly Resolution 2625, 24 October 1970) but the break-up of the Soviet Union, and especially of the former Yugoslavia, has abandoned this limitation. What was significant was not only the claims of state-shattering political independence by the former federal units in these two countries but the readiness of the international community to abandon its own doctrine of statist unity for the sake of geopolitical expediency, that is, welcoming these particular instances of break-up. Such doctrinal opportunism inevitably weakens the inhibition on the assertion of other comparable claims. The opposition to Albanian Kosovar insistence on full political independence is difficult to oppose on principled grounds.
2. The state responds, characteristically, with a technological fix by way of warfare without casualties.
3. The exceptional challenges that do occur arise from issues related to Eurocentrism and geopolitical policy imperatives, as in the NATO War over Kosovo.
4. There are admittedly some ambiguities. For instance, 'cults' may both espouse unorthodox belief systems that should be tolerated in a democratic society, and dangerous forms of absolutism that need to be regulated, if not altogether prohibited. An example of the latter is the Aum Shinrikyo cult in Japan, which made an indiscriminate attack in 1995 on Tokyo subway riders with sarin gas killing twelve and injuring thousands of civilians (Lifton 1999). See also Buruma (2001) on the menace posed by what he calls 'killer cults'.
5. The experiences of the 1990s relating to Somalia, Bosnia and Rwanda have been crucial.
6. This view that I favour contrasts with what I understand Martin Shaw (2000) to be advocating. Shaw's stress is a pragmatic one that builds on current trends, especially on the democratising projects of transnational social movements and their links to Western power, and culminates with the development of a system of global governance that inhibits war, see esp. 259–70 in particular.

# 2. GLOBAL CITIZENSHIP: YES OR NO?

## Nigel Dower

The idea of global citizenship or world citizenship – I shall use the phrases interchangeably – is remarkably controversial. Many claim that we are at least in the early twenty-first century world citizens, whilst others dismiss the idea as absurd. One way of seeing why such different positions on whether we are global citizens can be taken up is to address the issue via a series of further, more specific, contradictory statements and examine the reasons which might be given for each statement. At the very least this will reveal how complex the field is. In each case I offer a further critical comment which is sometimes a resolution of the opposition, sometimes support for one position but with recognition of important points made on the other side.

### 1. Ethical or Institutional?

(a) World citizenship is an essentially ethical conception about what people ought morally to do.
(b) World citizenship is an essentially institutional conception about membership of institutions of a specifically global kind.

*For (a):* The essential idea of world citizenship came from the Stoics and was about a relationship we had in a non-artificial way with the universe (which we could recognise if we were wise enough); what it rejected was the importance of artificial and contingent identities of living in particular political communities (for example, Heater 1996). Political communities are artificial in the sense that they are created and modified by the will of human beings and they are contingent in that it is an accident what political community I am born into and my contingent membership of one is quite distinct from my essential nature as a human being. In the modern world,

world citizenship may express itself in various forms of institutions (and might one day express itself through the artificial institutions of world government). But it still remains the core of world citizenship that one affirms a basic moral commitment, based on natural law, human rights, Kantian respect for persons or some similar ethical theory which does not base ethics on convention or agreement. From this vantage point one may wish to distance oneself from any actual institutions, global or otherwise (as many Stoics did in relation to what was, in effect, world empire at the time, namely the Roman Empire). For instance, a future world state might make one undoubtedly a world citizen in a legal sense, but one might for all that be profoundly discontented with it in terms of its policies and as a true world citizen answering to a higher moral law.

*For (b):* World citizenship makes no sense unless it is understood in institutional terms since citizenship is itself an institutional concept. We may be by nature human beings (with certain moral duties and rights as such) but the status of *citizenship* is essentially an artificial one, depending upon the construction of particular kinds of institutions by virtue of which one is a citizen.

This position might be adopted first by someone who wished to reject the idea of world citizenship on the grounds that the relevant institutions are not in place. For example, David Miller's support for nation-state citizenship takes this sort of form (Miller 1999). Thus the idea is dismissed except as a moral conception of doubtful interest and relevance (and misleading in the modern world with its well-established ideas about citizenship, whatever may have been the case in the ancient world).

On the other hand the position might be adopted by others who welcomed the idea of global citizenship. That is, whilst the *idea* of world citizenship can be extended beyond the conventionally political, that extension does indeed crucially depend upon an institutional factor, namely *there actually being* and/ or there being *intended* certain kinds of institutions through which world citizenship can get expressed. On the latter view, are we world citizens? Some might say that we aren't yet but that we ought to work for it by creating the relevant institutions; others that we are already global citizens given present institutions (see 3 below). Much depends upon how strong one thinks existing institutions are in what may be called 'global civil society' and how important what now exists is compared with working towards creating it.

*Critical comment:* Although there are contexts in which it is perfectly appropriate for someone to make a purely moral claim (in line with the Stoics), and there could be future circumstances where the institutions (for example, of a world state or some form of global governance approaching it) made it an uncontroversial institutional statement of an empirical kind, in the modern world the claims of world citizenship are a combination of moral and institutional components. The moral claim is that we have obligations in principle of a global kind which for their adequate expression require the development of appropriate institutions, and the institutional claim is that those institutions already exist albeit in a radically incomplete form.

Objectively the ethical framework and the institutional framework are to be accepted (whether or not individuals do accept it). Subjectively people can be said to be 'world citizens' in so far as they acknowledge such obligations and institutions. Of course the robustness of such institutions is a function of how many people actually acknowledge this framework. Undoubtedly we need what H. G. Wells called a 'mental cosmopolis' (through which we 'intend world community' in John Macmurray's phrase before the intention is fully actualised (Macmurray 1957)) and this has to precede its embodiment in institutions (quoted in Heater 1996). This is analogous to F. H. Bradley's conception of morality having a body (institutions, shared public rules and practices) and soul (individual moral wills) (Bradley 1876). There is a dialectical relationship between the two. In fact there are three elements here: (i) the *objective moral claim* made by a thinker, such as Piet Hein's striking statement 'we are global citizens with tribal souls' (quoted in Barnaby 1988), where the thinker is able, perhaps only temporarily, to transcend that limited perception and see things for what they are; (ii) the need for a *mentality* (our 'global' souls); and (iii) the need for *embodiment* (in public institutions and shared culture).

## 2. VACUOUS CONCEPTION?

(a) World citizenship is a vacuous and incoherent conception; it debases the currency of citizenship and is redundant in terms of the adequate expression of a global ethic.

(b) World citizenship is not a vacuous but a potentially rich and dynamic conception; given the acceptance of a global ethic, it is better to adopt a world citizen category than not.

*For (a):* By extending the idea of 'citizenship' beyond its twin context of political community and the moral community in which such membership occurs, the idea is emptied of its real meaning. This is partly an argument based on the special political nature of citizenship (as Miller claims) and partly on the more general idea that we gain our identity from particular moral communities (as MacIntyre and other communitarians claim). Thus MacIntyre sees world citizens as 'rootless' and claims that by becoming citizens of everywhere we become citizens of nowhere (quoted in Almond 1990). In a similar vein Cooper sees academics concerned with the environment who jet around the world waxing eloquently about the global environment as actually losing what it means to be in an environment as *a field of significance* (Cooper 1992). We are not then in reality global citizens, since citizenship is restricted to membership of a political community, and any attempt to use the language in this extended sense can at best be metaphorical, at worst misleading. If pragmatically it served to strengthen motivation, then there might be some justification for an incorrect or misleading use of language. But this is not the case. The extent to which agents respond to global duties is a function of what ethical theories they accept and what the general moral culture surrounding them is like, not particularly a function of this specific language.

*For (b):* Politically there are various ways in which the institutions we can act through can be extended beyond the nation-state. Ethically we do not become rootless unless we reject altogether our other levels of identity and community. Such rejection is not required by the acceptance of world citizenship. Analogously no one supposes that a child starts by being a world citizen rather than a member of his own family or gives the latter up when she accepts being a citizen! Modern states are already far too big for most individuals to feel much identity with the whole but their attachment shows itself through their involvement in smaller organisations and communities which are part of the whole. Likewise, most world citizenship action will express itself through involvement in a wide variety of organisations and communities of concern (often local). What is significant is that the interests and concerns of such groups are global in character. We may adapt the adage 'think globally act locally' to 'intend globally act locally'.

The idea of being a global citizen will, if accepted, reinforce the motivation of actors and make persuasion of others more achievable, since it does not merely assert the duties involved but describes us as members of a global *community*. In any case, any adequate ethical response to the problems facing the world must involve action through various institutions which are the appropriate embodiment of global citizenship. If the reality is that we are global citizens, that is, we are acting within the framework of global community, then truth requires that we acknowledge this dimension of our lives.

*Critical comment*: Although the sceptics are wrong to suppose that the category of world citizenship cannot become psychologically dynamic (both politically and ethically), they are right to stress the danger that a purely ethical conception of world citizenship will be inadequate; attention needs to be given to the creation of the right conditions of identity, motivation and a sense of being rooted in relevant communities of concern, which of course need not be located in one specific geographical area. One kind of non-localised community of concern would be an Internet interest group.

One of the key issues involved is over the nature and character of the global ethic accepted. Moral theories which require extensive action at a global level are likely to lead to the recognition of the efficacy of global citizenship discourse, even if the initial arguments do not start with it. For instance

Peter Singer's well-known radical ethic of sacrifice for alleviating world poverty is stated and defended without reference to world citizenship. ('If it is in our power to prevent an evil happening without thereby sacrificing anything of comparable moral importance, we ought to do it') (Singer 1979: ch. 8). Understanding one's responsibilities as a member of a global moral community would, however, help convert acceptance of the principle into concerted action. It has nevertheless to be recognised that whilst the discourse of world citizenship may be necessary if one does accept a robust global ethic (though not necessarily as demanding as Singer's principle), it by no means follows that all and everyone who accept such an ethic will need to use or accept that category. There may be very many different ways of being motivated.

## 3. WORLD GOVERNMENT?

(a) World citizenship is conceptually tied to world government.
(b) World citizenship is not conceptually tied to world government but involves commitment to working through other kinds of global institutions and the development of the same.

*For (a):* If citizenship is to make any sense in this context, it must be on all fours with citizenship in the nation-state context, so world citizenship would have to be citizenship of a world state with all the analogous structures of allegiance, taxation and so on.

This position could be adopted by someone who rejected the idea of world citizenship for the world as it is now, on the grounds that we do not have nor are near having a world government, whether or not he thought such a thing was desirable. However, it is more likely that someone who thought it was desirable would not deny that world citizenship exists, but rather take the view that we are (or at least those who accept the positions are) world citizens in virtue of a commitment to work for the creation of a federal world state (through all channels including existing institutions).

*For (b):* World citizenship is not to be understood as requiring reference to world government (or as requiring reference to institutions of any one particular kind) but to a variety of institutions – national parties, NGOs, global networks of various kinds – through which global concerns can be expressed. These institutions partly exist already but can, of course, be developed and part of the commitment of global citizenship is precisely to the development of these institutions, so that global responsibilities can be more effectively exercised.

*Critical comment:* This issue flags up the importance of giving an account of institutions in order to make sense of a robust conception of world citizenship.

If we were world citizens in a world state, then of course we would all be global citizens in virtue of the political community we belonged to (whether we wanted it or liked the order in question). What, however, about other kinds of institutions now? On the one hand, there is a sense in which working through these for certain global goals is *optional* and therefore depends on what agents decide to do. On this view it makes less sense to talk of *all* people being world citizens (see also 5 below). On the other hand, this runs counter to strong motives for wanting to say that people are global citizens without realising it. So if the claim that we are all global citizens is to stick (beyond a moral claim about responsibility), we need a more robust account of what these global institutions are which make us all members of global institutions whether we realise it or not. It may be that we need to make more of three ideas which are becoming the focus of much attention – global governance (for example, World Commission on Global Governance 1995), global democracy (for example, Held 1995a) and global civil society (for example, Linklater 1999a). Furthermore there is the international legal framework, especially the human rights framework, which provides a framework for thinking of all humans as citizens of the world in more than a merely moral sense.

## 4. OBJECTIVE ETHICAL BASIS?

(a) World citizenship presupposes a traditional objectivist ethic and is a universal concept with timeless and unchanging central norms.
(b) World citizenship does not presuppose a traditional objectivist ethic but can be fashioned out of any kind of ethic with the appropriate content, and its central norms are relative to time and place.

*For (a):* World citizenship is a conception which has arisen out of a certain style of western thought associated with the Enlightenment. It assumes a global order informed by a set of shared values. Whilst the detailed character of these ethics varies – Natural Law, Kant, Utilitarianism, Natural Rights – they all share the common feature of being objectively true or valid, universal and discovered a priori, that is, by a theorist, in Bull's sense, in an armchair rather than empirically investigating what is established. (Bull prefers what he calls the a posteriori approach which grounds moral values on what is generally agreed (Bull 1979); for a survey of traditional ethical theories of a cosmopolitan kind see Dower 1998). According to this view, if the opposite view is accepted that moral values are not universal, but vary from culture to culture, then there can be no global ethics and no basis for a set of universal norms underlying world citizenship. There is nothing peculiarly modern about world citizenship, since the ancient Stoics advocated the idea; it certainly does not depend on modern political conditions or the presence of modern technology.

This position could again be held by one or other of two different kinds of thinkers. First there are those who, because of a suspicion of objectivist ethics of the traditional kind, reject world citizenship discourse on the grounds that it rests on a theoretical error and is in danger of being culturally imperialistic in practice, partly because it is based on ideas emanating from the European Enlightenment. On the other hand, there are those who advocate world citizenship precisely because they do assert such an ethical approach and believe that it is the only sound basis for constructing such a discourse.

*For (b):* World citizenship no more presupposes any one particular kind of ethical theory than does national citizenship. National citizenship is based on *some* shared values, even though different groups in a pluralist society will have divergent values as well. How these values come to be shared, or what their source is, are questions of secondary importance. What matters for a global ethic is that agents accept that they have moral reason to act responsibly in relation to the whole world and to cooperate to protect common interests and so on. Such an ethic could well be constructed, gradually evolved or develop through negotiation. In this respect modern conditions are crucial, especially the way modern technologies of communication enable forms of identity and cooperation and kinds of institutions which were not easy in the past. Alternatively the ethic of someone who calls herself a global citizen may be one she sees as based on personal or subjective values, derived neither from objective facts nor from consensus or agreement.

*Critical comment:* Since the position (b) is open in the sense that allows both traditional ethical theories as well as other ethical bases, and since clearly there are people who in the modern world reject traditional thinking but think of themselves as global citizens, it seems as though (b) needs to be accepted. But we need to be cautious. Certainly, global citizenship in an institutional sense may be a peculiarly modern development, because it is in the context of shared global problems that people cooperate and hence develop shared ethical norms and values. But here the twin aspects of world citizenship – the moral and institutional – may point in opposite directions. Anyone who has reason, perhaps because of the perception of common global problems, to seek consensus with people with very different ethical theories has some kind of global ethic, which, if not traditionally objective, is a theory which he himself endorses from within his own thinking. If it is traditional (for example, Kantianism; Utilitarianism; Christianity), such an approach may well be of a kind which could have been held by thinkers in different ages.

In so far as world citizenship involves evolving common institutions through which individuals work, the extent to which those institutions become more developed, the more there will be a working sets of norms which have come to be agreed (often by a process of negotiation). These norms arise not from theory but from consensus and will be supported by a wide range of agents whose theoretical starting points will be very varied. Thus at one level world citizenship need not presuppose any particular ethical theory or kind of ethical theory, but at another level each person who accepts that she is a world citizen is likely to have her own ethical theory (Dower 1998: ch. 6).

## 5. ALL OR SOME?

(a) We are *all* world citizens.
(b) We are not all world citizens, only some who by their actions or attitudes or self-descriptions have the status of world citizen.

*For (a):* We have duties in principle towards all human beings, for example, not to undermine the bases of their well-being. We all have moral rights recognised by the international community. The world is so interconnected and interdependent that what is done in any part of the world can in principle impinge on the situation of others, so in principle we all have a share in a combined responsibility to avoid, reduce or address common problems.

*For (b):* It is quite absurd to suppose that most people have duties towards others in distant parts of the world. Many people, particularly poorer people in the South, are rightly concerned entirely with their own local problems and challenges. As an extreme example, the people living in the rainforest with no contact with the outside world cannot be said to be global citizens. Citizenship can only apply to those whose activities do have significant global impacts for which they are in real terms responsible and additionally requires an awareness of this category in the agents involved.

*Critical comment:* There are really two interconnected issues here. First, is the idea of global citizenship more about *duties* or more about *rights*? Certainly if it is more about rights, then these rights may be said to be universal and belong to all human being as *human rights*, whether or not people are aware of or claim these rights. Thus the *Universal Declaration of Human Rights* (1948) and numerous others legal instruments, international, regional and national, which give more detailed expression to such rights, all provide the framework for thinking of universal rights that world citizens possess. In a parallel way an influential conception of citizenship at national level was put forward by T. H. Marshall (Marshall 1973). He defined citizenship in terms of three kinds of right – civil, political and social. In contrast to this, others have developed a more 'republican' conception of citizenship as involving the duties of active participation in the affairs of one's state. In this sense citizenship is less secure at a global level, at least as applying to *all*, because it is unclear whether everyone does have a duty to participate in global institutions in global civil society. Certainly only a few do as a matter of fact so participate.

Second, there is the issue of whether *active* participation and *explicit adoption* of responsibility are the preconditions of being a global citizen in a full sense. Certainly a judgement of a particular person like 'she is a global citizen' implies such a full sense. On the other hand it seems counter-intuitive to say that people's obligations depend upon whether they act on them or accept them.

Perhaps a resolution of this would be to say that all human beings are in principle world citizens but to allow a wide spectrum of cases from a fully fledged form of self-conscious engagement and active responsibility, especially through appropriate institutions (political parties, NGOs and so on), through to cases where the category applies *hypothetically*, in order to cover cases where people have no wider 'causal footprints' beyond the local and thus have no need for active engagement at other levels. In the middle there is a way of understanding world citizens as bearers of universal human rights which does not imply active engagement in or even self-conscious acceptance of this category by those who have the rights. (In the case of a tribe in Amazon rainforest, it would certainly be inappropriate that they should be introduced to the 'conceptual package' with all that that would entail, or to regard a theory of global citizenship as doomed if one does not want that to be done. In many ways if their relationship to their environment is benign and they are not harming other people, they could be regarded as 'implicitly' good world citizens.)

## 6. CHALLENGE TO NATIONAL CITIZENSHIP?

(a) World citizenship challenges national citizenship/loyalty.
(b) World citizenship does not challenge national citizenship/loyalty but complements it.

*For (a):* World citizenship, even if it falls short of world government, inevitably involves a commitment to a moral ideal and to certain moral priorities which will reduce the level of commitment to the nation-state, whether this is at the level of feeling less than truly patriotic, or not putting energies into the well-being of one's own community (because of other commitments) or even weakening the commitment to obeying the law. In any case loyalty to the nation-state, which is different from obedience to its law, is an attitude of allegiance which is bound to be challenged by wider commitment or allegiance to a global common good.

This position may be adopted again both by those who are opposed to world citizenship on the grounds that the relation of a citizen to his state is morally important; but also by those who, in advocating world citizenship, precisely wish to challenge the current sets of priorities and attachments of citizens to their state.

*For (b):* The opposition is founded on an exaggerated contrast between what things are like within the state without world citizenship and what they are like with it. The idea of absolute loyalty to the state simply is not a reality or required for an adequate conception of national citizenship. Apart from a wide range of reasons for which people accept the possibility of justified civil disobedience (which may have no particular relation to global issues), people combine many moral commitments (to their church, charities, particular passions) with their commitments as citizens without any problem of a general kind. In any case the Stoic conception of concentric circles of family, immediate community, political community, the world (or the universe) can be adopted (Nussbaum 1996). Much expression of world citizenship concern can indeed be mediated through existing political structures or via NGOs which all work through the national political system.

*Critical comment:* whilst it is correct to say that acceptance of world citizenship need not lead to any formal opposition, it would be disingenuous not to accept that active world citizenship, in terms of not merely moral commitments but also sense of identity and allegiance to a wider constituency, has implications for how we think of state citizenship. These commitments go beyond the existence of other more normal attachments within a society. But there is no reason not to see this relationship as generally complementary, just as a layer of European citizenship can be meshed into the national citizenship of Member States. In any case the more citizens come to adopt global perspectives, the more a country's interests will come to harmonise with the good of all.

## CONCLUSION

What conclusions can we draw from this series of opposing views on global citizenship? It is tempting to say that there are no right answers or that it does not matter which answers we give, since it all depends upon how you decide to define the phrase or on what values you happen to believe in. But this would be too easy a verdict, since there are advantages and disadvantages to different definitions as well as important consequences for the different ethical positions we are prepared to argue for.

Certainly we have seen that different definitional moves can be made. Is the claim that we are global citizens an ethical claim or is it an institutional claim, like the claim that we are ordinary citizens, or is it both? If it is institutional, what forms does it or should it take? If we take the parallel with citizenship seriously, is it primarily about rights, about rights and correlative duties, or also about wider responsibilities and participation in (global) public affairs? Are we all global citizens or are only some, or is it better to think of two levels of basic and active citizenship?

We have seen that many issues turn on ethical positions. The most fundamental question is whether we should accept a global ethic or not. Certainly there are those who are sceptical about this. But even if we do accept one, how important is it to express this through the language of global citizenship? If we accept a global ethic, what is its content and what kind of justification do we give for it? And if we do accept this approach, does it require revision to our attitudes to national citizenship and patriotism?

My own preferred way of thinking of global citizenship is this: all human beings are global citizens in virtue of rights and duties which we all have as human beings. Such a global ethic may be thought of in different ways (ranging from traditional objectivism to subjectivism) and its content can vary. Only some human beings are 'active' global citizens because they accept responsibility to pursue global concerns. Being a global citizen is not merely a matter of accepting a global ethical framework; it is belonging to and participating in a wider community which finds expression in a variety of institutions within global civil society which already exist but which a global citizen is committed to develop and strengthen.

---

### QUESTIONS

1. Does the answer to the question 'Are we global citizens?' depend simply on how we choose to define the phrase 'global citizens'?
2. If you think of yourself as a global citizen, do you think that other people who do not are not global citizens? If you don't think of yourself as one, do you accept that other people are? Why do you take the line that you do?
3. If global citizenship is more than a claim about global responsibility, what developments in the world would determine conclusively that we are global citizens?
4. Is global citizenship more a claim about universal rights or about universal obligations?

---

# 3. GOOD INTERNATIONAL CITIZENSHIP

## John Williams

INTRODUCTION – THE IDEA OF 'GOOD INTERNATIONAL CITIZENSHIP'

The idea of Good International Citizenship is in many ways a remarkably simple one, although, as will hopefully be shown, it comes with some complicated baggage. Good International Citizenship proposes that states be regarded as citizens of the international community. The idea of states as citizens will thus establish certain expectations, akin to those we apply to individual citizens within a political community. States are the possessors of certain rights and owe commensurate duties within an established, regulated and codified framework which includes both formal international law and a more customary or informal framework of rules and principles of behaviour. The 'provision of national security, the strengthening of international order and the promotion of human rights' are mutually beneficial and underpin the idea of Good International Citizenship (Wheeler and Dunne 1998: 854). These rights and duties apply most strongly to those states which are predicated upon the idea of individual citizenship; that is, liberal democracies (Linklater 1992: 38).

Thus the 'good' in Good International Citizenship is linked to the idea of a concern for human rights within a framework that values respect for the sovereignty of states and recognises and accepts that questions of state security and order amongst states have a legitimate place in foreign policy. The language is not just a rhetorical ploy to try and establish a rather crude distinction between this approach and 'bad' international citizenship. It is, instead, appealing to a particular view of what constitutes goodness in the conduct of state policy in international relations. This view is something we will return to later in the chapter. However, it is worth noting here that this 'human rights within sovereignty' type of definition of goodness is not uncontroversial or immune from challenge. It is possible to agree with the premise of states as citizens of an international community or society of states, but to argue that 'goodness' ought to be viewed differently. For the sake of argument, though, the chapter shall proceed as though this notion of goodness is acceptable.

The motivations behind the idea of Good International Citizenship are unashamedly pragmatic. Indeed, the idea first came to some prominence when it was proposed by Gareth Evans, foreign minister of Australia in the mid and late 1980s, as a framework for Australian foreign policy (Wheeler and Dunne 1998: 854). It has recently been revived as a way of assessing UK foreign policy following Robin Cook's famous announcement of an 'ethical dimension' to UK foreign policy in May 1997 (Wheeler and Dunne 1998: 848). As such, the idea bears the imprint of practical politics, and we shall see how this has both costs and benefits. However, this practical pragmatism is evident in the framing assumptions of Good International Citizenship.

Firstly, it assumes that states are the dominant actors on the international stage. Individual citizens of these states find it almost impossible to achieve political results in international politics without going through the mechanisms of the sovereign state. The state enjoys all sorts of legal, institutional and power-political advantages and privileges in international politics and these have to be recognised and worked with, or perhaps round. In the effort to grant prominence to the sorts of issues often associated with global citizenship – human rights, the environment, development and political freedom – the states and the states-system are, at the very least, mechanisms which have to be engaged with and utilised. Therefore, it makes practical sense to think through ways in which the state can be thought of as an ally, or potential ally, in this process, rather than being the blockage it is often portrayed as. Good International Citizenship thus offers the attractive possibility of a practical and pragmatic way of promoting such issues but without having to first dismantle the sovereign states system. Good International Citizenship may thus appeal to advocates of global citizenship because it offers both a method of promoting progress on issues like human rights that are often linked to global citizenship and because it enables the holding of states to account as being themselves citizens of an international community and thus owing certain duties and bearing certain obligations. States may thus be brought more thoroughly, and more positively, into discussions about the nature of global citizenship and how it relates to and can be implemented in contemporary political circumstances.

The second assumption underpinning Good International Citizenship is potentially more problematic, if no less pragmatic. That is the implicit acceptance that the state to a considerable extent represents a coherent and unified national community. The state is like an individual writ large with the unity of identity and purpose we often associate with the individual. Good International Citizenship thus appeals, at least implicitly, to the individual analogy – that the state in international politics is akin to the individual in domestic politics. Unlike arguably the most famous appeal to the individual analogy in international relations – the idea of the state as being like an individual in a Hobbesian state of nature (for example, Beitz 1979: 27–50) – Good International Citizenship posits a fairly highly developed legal and customary framework in which the rights and duties of states are relatively well-defined, relations between states are generally orderly and where there is substantial agreement on issues of right and wrong. International politics may lack the clarity and solidarity of a well-run state but it is not a 'war of all against all' where there is no law and thus no justice.

The final assumption worth discussing is the prominence of universal human rights. National security, international order and human rights go together in Good International Citizenship. It thus appeals to the cosmopolitan idea of universal humanity – we are all people and we all have certain rights because we are people and these rights are inalienable. The idea that there is a radical split between human rights – which are a domestic matter – and international relations is dismissed in Good International Citizenship. States' foreign policies can, and must, take account of human rights and it is entirely proper they be judged on the basis of human rights, although not wholly or exclusively on this basis.

It is this that establishes the most obvious link between Good International Citizenship and global citizenship more generally. For many, as Nigel Dower discusses in 'Global Ethics and Global Citizenship' (Chapter 11), a cosmopolitan or universal ethical framework, such as human rights, is a common, some would argue inescapable, element of global citizenship thinking. The stress upon rights also brings weight to the claim of 'goodness' in the idea, for the growing prominence of human rights in international politics, especially in the West, has contributed to the challenge to ideas of foreign policy, and international relations more generally, being amoral or even immoral (Frost 1998: 1–74).

## GOOD INTERNATIONAL CITIZENSHIP AND FOREIGN POLICY

This brief outline of the idea of Good International Citizenship points to its principal appeal as a tool for assessing, and perhaps even formulating, foreign policy (Wheeler and Dunne 1998: 848). Good International Citizenship is a problem-solving way of thinking about global citizenship issues. Given where we start from – a states system predicated upon sovereignty and where states are very firmly entrenched and privileged in the prevailing order – how can we try to ameliorate the problems such a system generates in areas like human rights, the environment, development and political freedom? Good International Citizenship appears to provide a set of guidelines and principles rooted in existing foreign policy practice and environment. States are not expected, or required, to engage in a radical transformation of their understanding of their role as protectors and promoters of particular and specific interests but they are expected to take into account global issues and to act where they can do so without damaging vital national interests (Linklater 1992: 28–9; Wheeler and Dunne 1998: 855). Thus, issues such as the promotion of human rights should come ahead of short-term commercial gain, although a state would not be expected to sacrifice large numbers of its own troops (Wheeler and Dunne 1998: 868). As such, Good International Citizenship privileges the traditional mechanisms of diplomacy, occasionally backed by 'the big stick', and the manipulation of levers of influence and persuasion rather than appealing for a fundamental transformation in our understanding of the nature and role of states as international political actors. Thus there are no appeals to wholesale resource transfers or a radical utilitarianism which requires governments to regard citizens of other states as being of equal moral worth to their own and to significantly damage the living standards of their own people to help others (for example, Singer 1985).

Where Good International Citizenship is more radical is in its commitment to multi-lateralism (Wheeler and Dunne 1998: 854, 858). As 'citizens' of the states system states should abide by and support the 'international community mechanisms' of the United Nations and other multilateral institutions. Gareth Evans was explicit in his commitment to multilateralism as a central element of Good International Citizenship. Recent consideration of UK foreign policy on these grounds has stressed the ability of the UK as a Permanent Member of the Security Council, leader of the Commonwealth and EU member to set an example (Wheeler and Dunne 1998: 854–5). Indeed, the idea of the EU as a Good International Citizen able to follow this new foreign policy path as a new sort of foreign policy actor has been mooted (Dunne and Wheeler 1998: 9–22).

Such a commitment to multilateralism inevitably brings Good International Citizenship up against familiar realist criticisms of the effectiveness, or ineffectiveness, of multilateral institutions such as international organisations in the face of powerful states pursuing perceived national interests regardless of international law or the resolutions and declarations of such organisations. Good International Citizenship, as a pragmatic notion, does not deny that such events happen but believes that, wherever possible, states should be made aware of their commitments and be made to pay a price for breaking them. This may include the collective use of armed force or even, in extreme circumstances, unilateral use of armed force. There are occasions where a state pursuing a foreign policy based on the principles of Good International Citizenship may resort to unilateral force, perhaps where the route to collective armed force is being blocked by the naked self-interest of a particular power. Nicholas Wheeler has made an eloquent case for this in the face of what he describes as 'supreme humanitarian emergency' (Wheeler 2000).

Multilateralism may thus have to be abrogated on occasion and where the demands of Good International Citizenship generate a powerful case. Echoes of Good International Citizenship ideas can be heard in the Independent International Commission on Kosovo's conclusion that NATO's campaign in response to human rights abuses in the province in 1999 was 'illegal, but legitimate' (IICK 2000: 4). Its illegality resulted from the failure to gain United Nations Security Council authorisation, something that was impossible in the face of Chinese and Russian opposition. Its legitimacy stemmed from the need for an international response to the gross abuses of internationally recognised and codified human rights being perpetrated principally by the state authorities in the Federal Republic of Yugoslavia against their own citizens.

This appeal to the honouring of existing commitments is an important element of Good International Citizenship as it is the way in which proponents attempt to avoid the charge of cultural imperialism or the imposition of particular values (Wheeler and Dunne 1998: 852). Good International Citizenship is about fulfilling a state's commitments and encouraging, cajoling or occasionally forcing others to do the same and being prepared to bear some costs in the pursuit of these goals. Careful consideration has to be made of the effects of actions to encourage China, for example, to fulfil its international obligations under various human rights instruments. Equally, the chances of success are also an important issue, but as a Good International Citizen a state should be prepared to forego commercial or diplomatic advantages rather than be seen to condone human rights abuses (Wheeler and Dunne 1998: 863–6). The argument that 'if we don't sell this to them, somebody else will' is not a sufficient excuse, and one which would be unacceptable if states attempted to utilise it in defence of involvement in drugs running or the production and supply of child pornography (Wheeler and Dunne 1998: 868).

Good International Citizenship offers an attractive way of enabling states to make more explicit the linkage between domestic standards of political ethics and foreign policy behaviour via existing treaties, declarations, covenants, commitments, rules, norms and principles. It encourages law-abiding, community-spirited behaviour which recognises the difficulties of international politics and the sometimes terrible moral dilemmas facing the makers of foreign policy.

The commitment to the preservation and improvement of a state-centric, but rule-governed and orderly, international political system based on sovereignty points to the connection of Good International Citizenship to the 'English School' tradition in international relations theory (Linklater 1992: 29–31, 34–6). This posits the existence of an 'international society' of states characterised by states' shared recognition and acceptance of certain basic rules and principles of behaviour. These enable them to co-exist on an orderly, if not always peaceful, basis and to regard the maintenance of this system as being in both their own interests and in the common good (Bull 1977). Indeed, Dunne and Wheeler support the applicability of Good International

Citizenship to UK foreign policy in part because of its ability to offer a bridge across a divide in English School theory. This is between those who would privilege the promotion of a cosmopolitan justice in international politics and those who defend the orderliness generated by the principles of sovereignty and non-intervention at the cost of being unable to effectively address matters such as human rights abuses (Dunne and Wheeler 1998: 4; Bull 1977: 77–98).

If Good International Citizenship is viewed as part of the English School tradition, giving a new focus to the analysis of how foreign policy might be made within a normatively charged states system, then Good International Citizenship also becomes the target of some of the attacks upon international society (for example, Brown 1995b). Perhaps the most significant in terms of Good International Citizenship as a pragmatic, practical tool for assessing policy-making is the charge of conservatism, particularly in the face of the challenges of global issues such as human rights, the environment, development and political freedom.

## THE CONSERVATISM OF GOOD INTERNATIONAL CITIZENSHIP

Good International Citizenship, as already noted, bears the hallmarks of pragmatic politics, reflecting its genesis within the Australian Department of Foreign Affairs and Trade. As already suggested, its presuppositions about the nature of international politics are state-centric and rest on an assumption about the state as the representative, if not the manifestation, of a unified community. Good International Citizenship offers a way to protect this privileged position of the state and, hopefully, reinvigorate it as a mechanism for promoting and extending already existing positive trends in international politics. This perhaps helps explain the emphasis on issues such as human rights where there exists a number of well-known instruments and declarations to which states pursuing a policy of Good International Citizenship can tie their colours and urge others to do the same. In areas where developments are patchier and more recent, such as international environmental agreements, then the ability of any Good International Citizens to play the same cards are reduced.

Neither does a policy of Good International Citizenship suggest much in the way of radical developments in the ways in which international agreements are reached, implemented and policed. Again the environmental area is one where it has been argued that reaching agreements is regarded as the standard of success, almost regardless of whether or not the agreement is adequate to address the problem (Kütting 2000). This raises the question of whether or not Good International Citizenship can develop and react quickly enough to emerging global crises.

The environmental issue points to a more fundamental question about the desirability of Good International Citizenship as a pragmatic solution to addressing global issues within the existing political framework. This returns to our initial recognition of the debatable nature of 'goodness' in the conduct of international politics. It also goes further to ask if the conduct of international politics, as presently conceived, can ever reach adequate levels of 'goodness'. Is an evolutionary, or even teleological, approach such as this desirable? Or is a revolutionary change in the way in which international politics operates necessary? In relation to human rights, one of the areas where proponents of Good International Citizenship argue the idea is at its strongest, the very possibility of handling such issues within the states systemic framework has been strongly criticised. Ken Booth has described the states system as being a 'global gangster' perpetuating the dominance of the leading powers in the world and allowing them to avoid their responsibilities to the real citizens of the word – individual human beings (Booth 1991; Booth 1995).

Such concerns about protecting the leading liberal democratic states, as the most likely Good International Citizens and the possessors of the best records on issues such as human rights, also extend to development issues. The failure of most industrialised liberal democracies to reach the UN target of donating 0.7 per cent of GNP to international development aid is just the tip of the iceberg. The dominant role played by these states in institutions such as the WTO, the IMF and the World Bank and their general support for the further liberalisation of trade and the extension of a capitalist global economy may well be viewed as inimical, or at least very damaging, to the development opportunities and prospects for the Less Developed Countries. The inability, or unwillingness, of governments in the developed world to restrain the activities of transnational corporations can also be seen as suggesting that Good International Citizenship may be about re-entrenching and legitimising existing distributions and locations of power.

Thus Good International Citizenship's emphasis on furthering existing positive trends within international law and politics via the mechanism of states and their foreign policies can be accused of undue conservatism in the face of pressing global challenges. The need, rooted in English School theory, to protect the order-generating aspects of states-systemic practice out of fear of descending into the Hobbesian abyss of chaos may well hamstring Good International Citizenship in the face of non-state based challenges such as the environment and, perhaps to a lesser extent, development. Therefore the practical politics appeal of Good International Citizenship may be over-stated. Its ability to grant direction and purpose to foreign policy in a way which protects order but without ruling out justice or condemning it to an inevitable second place remains too restricted by the corset of established understandings of the states system to adequately address the global challenges we face.

INTELLECTUAL PROBLEMS OF GOOD INTERNATIONAL CITIZENSHIP

So far this chapter has looked at Good International Citizenship on its own level – as a foreign policy tool and guide. Whilst cautious about its ability to go far enough in meeting global challenges, this assessment has been generally positive. A world in which the major liberal democratic states adopted a foreign policy of Good International Citizenship would be a better one than that in which we currently live. However, there are a number of intellectual difficulties with the idea that may undermine these practical benefits.

The first is the familiar idea of applicability of the individual analogy and, along with it, comes the second, whether states can be morally autonomous (Brown 1992b: 109–28). The individual analogy is a commonplace of much discussion of international politics. We find it difficult to avoid talking of the United States doing this, the Russian reaction being that and the French concerns being something else. This is particularly true in relation to issues of foreign policy and the concerns of traditional 'high politics' such as security and the use of military force. Whilst this assumption of states as individuals writ large is widespread, particularly in popular understandings of international politics, it does not mean it is unproblematic. At a very basic level, the idea that the decision-making process of a state can be viewed as the same as that of an individual is obviously false, despite the appeals to ideas of rationality. Equally, the condition of relative equality amongst individuals, cited by Hobbes as an important reason for the brutality of his state of nature, is not matched by a relative equality of states, with some states enjoying enormous and insurmountable advantages over others. The familiar analogy of David and Goliath does not even begin to approach the disparities between Vanuatu and the United States.

In addition to these empirical points, the idea of states as individuals writ large results in a number of difficulties for an idea like Good International Citizenship which is attempting to establish a powerful and vibrant normative agenda aimed at promoting issues like human rights. Whilst Evans was quick to acknowledge that for a policy of Good International Citizenship to be credible Australia would have to be largely immune to charges of hypocrisy in terms of its own human and minority rights record this does not solve the problem (Wheeler and Dunne 1998: 856). Good International Citizenship implicitly appeals to the moral autonomy of states predicated on the notions of sovereignty, non-intervention and self-determination. Good International Citizenship accepts that states are the 'units' of international politics and possess certain rights, as well as certain duties that they should be encouraged to fulfil rather more thoroughly than they do at present.

How persuasive, though, is the idea of a state possessing moral status and particularly a right to sovereignty and its attendant corollaries? Many cosmopolitans would argue that the moral worth of states is contingent upon their ability to fulfil the needs of the people who live within them (for example, Booth 1991). States are means to an end of human freedom, fulfilment, emancipation or some other universal goal. As such, ideas such as human rights should be regarded as 'trumping', in the words of moral philosophy, the rights of states at every turn because the state has rights only to the extent that these do not infringe upon or threaten the prior rights of human beings. The state is an instrument of society and society, in Rawls' words, is 'a co-operative venture for mutual advantage' and as such is a servant, not master, of the individual members of society (Brown 1992b: 115). Those advocating a version of global citizenship strongly predicated on human rights may find these arguments particularly compelling.

Assuming this relationship is accepted, Good International Citizenship is thus in trouble because it does not recognise this contingent relationship between the rights of states and the rights of individuals. Whilst a state pursuing a policy of Good International Citizenship may, in very extreme circumstances, be justified in taking unilateral military action against another state in defence of human rights, this still allows widespread, lower level abuses to continue subject only to diplomatic appeals and commercial inconvenience. The threshold for action is set very high and with an assumption that action will not result in the dismembering of the target state, but perhaps only the removal of a particular regime. Within Good International Citizenship states have a right to exist and a right to enjoy the privileges of sovereignty and governments have a right to rule their people as they see fit subject to fulfilling certain international commitments. This is justified in part on pragmatic grounds of having to make a better world by starting from where we are – a sovereign states system – rather than where we might like to be, but also by appealing to the individual analogy and the assumption that states represent a largely homogeneous population. This is despite the problems identified with the individual analogy and the obvious empirical nonsense of the notion that the majority of states contain a population lacking significantly differing groups. Sovereignty, territorial integrity, non-intervention and a very specific and limited understanding of national self-determination are protected by Good International Citizenship and establish tight limits on its ability to address global issues.

A further line of criticism of the Good International Citizenship ideal stems from these efforts to portray states as individuals writ large inhabiting an international community made up of similar individuals. Is the idea of citizenship an appropriate model to follow? The development of citizenship as a means of conceptualising the relationship of an individual to the state rests on a basis famously absent from international politics – the existence of a central authoritative governing institution with the ability to act coercively and possessing the monopoly of the legitimate use of force. The need to establish limits to Leviathan to protect the autonomy of individuals, resist tyranny and ensure access to civil, political and social rights underpins the development of citizenship as an idea in domestic politics (Linklater 1992: 24–5; Linklater 1998b).

We have already seen that the analogy between states and individuals is a dubious one. How much more dubious is the application of the idea of 'citizenship' to states given the lack of a central government in international politics? It is arguably inappropriate to use a device designed to protect individuals from over-mighty government to grant protection to certain states from a near absence of effective government and instead enable them to appeal to a right to press other states to behave in certain ways.

This brings us to the fourth major difficulty with Good International Citizenship – its appeals to be immune to charges of cultural imperialism or the imposition of particular, Western values. The defence that a state acting as a Good International Citizen will merely attempt to hold other states to their stated commitments in areas like human rights and the environment and cannot be seen to be 'imposing' its will is problematic, particularly so, as we have seen, in the area of development. The status of documents such as the *Universal Declaration of Human Rights* is rarely as straightforward as Good International Citizenship's proponents require if they are to make such matters the basis for pressuring states such as China or Algeria, to take two cited examples (Wheeler and Dunne 1998). The debate between the relative importance of political versus economic rights is well known but more fundamental is the disputed nature of the idea of universal human rights, not just their content (for example, Williams 1999). The assumed universalism and validity of human rights apparent in Good International Citizenship is both politically and theoretically difficult in the face of powerful defences of cultural specificity and the particularities of certain religious or civilisational approaches to the moral standing of human beings (for example, Walzer 1985).

Indeed, whether or not the language of rights is the most appropriate way of thinking about such issues is not addressed by Good International Citizenship, although the use of the term 'citizen' almost requires the adoption of rights as the vehicle for thinking about moral agency. This is because of the way that citizenship has worked out in liberal democratic states that have placed this idea at the heart of their understanding of the state-individual relationship. As such, Good International Citizenship glosses over an area of immense philosophical and political dispute with serious implications for assessing the morality or desirability of international political conduct. Whilst a pragmatic approach such as Good International Citizenship is hardly the place to look for a resolution of serious philosophical questions, the proponents of Good International Citizenship may be accused of naïveté in failing to recognise more explicitly the problematic nature of the claim to avoid the cultural imperialism charge.

## CONCLUSION

As a way of addressing the issues we have come to associate with global citizenship, the idea of Good International Citizenship offers the appeal of a pragmatic politician's halfway house, rather than a radical challenge to our conceptualisations of international relations. Appeals to re-think international politics in order to address issues such as human rights, development, the environment and political freedom are often criticised for being 'utopian', 'unrealistic' or 'wishful thinking'. These are not charges that can be levelled at Good International Citizenship. As such it offers a valid and useful contribution to debates about how to move international relations forward in its efforts to address such issues. As already stated, a world in which more states based their foreign policy upon the principles of Good International Citizenship would be a better world.

However, the criticisms are also serious ones. In practical terms the ability of the states system to control the environmentally damaging and developmentally questionable processes of global capitalism is in doubt, especially given the support for such developments by many states likely to be amenable to Good International Citizenship.

Concerns about the practical effectiveness of Good International Citizenship lead to deeper issues about the sustainability and suitability of the supporting framework of international society. It is perhaps not surprising that the supporters of Good International Citizenship are also at the forefront of efforts to revitalise English School theory. Good International Citizenship offers a way to make the best of the non-ideal circumstances represented by the states system that history has lumbered us with in terms of its ability to act as a framework within which global issues can be addressed. However, we should not overlook the valuable role the states system and its supporting rules, norms and principles of behaviour plays in terms of containing the worst effects of the lack of overarching authority. The states system generates a degree of orderliness, stability and predictability in international politics without which the consideration of global issues would be near impossible. Good International Citizenship offers a revitalising foreign policy agenda with a strong normative element for the basically sound institution that is the states system.

This is the optimistic version of Good International Citizenship. We have also seen that concerns about the practical effectiveness of Good International Citizenship are rooted in harsher judgements of the states system. These see international society – and, by extension, Good International Citizenship – as an effort to legitimise and justify a system predicated upon inequality, injustice and the maintenance of an overly static and highly prejudicial distribution of power. Good International Citizenship requires tiny sacrifices by the powerful in terms of marginal commercial advantage and diplomatic discomfort. What the world needs is a radical transformation of the way in which international politics works which replaces state-centrism with anthropocentrism or, even more radically, a downgrading of human beings to being simply one inhabitant of the planet with no greater or lesser moral standing than any other. Many see global citizenship as part of these demands.

Such criticisms are perhaps too harsh. Good International Citizenship does have significant virtues. These are not just in terms of its practicality and potential effects but also in terms of putting global issues more firmly on the agenda. The pragmatism of Good International Citizenship makes it harder for political elites to declare that nothing can be done, that hard-headed concerns for the 'national interest' and the difficulties and dangers of international politics means that foreign policy must be insulated from such pressures. Once, in part via Good International Citizenship, this defence is rendered untenable the debate and agenda can move on to consider the more radical challenges to and charges against the states system. There remains a powerful tendency in foreign policy and political elites to postulate a radical dichotomy between realism and utopianism, with realism as the only practical choice. Good International Citizenship challenges this and perhaps offers a battering ram behind which a more radical storming of the bastions of foreign policy and the states-system can take place.

---

### QUESTIONS

1. Is it true that the state offers the best, or indeed only, mechanism for individuals to pursue global citizenship issues?
2. Why do states that are committed to the idea of citizenship domestically currently fail to act as Good International Citizens?
3. Can Good International Citizenship adequately address a full range of global citizenship issues?
4. Does it make sense to view the state as a Good International Citizen, or potential Good International Citizen, in an international community of states?

# 4. FEMINISM AND GLOBAL CITIZENSHIP

## Kimberly Hutchings

### INTRODUCTION

The idea of global citizenship can be characterised generally as involving the notion that the rights and duties of the individual either do or should extend beyond the boundaries of the nation-state. This is an idea which is shared by a variety of international and transnational social movements in the fields of ecology, peace and human rights. This chapter explores the resources of one particular political movement, that of feminism, for the theory and practice of global citizenship. This is not a straightforward matter, since feminism is not a monolithic ethical and political programme in either theory or practice. Although feminist movements, to the extent that they identify their goal as the liberation of women, are transnational in principle, different feminists have different understandings of the goal to which they are committed and this frequently reflects the very different nation-state contexts within and across which feminist political struggles take place. For this reason it might seem initially that the whole notion of a feminist global citizen is misconceived, since the language of global citizenship tends to be highly universalistic and to operate with a generic conception of the human individual – one indifferent either to sex or to political ideology. This chapter seeks to demonstrate that in fact feminism is compatible with ideals of global citizenship. Falk defines global citizenship in terms of the figure of the 'citizen pilgrim', who is someone committed to 'an imagined human community of the future' (Falk 1995: 95). In this sense, feminists are a good example of Falk's notion of the 'citizen pilgrim' because they are committed to a future in which the situation of women as such is transformed (regardless of nationality or ideology). However, as we shall see, the nature of the 'imagined future' in question, and the problem of how it is to be arrived at, continue to be matters of considerable debate within feminism itself.

## FEMINIST POLITICS IN A GLOBAL CONTEXT

Over the past quarter of a century international forums for the articulation and advancement of women's interests/rights have been set up and phenomena such as the UN Decade for the Advancement of Women (1975–85) and the United Nations Conference for Women at Beijing in 1995 have given a higher profile to women's position and concerns within the international community. This, along with the flourishing of feminist work within the academy, has publicised the cause of feminism internationally and also prompted much consideration within the feminist movement of what it might mean to be an international or global feminist citizen.

One example of such a feminist contribution can be found in the arguments which have gone on within the international women's movement over the value and significance of the idea of international human rights for women. Ashworth notes how the *Universal Declaration of Human Rights* (*UDHR*) and the covenants on civil and political, social and economic rights respectively have been ineffective even in recognising the violation (or vulnerability to violation) of women's rights (Ashworth 1999; Peterson 1990). For instance, although the *UDHR* specifies rights to bodily integrity and freedom from torture this provision was never explicitly associated with practices such as female circumcision or domestic violence. Until feminist groups began to campaign for more explicit recognition of the differential position of women as rights-bearers, there was no accepted understanding that human rights might need to be specified as women's rights. Over the past twenty-five years international organisations have been increasingly subject to pressure from feminist campaigners to make sure that women are explicitly included in the category 'human'. One example of this is the way in which the recent experience of the systematic rape of women which featured in the conflicts in Rwanda and Bosnia in the mid 1990s pushed feminist groups into a successful campaign for the international recognition of rape as a war crime. The campaign centred around feminist claims as to the 'gender blindness' of accepted cosmopolitan moral and legal discourses and practices, and the need always to look carefully at how women suffered or benefited from specific supposedly universal human rights provisions (Allen 1996).

The discussion of the category of human rights is only one aspect of both generic and feminist global citizenship discourse. Global citizenship is concerned with the specification of duties as well as rights and more broadly with issues to do with sustainable development, the environment, war and peace and global distributive justice. Feminist activists and feminist theorists have been involved in all of these arenas of political struggle and debate across the globe, from women's groups campaigning against deforestation in the Third World, to women's peace activism in Europe to the activities of feminist groups in INGOs working on issues of health and poverty (Basu 1995; Pettman 1996; Steans 1998). In all of these instances ways both of conceiving and of enacting global citizenship as and for women are being implicitly or explicitly evolved. This is not to say, however, that a single picture of what it means to be a feminist global citizen emerges from all these threads of thought and activity. For some women's groups and movements, the very concept of 'feminism' is suspect, associated as it is with the priorities of affluent, First World women. Even where the label 'feminism' is accepted, there are significant differences between different feminist movements. For some feminists (often labelled 'liberal') the idea of sex-specific rights and duties in thinking about global citizenship is only a stage on the way to achieving a truly generic model. The point of global citizenship for such feminists is the abolition of the idea of any moral and political significance being carried by sexual difference. In contrast, for so-called 'radical' feminists there are significant and enduring features of being a woman in the world (not necessarily biologically given), and these features entail that women's needs and interests are distinct from those of men and this therefore needs to be reflected in a sex-differentiated understanding of global citizenship. In contrast to either of these approaches are 'difference' feminism arguments which point to the ways in which there are often relevant differences between women as well as between men and women and that there follows a need to devise a more pluralistic and context-sensitive way of articulating the rights and duties of any particular woman considered as a global citizen.

In the light of this complexity of different feminist positions, it is obvious that there is no one account of the ways in which feminism might contribute to the theory and practice of global citizenship. For the purposes of this chapter, therefore, in order to demonstrate the richness of feminist theory and practice as a resource for global citizenship I will concentrate on one feminist model of what it means to be a global citizen. This model, commonly referred to as the 'ethic of care', can be seen as exemplified in practice by feminist peace campaigners in the 1980s and in theory in the work of Sarah Ruddick and her notion of 'maternal thinking'.

## WOMEN, WAR AND PEACE

One of the key traditional components of the theory and practice of citizenship within states has been the obligation of citizens to bear arms in defence of their state. This understanding of the meaning of citizenship goes back to the Greek polis and is at the heart of republican conceptions of citizenship. One of the main reasons cited for the refusal to grant full citizenship rights to women within modern states was that they could not be called upon to fulfil this ultimate citizenly duty. As Elshtain argues, in dominant thinking about war, women have been placed in the position of the naturally peaceful sex whose role is to provide comfort and care for the 'just war hero' and who is invoked (along with the children) as the party on behalf of whom resort to political violence has been necessary (Elshtain 1987). This traditional picture places women in the private sphere away from war zones, 'keeping the home fires burning'. However, the experiences of women as protagonists and victims in modern warfare over the last quarter of a century is very different to that suggested by the traditional picture. Research has shown that at the same time as women are gaining entry into the military and engaging in combat in increasing numbers, women also make up the vast majority of those dispossessed by war (whether as refugees or as the mediators between international sanctions and the needs of their families), as well as bearing the burden of responsibility for re-building lives in the aftermath of war (Enloe 1983; Vickers 1993; Pettman 1996: 126–53; Steans 1998: 81–103). Moreover, in contemporary warfare the deaths of civilians now vastly outnumber those of soldiers – rendering the assumption of a neat distinction between war zone and home front redundant. Feminist reactions to the changing nature of war have been various but have continued to draw on elements of the traditional picture. On the one hand, feminists have seen the right to bear arms as the mark of citizenship and have sought entry into the military on the same terms and with the same duties as men. On the other hand, feminists have drawn on the idea of women as the peaceful sex to challenge the link between fighting and citizenship and between state and citizenship. The latter phenomenon provides a practical example of how some feminists see themselves as global citizens.

The early 1980s was marked by the emergence of a distinctively feminist anti-nuclear peace politics in several Western European countries as well as the USA and Australia. Although clearly sharing much ground with other anti-war and pacifist movements, this feminist peace politics was premised on the idea of a special link between women and peace (Harris and King 1989; Warren and Cady 1994). Essentially, these feminist peace activists reversed the dominant hierarchy of evaluation of masculine civic virtue and feminine private virtue in which the former takes priority over the latter and the latter is essentially supposed to sustain the former. In the feminist peace activism of the 1980s, feminine private virtue was taken into the public realm and held up as the (subversive) yardstick of ethical conduct within that realm. A key part of the tactics of these campaigners was, quite literally, to make themselves visible to a world which recognised states as friends or enemies and humans as elements to be aggregated in statistics of putative death tolls, but not women as women. These tactics ranged from mothers taking babies and children with them on demonstrations (thereby quite literally putting the realm of private virtue in the public domain) to counterposing traditional symbols of women's work and femininity to the machinery of militarism held within the bases where nuclear weapons were kept.

Flowers, ribbons and wool were woven into the fences surrounding military bases. Women broke into bases and danced on or decorated missile silos. Camps were set up at the gates of bases as a constant reminder of a world which included women and families, not simply states and individuals. These tactics were designed to demonstrate the absurdity of the two most common ways of thinking and making judgements about war which had survived into the nuclear age: strategic thinking and just-war theory. The first of these reflects a 'realist' attitude to war, in which war is seen as purely a matter of power politics, wherein the only important question is a cost/benefit analysis of the justification for going to war. The latter mode of thinking is a normative one in which there are established principles which can be invoked to justify going to war and to limit what goes on within warfare. Both strategic and just-war thinking argue that in certain circumstances war is a rational option for states.

Implicit in the activities of the feminist anti-nuclear campaigners are ways of conceiving of and practising global citizenship. The campaigners at peace camps such as Greenham Common in England were not simply declaring their presence on the international stage but were also arguing that that international stage should learn from them. The tactics employed at Greenham Common were imbued by the idea of the ethical superiority of the notions of care, connection and responsibility embedded in women's work within the family over the strategic and just-war thinking which could even contemplate the destruction of large swathes of the human race in the pursuit of some greater goal. In addition, these campaigners were practising global citizenship through direct action in a way which has become familiar in the work of other social movements, particularly in relation to environmental issues. According to this understanding of global citizenship, considering oneself as a global citizen does not depend on anything other than identification of oneself as a member of the human race with an interest in its survival. Like Falk's 'citizen pilgrims', these peace activists acted as if national boundaries were irrelevant, as if they (the activists) were always already citizens of a global society. Moreover the forum for political action could be anywhere considered appropriate – it did not have to be either the political institutions of the state or international organisations – and it also was not dependent on any transnational framework of law or law enforcement. As with the actions of groups like Greenpeace, these women peace campaigners were constructing an international public sphere purely through their own actions. According to these women, global citizenship was not an aspiration but a reality brought about by the potential for the destruction of the entire world carried by nuclear weapons and the concomitant responsibility to resist this possibility. In order to examine this feminist model of global citizenship more closely I will now go on to examine its theoretical articulation in the idea of an ethic of care.

## AN ETHIC OF CARE

The idea of an ethic of care was pioneered in the work of Carol Gilligan and has become one of the most influential ideas in feminist moral and political theory (Gilligan 1982; Bubeck 1998). The key feature of an ethic of care is that it is embedded in the practicalities of relationships of responsibility for others. Crucial to ethical judgement from the perspective of care is the importance of particularity (knowing who and what you are making a moral judgement about); connectedness (recognising your actual relationship to others in the process of judgement); and context (paying attention to the broad and narrow context of ethical judgement). In her book, *Maternal Thinking: Towards a Politics of Peace*, Ruddick draws on the idea of an ethic of care as a central part of her argument for a feminist moral orientation in the context of international politics, and in doing so suggests what a feminist global citizen might be like (Ruddick 1990).

> When maternal thinking takes upon itself the critical perspective of a feminist standpoint, it reveals a contradiction between mothering and war. Mothering begins in birth and promises life; military thinking justifies organised, deliberate deaths. A mother preserves the bodies, nurtures the psychic growth, and disciplines the conscience of children; although the military trains its soldiers to survive the situation it puts them in, it also deliberately endangers their bodies, minds and consciences in the name of victory and abstract causes. (Ruddick 1990: 135)

For Ruddick, both the strategic thinking inherent in militarism and just-war theory share a commitment to the expendability of concrete lives in abstract causes to which maternal thinking is inherently opposed. In this sense she clearly echoes the points which feminist anti-nuclear campaigners sought to demonstrate which were described above. Ruddick claims that this means that the implication of maternal thinking is not just the rejection of war but the active embracing of peace politics, a fight against war which draws on the acknowledgement of responsibility and relationship and the specificity of need and obligations which are inherent in a proper understanding of what it means to care for others (Ruddick 1990: 141–59). In Ruddick's theory the logic of domestic relations in the restricted sense of the domestic or private sphere of family and personal relations is set against the logic of the public sphere of both state and inter-state relations. The former involves relating to individuals as specific, real human beings with particular needs, who cannot be traded in any kind of cost/benefit calculation, whereas the latter is characterised by a willingness to trade in some people's lives for others, in the pursuit of state interest or of principles such as national self-determination. For Ruddick, then, the realm of international politics and of global citizenship is primarily a realm of human relations, not of human, nation or state rights or an international state system. Ruddick assumes that ethical perspectives are the outcome of concrete practices and can never be neutral, but at the same time clearly suggests that some kinds of practice are inherently better than others. This distinction draws attention to the fact that although Ruddick presents an understanding of the international realm very different from mainstream ethical theories, she nevertheless argues for the notion of a standpoint from which critical judgements of international politics can be made.

As well as suggesting new ways of conceptualising the basis of judgement as a global citizen, Ruddick's maternalist ethic of care has specific implications for practical ways of addressing classic problems of violence and oppression in the international context. At the broadest level, maternal thinking involves commitment to peace politics. In other words, violence is outlawed as a political tool, even for the righting of injustices. One of Ruddick's key preoccupations is that of working out non-violent strategies to combat violence and oppression. She is clear that such strategies are as risky as the use of violence in the contemporary world and require levels of organisation and commitment just as great as those used to support any military machine. But she also emphasises the resources already present in women's lives which can be turned from sustaining political violence to resisting it. In Ruddick's work the example of the Argentinian mothers of the disappeared, whose movement gradually grew to embrace concerns with children across the world, is taken as exemplary. Through non-violent protest, drawing on the generally recognised private feminine virtues of motherhood, these mothers operated effectively to help to bring about political change (Ruddick 1990: 225–34). This example confirms for Ruddick both the connection between maternal virtues and peace politics and the potential effectiveness of peace politics. There is no doubt also that the kinds of activities of the feminist anti-nuclear campaigners mentioned above would serve as exemplary practices of global citizenship for Ruddick. More generally Ruddick's peace politics has elective affinities with a variety of examples of new ways of doing politics pioneered by peace movements, human rights movements and green movements which emphasise the idea of local non-violent resistance to the powers of states, international organisations and corporations. Such politics frequently makes use of the technique of subverting or overturning the dominant value hierarchy by asserting the value of that which has been marginalised or excluded, whether it is women's work, traditional economic practices or particular cultural identities (Walker 1988). Ruddick argues that the idea of maternal thinking has its origin in maternal practice, features of which, she argues, are present in the work of mothering in radically different cultures. She therefore claims that her account of maternal thinking is likely to be generalisable across contexts, providing 'at hand' an accessible basis for criticising and resisting political violence of all kinds, as well as suggesting limitations to the kinds of strategies it is permissible to employ in critique and resistance.

## CRITICAL REFLECTIONS

Ruddick's work provides one particularly influential example of feminist thinking about war and typifies an argument common in feminist literature in the 1980s, that women and/or feminists, as global citizens, have a particular role in the moral assessment of war and in peace politics (Harris and King 1989; Warren and Cady 1994). Feminist theorists seeking to build on the concept of care in the context of international ethics have stressed the value of the relational account of human individuals, the concrete location of the ethic of care perspective in actual responsibilities and attachments and the way it puts realist assumptions into question without drawing on the abstract universalism characteristic of much cosmopolitan moral and legal discourse (Hutchings 1994; Robinson 1999). Nevertheless, from the beginning, the work of feminist theorists such as Gilligan and Ruddick who privilege the ethic of care or the labour of care as a starting point for ethical judgement and political practice has also come under strong criticism from other feminist theorists. Generally speaking, critical responses to the ethic of care associate it with the radical feminist position in which an essential connection is claimed between being a woman and certain kinds of virtues. Unsurprisingly, therefore, there are two main theoretical positions from which the ethic of care and its implications for global citizenship tend to be criticised: the liberal feminist position and that of difference feminisms (see the subsection 'Feminist Politics in A Global Context' above).

For liberal feminists the problems with the ethic of care boil down to the charge that reliance on embedded relations with and responsibilities towards others as the basis for ethical judgement and political practice renders them both parochial and relativistic, and therefore inadequate as a basis for global citizenship (Benhabib 1992). The ethic of care is argued to be parochial because it cannot account for how you bridge the gap between the particular context and experience of certain specific people to whom you are related and the needs and rights of strangers. This is in contrast to universalist doctrines, which are based on the presumption of the equal moral significance of every individual regardless of context. Similarly, it is argued to be relativistic because it rejects the idea that there can be universal principles which are known to be right in advance of their application to a specific situation. For thinkers like Ruddick, what is right depends on context and cannot be established independently from context. For liberal feminists this is a worrying position, since it implies, for instance, that what is deemed to be ethically permissible may vary from culture to culture. Given the fact that women are more oppressed in some cultures than in others, this might be seen as opening the way to toleration of oppressive practices such as female circumcision or exclusion of women from the public sphere.

The criticism of care ethics offered by difference feminisms such as post-modernist and Third World feminisms is concerned not so much with care's lack of universality as with the way in which it depends on a particular account of women's virtues. It is argued that this account is based primarily on the experience of middle-class, white, Western women which is then taken to stand for the experience of 'women in general'. Over the past twenty years feminists, both within multicultural states and internationally, have been arguing that the predominant political campaigns and accounts of women's oppression within the feminist movement have reflected the position (and served the interests) of white, middle-class, Western women rather than those of the majority of women. What has emerged from this debate has been a growing dissatisfaction with any feminist account which relies on a gener-alisable notion of a feminist perspective. It is argued that the inclusive ambition of such theories is in practice exclusive, since no single under-standing of the feminist standpoint can possibly reflect the multiple and often contradictory positions in which different women and different feminists stand. In other words, rather than being parochial, Ruddick's approach is accused of being culturally imperialistic (Nicholson 1990; Mohanty, Russo and Torres 1991; Marchand and Parpart 1995).

The criticisms of liberal and difference feminists suggest that the model of global citizenship put forward in the work of people like Ruddick (and exemplified in practice in the actions of the Greenham Common women and the Argentinian mothers) is either too specific or too general. It is too specific in that it relies on particular aspects of who a person is and how a person is related to others as the starting point for criticism and political action; it is too general in that it generalises features of the caring practices and virtues associated with mothering in a specific cultural context and makes them into the basis of a feminist global citizenship with which all women are claimed to be identified. Central to both of these arguments is the question of how feminists can move from the local to the global in their moral and political identity, judgement and practice. Here I think it is instructive to return to Ruddick's claim that maternal thinking is generalisable across contexts and the examples of the peace campaigners and Argentinian mothers which can be used to illustrate this claim. As noted above, Ruddick claims that maternal thinking provides a critical standpoint from which to make moral and political judgements and she also claims that there is sufficient cross-cultural commonality in practices of care to prevent maternal thinking from being seen as parochial or imperialistic. I stated at the beginning of this chapter how the universalistic language of global citizenship appears to be in tension with feminist political ideology, since the latter clearly gives priority to the interests of women rather than 'humanity' as such. However, Ruddick's argument and the concrete examples of feminist political campaigning which cross national boundaries and link together radically different women in different places suggest that this is a tension which is apparent rather than real. Her point is that in practice people's actions as global citizens are rooted in the particularities of their identity and experience. It is through those particularities, she argues, that it becomes possible to recognise commonalities and to identify with the plight and interests of strangers.

## CONCLUSION

I have suggested in this chapter that the feminist movement provides interesting examples of the theory and practice of global citizenship. At the same time, however, the experience of the feminist movement has drawn attention to the problem of basing ideas of global citizenship on a model of generic humanity which takes insufficient notice of the many ways in which people differ from each other, including sex and gender. The viewpoint of the ethic of care is an example of a way of thinking which attempts to draw resources for the practice of global citizenship from the actualities of women's lives as carers. In doing this it offers a way of connecting local and global concerns without requiring a pre-established set of universal principles or the assumption that all people are somehow ideally the same. The question we are left with is whether the account offered by people such as Ruddick is strong enough to outweigh the arguments of critics both within and beyond the feminist movement.[1]

---

### QUESTIONS

1. In what sense, if at all, is the action of threading flowers through the fence of a military base in which nuclear weapons are kept the action of a global citizen?
2. What makes it possible to define whole populations as 'killable enemies'?
3. Is Ruddick right to suggest that the practice of mothering can be the basis of a globally relevant ethic?
4. Can men be maternal thinkers?
5. Does the emancipation of women mean the same thing universally?
6. Assess the strengths and weaknesses of liberal, radical and difference feminist approaches to the idea of global citizenship.

---

### NOTES

1. Parts of this chapter have previously appeared in 'Towards a Feminist International Ethics', *Review of International Studies*, Volume 26, Special Issue, December 2000, pp. 111–30.

# SECTION 2

# INSTITUTIONAL ISSUES AND THE BASES OF SCEPTICISM

# SECTION INTRODUCTION

## John Williams

The idea of citizenship is most usually encountered in the relationship between an individual and the sovereign state. For the vast majority of us, this relationship is with a single sovereign state; the number of people possessing dual nationality is very small and, indeed, a number of states refuse to countenance granting citizenship to an individual on anything other than an exclusive basis. Equally, the number of people who are citizens of no state is also small, thankfully so in most cases as being a stateless person can be a dangerous position, as well as an inconvenient one.

This tight connection between citizenship and the sovereign state reflects the development of citizenship as a mechanism for establishing a reciprocal framework of rights and responsibilities in the relationship between states and individuals.

Citizenship is, in one sense, an ongoing bargain in which the individual citizen accepts the right of the state to make certain legitimate demands upon them such as the imposition of taxation, law and military service. In return, the citizen expects the state to treat them fairly, especially before the law, and to oversee the provision of certain public goods, such as infrastructure, law and order, defence, welfare functions such as health and education provision, and others. Most important, perhaps, is the citizen's expectation that the state will not exceed the terms of the agreement and interfere or pry into aspects of the citizen's life that are deemed to be 'private'. Where it does so, the individual should be able to seek redress against the state through law. Thus, in normal circumstances, we would expect the state to have very little to do with what we choose to buy; how we raise our children; which leisure pursuits we enjoy; how we choose to participate, or not, in the political process; and so on.

This kind of classic, liberal conception of citizenship is, of course, worked out very differently in different state contexts. We can think of examples from the list of 'private' activities just given to illustrate this diversity in states that espouse a liberal ethos. In many states in the United States, for example, people are forbidden to buy alcohol before they are twenty-one. In Sweden, parents are legally prevented from exercising any form of corporal punishment against their children. In the United Kingdom there is an ongoing and very active debate that looks likely to see the banning of hunting foxes and other animals with dogs. In Australia it is a legal requirement to vote in certain elections.

These, and many other variations on the theme, should not disguise the common elements of citizenship in contemporary practice. In addition to this classic liberal bargain, though, is a further element that has tied citizenship to the state. This is nationalism and the idea of individuals owing loyalty to the state because the state is the institutional embodiment of a community establishing a sense of belonging amongst citizens. This may be rooted in many things, most commonly a shared history, culture, language and religion, and linked to a specific territory. The state as, ideally, a nation-state is thus more than an instrument for enabling individuals to live the sort of life they want to – it becomes the 'mother-' or 'fatherland'. Individuals owe loyalty to the state because it is through membership of the state that we become a rooted member of a community that gives us our identity. We are more than just an individual related to other individuals by our shared subjection to political authority and our shared enjoyment of the freedoms and privileges granted us as citizens.

This kind of nation-state ideal is extremely rarely reproduced in practice. Only a tiny number of states in the world contain a homogeneous national population and do not have significant numbers of the homogeneous community living in other states. Iceland and Japan are the two most commonly mentioned and few people can add significantly to this list.

Nevertheless, the power of the nation-state ideal and the bonding of citizenship to the state in the origins, development and practice of the idea of citizenship are importantly demonstrated in this section of the book. Institutional questions often focus on whether or not it is possible for an institution other than a state to participate with individuals in a relationship of citizenship. A negative answer to this enquiry, arguing that it is only possible for an individual to be a citizen of a state and nothing else, may be one basis for scepticism about the idea of global citizenship. This is likely to appeal to the unique concentration of power and authority in the modern state, arguing that this concentration of power makes citizenship necessary only in this context. There can be two bases for this claim. The first is that the individual does not need the protection that citizenship brings in any other context because it is only the state that wields the sort of might that leads to totalitarianism, apartheid, genocide and other kinds of political relationships that deny individuality, equality, justice and liberty. We do not need to be a citizen of anything else because nothing else threatens us like the state potentially does. The second is that only the state can fulfil the positive side of the bargain by providing public goods and services, law and order, defence and other core aspects of state provision. We do not need to be citizens of anything else because nothing can help us like the state can.

Another basis for scepticism about global citizenship may be to argue that nationalism is essential to citizenship and that only the state can generate the sense of identity and belonging that is necessary. We are unprepared to compromise our liberty, our wealth and possibly even to sacrifice our life for things other than the state and the national community that it helps to create, sustain and promote.

Both of these elements of critique are present in the contributions to this section, alongside efforts to persuade us to break this iron linkage between citizenship and the state. Andreas Follesdal and David Miller look specifically at one way in which a non-state based citizenship has been institutionalised in the idea of citizenship of the European Union. Follesdal sets out the content of EU citizenship, possessed automatically by all citizens of EU Member States, and explains the reasons behind its introduction. He emphasises the role of trust in trying to connect individuals to one another and to the EU and its institutions. He argues trust is necessary to legitimise the EU in the eyes of its 'citizens'. He sees trust as helping to establish the ties and connections amongst individuals and between individuals and institutions that are essential to the effective operation of the EU, especially as it continues to grow in size and to take on new functions, such as the single European currency.

Follesdal emphasises that this is a very unusual form of citizenship as it rests only on the 'bargain' basis outlined above. There is no widespread and deep-seated 'European' identity amongst the people who hold EU citizenship. Instead the EU is attempting to build citizenship on the basis of what it can do for individuals to help them lead better lives and, in return, what it needs individuals to do for it to help in this endeavour. Follesdal, however, is persuaded that such an ambitious project can be achieved on the basis of reason and mutual advantage alone and in the absence of a stronger sense of identity. As such, European citizenship has important lessons for global citizenship as it, too, faces the hurdle of generating trust and legitimate institutions in the absence of strong common identities.

Miller is convinced about European citizenship – convinced that it is a bad idea that will not work. More particularly, Miller argues that for the political left in Europe hopes are misplaced that European citizenship will further goals of social justice and democracy. He emphasises the identity element of citizenship, arguing that the goals of democracy and social justice, which he sees as being at the core of the left's political project, require sacrifice. Social justice in particular is likely to require restrictions on liberty and the redistribution of wealth from rich to poor. Miller believes that this is extremely unlikely to take place without a sense of loyalty, unity and belonging to a community. He sees no sign of such a community existing at the level of the EU and is sceptical about the possibility of creating one in anything less than the very long term. Instead, Miller urges the left in Europe to focus upon retaining and strengthening national communities as the essential condition for the furtherance of democracy and social justice. European citizenship can only be an adjunct to this and the hopes of some on the left in Europe that the EU can be a progressive force are the product of special and specific circumstances, rather than reflecting a more deep-rooted change in the politics of citizenship.

Those sceptical about global citizenship may feel that doubts such as these in relation to European citizenship operate with even more force at a global level. Europe may be linguistically diverse but it shares many common bases: the predominance of the Christian religions; a widely shared culture, both mass and elite (Eminem and Beethoven, *Who Wants to be a Millionaire* and *Waiting for Godot, Cats* and *Tosca*, for example); and a deeply entwined history (including periods of partial unity). How much harder will global citizenship prove without these?

Miller's emphasis upon the state as being the principal site of political action is reinforced by Roland Axtmann's critique of David Held. Held is a leading advocate of what he calls 'cosmopolitan democracy', an analysis and argument that urges the development of democratic political systems and structures that are detached from the state. Whilst not explicit on this, it seems fair to say that Held views these as necessary vehicles for the expression of global citizenship. Held bases the need for cosmopolitan democracy on the rapid development and expansion of non-state based political issues and forces in the world. Environmental issues and the boom in the number of trans- or multinational corporations, for example, raise important issues of democratic accountability. Held feels that these are inadequately addressed within a state-centric democratic framework. Instead, he argues for the development of democratic political systems and institutions that are responsive to the different constituencies affected by transnational actions and actors.

This would have the effect of ending the state's dominance of democracy and democratic accountability, although, as he notes, the state will remain one, very important, location of democracy. Instead constituencies ought to be thought of more in terms of those upon whom actions have an impact. This would generate a range of different groups within and across states who would be involved in the democratic process of holding power to account. Some of this can be done by reforming existing institutions but in the long run there will need to be a radical overhaul of the way in which politics and especially democracy is thought about and practised.

Axtmann is far from convinced of this. His critique of Held is rooted in a defence of the state as the principal political institution and site of democracy. At one level this critique is institutional in the sense that Axtmann finds Held's description of the mechanisms of cosmopolitan democracy to be unpersuasive. It is difficult to see, Axtmann suggests, how democratic processes could be organised on the basis of what we might call 'constituencies of concern', that is to say, that those entitled to take part in democratic processes relating to a particular actor or action ought to be those substantially affected by it.

More substantially, though, Axtmann defends the state as being a superior mechanism for achieving democratic accountability and participation, even in an increasingly global politics. He feels that the state has all the trump cards in terms of power, authority, experience and the loyalty of people. What is required is not an abandonment of the state as the locus of politics and democracy but its reinvigoration. Those who want to achieve the goals of Held's cosmopolitan democracy need to make more and better use of the existing democratic institutions of the state, including the idea of state citizenship.

Mark Imber's analysis of the United Nations (UN) further dents the institutional aspirations of global citizenship. Offering a critical account of the nature of the UN and its role in peace and security, development and human rights, Imber suggests that there are very few reasons to be optimistic about the UN as a device for promoting global citizenship. He recognises the aspirations and hopes that many have invested in the UN as the only global political institution and one whose charter includes many commitments to ideals such as peace, development and human rights that are prominent in discussions of global citizenship. However, Imber feels these hopes and aspirations are very significantly undermined by the way in which the UN operates and the kinds of activities it engages with. This is particularly so in relation to the most prominent activities in the field of international peace and security, where he argues that the narrow national interests of the leading states dominate where, when and how the UN is permitted to act. Imber is more positive about the specialist agencies, like the United Nations Children's Fund (UNICEF) and the World Health Organisation (WHO). Nevertheless, he points to the difficulties of UN reform and especially the reliance on Member States for money as ensuring that even here national interest will always have a role to play, and one detrimental to the hopes of global citizenship.

Held, Axtmann, Miller, Follesdal and Imber thus all view the idea of citizenship as being framed by the kind of liberal nationalist framework outlined at the start of this introduction. All are aware of the difficulties involved in institutionalising such a relationship on a global, or even European, basis. Whilst Held and, to a lesser extent, Follesdal argue that these difficulties are not insurmountable, they acknowledge the great difficulties of forging citizenship beyond the sphere of reasonably strong national identities and in a non-state context. Axtmann and Miller see this as a very serious obstacle to global and European citizenship respectively. Imber, too, sees the experience of the UN as demonstrating just how difficult it is to make global citizenship meaningful in a world of states and where world government is not only unlikely but almost certainly undesirable.

However, as the chapters in Section I suggest, it may be the case that global citizenship does not require the acceptance of a liberal nationalist model of citizenship or an institutionally- and community-focused manifestation. If global citizenship is conceived of in a less restrictive way it may be that the apparent distance between Held and Axtmann, for example, is less than at first sight. Both would seem to subscribe to the idea of a universal community of responsibility suggested as being at the core of global citizenship. Follesdal and Imber, too, write in ways that do not take issue with this basic tenet of global citizenship. Thus it may be that what Held and Axtmann are in dispute over is the best ways in which one should be a global citizen rather than over the possibility of global citizenship. A looser conception of global citizenship does not seem to rule out focusing on reinvigorating political activity within the state and does not seem to require cosmopolitan democracy. Instead, they may even be complementary strategies for establishing, promoting and institutionalising recognition of a universal community of responsibility in addition to local communities.

# 5. CITIZENSHIP: EUROPEAN AND GLOBAL

## Andreas Follesdal

### INTRODUCTION

Talk of citizenship beyond state borders is not new. To the contrary, we find competing conceptions already in ancient Greek and Roman political thought. When asked which was his country, Socrates insisted that he was a citizen of the world, rather than an Athenian or a Corinthian. Likewise, when asked where he came from, Diogenes answered that 'I am a citizen of the world'. Their notion of citizenship beyond the city-state did not include any legal rights beyond borders. In contrast, Athenian citizens – that privileged set of free men – enjoyed active rights to political participation. Yet, for Socrates and Diogenes, citizenship of the world seemed to replace traditional citizenship rights and duties. In comparison, the Roman Empire recognised and even encouraged dual citizenship, with loyalty both to the local community and to Rome. This arrangement allowed citizens of Rome freedom of movement and trade within the Empire. Still, the Roman notion of dual citizenship had its drawbacks, both for the individual and for the political order. To be a citizen of Rome usually only provided status or passive citizenship in the form of protection, rather than active citizenship rights to political participation enjoyed only by the patrician class. Dual citizenship also created dual loyalties in the populations of the Empire, causing unresolved conflicts (Toynbee 1970; Clarke 1994).

European Union citizenship is closer to this Roman practice than to the Greek vision of cross-border citizenship – for better and worse. Union citizenship carries clear legal implications fostering freedom of movement and trade, and is intended to supplement, rather than to replace, national citizenship. Dual citizenship also means that the European Union must come to grips with challenges of institutionalisation and multiple loyalties. Reflection on the roles and challenges of Union citizenship may teach lessons for global citizenship. Both forms of citizenship create aspirations to a democratic political order with a scope beyond existing states, and face challenges regarding institutions and political culture aspiring to treat all affected individuals as equals.

Part 1 below provides a brief overview of the content of Union citizenship. Part 2 discusses the need for trust among individuals creating and sharing European-level institutions. Part 3 explores how trust can be secured by Union citizenship based on shared commitments rather than on common history and broader culture. Part 4 draws lessons for the roles and preconditions of global citizenship.

## 1. UNION CITIZENSHIP

Union citizenship was a conceptual innovation of the 1993 Maastricht Treaty, restated most recently in the Treaty of Nice (December 2000). Every person who is a national of a Member State of the Union is also a Union citizen. Union citizenship confers four main rights (EC Treaty 1992 Art. 17, 21). They include both protections (passive rights) and political control (active rights):

(i) The right to move freely among, and stay in, other Member States.

(ii) The right to vote and run in local and European Parliament elections in the Member State where one resides. The European Parliamentarians are elected directly by citizens of the various Member States, forming a representative body across state borders. Through successive treaties, the European Parliament's power over Union legislation has gradually increased. Union citizenship enhances the political rights to the European Parliament of those who have exploited the opportunities for mobility.

(iii) Protection in a non-EU country by the diplomatic or consular representatives of other Member States if one's own Member State is not represented.

(iv) The right to petition the European Parliament, and to petition the European Ombudsman.

The Amsterdam Treaty (1999) clarified the relationship between national and Union citizenship, insisting on the supplementary role of Union citizenship. Union citizenship did not replace national citizenship but was intended to complement it. One reason for introducing Union Citizenship was the perceived need to facilitate free movement and residence within the Union. Citizens of Member States were no longer foreigners when travelling and living elsewhere in the Union (Preuss 1996: 139).

## 2. CITIZENSHIP AS A SOURCE OF TRUST

The label 'citizenship' hints at another important reason why governments agreed to these rights; namely to foster a sense of European identity among those belonging to the same political unit. Union citizenship was introduced to foster trust among citizens of the Union, and to engender popular support and allegiance to Union institutions and policies (Closa 1992: 1155; Shaw 1997; Wiener 1997).

The need for popular support has increased with the expansion of EU activities and powers. Community-level institutions increasingly shape the lives, circumstances and aspirations of Europeans. Union law enjoys status as a new legal order, exercising direct legal authority over Europeans (Weiler 1991; MacCormick 1997). Many citizens and organisations were critical of the increased powers of Union-level institutions, particularly because they appear to be beyond the control of any single accountable government. This legitimacy deficit hindered trust among Europeans and prevented compliance with common rules.

Mutual trust is central to ensuring a stable political order over time, in several ways.

### 2(i) The need for trust among individuals – impersonal reciprocity

One possible role for Union citizenship is to foster and maintain the mutual, legitimate trust required among Europeans. Trust is important when individuals need to cooperate but will only do so if they expect the others to do their part. Suspicion that others will exploit rather than reciprocate one's efforts can easily prevent or unravel complex practices of cooperation. Trust is therefore crucial for 'social capital' – 'social connections and the attendant norms and trust' (Putnam 1995: 665; Loury 1987; Coleman 1990).

Robert Putnam argues that the operative norm in trust is what he calls 'generalised reciprocity' fostered in civil society:

> [N]ot 'I'll do this for you, because you are more powerful than I,' nor even 'I'll do this for you now, if you do that for me now,' but 'I'll do this for you now, knowing that somewhere down the road you'll do something for me' (Putnam 1993: 182–3)

To prevent suspicion and ensure stable cooperation, actual compliance is not enough: each must also appear trustworthy, so that others can count on their compliance (Hardin 1996). I submit that institutions such as those of the European Union can be an important means for fostering trust and trustworthiness, even among strangers, by engendering impersonal reciprocity, of the form:

I'll do this for you, knowing that somewhere down the road *someone else* will treat me in the appropriate way.

## 2(ii) Shaping institutions that in turn shape us

Such *impersonal* reciprocity is fostered by confidence in the general compliance with social institutions – including abstract, aggregated political systems (Inglehart 1970; Giddens 1995). Institutions can monitor and sanction defection, thus reducing the temptation to free ride. In turn, this reduces the likelihood of defection by those who do not mind cooperating as long as they are assured that others do likewise. These arrangements are especially important when establishing practices, as in the European Union at present, where institutions are crucial for facilitating cooperation.

Social practices and institutions rely on norms of impersonal reciprocity, but can also foster them – though slowly (Putnam 1993: 184; Rawls 1993b: 168). Institutions not only enable cooperation and shape individuals' strategies, they can also shape our identities: how we conceive of ourselves, our values, norms and interests. This is another way that institutions can create and sustain trust. They shape individuals' interests and perceptions of alternatives, and can foster trust in others' benevolence (Becker 1996). Trustworthiness is further enhanced if individuals do not act on the basis of calculations, but instead are socialised to regard certain behaviour as obvious and appropriate (Stinchcombe 1986; March and Simon 1993; Olsen 2000).

## 2(iii) Increased need for compliance in the European Union

As the Union increases its influence, individuals and government representatives are required to adjust or sacrifice their own interests for the sake of other Europeans. Several aspects of Union regulations make trust in other Europeans more important. One feature of the European Union that makes compliance especially dependent on trust is that it is national governments that implement EU decisions and directives. If Union legislation is perceived as 'interference' or an improper imposition on domestic government, and this becomes widely known, it will be difficult to secure compliance.

Veto powers intended to protect vital interests easily lead to deadlock in the absence of trust. No one must suspect that others will veto extensively to their own advantage – otherwise veto easily turns into a bargaining chip. Majority voting also requires trust. The minority that loses in decisions is required to act contrary to their own interests, possibly against the majority of their fellow domestic citizens, out of respect for the majority decisions made in European institutions (Scharpf 1997: 21). The minority that submits must trust that future minorities will do likewise (Taylor 1969; Barry 1991). Minorities must also be confident that the majority will take their interests into account.

Legislators must be trusted by each other, and by the populations, to consider the impact on all Europeans when making law.

The population at large must trust the legislators and executive branch. For instance, if the population perceives that the Commission abuses trust, acceptance and compliance with its decisions are at stake (Wessels 1999: 268). Another source of mistrust could be whether the domestic government officials attending Commission committees shift their loyalties, from government representatives towards evoking roles as supranational, pro-integrationist agents (Egeberg 1999; Egeberg and Trondal 1999; Trondal 2000).

## 2(iv) Willing support for institutional change

Trust is also important when institutions are created or modified in (quasi-) constitutional conventions. The Intergovernmental Conferences of the European Union regularly recast institutions in such ways, most recently in Nice in December 2000. These institutions are important both because they give the decision rules for the Union, and because of the long-term role that institutions may have in shaping Europeans' motivations and values (Checkel 1999; Checkel and Moravcsik 2001). Given these high stakes, citizens and their representatives must be reasonably secure that their interests are considered and respected by other participants. Individuals must not believe that others will change institutions guided by shared values or ideals, for example, concerning the proper allocation of tasks between the Member States and the Union.

If the Union remains a 'polycentric' political order with competences split and shared between Member States and Community institutions, the question of institutional stability becomes even more important. Historically, the institutions of such multinational federations have been less stable than those of unitary states (Kymlicka 1998; Lemco 1991). A central challenge will be to maintain trust in the cooperation of others in the face of protests concerning the appropriate allocation of powers between the central unit and sub-unit, all the while maintaining loyalty both to the particular group and to the state (cf. Lijphart 1977: 81–3; Mason 1999: 282).

## Subsidiarity as a solution?

An important challenge, then, is to agree to the proper allocation and use of such powers. Within the European Union, the so-called Principle of Subsidiarity shall serve this role. This principle holds that community action is appropriate only if 'the objectives of the proposed action cannot be sufficiently achieved by Member States' action in the framework of their national constitutional system and can therefore be better achieved by action on the part of the Community'. The Principle of Subsidiarity faces several challenges (Follesdal 1998). First, there are various conceptions of subsidiarity. Some versions hold that larger-scale institutions shall support the smaller-scale institutions in carrying out their tasks, while other versions hold that smaller-scale institutions must enjoy immunity from interference. The conception of subsidiarity in the EU Treaty is reasonably clear on such issues. The aim of the principle is to limit but also warrant actions by the community to those necessary to secure the objectives of the Treaty. Decisions shall not go beyond what is necessary to achieve the objectives of the Treaty and this must be substantiated. A global principle of subsidiarity awaits a clear interpretation. David Held, for one, suggests a similar standard of comparative efficiency for deciding whether to allocate powers to the global level (Held 1995a: 236).

Second, the application of the Principle of Subsidiarity requires agreement on the ends of the political order, and the appropriate tasks of each level. This is currently not in place in Europe, and certainly not regarding global-level institutions.

Third, and related, a particular problem arises in so far as the multi-level political order is asymmetric, in the sense that some sub-units will enjoy certain competences, while others will not. In Europe today this finds expression in European Monetary Union uniting some but not all Member States. States will disagree about the proper tasks and responsibilities of the Union, and some citizens and their politicians may plausibly claim a larger say in matters monetary. This is even more so if the future holds 'multiple Europes' of asymmetric federal arrangements where Member States have different bundles of competences.

These remarks suggest that a fundamental challenge to the future European Union is to ensure that Europeans develop and maintain trust in one another and in their common institutions, particularly if the Union increases its power and remains a polycentric, asymmetric political order. Europeans must have reason to believe that they will all comply with common laws and regulations, and that their new institutions and rules deserve compliance.

One important function of Union citizenship can be to bolster such trustworthiness.

## 3. THE BASIS OF CITIZENSHIP

An immediate objection to Union citizenship as a facilitator of trust might be that this is implausible. It is unrealistic to believe that Europeans will act on feelings of solidarity and charity across hundreds of miles (Preuss 1995: 275). The shared culture and common heritage of Europeans seems too thin to support the required trust, especially when compared to the national heritages bolstering compliance within the European welfare states. There is no 'demos' in Europe (Preuss 1995), no shared sense of destiny or broad set of common values.

However, a 'thick' common basis of shared beliefs, values and traditions is not needed. There are states without 'thick' shared values and sense of community. Indeed, the search for a common ethnic or cultural base for 'belonging' worries many Europeans, due to the memory of past wars based on such grounds.

Instead, I submit that a satisfactory account of Union citizenship need not build on a broad base of common identity, culture and history. It can build on a shared sense of justice and more limited commitments to the equal dignity of all Europeans, motivated by a 'desire to arrange our common political life on terms that others cannot reasonably reject' (Rawls 1993b: 124; and see Ackerman 1980: 69ff.; Weiler 1995 Preuss 1996: 275; MacCormick 1996: 150; MacCormick 1997: 341; Habermas 1998).

On this view, the motivating force is not a feeling of altruism, but a sense of justice, a preparedness to comply with those institutions that apply to us that are just (Rawls 1980: 540). Day-to-day compliance with laws and regulations is required by the duty to honour others' legitimate expectations, and the sense of justice as it binds us to the institutions that surround us. This is a different motivation for individuals' compliance than 'sentiments of affinity', the emotional bonds between individuals. A central question to this account is whether this inherently 'abstract' sense of solidarity based on universalistic principles of social justice can motivate, and be sustained over time (Preuss 1995: 275). However, even existing nation-states are usually too large to foster empathy and sympathetic concern for the well-being of all others (Calhoun 1996: 3; Goodin 1988). And still they seem to enjoy support from their citizens – at least for the time being. The account I sketch below assumes this more 'impersonal' motivation: a sense of justice, an interest in doing our moral duty and expressing respect for others, rather than from a sense of community, 'thick' identity, or empathy.

### 3(i) Citizenship: Commitment to institutions and to a political theory

For trust among citizens, it seems that they must be habituated to three sets of commitments.

First, citizens must be committed to their institutions and the decisions and rules that their officials make. In practice, this means that they must generally be prepared to abide by the laws and other rules that apply to them. In this way they respect the legitimate expectations of those around them who depend on their compliance.

Citizens must also have reason to believe that others will continue to comply in the future. Such trustworthiness, essential for stability, can be maintained by a publicly known, generally shared commitment to comply for what each person regards as good reasons. The second commitment is therefore to principles of legitimacy for institutions.

Such principles of legitimacy, duly worked out for polycentric polities, serve several roles in accounting for stability. One is to provide critical standards for assessing existing, concrete institutions. Another is to secure some shared bases for compliance with just institutions, since these principles provide justification for such existing institutions.

The third common commitment is to the immediate premises for such principles, for instance in the form of a conception of citizens as equal members of the polycentric political order. To illustrate this commitment, consider John Rawls' suggestion that the social institutions should be regarded as a system of cooperation among individuals regarded for such purposes as free and equal participants (Rawls 1971). That particular conception is insufficient for the challenges facing the European Union, since the Member States and community institutions split and share sovereignty. A shared conception of the proper responsibilities of Member States and the Union seems necessary to allocate powers between them, for instance by specifying the Principle of Subsidiarity further.

There are two reasons for this third kind of commitment. A consensus on institutions and principles of legitimacy is insufficient to convince others of one's trustworthiness regarding future compliance with these procedures. Others' present compliance does not by itself give us reason to trust that they will continue to respect the principles of legitimacy – we also need assurance that they regard themselves as having reasons to continue to comply in the future. Moreover, the trust needed in the European Union now also concerns the creation of institutions. Such tasks must be guided and seen to be guided by a sense of justice, including a commitment to a shared conception of the equal standing of Europeans within the polycentric European political order.

### 3(ii) Talk of citizenship may erode trust in the Union

The label 'Union citizenship' indicates that the future European order must satisfy democratic principles harking back at least to Jean-Jacques Rousseau and Immanuel Kant. Equal respect requires that those subject to laws should also have an equal say in legislation and other matters European.

By invoking the notion of citizenship, the European Union commits itself to the normative ideals and requirements developed over centuries in Europe. Long-standing European theories of political legitimacy insist, for instance, that a legitimate political order must provide terms for living together that in some sense could secure the consent of all (Locke 1963; Rousseau 1978; Kant 1970). Constitutional democracy has come to be seen as one such condition, where citizens can hold their rulers accountable on the basis of unconstrained common debate and deliberation.

However, many observe that the European Union falls short of such conditions for legitimate rule: there are few opportunities both for deliberation and for accountability. In so far as talk of 'Union citizenship' highlights these deficits, it may serve to reduce, rather than enhance the support and trust Europeans exhibit towards each other and their common institutions. So Union citizenship destabilises rather than consolidates the European political order.

In response to this worry, it seems clear that talk of citizenship may fail to provide the desired support for existing institutions. However, the conclusion is not automatically that the normative political ideals and standards of democratic governance should be scrapped. This would run counter to the traditional critical function of normative political theory in the Western tradition.

The need to enhance democratic control appears unavoidable given the political impact of the Union. Talk of 'Union citizenship' does not create these tensions, nor do the tensions disappear by abolishing the term – for that, institutional reforms are required. And it remains to be seen whether there is political will and resources for such political craftsmanship (Olsen 2000; Joerges, Mény and Weiler 2000).

In response to this worry, I submit that pessimism on the basis of current absence of trust is premature (Follesdal 2000b). The development of a European sense of commonness can be a dynamic process. Given that institutions can shape citizens, common institutions may help create the requisite commitments and will to live together, thus building trust (Preuss 1995: 277–8; Preuss 1996; Streeck 1996: fn. 64 and 74; cf. Putnam 1993: 184; Rawls 1999: 112; Habermas 1998; MacCormick 1997: 353).

The arenas for public debate may also emerge with time. The impact of the lack of a common language may be less severe in so far as the agenda can be limited to political issues, and among them only those that are of common European concern (La Torre 1998; Habermas 1992: 7).

Nevertheless, the relatively feeble European public sphere and weak socialisation to a common European sense of justice may warrant caution about a premature reliance on majoritarian decision-making (Grimm 1995: 293–4). Institutions should economise on trust while at the same time fostering the means for credible commitments among Europeans.

### 3(iii) The challenge of multiple citizenship – conflicting loyalties?

Historically, citizenship has often been regarded as exclusive. One is hopefully a citizen of one state – but only of one. Many states have traditionally prohibited multiple citizenships. One long-standing worry about multiple citizenships is that individuals will suffer from conflicting loyalties and split identities. Union citizenship is explicitly a second citizenship, supplementing rather than replacing citizenship in a Member State. This would lead to a fear that instead of bolstering trust, Union citizenship will foster split loyalties.

In response, we can note that the basis of citizenship sketched above is not exclusionary. It does not rely on a broad cultural basis or a thick sense of national identity and pride. It is thus – at least in principle – compatible with other, concurrent commitments and loyalties. Conflicts may still occur, of course, in so far as the Member State governments and Union institutions issue conflicting orders or legislation and there is no final judicial authority.

Such occasions can be drastically reduced in so far as courts with European jurisdiction have the final word on the basis of a clear delineation of authority and competences.

I have suggested that one important task that Union citizenship can play is to facilitate the trust and trustworthiness required for stable compliance and support of Union institutions. To secure such trust, all Union citizens must share some common grounds that include the commitment to existing institutions and to shared principles of legitimacy. Moreover, citizens must also share the immediate grounds for principles, for instance conceptions of the ends of the political unity, and some conception of the proper relationship between individuals and non-unitary European political order, where Member States and community institutions split and share sovereignty. These three commitments would seek to avoid contested parts of specific religious or philosophical worldviews. At the same time, the shared basis goes beyond 'constitutional consensus' or a 'constitutional patriotism' that require consensus on procedures for making and interpreting authoritative decisions (Baier 1989; Habermas 1998). Agreement on procedures seems insufficient for maintaining the mutual trust necessary for constitutional changes and institutional development.

Critics will point out that there are broad discrepancies between the institutions of the European Union, including Union citizenship, and the requirements of normative political theory. But such deviations are not necessarily a flaw of the theory. They may equally well be weaknesses of the institutions, highlighted by a normative theory. That talk of citizenship may increase conflicts, and not only induce support, should come as no surprise: governments have often discovered that citizenship rights have 'the potential for exacerbating, as well as diminishing the conflict of classes' (Goodin 1988).

## 4. EUROPEAN AND GLOBAL CITIZENSHIP

Union citizenship may help clarify the notion and possible political roles of global citizenship.

Union citizenship invokes the notion of citizenship. This commits the European political order to the equal standing of all individuals, including democratic control over the institutions that shape their lives. We may call this underlying normative commitment 'normative cosmopolitanism'. It is universal in scope, insisting that if someone is affected then they should receive equal consideration regardless of race, gender, social status or citizenship.

Normative cosmopolitanism does not in itself require global institutions. But those equally affected by practices and institutions should also have an equal say in how the institutions should be shaped. Such arguments apply at the European level: Europeans are now so interdependent due to their common institutions that they must also have an equal say in how they are governed (Follesdal 1997b). The institutions of the Union, including Union citizenship, must be shaped to ensure such democratic accountability.

This line of argument can serve as a model with regards to claims to institutionalise global citizenship. Globalisation reduces the significance of state borders, due largely to the digital and transnational economy. Our decisions increasingly affect others across borders, increasing the interdependency of foreigners. In so far as global regimes have global implications, normative cosmopolitanism requires that they must also be under political control where all have an equal say. The fact of globalisation, as indeed a fact with drastic implications on individuals' life-chances, supports a normative requirement to address the global democratic deficit.

The requisite legal protections and controls may take at least two forms, reminiscent of the classical distinction between passive and active citizenship. First, there may be institutional arrangements that provide immunity to individuals and communities against severe damage wrought by others. A wide range of human rights and practices of sovereignty are examples of such protections. Second, individuals may enjoy institutionalised influence in the form of political rights over the institutions and regimes. National citizenship typically provides both forms of controls. Europeans also enjoy both forms of controls: passive rights are expressed in the form of European human rights regimes, including the recent Union Charter on Fundamental Rights; active rights are enjoyed in the form of voting rights of two kinds – through democratic control over domestic governments represented in the EU Council, and secondly regarding directly elected representatives to the European Parliament. Union citizenship ensures the latter political influence for Europeans residing in Member States other than their own.

Hitherto, in so far as global citizenship is institutionalised it primarily consists of passive rights in the form of universal human rights standards. Elements of the United Nations may be enhanced to provide equal political influence over various regimes but such global political rights are not well developed – yet.

The discussion of Union citizenship indicates that institutionalising active global citizenship faces several challenges.

Global political authorities do not automatically alleviate the problems of globalisation – to the contrary, they can easily be abused to the further detriment of the powerless. To ensure that a global political order expresses respect for all on a footing of equality, the institutional design is of utmost importance. Moreover, if these decision-making bodies are to enjoy compliance and support, they must be trusted to make just decisions. If they are to be representative, this entails that most global citizens must be committed to a common normative basis. The account of Union citizenship sketched above suggests that such a basis need not draw on a broad shared history and culture. Nevertheless, several commitments must be broadly shared, including a conception of the proper tasks of state governments, regional bodies such as the EU, and global institutions. Such a shared political culture must be fostered and maintained. The risks of abuse of such global institutions are obvious, particularly in the absence of global arenas for political deliberation and habituation. But gradual development in this direction may still be feasible – and the alternatives may be even worse, judged from the point of view of normative cosmopolitanism.

## CONCLUSION

The present reflections have focused on the role of citizenship in securing trust, and thereby contributing to compliance with legitimate institutions. This concern for trust seems to have fuelled the call for Union citizenship. Similar needs arise at the global level in the wake of globalisation, and global citizenship might be considered a solution.

If Union citizenship is to secure trust and trustworthiness in the population, a common normative basis is required. I have suggested that this basis need not primarily focus on a common history and culture in a broad sense. Instead, three commitments may suffice: to the institutions and hence the legislation they engender; to principles that justify these institutions; and to a political theory that grounds these principles in a conception of the proper role of individuals, of Member States and of the Union. Such common grounds may suffice to ensure trust and stable compliance.

Talk of Union citizenship sets standards of legitimacy for such a shared basis, but the actual institutions and shared commitments fall short of these standards. In so far as Union citizenship highlights these deficits it may reduce rather than enhance the support and mutual trust of Europeans.

The response should not be to dismiss the normative political ideals and standards of democratic governance. Given the impact of the Union, the need to enhance democratic control is unavoidable. Long-term trust among Union citizens depends on resolving the legitimacy deficit of the Union. However, it remains to be seen whether there is the political will and resources for such changes.

Similar considerations appear to hold concerning institutions for global governance. Present global regimes regarding issues such as trade, environment and human rights fall short of the normative standards of global justice. These conflicts cannot be resolved by dismissing any attempt at bringing normative political theory to bear. Resources, competence and political will are required to increase the legitimacy of the political orders both in Europe and globally. Reflections on Union citizenship and global citizenship might motivate and guide such changes.[1]

QUESTIONS

1. Union citizenship seems intended to strengthen mutual trust between the diverse peoples in the European Union. Is similar trust needed at the global level? Could global citizenship serve a similar role among individuals globally?
2. How can trust across borders be fostered?
3. If citizenship today requires democratic institutions, what bearing does that have on world citizenship?
4. Is Union citizenship different from both state citizenship and global citizenship?
5. If you are from Europe, does being a Union citizen mean anything to you? If so, what? If not, why? If you are not from Europe, when would it be important for you to be a citizen of a political order like the EU?

NOTES

1. The research for this paper was funded by ARENA – a programme of Advanced Research on the Europeanisation of the Nation-State, under the Research Council of Norway, and by the EU TSER program (SOE 2973056) on European Citizenship and the Social and Political Integration of the European Union. I have benefited from comments from the editors, and from Stefan Gosepath, Jos de Beus, Carlos Closa, Hans Peter Graver, Pablo De Greiff, John Erik Fossum, Percy Lehning, Neil MacCormick, Johan P. Olsen and Ulf Sverdrup. This paper explores further some themes addressed in earlier works, particularly Follesdal 1997a and Follesdal 2001.

# 6. THE LEFT, THE NATION-STATE AND EUROPEAN CITIZENSHIP

## David Miller

As the European Union (EU) moves steadily towards fuller political integration in the form of the single European currency, attitudes on the left towards projects of supranational governance remain ambivalent. Currently in Britain, the Labour Party under Tony Blair presents itself as markedly more Euro-friendly than the defeated Conservatives but historically the two parties have not always aligned themselves in this way. Both parties have been divided between pro- and anti-Europeans but until the arrival of Margaret Thatcher enthusiasm for the European project ran higher among the Conservatives. On the Labour left, membership of the European Economic Community (as it was called then) was seen as imposing a straitjacket of economic orthodoxy on the policies of national governments, and although this point of view has become heretical under New Labour, we can expect to see it expressed more often as the debate about whether to join the single currency heats up. Equally, pressures from big business will in due course force the Conservative Party to moderate its present Euro-sceptic stance.

The same confused picture, with parties swapping positions over time, can be found in other EU Member States. Can we say any more here? Should parties of the left be more enthusiastic, or less enthusiastic, than parties of the right for transnational groupings like the EU as a matter of general principle, or is it simply a matter of assessing each proposal as it comes along? How should we try to think about this question?

If we look back to the socialist tradition for inspiration, we find that it contains strong currents both of nationalism and of internationalism. The internationalist strain stems philosophically from the Marxist belief (like most Marxist beliefs not held in its crude form by Marx himself) that national divisions are created artificially by the capitalist class to divide the proletariat, and politically from the belief that socialism in one country could never be a feasible possibility. The nationalist strain derives first from the fact that all socialist projects, whether communist or social-democratic, have been national projects in the sense that they have been undertaken by parties and movements working within national borders; second from the fact that in order to carry these projects through, socialists have needed to invoke the idea of the nation. This can be seen only too clearly if we consider the Soviet Union and the People's Republic of China, where appeals to national solidarity and pride always played a central role in socialist propaganda, but even mild social democrats such as Bill Clinton and Tony Blair pepper their speeches with references to 'our nation' or 'this great country of ours' as a way of inducing the audience to consider some small sacrifice of personal gain for the good of the whole.

Faced with this apparent conflict between socialist internationalism and the practical significance of national loyalties, many on the left have responded by saying that the socialist invocation of nationhood is simply a matter of political realism. Given that most of the people to whom they want to appeal, especially most members of the working class, have fairly strong nationalist sentiments, it makes sense to use those feelings constructively in building a socialist movement – or at least not to trample upon them overtly. George Bernard Shaw once said that if you wanted to rebel against high-heeled shoes, you should take care to do it in a very smart hat. But that is the beginning and the end of the matter. To the extent that the public can be weaned away from their national prejudices toward a more cosmopolitan outlook, it should be. There are no reasons of principle to embrace the nation-state as a unit of political mobilisation.

This common response seems to me badly mistaken. To see why, we need to think about the values underlying the political projects of the left. These are, of course, disputed but among them we must surely count *democracy* and *social justice*. We want to live in societies in which there is a far greater degree of popular control over policy-making, in which people are not simply asked to vote for representatives every four or five years but have more direct input into the way those societies develop. We also want to live in societies in which the huge resource inequalities generated by capitalist markets are combated by public action, whether this takes the form of redistribution through social security and the welfare state, or more radically through new forms of economic organisation (employee ownership schemes, for instance) that alter the primary distribution of income in the direction of greater equality.

For present purposes there is no need to be more specific than this about the goals of the left. What interests me is the way in which these aims are linked to something like the nation-state in its familiar form. Take democracy first. If political decisions are going to be made in a genuinely democratic way – through public discussion in which all sections of society have their voice heard – one crucial requirement is a sufficient degree of trust among the debating constituency. For democratic decision-making to work successfully, each participating group must be willing to listen to opposing points of view, and be willing to moderate its own demands in order to reach a compromise that everyone can accept. Equally, when a decision has been reached, those who find themselves in a minority – we cannot expect decisions to be unanimous – must be willing to comply with the outcome, knowing that their point of view has at least been taken seriously, and that on future occasions they may find themselves on the winning side. All of this requires confidence in, and understanding of, those one disagrees with politically. Trust of this kind is much more likely to exist among people who share a common national identity, speak a common language and have overlapping cultural values. Conversely, in multinational states, where trust exists much more within the national groups than among them, politics tends to take the form of bargaining, and each decision is regarded as a victory or a defeat for the group that one belongs to. As Michael Lind has argued (1994), prospects for democracy of any kind are fragile in these circumstances, and the more radical form of democracy is clearly a non-starter.

Next, what about social justice? Every system of social justice requires people to limit to some degree their pursuit of private advantage through the market system. This is not simply a matter of taxing or expropriating the very rich. Ordinary working people must be taxed, or pay into social insurance schemes, to provide social services and income support for the unemployed. Everyone must comply with fair, non-discriminatory rules for job appointments and promotions. What can motivate people to make the sacrifices that social justice requires, whether this takes the form of supporting parties that promise redistribution, or simply behaving in a fair way in their everyday lives? There is a wealth of evidence that shows that people are more willing to make such sacrifices the more closely they feel themselves tied to the likely beneficiaries of their actions. (Psychological studies of justice, for instance, show that people are more likely to afford equal treatment to others with whom they share a common identity or common values.)

From this point of view, nationhood is a very important source of common identity, particularly in societies that are sharply divided along lines of race, ethnicity, religion or lifestyle. I may not approve of, or sympathise with, the personal beliefs and values of the people in the next house or the next street, but because I see them as my compatriots I feel a sense of responsibility towards them and also a degree of confidence that if they are now benefiting from my contribution (as a tax-payer, say) they would be prepared to return the benefit if the roles were reversed and it was I who needed income support or medical care. As Richard Rorty has argued, programmes to help disadvantaged minorities in the inner cities sound much more persuasive when presented as programmes to help 'our fellow Americans' rather than simply 'our fellow human beings'. To say this does not mean that we should be indifferent to the fate of human beings worldwide, but it does recognise that aspirations to social justice are linked to distinct communities whose members feel a special responsibility to one another.

So if the left continues to value democracy and social justice, as it surely must, it must also acknowledge that pursuit of these goals presupposes national communities in which mutual trust stems from a shared identity. At the same time it is important not to present these identities as though they were God-given and eternal. Many studies have shown how the national divisions that now exist were generated historically, sometimes from above by political leaders anxious to consolidate newly-formed states, sometimes from below by minority ethnic groups seeking to escape from the clutches of governments controlled by the majority. So this raises the possibility that nations in their present form might be superseded by larger units – in the European context, the possibility that Europe itself might come to serve as a source of identity and citizenship that overrides existing national allegiances. This certainly is the hope of some European leaders today. But is it a realistic hope, and should the left be supporting moves in this direction?

Let's begin with the current situation. It's fairly clear that for people across Europe the nation remains their primary focus of political identity and allegiance. If asked who they are willing to fight to defend, or who they are willing to support by paying taxes, the answer given by people in each country is their fellow nationals. Attitudes to the general idea of European unity are broadly positive – though views about the European Union as an institution are more divided, with majorities in some countries saying that on balance they would be better out than in. But Europe does not command loyalty in the ways that nation-states do. A united Europe is seen as a useful arrangement that provides benefits like freer travel and greater access to jobs and economic markets but it does not generate a sense of emotional identification.

Even if Europe cannot yet provide the sense of identity that nations can, does it not at least provide a transnational form of citizenship that might be a model for other parts of the world? Certainly European citizenship exists in a legal sense. But what does this mean in practice? European citizens enjoy some rights that are not available to outsiders, for example, the rights to travel freely across borders within Europe, and to work and study in other European countries. They also have the right to challenge national legislation or policy by bringing a case before the European Court of Justice. This latter right has had some significance in forcing national governments to come into line with European practice in some areas. But its reach should not be exaggerated. The European Court has been careful to construe its remit quite narrowly so as not to challenge the right of Member States to pursue different policies in areas such as health, education and industrial relations according to national traditions and preferences.

If we look at European citizenship in the light of T. H. Marshall's classic account of citizenship as a common status uniting civil, political and social rights, we find that to date at least only rights of the first kind are included. In a technical sense it could be argued that European citizens enjoy political rights in the form of rights to elect MPs to the European Parliament. However, knowledge of and interest in the doings of this parliament remain minimal among ordinary voters, and European elections are fought very largely by national parties on national issues. Politically speaking, people continue overwhelmingly to think and act as members of national electorates. As for social citizenship, rights to health, education, social security, pensions and so forth remain under the control of national governments, subject only to such common standards as are imposed by the European treaties and enforced by the Court of Justice. However this still leaves room for considerable variation in how these rights are defined. It would be hard to claim that European social citizenship exists in any concrete sense.

If this is a correct assessment of the current situation, what are the prospects of the European Union changing in such a way that it can accommodate the ideas of democracy and social justice that I sketched earlier? Could we see, for instance, the development of a Europe-wide practice of democratic citizenship? One serious obstacle to this, as Tony Judt has emphasised in his book *A Grand Illusion* (1996), is the continuing existence of language divisions among the peoples of Europe. Although negotiations among political elites are increasingly carried out using English as a common language (French resistance to this practice seems finally to be crumbling), if we are looking toward a form of democratic politics in which the public at large is involved in political debate, we must recognise that such debate will necessarily be carried out in the vernacular language of each community. We cannot expect the ordinary citizens of Italy, Denmark or Greece to conduct their political discussions using English, or any other second language for that matter. So these debates will remain opaque to those who speak a different language, and instead of a European public opinion which might form the basis of a Europe-wide form of democracy, the best we can hope for are separate bodies of public opinion that could then be fed into elite negotiations at European level. There seems to be a simple trade-off here: the wider the scope of citizenship is drawn, and the more publics it has therefore to embrace, the weaker its democratic credentials become.

We need to ask similar questions about social justice on a European scale. At present some redistribution does take place between richer and poorer European states but this is as a result of regional and other policies negotiated between elites in Brussels, and most people remain unaware of the transfers unless they happen to be the direct beneficiaries. The evidence suggests that people's sense of their responsibilities does not extend to having their tax revenues used to support poorer citizens in other nation-states. So there is a gap between citizens' sense of social justice and what is actually happening on the ground, a gap that, if my earlier argument is correct, will not be bridged unless a common sense of European identity emerges that transcends national borders.

This problem is likely to get far worse if and when the European Union is enlarged to include those central and eastern European states that are currently in the process of applying for membership. To bring the economies and welfare regimes of these states up to the point where they can properly be integrated into the European economy (with free movement of labour and so forth) would require redistribution of resources on a scale well beyond that so far attempted. It is hard to see why the relatively prosperous citizens of Britain or France would be willing to supply the means to raise Poles or Hungarians to a position of near equality in the absence of a strong sense of mutual identification. (It has often been pointed out that the economic costs to the former West Germany of German reunification were only tolerable because of the powerful feelings of pan-German national identity that came to the fore in those dramatic moments when the Berlin Wall came tumbling down.) Once again there appears to be a trade-off. Europe can choose to expand, and there may be good political arguments for bringing the states of eastern Europe into the Union, but only at the cost of a loosening of the economic bonds that have developed among the members of the existing core.

None of this should be taken as a root-and-branch argument against transnational federations or other forms of transnational governance. Linking states together by such institutions serves important values, most obviously the peaceful resolution of international conflicts. But our question is whether the distinctive values of the left are promoted when political decisions are removed from the competence of existing nation-states and transferred to larger units, and my argument has been that the causes of democracy and social justice are unlikely to be advanced. The left should welcome the forging of friendly bonds between erstwhile adversaries such as has occurred within the European Union but it should not move too quickly to dismantle or marginalise the nation-state. It is not accidental that left causes have been advanced furthest in communities that have combined a strong sense of national solidarity with effective political institutions: the Scandinavian social democracies are the clearest example.

Many would argue that the nation-state, whatever virtues it might have had until recently, is rapidly becoming obsolescent. The changing structure of the global economy means that only larger political units have any chance of controlling market outcomes. The Scandinavian example cuts both ways: with some reluctance, both Denmark and Sweden felt impelled to join the European Community, despite its defects in terms of inequality and high levels of unemployment, feeling that their economies were too exposed to the forces of international trade and investment if they stayed outside. Only the Norwegians have remained determinedly autonomous. This is a large issue, and all I can do is signal my agreement with those who argue that states still have more freedom in their economic and social policies than strong globalisation theses would suggest. The state cannot challenge international capital and currency markets head-on – or at least it will pay a very heavy price if it tries to do so – but there are many areas of policy in which a strong commitment to social justice can go hand in hand with creating conditions that will attract foreign investment and help the economy to remain competitive. Providing, at public expense, the education and training needed to create a skilled and flexible workforce is one obvious example.

Unquestionably there are some problems – global environmental problems, for instance – that cannot be solved by nation-states acting independently of one another. The fact that groups such as Greenpeace and Friends of the Earth have been able to unite activists across borders has led some commentators to argue that we are witnessing the emergence of new forms of citizenship that are not tied to any geographical location, not even such a broad location as Europe. But should we be describing politics in this vein as citizen politics at all? In what sense is the Greenpeace activist a citizen? There is no determinate community with which she identifies politically, and no one, except perhaps other members of her group, with whom she stands in relations of reciprocity. So there is no group of fellow citizens with whom she is committed to seeking grounds of agreement. If confronted by individuals who do not share her commitment to the cause, she must either convert them or oppose them by whatever means she has at her disposal. To say this is, let us be clear, not to condemn her. If the cause is a good one, and she pursues it in a way that respects the rights of others (non-violently, for instance), she may act heroically and well – many of us, I am sure, will feel this about the Greenpeace campaigns on nuclear testing and whaling. But this is not citizenship in any recognisable sense. It does not involve democratic debate with others with different interests and views. It may supplement, but it cannot replace, the form of citizenship that has emerged in national communities whose members seek to practice justice among themselves.

The distinctive aims of the left must, I believe, be promoted by strengthening citizenship and fighting for social justice primarily at the national level, through movements and parties organised at that level. Collaboration with like-minded movements abroad is, of course, fine, and so is participation in transnational and international institutions; but we should avoid the error of thinking that membership in these bodies can somehow achieve socialist or social-democratic aims that fail to win democratic support at home. Europe has sometimes looked like that to Labour supporters in Britain, particularly during the Thatcher years: if only we were fully paid-up members of the European club, somehow that would safeguard cherished social-democratic programmes against the ravages of domestic politics. But that is an illusion, and Tony Blair, if he did succumb to it, will soon be disabused.

QUESTIONS

1. Why does Miller identify issues of democracy and social justice as being of central concern for the left in relation to European citizenship?
2. In what ways does European citizenship fail to generate the loyalty and identity that Miller argues are vital to the pursuit of the goals of democracy and social justice?
3. What important roles can the state play that the European Union cannot in relation to promoting citizenship and associated goals?
4. Why does Miller argue that NGOs and other organisations and institutions are inadequate alternatives to the state in this context?

# 7. THE TRANSFORMATION OF POLITICAL COMMUNITY: RETHINKING DEMOCRACY IN THE CONTEXT OF GLOBALISATION

## David Held

*In the first section of this chapter – a much shortened version of a chapter published in 1999 – Held summarises the development of modern ideas of the nation-state, the nation-state system and liberal democracy. He contrasts this with previously existing political arrangements in Europe and elsewhere. These possessed greater diversity within political communities, but greater homogeneity across them, although he recognises this was partly due to the limited geographical extent of politics prior to the expansion of the European empires between the sixteenth and nineteenth centuries.*

In Europe from the sixteenth century onward political power became increasingly concentrated within more strictly defined territorial borders. This reduced social, economic and cultural variation within these emerging states but increased diversity among them. By the eighteenth century this had become formalised in notions of territorially-defined sovereignty, initially embodied in the monarch, and emerging 'national' identities highlighting shared features such as history, culture and language that united the people of one state and distinguished them from the people of other states. Alongside state-formation, the states system developed in a symbiotic relationship. Often seen as being enshrined in the Peace of Westphalia (1648), the 'Westphalian system' culminated in ideas of sovereignty, sovereign equality among states, non-intervention in domestic affairs and states' consent as the basis of legal obligation becoming widely accepted principles. Within these *confines, competing national interests, often resolved via war, rendered cooperation difficult and dangerous. Power and security were essential goals of foreign policy but ones that could only be acquired at the expense of others, ensuring confrontation and competition.*

*This framework of domestically centralised and homogeneous states co-existing in an international environment without central authority and where war is common and legitimate had a major effect on the development of democracy. The eighteenth-century advent of representative democracy – whereby people exercise democratic authority and accountability through elected representatives rather than direct participation – made democracy practical in these new, large states. Questions about who could participate in elections and other democratic practices were answered by reference to the state: those within its borders and sharing in a common identity were the democratic constituency. As importantly, politics in the states system identi-fied members of other states as potential enemies and threats to security, thus justifying their exclusion from democratic processes. The hardening lines on the map that defined the limits of sovereignty neatly defined the state, the nation and the demos – those entitled to democratic representation and those to whom politicians are accountable. Those living in other states were different – 'foreign' – and justifiably excluded.*

*Held concludes thus . . .*

Accordingly, the heart or 'deep structure' of the system of democratic nation states can be characterised by a number of striking features, which are, broadly: democracy in nation-states and non-democratic relations among states; the entrenchment of accountability and democratic legitimacy inside state boundaries and pursuit of reasons of state (and maximum political advantage) outside such boundaries; democracy and citizenship rights for those regarded as 'insiders', and the frequent negation of these rights for those beyond their borders.

### Changing Forms of Regional and Global Enmeshment

At the centre of the dominant theoretical approaches to democratic politics is an uncritically appropriated concept of the territorial political community. The difficulty with this is that political communities have rarely – if ever – existed in isolation as bounded geographical totalities; they are better thought of as multiple overlapping networks of interaction. These networks crystallise around different sites and forms of power – economic, political, military, cultural, among others – producing diverse patterns of activity which do not correspond in any simple and straightforward way to territorial boundaries (Mann 1986: ch. 1). [. . .]

The term 'globalisation' captures some of the changes which shape the nature of the political and the prospect of political community; unpacking the term helps create a framework for addressing some of the issues raised above. Globalisation can be understood, I believe, in relation to a set of processes which shift the spatial form of human organisation and activity to transcontinental or interregional patterns of activity, interaction and the exercise of power (see Held et al. 1999). It involves a stretching and deepening of social relations and institutions across space and time such that, on the one hand, day-to-day activities are increasingly influenced by events happening on the other side of the globe and, on the other, the practices and decisions of local groups or communities can have significant global reverberations (Giddens 1990). It is possible to distinguish different historical forms of globalisation in terms of: (1) the extensiveness of networks of relations and connections; (2) the intensity of flows and levels of activity within these networks; and (3) the impact of these phenomena on particular bounded communities. It is not a case of saying, as many do, that there was once no globalisation, but there is now; rather, it is a case of recognising that forms of globalisation have changed over time and that these can be systematically understood by reference to points 1–3 above. Such an historical approach to globalisation contrasts with the current fashion to suggest either that globalisation is fundamentally new – the 'hyper-globalisation school', with its insistence that global markets are now fully established (Ohmae 1990); or that there is nothing unprecedented about contemporary levels of international economic and social interaction since they resemble those of the gold standard era – the 'sceptical school' (Hirst and Thompson 1996). [. . .]

From the foundation of the International Telegraph Union in 1865, a plethora of international organisations developed with responsibility for regulating and ordering diverse domains of activity including trade, industrial infrastructure, agriculture, labour, public order and administration, elements of individual rights, health and research. At issue was not the creation of a single institution or authority to manage world affairs but rather the establishment of regulatory regimes for, in principle, the predictable and orderly conduct of pressing transnational processes. By 1914 many aspects of global affairs had been brought within the terms of these offices and rule systems. Accordingly, a new infrastructure for the regulations and control of economic, social and cultural affairs was slowly founded, stimulating telegrams, letters, and packages to flood the international networks by the beginning of the twentieth century (Murphy 1994: ch. 2–3).

Virtually all countries in the world became enmeshed in and functionally part of a larger pattern of global flows and global transformations (Nierop 1994: 171). Goods, capital, people, knowledge, communications and weapons, as well as crime, culture, pollutants, fashions and beliefs, readily moved across territorial boundaries (McGrew 1992). Transnational networks, social movements and relationships extended through virtually all areas of human activity. The existence of interregional systems of trade, finance and production bound together the prosperity and fate of households, communities and nations across the world. Far from this being a world of 'discrete civilisations', it became a fundamentally interconnected global order, marked by dense patterns of exchange as well as by power, hierarchy and unevenness.

Against this background, the meaning and place of political community, and particularly of the democratic political community, needs to be re-examined. At least two tasks are necessary in order to pursue this objective. First, it is important to illustrate some of the fundamental alterations in the patterns of interconnectedness among political communities and the subsequent shifts in the structure and form of political community itself. Second, it is important to set out some of the political implications of these changes. [. . .]

1. Among the significant developments which are changing the nature of political community are global economic processes, especially growth in trade, production, and financial transactions, organised in part by rapidly expanding multinational companies. Trade has grown substantially, reaching unprecedented levels, particularly in the post-Second World War period. [. . .]

Underpinning this economic shift has been the growth of multinational corporations, both productive and financial. Approximately 20,000 multinational corporations now account for a quarter to a third of world output, 70 per cent of world trade and 80 per cent of foreign direct investment. They are essential to the diffusion of skills and technology, and they are key players in the international money markets. In addition, multinational corporations can have profound effects on macroeconomic policy. They can respond to variations in interest rates by raising finance in whichever capital market is most favourable. They can shift their demand for employment to countries with much lower employment costs. And in the area of industrial policy, especially technology policy, they can move activities to where the maximum benefits accrue. [. . .]

Although the rhetoric of hyper-globalisation has provided many an elected politician with a conceptual resource for refusing political responsibility, globalisation has significant and discernible characteristics which alter the balance of resources – economic and political – within and across borders. Among the most important of these is the tangible growth in the enmeshment of national economies in global economic transactions (that is, a growing proportion of nearly all national economies is involved in international economic exchanges with an increasing number of countries). As a result, the autonomy of democratically elected governments has been, and is increasingly, constrained by sources of unelected and unrepresentative economic power. [. . .]

2. Within the realms of the media and culture there are also grounds for thinking that there is a growing disjuncture between the idea of the democratic state as an independent, accountable centre of power bounded by fixed borders – in this case, a centre of national culture, able to foster and sustain a national identity – and interlinked changes in the spheres of media and

cultural exchange. A number of developments in recent times can be highlighted. English has spread as the dominant language of elite cultures throughout the world: it is now the dominant language in business, computing, law, science and politics. The internationalisation and globalisation of telecommunications had been extraordinarily rapid: international telephone traffic has increased more than fourfold between 1983 and 1995; there has been a massive increase in transnational cable links; there has been an explosion in satellite links; and the Internet has provided a remarkable increase in the infrastructure of horizontal and lateral communication capacity within and across borders. Moreover, substantial multimedia conglomerates have developed, such as the Murdoch empire and Time Warner. In addition, there has been a huge increase in tourism – for example, in 1960 there were 70 million international tourists, while in 1994 there were nearly 500 million. And in television and in film there are similar trends. [. . .]

3. Environmental problems and challenges are perhaps the clearest and starkest examples of the global shift in human organisation and activity, creating some of the most fundamental pressures on the efficacy of the nation-state and state-centric democratic politics. There are three types of problems at issue:

(i) The first is shared problems involving the global commons, that is, fundamental elements of the ecosystem – among the most significant challenges are global warming and ozone depletion;

(ii) A second category of global environmental problems involves the interlinked challenges of demographic expansion and resource consumption – pressing examples under this heading include desertification, questions of biodiversity, and threats to the existence of certain species;

(iii) A third category of problems is transboundary pollution such as acid rain, or river pollutants, or the contaminated rain which fell in connection with Chernobyl.

In response to the progressive development of, and publicity surrounding, environmental problems in the last three decades, there has been an interlinked process of cultural and political globalisation as illustrated by the emergence of new cultural, scientific and intellectual networks; new environmental movements with transnational organisations and transnational concerns; and new institutions and conventions such as those agreed in 1992 at the Earth Summit in Brazil. Not all environmental problems are, of course, global; such an implication would be entirely false. But there has been a striking shift in the physical and environmental conditions – that is, in the extent and intensity of environmental problems – affecting human affairs in general. These processes have moved politics dramatically away from an activity which crystallises first and foremost around state and interstate concerns. It is clearer than ever that the fortunes of political communities and peoples can no longer be simply understood in exclusively national or territorial terms. [. . .]

4. Changes in the development of international law have placed individuals, governments and non-governmental organisations under new systems of legal regulation. International law recognises powers and constraints, and rights and duties, which have qualified the principle of state sovereignty in a number of important respects; sovereignty *per se* is no longer a straightforward guarantee of international legitimacy. Entrenched in certain legal instruments is the view that a legitimate state must be a democratic state that upholds certain common values (Crawford 1994). One significant area in this regard is human rights law and human rights regimes. [. . .]

5. While all the developments described so far have helped engender a shift away from a purely state-centred international system of 'high politics' to new and novel forms of geogovernance, a further interesting example of this process can be drawn from the very heart of the idea of a sovereign state – national security and defence policy. There has been a notable increase in emphasis upon cooperative security. [. . .] Indeed, even in this realm, any conception of sovereignty and autonomy which assumes that they denote an indivisible, illimitable, exclusive and perpetual form of public power – embodied within an individual state – is increasingly challenged and eroded.

### DEMOCRACY AND GLOBALISATION: IN SUM

At the end of the second millennium, as indicated previously, political communities and civilisations can no longer be characterised simply as 'discrete worlds'; they are enmeshed and entrenched in complex structures of overlapping forces, relations and movements. Clearly, these are often structured and hierarchical but even the most powerful among them – including the most powerful nation-states – do not remain unaffected by the changing conditions and processes of regional and global entrenchment. Five central points can be noted to help characterise the changing relationship between globalisation and democratic nation states. All indicate an increase in the extensiveness, intensity and impact of globalisation, and all suggest important points about the evolving character of the democratic political community.

First, the locus of effective power can no longer be assumed to be national governments – effective power is shared, bartered and struggled over by diverse forces and agencies at national, regional and international levels. Second, the idea of a political community of fate – of a self-determining collectivity – can no longer meaningfully be located within the boundaries of a single nation-state alone. Some of the most fundamental forces and processes which determine the nature of life-chances within and across political communities are now beyond the reach of nation-states. Third, there is a growing set of disjunctures between the formal authority of the state – that is, the formal domain of political authority that states claim for themselves – and the actual practices and structures of the state and economic system at the regional and global levels. [. . .]

Fourth, it is not part of my argument that national sovereignty today, even in regions with intensive overlapping and divided political and authority structures, has been wholly subverted – not at all. But, it is part of my argument that there are significant areas and regions marked by criss-crossing loyalties, conflicting interpretations of rights and duties, interconnected legal and authority structures and so on, which displace notions of sovereignty as an illimitable, indivisible and exclusive form of public power. [. . .]

Fifth, the late twentieth century is marked by a significant series of new types of 'boundary problem'. If it is accepted that we live in a world of overlapping communities of fate, where the trajectories of each and every country are more tightly entwined than ever before, then new types of boundary problem follow. [. . .]

## RETHINKING DEMOCRACY IN THE CONTEXT OF GLOBALISATION

In the liberal democracies, consent to government and legitimacy for governmental action are dependent upon electoral politics and the ballot box. Yet the notions that consent legitimates government, and that the ballot box is the appropriate mechanism whereby the citizen body as a whole periodically confers authority on government to enact the law and regulate economic and social life, become problematic as soon as the nature of a 'relevant community' is contested. What is the proper constituency, and proper realm of jurisdiction, for developing and implementing policy with respect to health issues such as AIDS or BSE (bovine spongiform encephalopathy), the use of nuclear energy, the management of nuclear waste, the harvesting of rain forests, the use of non-renewable resources, the instability of global financial markets, the reduction of the risks of the chemical and nuclear warfare? [. . .]

Against this background, the nature and prospects of the democratic polity need re-examination. I have argued elsewhere that an acceptance of liberal democratic politics, in theory and practice, entails an acceptance of each citizen's equal interest in democracy; that is, a recognition of people's equal interest in self-determination (Held 1995a: part III). Each adult has an interest in political autonomy as a result of his or her status as a citizen with an equal entitlement to self-determination. An equal interest in political autonomy requires, I have also argued, that citizens enjoy a common structure of political action. A common structure of political action entails a shared enjoyment of a cluster of rights and obligations. This cluster of rights and obligations has traditionally been thought of as entailing, above all, civil and political rights and obligations. Again, elsewhere, I have argued that this cluster has to bite more deeply than civil and political rights alone; for the latter leave large swathes of power untouched by mechanisms of access, accountability and control. At stake, in short, is a recognition that a common structure of political action requires a cluster of rights and obligations which cut across all key domains of power, where power shapes and affects people's life-chances with determinate effects on and implications for their political agency.

I think of the cluster of rights and obligations that will create the basis of a common structure of political action as constituting the elements of a democratic public law. If power is to be held accountable wherever it is located – in the state, the economy, or cultural sphere – then a common structure of political action needs to be entrenched and enforced through a democratic public law. Such a notion, I believe, can coherently link the ideas of democracy and of the modern state. The key to this is the notion of a democratic legal order – an order which is bound by democratic public law in all its affairs. A democratic legal order – a democratic *Rechtstaat* – is an order circumscribed by, and accounted for in relation to, democratic public law.

The idea of such an order, however, can no longer be simply defended as an idea suitable to a particular closed political community or nation-state. We are compelled to recognise that we live in a complex interconnected world where the extent, intensity, and impact of issues (economic, political, or environmental) raise questions about where those issues are most appropriately addressed. Deliberative and decision-making centres beyond national territories are appropriately situated when those significantly affected by a public matter constitute a cross-border or transnational grouping, when 'lower' levels of decision-making cannot manage and discharge satisfactorily transnational or international policy questions, and when the principle of democratic legitimacy can only be properly redeemed in a transnational context (Held 1995a: ch. 10). [. . .]

In the context of contemporary forms of globalisation, for democratic law to be effective it must be internationalised. Thus, the implementation of what I call a cosmopolitan democratic law and the establishment of a community of all democratic communities – a cosmopolitan community – must become an obligation for democrats; an obligation to build a transnational, common structure of political action which alone, ultimately, can support the politics of self-determination. [. . .]

Thus, sovereignty can be stripped away from the idea of fixed borders and territories. Sovereignty would become an attribute of the basic democratic law but it could be entrenched and drawn upon in diverse self-regulating realms, from regions and states to cities and local associations. Cosmopolitan law would demand the subordination of regional, national and local sovereignties to an overarching legal framework, but in this framework associations would be self-governing at different levels. A new possibility is anticipated: the recovery of an intensive and more participatory democracy at local levels as a complement to the public assemblies of the wider global order; that is, a political order of democratic associations, cities and nations as well as of regions and global networks. I call this elsewhere the cosmopolitan model of democracy – it is a legal basis of a global and divided authority system, a system of diverse and overlapping power centres, shaped and delimited by democratic law (Held 1995a and 1996). [. . .]

In this system of cosmopolitan governance, people would come to enjoy multiple citizenships – political memberships in the diverse political communities which significantly affect them. They would be citizens of their immediate political communities and of the wider regional and global networks which impacted upon their lives. [. . .]

It would be easy to be pessimistic about the future of democracy. There are plenty of reasons for pessimism; they include the fact that the essential political units of the world are still based on nation-states while some of the most powerful socio-political forces of the world escape the boundaries of these units. In reaction to this, in part, new forms of fundamentalism have arisen along with new forms of tribalism – all asserting the a priori superiority of a particular religious, or cultural, or political identity over all others, and all asserting their sectional aims and interests. [. . .]

But there are other forces at work which create the basis for a more optimistic reading of democratic prospects. [. . .] There are forces and pressures which are engendering a reshaping of political cultures, institutions and structures. First, one must obviously note the emergence, however hesitatingly, of regional and global institutions in the twentieth century. The UN is, of course, weak in many respects but it is relatively recent creation and it is an innovative structure which can be built upon. [. . .] Furthermore, there are, of course, new regional and global transnational actors contesting the terms of globalisation – not just corporations but new social movements such as the environmental movement, the women's movement and so on. These are the 'new' voices of an emergent 'transnational civil society' heard, for instance, at the Rio Conference on the environment, the Cairo Conference on Population Control and the Beijing Conference on Women. In short, there are tendencies at work to create new forms of public life and new ways of debating regional and global issues. [. . .]

---

### QUESTIONS

1. What is the connection between the nation-state and democracy?
2. In what ways are states 'globally enmeshed'?
3. How is democracy within the nation-state affected by globalisation?
4. What light does the development of a global democratic legal order throw on the idea of global citizenship?

# 8. WHAT'S WRONG WITH COSMOPOLITAN DEMOCRACY?

## Roland Axtmann

### GLOBALISATION AND COSMOPOLITAN DEMOCRACY

In the past, the sovereign nation-state was considered to be the 'ultimate power' that could impose, and enforce, order within a territory. Political rule in general, and the regulatory, steering and coordinating capacities of the state in particular, have been territorially bounded in their reach. The success of the nation-state in the last two hundred years or so, as well as its universality and legitimacy, were premised on its claim to be able to guarantee the economic well-being, the physical security and the cultural identity of the people who constitute its citizens. However, ever more societal interactions cross borders, becoming transnational and hence detached from a particular territory. Global capitalism and the global division of labour, the global proliferation of nuclear weapons, the global reach of environmental and health risks, global tourism and mass migration, or global media and communication networks, now challenge the effectiveness of the organisational form of the nation-state. The links between the citizens and the nation-state are becoming ever more problematic. The citizens demand political representation, physical protection, economic security and cultural certainty. Yet we are moving into a world of diffused and decentralised power. In this world that is made up of states, (politically organised) regions, international and supranational organisations, non-governmental organisations and transnational corporations, the nation-state finds it increasingly difficult to accommodate these interests and mediate between its citizens and the rest of the world.

In the current age, then, the conception of the state's *summa potestas* has become problematical. And so has the notion of the sovereignty of the people as a united, homogeneous body legitimating the sovereign power of 'its' state through a constitution that manifests the principle of *voluntas populi suprema lex* (that is, 'the will of the people be the highest law'). In this complex and fragmented world, where is the place of 'democracy'? If there is no longer a *summa potestas*, who, then, can be held accountable by the 'people'? And if we, as individuals and members of groups and communities, are 'embedded' in a plethora of cross-border or transnational power networks, bringing us into relationships of dominance and dependency with alternating sets of individuals, groups and communities, who is the 'people', and who or what 'constituency' can legitimately claim the democratic right of control and participation? In a global world, has the concern with the creation and maintenance of citizenship and rights attached to membership in a national community become anachronistic?

As a result of the increasing transnationalisation of a wide range of societal interactions, the effective political solution of an increasing number of societal problems is being sought at a level above or outside the nation-state. However, many transnational interactions, and the transnationalisation of economic action in particular, have hurried ahead of the current possibilities for their political regulation. At the same time, the structures and mechanisms of international regulatory policy-making – such as international governmental organisations (IGOs) – are, in turn, more advanced than the institutions for their democratic control. This creates a tension between the effectiveness of political problem-solving at the 'international' level, on the one hand, and democratic legitimacy which remains embedded in 'domestic' political institutional arrangements on the other. This tension is aggravated by the repercussions of international policy-making on domestic societies. Democratic politics at the nation-state level is increasingly curtailed as a result of the binding force of international political agreements. While 'democracy beyond the nation-state' remains weak, 'democracy within the nation-state' is weakened as well.

This is for mainly two reasons. First, extraterritorial 'global' forces both invade the political space of the nation-state and, because of their extraterritoriality, are operating outside its controlling reach. Both as space invaders and space evaders do they challenge the democratic polity. Second, international policy agreements restrict the range of democratically contested domestic policy options. The formation of the human rights regime since 1948, codified in a number of 'covenants', may serve as an example. For better or worse, human rights qualify the notion of the rightful authority of the state: 'How a state treats its own citizens, and even what legal and constitutional arrangements it has, can thus no longer be regarded as a purely internal matter for the government concerned' (Beetham 1998: 61–2).

According to David Held, one of the foremost analysts of these developments, globalisation poses the question as to how adequately to combine the system of territorially rooted democratic governance with the transnational and global organisation of social and economic life. Held pinpoints the problem succinctly:

> National boundaries have traditionally demarcated the basis on which individuals are included and excluded from participation in decisions affecting their lives; but if many socio-economic processes, and the outcomes of decisions about them, stretch beyond national frontiers, then the implications of this are serious, not only for the categories of consent and legitimacy but for all the key ideas of democracy. At issue is the nature of a constituency (how should the proper boundaries of a constituency be drawn?), the meaning of representation (who should represent whom and on what basis?), and the proper form and scope of political participation (who should participate and in what way?). As fundamental processes of governance escape the categories of the nation-state, the traditional national resolutions of the key questions of democratic theory and practice are open to doubt. (Held 2000: 28)

We face the challenge, so Held argues, to create and entrench democratic institutions at regional and global levels – complementing those at the nation-state level – which would enable the peoples of the world to express and deliberate upon their aims and objectives in a progressively more inter-connected global order (Held 1995a: ch. 10–12; Archibugi and Held 1995; Held 1996: 353–60; Held 1998; Held et al. 1999; Falk 1995; Linklater 1996; Linklater 1998a; Linklater 1998b; Linklater 1999b; Hutchings and Dannreuther 1999; Holden 2000).

For Held, the concept of 'cosmopolitan democracy' refers to 'a model of political organisation in which citizens, wherever they are located in the world, have a voice, input and political representation in international affairs, in parallel with and independently of their own governments' (Held 1995b: 13). Transnational socio-political movements and non-governmental organi-sations (NGOs) are to play a vital role in this process of global democratisa-tion (Della Porta et al 1999; Smith et al 1997). It has been calculated that there are well over 15,000 recognisable NGOs that operate in three or more countries and draw their finances in more than one country. Moreover, an increasingly dense network structure that connects NGOs globally has come to be established. As a result, the number of 'international' non-governmental organisations (INGOs) has increased. There are transnational federations of NGOs such as Save the Children, Amnesty International, Oxfam, Médicins sans Frontières, or the International Federation of Red Cross and Red Crescent Societies, all of which operate on a global scope and whose chapters in individual countries have a high degree of autonomy. Further prominent examples of INGOs are the Socialist International, the International Confederation of Free Trade Unions, the International Olympic Committee, PEN or the World Council of Indigenous Peoples. If we add the 'business non-governmental organisations' (BINGOS) such as multi- and transnational corporations to this list of non-governmental actors in the 'international' arena, a complex network of 'global' actors emerges. The concept of 'transnational civil society' is meant to refer to this plethora of non-state organisations and movements.

Held's model does not aim for a world government or a federal world state. He accepts that democracy must be institutionalised on many levels, ranging from the local/municipal to the subnational and national levels and through the regional level to the global level. Some of the institutional innovations are defined as long-term, others as short-term objectives. The short-term objectives aim, for example, at the reform of the United Nations with a modification of the veto arrangement in the Security Council and a reconsideration of representation on it to allow for adequate regional accountability; the creation of regional parliaments (for example, in Latin America and Africa) as well as the enhancement of the role and power of such bodies where they already exist (as in the case of the European Union); the creation of a new, international Human Rights Court; and the establishment of an effective, accountable military force. Within the UN context, Held proposes the establishment of an independent assembly of democratic peoples, directly elected by them and accountable to them, whose role would have been agreed upon in an international constitutional convention involving states, IGOs, INGOs, citizen groups and social movements. This new assembly could become an authoritative centre for the examination of the most pressing global problems: '[H]ealth and disease, food supply and distribution, the debt burden of the "Third World", the instability of the hundreds of billions of dollars that circulate the globe daily, global warming, and the reduction of risks of nuclear and chemical warfare' (Held 1995a: 274).

In this brief summary, I have only listed Held's short-term institutional innovations which he considers to be necessary for moving towards democratic global governance. And although there are many more facets to Held's model of 'cosmopolitan democracy', it is nevertheless possible to raise a few critical queries which will have to be addressed when this model is further developed.

## A CRITICAL VIEW ON COSMOPOLITAN DEMOCRACY

1. Held foresees that the new democratic political institutions would override states in clearly defined spheres of activity 'where those activities have demonstrable transnational and international consequences, require regional or global initiatives in the interests of effectiveness and depend on such initiatives for democratic legitimacy' (Held 1998: 24). This is an exceedingly vague statement. In the 'age of globalisation', which activities do *not* have demonstrable trans- and international consequences? Who, or which bodies, decide whether regional or global initiatives are warranted? Who enforces the

appropriation of decision-making powers by regional or global bodies? As Held himself argues, states are reluctant to submit their disputes with other states to arbitration by a 'supreme authority': who then enforces the decisions taken by these bodies? (Held 1995a: 276) How realistic is it to stipulate – as either a short-term or long-term objective – the formation of an 'effective' and 'accountable' international military force? In particular, it is inconceivable that the rich states of the North are willing to submit to any political will that is counter to their core political interests.

2. There is woefully little analysis of the 'prerequisites' of 'cosmopolitan democracy'. Philip Resnick has argued that prospects for global democracy are held back by uneven economic development, diverging political traditions, cultural and ethnic identities, and solidarities that are primarily local or national in character (Resnick 1998: 126–43). Above all, issues of economic and social equality will have to be put back on to the agenda if we wished to create the conditions for global democracy. The extreme inequality of living conditions between North and South must be addressed. Resnick is right to point out that 'the very parameters of global economic development further the concentration of wealth and power in the core countries' (Resnick 1998: 131). IGOs such as the International Monetary Fund, the World Bank or the World Trade Organisation have played an important role in shaping national public policies and creating a political and legal institutional infrastructure for global capitalism. They have been very much under the control of the richest and most powerful countries and have been implicated in retaining structures of inequality. To address these concerns adequately, Held would have to integrate economic issues more profoundly than has so far happened into his model of 'cosmopolitan democracy'. In his model, Held has listed under short-term objectives the 'foundation of a new co-ordinating economic agency at regional and global levels' and the 'introduction of strict limits to private ownership of key "public-shaping" institutions' such as the media (Held 1995a: 279–80). The long-term objectives include the 'establishment of the accountability of international and transnational economic agencies to parliaments and assemblies at regional and global levels' as well as a 'guaranteed basic income for all adults, irrespective of whether they are engaged in market or household activities'. Held would have to show how these objectives of a global 'social market' capitalism are likely to be achieved; how they could possibly be justified (for example, in terms of global justice); and whether capitalism as an inherently inegalitarian system organised around the profit motive can ever be the appropriate means of overcoming the division of the world as well as the divisions within its constituent states and societies into 'rich' and 'poor'. More broadly, he would have to theorise the connection between economic development and cosmopolitan democracy, or, to put it differently, the connection between democracy and economic power.

3. While a call for the establishment of regional parliaments appears to be unproblematic from within a democratic position, efforts at parliamentarisation

in the politically most advanced region, Europe, show that this is by no means the case. First of all, political development in the past has shown that it is around the conflict and cleavage structure within the bounded territory of the nation-state that intermediary institutions such as political parties, interest groups, voluntary associations, trade unions or the mass media have been organised. Citizens tend to avail themselves of the national intermediary institutions as the means of their political participation. To put it differently, the role of the citizen has been firmly institutionalised at the level of the nation-state.

Even after forty years of European integration, we still find that intermediary structures remain 'nationalised'. As yet, there is no European party system that would aggregate and articulate social and political interests on a Europe-wide level. So far, political parties are national actors that, at best, aim to translate interests of their *national* constituencies into the European political system. The degree of 'Europeanisation' of other than business interests has been low. With citizens still directing their interests, concerns and demands to their national, or subnational, government, not to 'Brussels', there is no European public opinion. Given that the intermediary structures necessary for interest and opinion formation are not in place, whom or what could a European Parliament possibly represent? Only if there is a genuine process of Europe-wide, transnational interest formation does it become necessary for reasons of democratic legitimacy to institute the European Parliament as that mechanism through which diverse interests have to be channelled, reconciled and acted upon.

Second, a key feature of parliamentary rule is policy-making on the basis of decisions taken by a parliamentary majority. Yet the principle of majority rule does not suffice to generate legitimacy of the political system as a whole. The application of majority rule as a legitimating principle is premised on a socio-political and socio-cultural context that is conducive to the defeated minority's acceptance of the majority decision. The existence of such a congenial context cannot be taken for granted. Democratic legitimacy as an effect of parliamentary majority rule has a number of preconditions: there must be no fundamental ethnic, linguistic, religious, ideological or economic cleavages in a society; and the political community must have developed a collective identity based on shared citizenship and political equality as well as shared normative orientations so that differences in specific policy areas will not be dramatised into fundamental differences over the institutional order of the political community. In national political systems it is the intermediary institutions that play a central part in the generation of a collective identity as well as in processing conflicts among interests and differences in cultural orientation in such a way that they can be integrated into the political system. And it is the dynamics of the intermediary structure that hold open the promise for minorities possibly to turn their current minority position into a majority position at some point in the future. Neither of these two preconditions for the acceptance of parliamentary majority decisions as legitimate is as yet in place in Europe with its historical, cultural, linguistic and political-institutional diversity and economic disparities. To expect that decisions by the European Parliament would meet with widespread acceptance under these circumstances would appear to be unwarranted, even foolhardy.

What has just been said about the socio-political and socio-cultural pre-conditions for the parliamentarisation of the European Union would also apply to David Held's envisaged 'assembly of democratic peoples' within the UN, and also, for example, to Johan Galtung's institutional reform of the UN (Galtung 2000: 153–9). Galtung envisages five UN assemblies: in addition to the General Assembly (UNGA) for governments, the UN People's Assembly (UNPA) would be ultimate sovereign, legitimised on the basis of direct elections. There would be a Third Assembly, for economic corporations (UNCA), and a Fourth Assembly for local authorities (UNLAA). The Fifth Assembly of NGOs (CONGO) would have, like UNCA and UNLAA, only consultative status. Whereas it is possible to conceive of UNGA, UNPA and UNLAA as possessing – in the long run – some degree of democratic legitimacy as a result of their grounding in elections, the same cannot be said of either corporations or NGOs. The former Secretary-General, Boutros Boutros-Ghali, while sharing Galtung's utopian and romantic ideas about political representation, is on firmer grounds in terms of legitimacy when he argues for a closer integration of the Inter-Parliamentary Union, the world organisation of parliamentarians, into the UN system (Boutros-Ghali 2000: 113).

## THE CONTINUING RELEVANCE OF THE NATION-STATE

These considerations about the place of a supranational parliament within a 'cosmopolitan democracy' turn our attention back to the nation-state and its role within a changing global structure. Evidently, the effects of globalisation on the modern state need extensive empirical analysis which are beyond the limited concerns of the current discussion. However, we should not assume without detailed argument that globalisation, of necessity, 'weakens' the modern state and undermines, if not destroys, its policy capacity. There are still certain functions and tasks that will have to be performed even in the 'global' world and which are unlikely to be performed well, or at all, by private agencies.

1. Economic globalisation affects different sectors and regions within each state differently. 'Deindustrialisation', for example, is bound to bring disadvantages to the manufacturing industries and industrial regions of advanced capitalist countries, whereas the internationalisation of financial services is likely to benefit other geographical locations and socio-economic groups within these countries. One of the effects of global capitalism on the advanced capitalist countries has been the occurrence of socio-economic and socio-political crises which used to be seen as unique to less-developed countries: for example, rising long-term unemployment, increase in income

disparities and in absolute poverty, depopulation of the countryside, decay of urban centres and an increase in organised crime. Neither for the global system as a whole nor for its constituent units does economic globalisation thus result in homogeneity and overall integration; rather, it is likely to accentuate heterogeneity and fragmentation. Global capitalism is best analysed as a system of structured inequality. There is a need for an agency that integrates society and takes care of the interests individuals share as members of a community. Who else but states (on their own or in cooperation with each other) could take care of this task?

2. The very real danger of a global eco-catastrophe is an important aspect of globalisation and of the formation of a global consciousness, the idea of a shared fate of humankind on 'Planet Earth'. There can be no doubt that, in the twenty-first century, a new balance will have to be found between the economy and ecology. Achieving 'sustainable development' and hence an economic system that is ecologically safe presupposes an agency that can instigate reform and see through fundamental changes. Who else but states (on their own or in cooperation with each other) could take care of this task?

3. We have come to recognise that 'local' (national) decisions may have 'global' effects – for example, policies regarding emission levels for power stations. Likewise, 'global' processes may have a 'local' impact – for example, the global dissemination of Western imagery through satellite-based communications systems and its effect on 'local' or 'national' cultures. There is a need for an agency that considers the possibly global effect of 'local' decisions but that also protects 'national' communities as best as possible against the 'local' effects of 'global' forces. Who else but states (on their own or in cooperation with each other) could take care of this task?

4. International governmental organisations (IGOs), such as the UN, the World Bank, the International Monetary Fund, or the World Trade Organisation, are a vital element in global governance. Furthermore, ever more policies and decisions are being taken in the setting of multilateral negotiations and agreements. Who, if not the state, could bestow legitimacy upon these international organisations and would have the legitimacy to participate in multilateral negotiations, agree to binding policy decisions, and then have the power to guarantee their 'local' implementation?

5. Around the world, political projects of regional integration are being pursued as an attempt to promote regional economies and create structures of regional political governance. The European Union (EU), the North American Free Trade Agreement (NAFTA), the Asian-Pacific Economic Cooperation (APEC), or the Association of South East Asian Nations (ASEAN) may serve as examples. These projects will put a premium on the cooperation of states. Who else but states could provide a legal and material infrastructure for such a regional, 'supranational' space and contain the political, economic and social dislocations which will necessarily arise in such an enterprise? As Paul Hirst

has argued, *democratic* practices within states make wider institutions both possible and legitimate:

> Democratic governments can credibly speak for their populations, since they are legitimated by majority vote. Democratic governments know that the international commitments they enter into will, by convention, be honoured by successor administrations. Other states know this too and can thus accept such commitments as binding. Democratic states, because they abide by the rule of law internally and accept decisions against them in the domestic courts, also tend to abide by international law and to respect international agreements. Without this lawful behaviour of states as members of the international society, international law would have little force and international governance above the level of the sovereign state would be virtually impossible. (Hirst 2001: 271; Bellamy and Jones 2000: 202–16)

## WHY WE NEED A STRONG AND DEMOCRATIC CIVIL SOCIETY

The argument put forward in the previous paragraphs re-focuses the question of democracy. As long as the state retains those functions and is expected to perform those tasks in discharge of its duties in relation to its citizens, it is imperative that democratic accountability of state elites is upheld at the level of the nation-state. Indeed, there is an urgent need to enhance the opportunities for political participation and citizen engagement 'at the local level'.

1. Arguably, a 'strong democratic civil society' (for example, Barber 1998) is a key prerequisite for the transnational movements and (international) non-governmental organisations mentioned above. For the most part, they are formed within national societies and depend for their success, and even frequently their very survival, on other institutions within this national political environment, such as political parties, trade unions, churches and the media. And we must not forget that one response to globalisation has been the formation of extreme national and racist movements which have been mobilising for the closing down of democratic spaces in Western societies. A 'global' civil society as part of a 'cosmopolitan' democracy that is built partially around the global linkages of these 'nationally' embedded 'transnational' movements is thus inherently fragile and premised on a national environment supportive of movement politics. It is through citizen participation that such an environment must be nurtured and sustained.

2. Casting a critical-analytical eye on the 'turbulent world' of the late twentieth century, James Rosenau saw new forms of 'global governance' emerging. For Rosenau, global governance is the (mainly) unintended consequence of the conscious pursuit of goals by distinctive collective actors through the exercise of control mechanisms that have transnational repercussions:

> To assess global governance . . . is to trace the various ways in which the processes of governance are aggregated. The cumulation encompasses individuals, their skills and orientations, no less than private and public collectivities at the local, provincial, national, transnational, international and global levels . . . Global governance is not so much a label for a high degree of integration and order as it is a summary term for highly complex and widely disparate activities that culminate in a modicum of worldwide coherence. (Rosenau 1997: 10–11)

In this world, governance is no longer the exclusive domain of national governments and the state, and the sites out of which authority can be exercised and compliance can be generated have been dispersed and authority has been relocated 'outwards to transnational and supranational organisations, sidewards to social movements and NGOs, and inwards to subnational groups' (Rosenau 1997: 43–4). If (for the sake of argument) we follow Rosenau, then we should ask: what makes for a *democratic* 'global governance'? In his study on 'governance in a turbulent world', Rosenau has spent, however, only 12 out of 450 pages on this issue of 'democracy'. Essentially, Rosenau organises his thoughts on democracy around the idea of 'checks and balances'. These checks and balances are the consequence of the disaggregation of authority and the multiplicity of actors in the global arena:

> The decentralization of rule systems in disparate and localised sites has greatly inhibited the coalescence of hierarchical and autocratic centres of power . . . authority is so widely dispersed that neither tyrannical majorities nor autocratic leaders are likely to gain much of a foothold in this emergent domain and, if they do, the constraints against their tyranny are likely to be too numerous and resistant for them to expand the scope of their power. (Rosenau 1998: 40–1)

This rather mechanistic model with its emphasis on the dispersal of power among a multiplicity of groups and collective actors is reminiscent of American pluralist political theory of the 1950s and 1960s. Let us disregard the obvious question as to whether there are no power differentials between, say, transnational corporations on the one side and Amnesty International on the other, which translate into power differentials in the 'global governance' structure. Let us ask instead: may we reasonably assume that the quality and scope of 'global democracy' would be enhanced should democratic structures and processes obtain within these non-state agencies and organisations implicated in 'global governance'? At issue are questions of intra-organisational democracy, the representativeness, responsiveness and accountability of organisational elites to the members and supporters of the organisation and the openness of organisations to outside scrutiny. If intra-organisational democracy contributes to the democratic character of global governance, then, arguably, the struggle for extending democracy to 'private' associations or corporations would have to be fought initially at the nation-state level where most of these organisations are 'incorporated'.

3. Such democratic involvement and struggle at the nation-state level is all the more imperative since economic 'globalisation' has had manifest 'political' roots in the decisions and non-decisions of national governments over the past three decades or so, mainly in the area of macroeconomic management (Jones 2000: 55–64): globalisation is not 'technologically' driven, but a political 'project'. State policies of liberalisation, deregulation and marketisation that have been presented by national and transnational political and economic elites as a necessary and inevitable 'response' to the 'challenges' of globalisation to the nation-state have propelled globalisation forward. Philip G. Cerny has analysed these policy changes in the context of a discussion of the transition from the industrial welfare state to the competition state:

> Rather than attempt to take certain economic activities *out* of the market, to 'decommodify' them as the welfare state in particular was organized to do, the competition state has pursued *increased* market-ization in order to make economic activities located within the national territory, or which otherwise contribute to national wealth, more competitive in international and transnational terms. The main features of this process have included attempts to reduce government spending in order to minimize the 'crowding out' of private investment by state consumption and the deregulation of economic activities, especially financial markets. (Cerny 2000: 122–3)

Any resistance to such 'national' policies has to be organised 'nationally'. In all the democratic nation-states in Western Europe, we find well-developed systems of interest formation and intermediation, of institutionalised conflict management and institutionalised norms of social justice. Amongst the forces that have had the greatest impact on the formation of these systems, the political, economic and cultural struggles around the formation of centralised, and secularised, state structures and of industrial-capitalist national economies stand out. Of course, the precise cleavage structure has been different in each country, and so have the course and outcome of the struggles caused by it. As a result, each country has developed complexes of interest formation and intermediation that are fairly idiosyncratic. In the process of democratisation and the formation of 'mass politics' each country has built up political parties, trade unions, professional associations, voluntary associations, special interest groups and media for the formation and expression of public opinion. Yet, for example, party systems, structures of industrial relations, the incorporation of interest groups into the political system, or the allocation of jurisdiction and resources to subnational, regional and municipal bodies, have developed in historically distinct ways in each case. And so, for example, has the specific mix of policies through which national welfare states became institutionalised. 'National' economies and national welfare states exhibit distinct structures and institutional features that influence the degree to which they are able to respond to 'globalisation'. Furthermore, public welfare services must be wanted, and demanded, by the citizens, and the citizens must be willing to pay for them. Such solidaristic values and attitudes must be embedded in a national political culture; but for them to be sustained, and acted upon, political mobilisation and citizens' involvement at the 'local' level are needed (Hirst and Thompson 1999: ch. 6). More generally, the 'local' (ill-) effects of 'global' processes need 'local' responses from within a 'strong' democratic civil society. Because of the historical path-dependency of state form and policy-formation, political struggle over policies must be organised 'nationally'.

Taken together, these criticisms and queries of some aspects of David Held's model of 'cosmopolitan democracy' should not be understood as a critique of a normative commitment to 'democracy beyond the nation-state'.[1] Rather they are an invitation to continue the important task of specifying more fully the political, economic and cultural preconditions and chances for democracy and democratisation in the age of globalisation. Nor should they be construed as a critique of the more modest claim that individuals ought to work for global goals and that the agendas of citizens within a state increasingly ought to include global concerns. Global goals such as the protection of human rights, peace, the reduction of poverty or caring for the environment, and action such as working for Oxfam, joining an Amnesty International letter-writing campaign or standing in vigil for peace at a time of war, may serve as examples of global commitment and forms of action geared towards achieving it (Dower 2000).

However, we live in a world of value conflicts. For example, some people may believe that 'global' capitalism is conducive to reducing world poverty, and that excessive environmental concerns and regulations will not only unduly restrict economic development but therefore also result in 'global injustice'. And even if we accepted that there is a 'global' consensus on certain elements of a 'global ethic' (such as 'human rights'), there are then still conflicts over the specific policies necessary (or appropriate) to enact such rights. Think, for example, in the case of abortion how the (human) rights of the mother are best balanced with the (human) rights of the unborn child. Politics may be about many things. But it finds one expression in the authoritative allocation of values for a political community as a whole. Given value conflicts, such allocation is, of necessity, contentious. Democracy aims to prevent the authoritarian or dictatorial allocation of such values by institutionalising mechanisms of popular participation in, and control over, political decision-making. The argument of this chapter has been that the establishment of such democratic institutions and mechanisms at the level 'beyond the nation-state' is suboptimal compared to the expansion of democracy at the level of the nation-state. The institutional framing, or balancing (if not the settlement), of value clashes above the level of the nation-state needs the mediation of the democratic nation-state. Without such mediation, there is – in a political sense – no 'democratic' global citizen(ship).

---

QUESTIONS

1. Should a distinction be made between 'global citizenship' and 'global democracy'?
2. If it could be shown that the democratic nation-state has retained its policy capacity in many important areas, how would this affect an argument in favour of establishing a 'cosmopolitan democracy'?
3. What is the relationship between a strong democratic civil society at the level of the nation-state and 'democracy beyond the nation-state'?

---

NOTES

1. For such a critique see Miller 1995; Miller 1999; Zolo 1997.

# 9. THE UN AND GLOBAL CITIZENSHIP

## Mark Imber

### Origin and Development

Global citizenship implies some sense of belonging to a larger political community than that of our own state alone. Global citizens believe they have duties beyond borders. Their concept of *rights* also extends internationally. It is concerned, in principle and in practice, with the protection of human dignity in several forms; such as human rights and the struggle to escape from poverty, lack of education and poor health that blight the lives of the global majority.

Global citizenship also implies a commitment to maintaining international peace and security within the system of states. The terrible violence unleashed by two world wars during the last century has led to calls for the instrument of warfare to be placed beyond national use, preserving it solely for purposes of collective security.

Global citizenship is also concerned with the good government of our shared environmental resources such as the climate system, the ozone layer and the high seas. These are beyond the ability of any one country to protect but are vulnerable to any one nation's ability to inflict damage.

The twentieth century witnessed two attempts to give institutional expression to these principles of wider citizenship, collective security and environmental protection. The League of Nations was created in 1919 with a very limited mandate to maintain the peace, and a limited membership base as colonial rule still prevailed in the Third World.

Its successor after the Second World War, the United Nations, was formally created at the San Francisco Conference of June 1945. Its subsequent growth to embrace 190 Member States has created the largest, and most nearly universal, membership international organisation in the world. In a fascinating history over nearly sixty years the UN has been the repository of many great ambitions for the improvement of the human condition. The hopes and fears of all the years have been brought to and played out in the General Assembly of all members in New York. Decolonisation, the *Universal Declaration of Human Rights*, nuclear non-proliferation, numerous peace-keeping operations and global conferences such as the Rio Earth Summit all emerged from UN initiatives. As will be shown, a wide range of functions from military security to collaborative scientific research are organised by the UN. That said, the organisation is also subject to much criticism of its limited efficiency and political disputes in attempting to develop norms and ideals into operational forms of global governance. Riven for over 40 years by Cold War tensions between its leading members, a decade of recent attention has focused on the role of the UN in delivering imaginative solutions and good government on a range of post-Cold War issues. Whilst this account of the UN's record is critical, it would be remarkable if an unreformed political institution created over fifty years ago was not capable of improvement. We would not indulge a government, a university or a corporation's claims to have been created perfect, and to have stayed perfect for half a century. Neither should we be afraid to criticise the UN. It is in a spirit of constructive engagement for the reform of the UN that this chapter will highlight the many deficiencies of the organisation.

The 'Atlantic Charter' of post-war aims, agreed by British Prime Minister Churchill and US President Roosevelt as early as August 1941, referred to the need for a post-war security organisation, and in January 1942 twenty-six allied nations signed the 'Declaration by United Nations'. These origins and dates are crucial to understanding the basis upon which the UN was founded as an inter-governmental organisation, and the limitations which those origins placed on its subsequent development. The UN was created in wartime, as an exercise in allied solidarity, to create an instrument of post-war international order. Its principal designers were the great powers of that time; American, Soviet, British and Chinese delegations drafted the UN Charter in strict secrecy at Dumbarton Oaks, in Washington DC, in 1944. The UN was created at a time of anticipated US-USSR alliance, two months before the first use of the atomic bomb, over Hiroshima on 4 August 1945. It was created at a time when just fifty-one sovereign states constituted the membership of the international political system. The UN's pre-Cold War, pre-atomic and pre-Third World origins are still embedded in its contemporary structure and partly explain the near impossibility of its reform (Mingst and Karns 2000).

The UN Charter identifies four specific purposes of the organisation. First, to 'maintain international peace and security, and to that end to take effective measures for the prevention and removal of threats to the peace'. Second, the UN was tasked to 'develop friendly relations among nations'. Third, to also 'achieve international cooperation in solving international problems of an economic, social, cultural and humanitarian character' including 'encouraging respect for human rights and fundamental freedoms'. Fourth, and somewhat self-evidently, the UN was to be a 'centre for harmonising the actions of nations in the attainment of these common ends' (UN 1945: Art. 1).

## INTERNATIONAL PEACE AND SECURITY

Although early enthusiasm for the UN in Western countries has gradually cooled, especially since the 1970s, only in the US is there an articulate and influential *anti*-UN faction advocating US withdrawal (Pines 1984). What can advocates of global citizenship expect of the organisation? It was created nearly sixty years ago by two soon-to-be superpowers. The US had acquired global hegemonic power in an astoundingly rapid time, from its pre-1939 isolationism, and the United States' democratic instincts and institutions were very influential in drafting the Charter. Stalin's USSR had murdered over 30 million of its own citizens before falling victim to Hitler's aggression that killed a further 20 million in the course of the war. Great Britain still had an empire and, despite its domestic democracy, still claimed the right to rule, unelected, over one quarter of the earth's population. China was then a collapsed quasi-state, riven by civil war and without effective control of its own territory. The question is particularly cogent in that each of these founders also gave themselves, and later France, a permanent seat on the highest governing authority of the UN, the Security Council. They also gave themselves the right to veto its decisions (UN 1945: Art. 27) and further powers to veto any reform of these entrenched arrangements (UN 1945: Art. 108).

The Charter makes no reference to democracy; the Charter *does*, however, make references to '. . . promoting respect for, and observance of, human rights and fundamental freedoms of all . . .' (UN 1945: Art. 62). Elsewhere, the Charter identifies 'higher standards of living, full employment, and conditions of economic and social progress and development' as specific goals, in words very reminiscent of the 'New Deal' economic policies pursued in the United States in the 1930s (UN 1945: Art. 55). The famous and redolent phrase from the Preamble, 'We the peoples of the United Nations', which introduces the Charter, implies a direct appeal to citizens. This is deceptive. This one use of 'we' is never repeated. At every turn thereafter, the Charter asserts the rights of Member States. This 'morality of states' – sitting in the UN and voting on the principle of one-member-one-vote – determines the efforts of the UN to implement the larger social and economic goals of the Charter. This morality of states is, however, a very partial basis on which to claim a *legitimate* basis for international policy and action. At best, the UN members' commitment to democratic causes has been selective. The South African, Namibian and Palestinian peoples have received recognition and succour in their struggles; whilst Tibetans, Biafrans and Sikhs have not. Their causes would either attract the veto of one of the five permanent members or would offend a majority of Third World governments with mutually defensive reactions to claims for post-colonial secession by their own minorities.

The most fundamental purpose and function of the state is to provide security. Hobbesian political theory, which has dominated Western political thought since 1650, argues that citizens contract with one another to create good government, the primary purpose of which is to protect the citizen from domestic crime and from foreign invasion. If defeated in war, the state has failed in its contract to protect. If, in a civil war, the state turns upon its own citizens, it breaches Hobbes' contract. Can the UN provide the defenceless with security?

The founding purpose of the UN was, as we have seen, to 'save succeeding generations from the scourge of war' (UN 1945: Preamble). The UN was created to deter and to punish aggression by one state upon another and so provide collective security. From 1945 to 1990 the UN members' ability to do this was fundamentally compromised by the five veto-wielding powers. In the period 1946 to 1998 a total of 246 resolutions were vetoed in the Security Council, 120 by the USSR/Russian Federation, 72 by the USA, 32 by the UK, 18 by France and 4 by China (Mingst and Karns 2000: 28).

Only in those situations where the five veto powers could all agree was it possible to activate the UN's mechanisms to limit warfare. Those highly specialised conditions were only created on 15 occasions between 1945 and 1990. The creation of so-called peacekeeping forces was not envisaged in the Charter, where the term does not exist. Nonetheless, the ad-hoc creation and dispatch of lightly armed forces into cease-fire situations to undertake third-party verification of compliance, policing and sometimes humanitarian relief, created a very special niche for the UN.

Since 1990 the number of operations launched is more than double the previous number. In March 2001 fifteen UN peacekeeping operations were active. Thirty-nine operations have been terminated. One of the most con-troversial of the latter terminations did not involve any agreed *resolution* of the issue at hand, but rather the now very rare veto of a great power opposed to the continuing efforts at stabilisation. The UN's forward deployment of a preventive force in Macedonia, UNPREDEP, was terminated abruptly on 28 February 1999 when China vetoed a routine, six-monthly renewal of UNPREDEP's mandate (Williams 2000: 174). Almost exactly two years later, in March 2001, ethnic Albanian irregulars operating from Kosovo, a province in southern Serbia, were able to make incursions into Macedonian territory, thus creating a new front in the one former Yugoslav republic to have hitherto avoided hostilities.

In some of the most elaborate post-Cold War peacekeeping operations – Namibia, Cambodia and El Salvador – the UN has, in practical terms, acted as a quasi-government. In other cases the UN's mandate has become so over-extended, and the consent of the hosts and other parties so partial and conditional, that serious and damaging failures have occurred. This was most notable in Bosnia and in Somalia. These attempts to intervene in the internal affairs of states have attempted to move that other bulwark of seventeenth-century political theory, the doctrine of sovereignty, enshrined in the Peace of Westphalia of 1648.

This doctrine severely limits the right of states to intervene in the internal affairs of other states. This presumption in favour of non-intervention persisted throughout the twentieth century until, amongst other things, the Holocaust of 1941–5 persuaded even the most conservative states to recognise some fundamental notion of *human* rights which justified interference in *states'* rights.

For the Muslims in Serbian-occupied Bosnia in 1995, and for the Kurds of northern Iraq in 1991, the UN's actions to create so-called 'safe-havens' protected by UN forces led the UN into its most ambitious role as a guarantor of the physical security of millions of persons. It can be charged that these efforts have frequently been too little, too late, and also very selective.

The high point of intervention was the creation of a 'safe-haven' for the Iraqi Kurds in March 1991, policed and very effectively protected by NATO air forces. An element of double standards attached to these efforts. Whilst Iraqi Kurds received NATO air protection, their neighbouring kin in Turkey were bombarded by Turkish air strikes until 1999. As Orwell might have observed, all Kurds are equal but some are more equal than others. More remote genocidal civil wars received only token concern from the Security Council. The international community effectively abandoned the Rwandans to their fate in 1994 (Melvern 1995).

The nadir of this pretended competence to extend the 'safe-havens' policy was reached just five years after its inception. On 16 April 1993, six Bosnian cities were declared to be safe-havens – Sarajevo, Bihac, Tuzla, Gorazde, Zepa and Srebrenica – a decision contained in Security Council Resolution 819. Two years later, in July 1995, the refusal of senior UN commanders to authorise air strikes to repel Serbian advances on the besieged town of Srebrenica led to the surrender and taking-hostage of the resident Dutch peacekeeping force. The massacre of 7,079 Muslim men and boys that followed was the largest single act of mass murder in Europe since the last days of the Holocaust. The figure is that calculated by the Red Cross (Rohde 1997: 348). Srebrenica was the low-point of the 'new peacekeeping'. It is unlikely that the UN will be asked, or will again seek to adopt, the role of proclaiming and defending a protectorate within a civil war.

HUMANITARIAN ASSISTANCE: DISASTERS, REFUGEES AND RIGHTS

Second to providing physical security, another source of UN legitimation is in the provision of global technical assistance, aid and humanitarian relief. The work of the UN High Commission for Refugees (UNHCR), the children's fund (UNICEF), and the High Commission for Human Rights (UNHCHR) is probably the most widely known 'public' face of the UN. The former two agencies also receive direct charitable donations from volunteers and supporters. As with peacekeeping, this is global citizenship in action. In extreme cases of natural disaster, famine, flood and drought, the state can again be said to have failed its citizens. These natural disasters are sometimes compounded by the indifference and occasionally the deliberately harmful actions of government. The Rwandan genocide of 1994 is a case in point. That said, some relief missions have actually institutionalised a 'refugee' situation. The quarter-million Arabs displaced in the first war with Israel in 1948, and their descendants, have lived in the most appalling poverty in UN-administered UNWRA camps in Jordan, Lebanon and Syria for three generations. They await a comprehensive political settlement that would include a Palestinian 'right of return' to match that which Israel extends to the Jewish diaspora.

Described by one commentator as 'notoriously venal' the UNHCR has for most of its history typified what is worst in UN practice (Righter 1995: 298). A Commission comprised of Member State governments, it has for decades refrained from all but the most predictable denunciations. Not until 1994 did the Commission adopt a resolution critical of any African country except South Africa, despite regimes such as those of Obote and Amin in Uganda, and the Emperor Bokassa of the Central African Empire, murdering their citizens by the hundreds of thousands in the 1970s. The Asian countries, from China to Singapore, have all benefited from mutual, respectful silence regarding each other's human rights records (Righter 1995: 299–300). The limitations and frustrations of this system drove UN Commissioner Mary Robinson to an announcement in March 2001 of her refusal to seek a second term in office.

## SCIENCE, ECONOMIC COOPERATION AND DEVELOPMENT

The specialised agencies are part of the so-called UN system but they are legally, financially and organisationally independent. This has generally helped to insulate them from the political disputes and Cold War tensions that characterised the UN itself. Some agencies pre-date the UN. The Universal Postal Union (UPU) and International Telecommunications Union (ITU) were nineteenth-century creations. They were established to manage the first of many technical innovations of the industrial era which required a degree of international cooperation to function most efficiently. Later, technical agencies such as the World Meteorological Organisation (WMO), International Civil Aviation Organisation (ICAO) and International Atomic Energy Agency (IAEA) were created to regulate new, twentieth-century technologies. Human rights and welfare underlay the need to create the International Labour Organisation in 1919 and thereafter the World Health Organisation and the scientific, educational and cultural agency, UNESCO.

A common theme after the inter-war depression of the 1930s was to provide independent states with the means to jointly and simultaneously improve labour rights, social security and public education without the fear of losing economic advantage by acting alone. The desire to manage the post-war international economy in ways which would prevent the reversion to trade barriers, as had happened in the 1930s, lay behind the third variety of specialised agency. The International Bank for Reconstruction and Development (commonly known as the World Bank), the International Monetary Fund (IMF) and General Agreement on Tariffs and Trade (GATT), now the World Trade Organisation, were created to stabilise the recovery of the world economy. Under their rules between 1944 and 1971 the Western and global economies enjoyed a quarter century of unparalleled growth. The dissolution of that system after 1971, the oil shocks of the 1970s and high rates of inflation were to lower averaged growth rates in the following quarter century. Only in the mid-1990s under entirely different conditions of de-regulation, the massive growth of foreign direct investment, and genuine free trade in industrial goods, did the world economy recover the vitality of the heavily rule-bound and internationally cooperative quarter-century 1944–71.

Simultaneously with this task of managing economic stability, the so-called Bretton Woods organisations attempted to address the imperative for development to assist the poor two-thirds of the world's citizens in the so-called Third World. The UN undertook a leading role, intellectually and normatively, in promoting economic development in tandem with de-colonisation. The UN's own largest programme, the UN Development Programme (UNDP), sought to coordinate the developmental activities of all the specialised agencies who were themselves delivering aid, infrastructure and training in each of their functional 'sectors'. The UN's achievements in development have been frequently and heavily criticised. Not least among these are successive internal accounts by Jackson (1969) and Bertrand (1985), for example. They have pointed to duplication in agency efforts, exotic staffing excesses, the inappropriate targeting of Official Development Assistance (ODA), favouring of failed models of socialist planning and the creation of a corrupting dependency culture inimical to both local entrepreneurs and the attraction of private investment. These criticisms are not new.

## REFORM AND DEMOCRATISATION OF THE UN?

Does the UN encourage global citizenship? Internationalism is not cosmopolitanism. The culture of *statism* is deeply rooted in the UN, and is consistent with its Charter, for example Articles 2.1 and 2.7. UN membership is for the newest, smallest and poorest states *constitutive*. The existence of a new country is confirmed by its membership of the UN. Sovereignty, which globalisers, Internet enthusiasts and others denigrate, is therefore central to status and participation within the UN system. The only non-sovereign actors permitted to hold observer status at the General Assembly were those pretended sovereign organisations such as the South West African People's Organisation (SWAPO) and the Palestine Liberation Organisation (PLO). During the 1970s and 1980s, they participated in the UN on the basis of their own *claim to sovereignty*, that is, the right to act as the 'sole legitimate representatives of the Namibian [or Palestinian] peoples'.

The reform of the UN is crucial to making the organisation more relevant and accountable to the people in whose name it was created. For successive US administrations and other conservatives, reform has been expressed mostly in managerial terms, that is, how to extract greater value for the tax-payer's dollar (Mingst and Karns 2000: 200–1). More ambitious theorists of cosmopolitan democracy wish to improve citizens' participation in the policy-forming and work of the UN and, by extension, other 'remote' organisations such as the World Bank. The European Union, for example, despite many criticisms, does have a directly elected parliament unlike any UN agency. The most literal way in which the reform of the United Nations could address the 'democratic deficit' in its institutions to become more representative of populations rather than governments would be to create a directly elected parliament or assembly. This 'Second Assembly' would operate alongside the existing General Assembly. A broad comparison would be the European Parliament and its role in relation to the European Council. Immediately the problems become apparent. A genuinely representative chamber of all the world's six billion population would be 20 per cent Chinese, 17 per cent Indian, 4 per cent US, and less than 1 per cent British in its distribution of seats. This contradicts the other democratic principle of one-Member State – one-vote. Second, why should the dictators, theocrats, generals and klepto-maniacs who govern many UN Member States show the slightest interest in permitting democratic participation for their citizens in the UN when they do not allow such freedoms at home? A similar case and a similar objection can be made to the call for binding global referenda (Commission on Global Governance 1995).

More feasible is the expansion of the already widespread role of non-governmental organisations (NGOs) or voluntary organisations within the UN system. The world's largest charities, humanitarian organisations, human rights groups, environmental campaigns and single-issue lobbyists are able to have observer status within the Economic and Social Council (ECOSOC), a committee of the General Assembly. Household names such as Amnesty International, the World Wide Fund for Nature and the Red Cross have enjoyed these rights for decades. In practice, this formal connection allows them a semi-permanent presence within the organisation where they represent their members' and subscribers' interests in constant research, lobbying and persuasion. It would be quite feasible to expand this presence into an 'NGO Assembly'. Meeting in September, in advance of the annual October opening of the UNGA, such an assembly could focus attention on the forthcoming agenda of the Assembly. By its combination of expert opinion and open debate it could highlight and, frankly, embarrass the grossly over-hyped October sessions of Assembly, which are traditionally addressed by heads of Government. These stage-managed 'debates' currently occupy several months of the UN calendar before the real work can begin, near to Christmas, in the committees of the UNGA, where negotiations are conducted amongst permanent, professional diplomatic staff.

The greatest single obstacle to the UN undertaking more independent initiatives is its complete lack of financial independence. The UN relies entirely upon the Member States' subscriptions, known as 'assessed contributions', and increasingly upon their voluntary contributions to specific programmes such as UNICEF. This makes each welfare, environment and development programme especially vulnerable to annual fluctuations and to political pressure.

Logically, an international organisation could raise additional revenues by taxing those activities in the global economy which transcend state boundaries and which therefore fall outside the revenue-collecting scope of states. Taxing the use of the global commons – such as outer space, the ozone layer, the climate system and the high seas – which all states *use* but do not *own*, would have additional gains in environmental protection. The global commons are largely 'free', resulting in over-exploitation, especially by environmental pollution. 'Taxing the commons' would therefore serve three related purposes. It would create a legal responsibility on the international community to protect and conserve these territories. Second, raising a charge for the use of the commons would deter their pollution and over-use. Third, revenues could be dedicated to UN services, most obviously the work of the UN Environmental Programme (UNEP), UNDP, UNICEF and UNHCR. Suitable candidates would be levies on geo-stationary orbits used by telecommunications and satellite TV broadcasting companies, and on high-seas fishing conducted beyond sovereign waters. The 1982 UN Convention on the Law of the Seas already provides for UN taxation of deep-sea mining revenues from the 'common heritage of mankind' zones beyond the 200-mile Exclusive Economic Zones allowed to coastal states. Marine pollution – for example, oil-tanker accidents – could be fined. The Framework Convention on Climate Change, adopted at Rio in 1992 and modified by the Kyoto Protocol, allows countries to trade unused national allowances for carbon-dioxide emissions. This market could be taxed for WMO or for UNEP to fund continuing climate research, and to assist developing countries with the costs of climate change. Other possible sources of international taxation are the Tobin tax suggested as a levy on international currency dealings, on aviation fuel, defence spending in national budgets and the international arms trade (Grubb et al. 2000; ODI 1996).

The US Senate has set itself against any international tax-raising powers for the UN. As part of its general hostility towards the Third World majority driven programmes of the UN, the US Senate is determined to prevent the UN from acquiring autonomous sources of funding. The damage being inflicted upon the UN by reliance on traditional funding is shown by its state of arrears. The US has applied what can only be called financial sanctions against the UN over a period of nearly twenty years since the early 1980s. Other major debtors currently include Brazil, Yugoslavia, Argentina and Iraq. The US made the first of its scheduled arrears payments in 1999. It would have lost its General Assembly vote had the arrears total exceeded two years' assessed contributions (UN 1945: Art. 19). As of 31 May 2000 the US owed $1,774.7 million, or 61 per cent of the total $2,914.3 million owed to the UN on that date. Two-thirds of these arrears constituted unpaid peacekeeping assessments (UNA-USA 2000: 275).

## CONCLUSION

The current state of the UN, after a decade of post-Cold War opportunities for reform and expansion, suggests that the recognition of global citizenship has not penetrated far into this most unchanging of international organisations. Relative to the enlargement and deepening of the European Union, the formation of NAFTA and the controversial expansion of the WTO's mandate in world trade, the UN has been entirely unreformed in its Charter and structure.

Secretary-General Kofi Annan has advanced internal administrative reforms, called 'Track One', almost all concerned with meeting the insatiable demands of the US for staff reductions and managerial tinkering. Structural reform, 'Track Two', is enmired. Not even the expansion of the Security Council to more representatively reflect the changed power structure of the past half-century can be agreed. Britain and France defend their permanent seats. Germany and Japan aspire to join them. Half a dozen Third World members, such as Egypt, South Africa, India, Pakistan, Brazil and Argentina cannot agree a regional formula for enlargement. The US anyway opposes enlargement. Development programmes are frozen, matching the stagnation and latter decline of bilateral aid programmes. The decline of ODA within the twenty-four democracies of the Development Assistance Committee (DAC), the aid agency of the Organisation for Economic Cooperation and Development, is a telling case study of declining commitment to internationalism during a decade of post-Cold War optimism concerning enlarged commitments to sustainable development. Only five countries – Norway, Sweden, Denmark, Netherlands and France – actually give above the 0.7 per cent of Gross Domestic Product (GDP) target adopted by the UN in 1970. In 1995 the USA gave just 0.10 per cent of GDP as ODA. The most generous of the DAC twenty-two was Norway at 0.87 per cent (DAC 1996: A22). The declining status of ODA is vividly stated thus: 'The ratio of ODA to Gross National Product, a measure of donor countries' performance effort, has fallen to just

0.27 per cent, the lowest level since the United Nations adopted the 0.7 per cent target in 1970' (DAC 1996: 66).

The decline of ODA illustrates an issue of global citizenship, in which the majority of the world's richest and most clearly democratic governments have under performed in their duties for a quarter of a century. It is an issue entirely within the domestic, sovereign grasp of each government to act to tackle. How much more difficult, therefore, is the task of modernising and energising UN mechanisms?

The UN is firmly rooted in the intergovernmental tradition and even its democratic member governments will resist the extension of direct or participatory models of democracy to these institutions. Manifestly, the non-democratic member governments will resist any attempt to enlarge the ability of the UN to inspect, challenge and hold accountable their human rights abuses and other practices. The 1990s saw extraordinary progress in extending democratic government in Eastern and Central Europe, in Latin America, selectively in East Asia and more partially still in Africa. Only when democratic government is established across the globe will the more exotic dimensions of global citizenship be addressed. Until then the UN will perform with very variable efficiency. Underfunded, and subject to political inter-ference in its humanitarian role, the UN's ability to help the world's poorest and most vulnerable, the one billion of the global underclass, will suffer most by this neglect. The only political choice for global citizens is to maintain the case for reform.

---

QUESTIONS

1. In what ways does the UN still reflect the times in which it was created?
2. How can the UN provide for the security of victims of aggression?
3. Global citizens should be concerned with the financial crisis of the UN and its impact on the UN's ability to meet the needs of the most disadvantaged. How might this be alleviated?
4. How might the UN be made more accountable to popular democratic opinions?

---

# SECTION 3

# ETHICAL BASES OF GLOBAL CITIZENSHIP

# SECTION INTRODUCTION

## Nigel Dower

In the Introduction and elsewhere the distinction is drawn between the 'ethical' component of global citizenship and the 'institutional' component. Whatever else may be claimed in the statement 'we are citizens of the world', at least there is an ethical claim that we belong to one global moral community within which we have global responsibilities and some shared universal values. Although the word 'citizen' may for some users of the phrase 'global citizen' be no more than a way of talking about agency or membership of a moral community, for many others it indicates something more, and many of the chapters in this reader try to make sense of this 'citizenship' component. The chapters in this section, however, are mainly concerned with the primary ethical issue: what global ethic should we accept? Whilst Küng and van den Anker are also concerned to some extent with the questions 'What needs to happen for a global ethic to exist?' and 'What institutions are needed to express global justice?' respectively, all the authors attend to the ethical issue itself. I shall first set out some of the salient points from each chapter and then offer a few general remarks on these approaches.

Hans Küng's 'A Global Ethic for a New World Order' is a forthright advocacy of an ethical vision, a particular global ethic seen as the basic ethical minimum which can be and is being accepted by different religions and cultures throughout the world. The twenty-first century faces problems like the so-called 'clash of civilisations'. But it is also the century in which it is possible that a 'universal civilisation' will emerge based on peace and mutual acceptance of different faiths and cultures. Peace amongst the religions is a prerequisite for peace in the world and it will not occur without dialogue between the religions. He documents various events and processes in the 1990s which show an acknowledgement of the importance of global ethics, such as the *Universal Declaration of Human Responsibilities* of the

InterAction Council in 1997. These witness to an important point about a global ethic: it must be one which stresses not only rights but responsibilities and duties as well. These responsibilities go beyond what law requires. Legal duties correlate with legal rights but what is needed is an ethical commitment to exercise one's rights responsibly, to underpin law and to make a better world. Küng ends by stressing that, despite the negative impact of some forms of religion, religions do have an extremely positive role to play in finding a common core of value and commitments. He claims that all religions agree (though one suspects that it is really some adherents of all religions that do this) to the following four commitments: to a culture of non-violence and respect for life; to a culture of solidarity and a just social order; to a culture of tolerance and a life of truth; to a culture of equal rights and partnership between men and women.

Nigel Dower's piece 'Global Ethics and Global Citizenship' has a more analytic intention in that he wants to show that any commitment to being a global citizen involves an ethical commitment of some kind, but that the content and character of this global ethic can vary considerably. The common core includes acceptance of global responsibility, and an attitude towards humanity which means one does not have uncritical loyalty towards one's own society or nation-state, and acceptance that what happens to human beings anywhere in the world matters (normally seen as an acceptance that there are *some* universal values). That said, there are many variations in approach. First, through a discussion of several examples of global citizenship action, he shows that global citizens may vary considerably over the means they pursue or endorse, even if they agree on the overall ends: the means adopted by some may – for instance, civil disobedience – be deemed immoral or ineffective by others. Second, acceptance of the same values and norms may well stem from quite different theories or worldviews – philosophical and religious; several examples of philosophical theories (Kant, Utilitarianism, human rights) are discussed. (This point is similar to Küng's concerning different religions agreeing on the same common core.) Third, there may be real differences in practical orientation between different global ethics. He advocates 'solidarist pluralism' in contrast to the dogmatic idealism of, for example, religious fundamentalism or the libertarianism underlying the global economy.

Christien van den Anker's piece on global justice focuses on moral principles underlying our global responsibilities as world citizens, and is concerned to defend a particular theory which justifies these. Like Ottonelli later in the reader, she asks the question in terms of a theory of global justice: what does justice require on a global level? What drives her account is the great disparity of wealth in the world and in particular the position of the very poor. Not only does she want to argue that justice requires redistribution of wealth, she also wants to defend a particular liberal approach to justice associated with John Rawls. Indeed the hallmark of Rawls' *A Theory of Justice* was to provide an intellectual justification based on liberal premises for 'welfare liberalism' – the claim that social justice requires not merely the protection of liberty but also the redistribution of wealth in such a way as to improve the position of the poor as much as is practicable (or at least to protect them from various kinds of need). Van den Anker follows several theorists (Beitz, Pogge and Barry) each of whom in different ways extends and adapts Rawls' theory to apply to the world. If these extensions work then justice requires extensive redistribution of wealth in favour of the world's poorer countries and peoples. She also addresses two other issues to do with the effective implementation of such principles. What international institutions are needed? Whilst she defines institutions (not uncontroversially) as bodies that can enforce rules, she is at pains to distinguish institutions which would constitute a world state and institutions of global governance, and in favour of the latter recommends various measures including cosmopolitan democracy (as advocated by Held). Finally she advocates a model of global citizenship which combines political freedom through democracy with social protection through distribution. Whilst she accepts that global citizenship can have a merely ethical sense, she is clear that global citizenship in a full sense involves the institutions of global governance or at least a commitment to create such institutions.

Sabine Alkire's chapter 'Global Citizenship and Common Values' has a quite different focus. Her concern is not with the principle of duty/responsibility/justice which underlies global citizenship but rather with an account of the 'good' (some account of which is presupposed in any theory of global obligation). A global ethic needs to include an account of the good as a universal value. Just what makes life 'go well' or makes a person flourish or achieve well-being? Alkire starts by inviting us to imagine an exchange student from another culture: how would we render intelligible to her our practices? For instance, handshaking may only become intelligible because it is seen as a gesture of sociability which can be seen as a universal value intelligible to anyone. After indicating some empirical evidence of the universal acceptance of certain values, she seeks to ground this in a philosophical conception (that of John Finnis) of dimensions of value which constitute basic reasons for action. Life, knowledge, aesthetic experience, work and play, for instance, are all seen as basic dimensions; there is no hierarchy amongst them and their relative weight will depend on circumstance. These are not as such *moral* values. The latter emerge when we apply the fundamental principle of practical reasonableness or morality which is to will those goods which are compatible with (and often conducive to) integral human fulfilment – that is, the fulfilment of all persons. On this basis Alkire claims the basic core values for global citizens are the dimensions of the good and these moral principles, but no more. This limit is a part of the point she wants to make: within this framework there are many ways of achieving human good and many ways of acting morally, that is, not marring the good of others. Thus she defends a theory of the good which is both universal but also fully sensitive to variations of expression (based on individual and cultural differences). It steers a middle course between a traditional universalism (often seen as emanating from the West and thus as culturally imperialistic) and a relativism which denies altogether that there are universal values.

It is a striking feature of all the discussions in this section that little or nothing is said about the process of globalisation. It is, of course, no accident that the current interest in global citizenship and associated ideas like global/cosmopolitan democracy and global civil society arises precisely because of the pervasive processes of economic, political and cultural globalisation, particularly in the 1990s. This is both because globalisation involves global impacts, especially on the environment and on the world's poor, and because globalisation creates through the greater ease of communication and cooperation the space in which effective agency at a distance becomes more realistic for many individuals (and not merely a privileged few, as in the past).

Many other chapters throughout this reader deal with the context of globalisation, especially those by Falk, Held, Axtmann, Newlands and Strijbos. Is it therefore a defect that this is not discussed here? This depends on whether one thinks that the existence or validity of a global ethic *depends* on processes of globalisation. If one thinks that an ethic depends on the shared agreement about values (the good) and norms (the right, that is, duties/oughts) among people (a form of communitarianism), then it would be a serious problem if one discussed ethical principles in the abstract without attending seriously to questions like: are these values already accepted universally? Or: are these values ones that have been agreed upon by some process of negotiation or mutual assimilation through extensive interrelations? Certainly Dower, van den Anker and Alkire all adopt an ethical methodology which is not based on communitarian assumptions. For them an ethic – global or otherwise – is one that is to be accepted for *reasons* or from rational reflection about human nature and the human condition. It might be thought that Küng's approach is somewhat different because he makes much of the importance of there actually being a common core for all religions and of the importance of acts of agreement like the Declaration Toward a Global Ethic of the Parliament of the World's Religions in 1993. But even here the differences are less significant than might appear at first sight. Küng takes the basis of the global ethic to be the pre-existing similarities in the worldviews of particular religions or cultures, and he stresses that these are not to be given up: a shared global ethic is not a substitute for the particular ethics of particular societies or cultures. They are already universal global ethics.

Küng and van den Anker are partly interested – and rightly so – in what processes will strengthen the process of explicit mutual acceptance of the common core of values. In Küng's case many will question the pivotal role religion is meant to play in the development of agreed ethical standards at a global level. In van den Anker's case a sharp distinction is drawn between democratic global institutions which can enforce global justice and other kinds of organisation such as NGOs, the latter not being seen as appropriate vehicles for being global citizens, and it is not at all obvious that either of these points need to be accepted. However, there is an important question to face: what developments in the world will facilitate the general acceptance of appropriate global norms and values? To answer this question we do need to know about the actual processes of globalisation and what the real possibilities are for developments. But to answer the question: 'what global ethics should we accept?' we do not need this. And it is worth reminding ourselves, as several authors note, that the idea of a universal ethic and of global citizenship is one that goes back to the ancient Stoics. The conditions of globalisation are not essential to a global ethic, only to its effective expression in the modern world.

In respect to the ethical strategies adopted by van den Anker and Alkire the following needs to be noted. Both argue for a particular conception – of global justice and human well-being respectively. Whilst their particular approaches may be right, of course, perhaps what is important is that the reader recognises that there are deep questions to be answered about the nature of global ethics. It could make a big difference to the world if enough global citizens accept a duty to alleviate poverty and to address North–South inequalities: whether one accepts a globalised version of Rawls' theory, or a principle based on extensive benevolence or appeal to subsistence rights, a world informed by people who accept *any* of these principles would be a rather better world than the world we have now. Likewise, whether or not one accepts Alkire's particular list of dimensions of value or her account of why they are to be accepted as values, it is likely that anyone who reflects seriously on the questions raised would come to a view about what is important in human well-being which at least questions and possibly challenges the dominant paradigm of development. This paradigm is one defined almost exclusively in terms of economic growth (and applies to rich and poor countries alike). Again, widespread acceptance of less economics-dominated accounts of development and welfare would be good news for the environment and for the world's poor. This critique of conventional assumptions is not, however, something Alkire explicitly stresses. For her the major merit of her account is that it provides a basis for a gentle universalism that allows for reasonable diversity of expression and thus underpins a world of tolerance and mutual respect amongst peoples.

On the other hand it has to be recognised that not all theories of justice will favour van den Anker's redistributive prescriptions. A more libertarian conception (such as that of Nozick (1974)) will stress liberty rights and question welfare rights or the rightness of redistributive measures. Not all reflection on the nature of the good and attempts to base values on the requirements of reason will lead to the kinds of flexible or latitudinarian conclusions which Alkire draws. As Dower remarks, we must recognise the real possibility of divergence of views amongst global citizens. Not all global citizens would necessarily accept the implied convergence of views on what is to be done or valued. The idea of being a global citizen is not quite the same as being, from the standpoint of any particular observer, a *good* global citizen!

# 10. A GLOBAL ETHIC FOR A NEW GLOBAL ORDER

## Hans Küng

1. The twenty-first century will not be a European one as the nineteenth century, nor an American century as the twentieth century, and it will not be an Asian century, but a World century. The age of imperialism and hegemonism is gone, and the damnation that is domination would be no lesser if it would be Asian domination.

2. But the world is faced with a new sense of East Asian self-worth, self-respect and empowerment; Asians today are aware of their own potentials, their possibilities, and their Asian values.

3. We should avoid any silly confrontation especially between the Western world (Christian or secular) and the world of Islam and should strive for a commonwealth of all nations where wealth is truly common, in other words: towards a single commonwealth of common wealth. In this sense we should strive for a universal civilisation.

Presupposing these three points of agreement, it is easier for me to analyse in my first point the fundamental challenges and responses we face in the twenty-first century. I do it very briefly in four steps (cf. Küng 1987; Küng 1989).

### 1. Challenges and Responses

1. We live in a time where humanity is threatened by a 'clash of civilisations', as some think, between the Islamic civilisation and the Western civilisation.[1] We are threatened, as I believe, not so much by a new world war but by all

sorts of cultural and religious conflicts between specific countries or in a specific country often even in the same city, the same street, the same school.

The reasonable alternative is: *peace among the religions. Because there will be no peace among the nations and civilisations without peace among the religions.* But many people all over the world will ask: do not precisely the religions often support and inspire hatred, enmity and war? Indeed:

2. We live in a time where peace in the Western and in the Islamic world is threatened by all sorts of religious fundamentalism; Christian, Muslim, Jewish, Hindu, Buddhist; often simply rooted in social misery, in reaction to Western secularism and in the desire of a basic orientation in life.

The alternative is: *dialogue between the religions. Because there will be no peace among the religions without dialogue between the religions!*

But many people will object: are there not many dogmatic differences and obstacles between the different faiths which make real dialogue a naïve illusion? Indeed:

3. We live in a time where in the Western and in the Muslim worlds better relations between religions are blocked by all sort of *dogmatisms* which exist within each religion: the reason for many clashes between dogmatism and pragmatism, fundamentalism and enlightenment.

The alternative will be: despite dogmatic differences *a global ethic, an ethical minimum common to all religions, cultures, civilisations. Because there will be no new world order without a global ethic.* This forthcoming 'world century' asks for a 'world ethic' which has to be the basis for an upcoming 'world civilisation' or 'universal civilisation'.

The idea of a 'universal civilisation' certainly does not imply the abolition of cultural and religious differences, which are tremendous not only in Europe but also in Asia, which is only a geographical entity and not a political, ethnic, cultural or religious one. The idea of a 'universal civilisation' means in a positive way a universality in the technological, economical, political and, as we hope, also in the ethical dimension. In this time of globalisation of markets, technologies and medias we need also the globalisation of ethics. Nevertheless, we, in Asia or in Europe, shall not and should not give up our specific cultures, the cultures of the different particular tribes, regions or nations with the particular history, language, custom, belief, law and art. Reaching out for a universal civilisation we must not strive towards a single unified religion, which would anyway be an illusion, but we should maintain a culture of tolerance which respects all cultural and religious minorities. Pre-supposing, therefore, the importance of a universal civilisation and at the same time the remaining differences in culture and religion, let us now talk about the emergence of a new world order in the political sense which, as I am convinced, needs an ethical basis (Küng 1997).

## 2. NEW WORLD ORDER AND WORLD ETHIC

1. In *negative* terms – a better world order will *not* be introduced on the basis:

(a) solely of diplomatic offensives which all too often are unable to guarantee peace and stability in a certain region and which are often, as in former Yugoslavia, characterised more by hypocrisy than by honesty;
(b) simply of humanitarian help which cannot replace political actions and solutions. The European powers, by substituting in Bosnia humanitarian aid for political action, put themselves in the power of the aggressors and became complicit in the crimes of war;
(c) primarily of military interventions. Of course an absolute pacifism would allow a new holocaust, a new genocide after the end of the 'never again' twentieth century. But indeed, the consequences of military interventions tend often to be more negative than positive;
(d) solely of international law, as long as such a law rests on the unlimited sovereignty of states and is focused more on the rights of states than on the rights of peoples and individuals. If moral convictions and moral intentions do not back a law, armistice or treaty, powers (as in Bosnia) are not even prepared to defend the principle that only peaceful and negotiated territorial change is acceptable in Europe.

2. In *positive* terms – a better world order will ultimately be brought in *only* on the basis of:

(a) common visions, ideals, values, aims and criteria; a minimal basic consensus relating to binding values, irrevocable standards and moral attitudes;
(b) heightened global responsibility on the part of peoples and their leaders;
(c) a new binding and uniting ethic for all humankind, including states and those in power, which embraces cultures and religions. No new world order without a new world ethic, a global ethic.

3. What is the *function* of such a global ethic?
A global ethic is not a new ideology or superstructure:

(a) it will not make the specific ethics of the different religions and philosophies superfluous;
(b) it is therefore no substitute for the Torah, Sermon on the Mount, the Qur'ān, the Bhagavadgītā, the Discourses of the Buddha or the Sayings of Confucius.

A global ethic is nothing but the necessary minimum of common values, standards and basic attitudes. In other words:

a consensus relating to binding values, irrevocable standards and moral attitudes, which can be affirmed by all religions despite their 'dogmatic' differences and should also be supported by non-believers.

This consensus of values will be a decisive contribution towards overcoming the crisis of orientation which became a real world problem. And in the recent discussion on human rights Asians insisted rightly on the fact that in their traditions there was from the beginning a great insistence on duties, obligations, responsibilities and that these rights are a relatively new development in Europe and America originating with the Enlightenment of the seventeenth century.

But one of the most astonishing and at the same time most welcome phenomena of the last decade of the twentieth century is the almost explosive spread of the notion of a world ethic, not only in theology, philosophy and education, but also in world politics and the world economy. The most important developments are:

### 3. WORLD POLITICS DISCOVERS THE GLOBAL ETHIC

When I published the book *Projekt Weltethos* (*Global Responsibility – In Search of a New World Ethic*) in 1991, there were hardly any documents on a global ethic from world organisations to which I could refer.[2] Of course there were declarations on human rights, above all the 1948 *Declaration* of the United Nations, but there were no declarations on human responsibilities. However, now, seven years later, I can refer to three important international documents which not only acknowledge human rights but also speak explicitly of human responsibilities. Indeed they programmatically call for a global ethic and even attempt to spell it out in concrete terms.

1. The report of the UN Commission on Global Governance bears the title *Our Global Neighbourhood* (1995) and calls for a neighbourhood ethic: 'Global values must be the cornerstone of global governance' (CGG 1995: 47). And for the ethical dimension of the world political order this document gives the Golden Rule as the main basic principle: 'People should treat others as they would themselves wish to be treated' (CGG 1995: 49). In connection with this a request is made. The authors were presumably unaware that it had already been made in a discussion in the Revolutionary Parliament of 1789 in Paris, one which could not be met at that time: 'Rights need to be joined with responsibilities' (CGG 1995: 56). For the 'tendency to emphasise rights while forgetting responsibilities' has 'deleterious consequences' (CGG 1995: 56). 'We therefore urge the international community to unite in support of a global ethic of common rights and shared responsibilities. In our view, such an ethic – reinforcing the fundamental rights that are already part of the fabric of international norms – would provide the moral foundation for constructing a

more effective system of global governance' (CGG 1995: 56). The international commission expresses the hope that 'over time, these principles could be embodied in a more binding international document – a global charter of Civil Society – that could provide a basis for all to agree on rules that should govern the global neighbourhood' (CGG 1995: 57).

2. The Report by the World Commission on Culture and Development bears the title *Our Creative Diversity* (1995). Here the presupposition is a 'commitment to pluralism', but this statement is preceded by a chapter which stresses what is held in common rather than the differences: 'A New Global Ethics', an ethic of humankind, a global ethic.

Why a global ethic? Because collaboration between people of different cultures and interests can be made easier and their conflicts diminished and limited if all peoples and groups 'see themselves bound and motivated by shared commitments' (WCCD 1995: 34). Hence the call for a global ethic: 'So it is imperative to look for a core of shared ethical values and principles' (WCCD 1995: 34). The Commission on Culture and Development emphasises the agreement between its concern and the efforts of the UN Commission for Global Governance, and states: 'The idea is that the values and principles of a global ethic should be common points of contact which offer a minimal moral stimulus which the world must observe in its manifold efforts to overcome the global problems mentioned'(WCCD 1995: 35). To this degree today there is a whole 'culture in search of a global ethics'(WCCD 1995: 35). Such a search is already in itself a cultural activity par excellence. Questions like 'Who are we? How do we relate to one another and to humankind? How do we behave to one another and to humankind as such? What is our meaning?' stand at the centre of culture.

What are the sources of such a global ethic? The formulation of a global ethic must draw its content from 'the cultural resources, the insights, emotional experiences, historical memories and spiritual orientations of the peoples' (WCCD 1995: 35). Despite all the differences between cultures, there are some themes which appear in almost all cultural traditions and which could serve as the inspiration for a global ethic.

3. The InterAction Council, which consists of former presidents and prime ministers (Helmut Schmidt of Germany, Honorary Chairman; Malcolm Fraser of Australia, Chairman) proposed in September 1997 to the United Nations to accept a *Universal Declaration of Human Responsibilities* (1997). This Declaration is based on the conviction that 'global problems demand global solutions on the basis of ideas, values and norms respected by all cultures and societies'. The Introductory Comment of this Declaration emphasises that 'it is time to talk about human responsibilities'. Therefore the *Universal Declaration of Human Responsibilities* 'seeks to bring freedom and responsibility into balance and to promote a move from the freedom of

indifference to the freedom of involvement. . . . The basic premise should be to aim at the greatest amount of freedom possible, but also to develop the fullest sense of responsibility that will allow that freedom itself to grow'. The Comment stresses 'that a better social order both nationally and internationally cannot be achieved by laws, prescriptions and conventions alone, but needs a global ethic. Human aspirations for progress can only be realised by agreed values and standards applying to all people and institutions at all times' (InterAction Council 1997: 1).

The responsibilities which 'should be taught and promoted throughout the world' contain 'Fundamental Principles for Humanity', 'Non-Violence and Respect for Life', 'Justice and Solidarity', 'Truthfulness and Tolerance' and 'Mutual Respect and Partnership' (InterAction Council 1997: 2–5).

## 4. NOT ONLY RIGHTS BUT ALSO RESPONSIBILITIES

Already in the debate on human rights in the French Revolutionary Parliament of 1789 the demand was made: if a declaration of the rights of man is proclaimed, it must be combined with a declaration of the responsibilities of man (*Declaration des devoirs de l'homme*). Otherwise, in the end all human beings would have only rights which they would play off against others, and no one would any longer recognise the responsibilities without which the rights cannot function. After a controversial discussion over three days a vote cleared the further proceedings by 607 voices against but also 433 in favour of this demand.

### 4(i) Human beings have responsibilities from the beginning

In our historical retrospect we saw that the responsibilities were formulated millennia before the rights. But 200 years after the 1789 Revolution we are living in a society in which individuals and groups constantly appeal to rights against others without recognising any responsibilities of their own. Hardly anyone can build a house or a street, hardly an authority can enact a law or a regulation, without an appeal being made to rights in connection with it. Today countless claims can be advanced as rights, in particular against the state. After all, we live in a society of claims which often appears to be a 'litigious society', and thus makes the state a 'judiciary state' – as it has been called in the Federal Republic of Germany. That is above all the case in the USA, where a third of all the lawyers in the world practise; there the costs of damages use up around 3 per cent of the Gross National Product. Don't we perhaps need a new concentration on responsibilities, particularly in our overdeveloped legalistic states, to balance all the justified insistence on rights? Responsibility, obligation, duty; in German all are expressed by the same word 'Pflicht'. And, of course, as *duty* it has been badly misused. 'Duty' (towards those in authority, the Führer, the people, the Party, the Pope) has been hammered home by totalitarian, authoritarian, hierarchical ideologies of every kind; fearful crimes are committed out of 'duty' or on the basis of some 'oath' which backs up obedience with divine authority. 'Duty is duty' and 'an order is an order'. Neither of these must again become slogans: blind obedience, whether in state or church, is immoral. But all the abuses should not prevent us from taking up the concept of duty in a discriminating way. It is a term which has had a long history since Cicero (*De officiis*) and Ambrose, Bishop of Milan (*De officiis ministorum*), and became a key concept of modernity through Immanuel Kant.

The fact cannot be overlooked that duty in particular – this was Kant's key thought – distinguishes man as a rational being from animals, who only follow inclinations, instincts, drives or external pressures and training. But human beings are not just rational, quite naturally following their reason and therefore needing no obligation. Human beings, who are both rational and subject to drives, have the possibility – which is both an opportunity and a risk – to make decisions in freedom and to act in accordance with their reason. In this sense, understood in modern immanent terms, an obligation is a claim of reason which is binding and yet aims at freedom. However, in principle it does not exclude other 'external' authorities (God, positive law), since a human autonomy grounded in theonomy need not mean heteronomy, that is, being governed from outside.

Moreover, it is important to see that while duty exerts a moral compulsion, this compulsion is not physical. Leaving aside external authorities, it follows from reason, which is not purely technical nor economic but ethical, prompting and compelling human beings to moral action. But in modern discussion of human rights one thing is overlooked. All rights imply responsibilities, but:

### 4(ii) Not all responsibilities follow from rights

I shall demonstrate this first by three examples, one more special, one more general and one quite universal, and then make a more precise definition of the relationship between rights and responsibilities.

A special example:

> the freedom of the press enjoyed by a newspaper or a journalist is guaranteed and protected by the modern constitutional state. The journalist, the newspaper, has a *right* to report freely. The law may not only not *attack* this right, on the contrary it must protect it actively, and if need be even establish it with its authority. Therefore the state and the citizen have the *responsibility* to respect the right of this newspaper or this journalist to report freely.
>
> However, this right does not in any way affect *the responsibility of the journalist or the newspaper itself*, namely to report objectively and fairly, not to caricature reality and not to manipulate the public, but to inform it truthfully.

A more general example:

> the right of each individual to property is guaranteed by the modern constitutional state. It contains the *legal* obligation for others (the state or the individual citizen) to respect this property and not to misappropriate it.
>
> However, this right does not in any way affect the *responsibility of the property-owner* himself not to use the property in an anti-social way but to use it socially, to restrain the unquenchable human greed for money, prestige and consumption, and to develop some sense of proportion and moderation.

A quite universal example:

> the freedom of any individual to decide in accordance with his or her own *conscience* entails the legal obligation that others (individuals or the state) should respect a free decision of conscience; the individual conscience is guaranteed protection by the constitution of the state.
>
> However, this right by no means entails *the ethical responsibilities of individuals* in every instance to follow their own consciences even, indeed especially, when this is unpleasant or abhorrent to them.

It follows from all this that rights imply certain responsibilities, and these are legal obligations. But by no means all responsibilities follow from legal rights. There are also original ethical obligations. The Protestant natural-law ethicist Samuel von Pufendorf (1632–94) and the Jewish philosopher Moses Mendelsson (1728–86) distinguished between:

> 'perfect' obligations, obligations in the narrower sense: these are *legal obligations*, for example, to respect freedom of conscience and religion, obligations which the state may enforce, punishing violations of them; and

> 'imperfect' obligations, obligations in the wider sense: these are *ethical obligations*, for example, the obligations of conscience, love and humanity which rest on one's own insight and cannot be compelled by the state unless it wants to be a totalitarian state. That constitutes their greatness but also their practical limits. Here, though, we should reflect:

### 4(iii) What would rights be without morals?

The distinction between legal and ethical obligations is important for a more precise distinction between the levels of law and ethic, which has many implications, in particular for the implementation of human rights. First of all we need to clarify the question: can one develop an ethic valid for the whole of humankind simply on the basis of human rights? The levels of law and ethic are related in many ways: the origin as well as the presence and application of the law already presupposes an ethic. On the other hand, an ethic is not exhausted in the law. The levels of law and ethic are thus to be distinguished in principle, and this is of particular significance for human rights.

Human beings have fundamental rights which are formulated in declarations of human rights. To these correspond the responsibilities both of the state and of individual citizens to respect and to protect these rights. These are legal obligations. Here we are at the level of law, the laws, the regulations, the judiciary, the police.

In practice that means that outward conduct in conformity with the law can be examined; the law can be appealed to in principle and if need be enforced ('in the name of the law').

But at the same time human beings have elementary responsibilities which are already given with their personhood and are not based on any laws: there are ethical obligations which are not fixed in law. Here we are at the level of ethics, customs, the conscience, the 'heart' . . .

In practice this means that the inner, morally good disposition cannot be examined; so it cannot be brought under the law, let alone be compelled ('thoughts are free').

The conclusion to be drawn from this is that no comprehensive ethic of humanity can be derived from human rights *alone*, fundamental though these are for human beings; it must also cover the human responsibilities which were there before the law. Before any codification in law and any state legislation there is the moral independence and conscious self-responsibility of the individual, with which not only elementary rights but also elementary responsibilities are connected.

The distinction between law and ethic has momentous consequences: because law and ethic are not a priori identical but can fall apart. The law very often does not function. That is particularly true of politics: if, as happened in the war in Yugoslavia in the 1990s, one or both partners in a treaty a priori do not have the ethical will (which cannot be directly examined, far less be compelled) to observe the cease-fire that has been negotiated, then the cease-fire treaties co-signed by the great powers and all their legal provisions are of no use; the parties will continue the war as soon as there is a favourable opportunity, with whatever political or legal justification. The realisation of the fundamental principle of international law, 'treaties are to be observed' (*pacta sunt servanda*), quite decisively depends on the ethical will of the partners in the treaty. It only needs Bismarck's secret addition 'as things are' (*rebus sic stantibus*, which also cannot be guaranteed) for even the most solemn legal treaty to be built on sand, and one-sidedly to be declared no longer valid in a changed situation.

On the level of international law, in 1955 Max Huber (1874–1966) pointed out the relevance of the distinction between law and ethic. In his reflections, Huber, who was not only a renowned Swiss international lawyer but also the

President of the International Court of Justice at The Hague (1925–28, and President of the International Committee of the Red Cross (1928–45), develops the concept of an 'international ethic' transcending the law, standing behind and above it, and therefore not grounded in law.[3] For the international lawyer it is a matter of principle that: 'Neither the law nor morality can assert themselves in the long run without the authority of an ethic which stands behind them and comes from another, higher, realm that elevates mere custom to morality.' In relation to international law, which accords the sovereign states very great freedom of movement for politics, the ethic has 'the task of giving criteria for this broad area of political action, and setting limits' (Huber 1955/56).

So, '*Quid leges sine moribus?*' runs a Roman saying: what is the use of any laws if no morals, no moral inclination, no obligation of conscience stands behind them? What is the use of a peace treaty which only exists on paper, which has not found its way into human heads and, since it is not just a rational event, into human hearts? There is no overlooking the fact that the realisation of peace, justice and humanity depends on the insight and readiness of human beings to give the law validity. In other words, the law needs a moral foundation! For a new world order that means:

> a better world order cannot be created or even enforced with laws, conventions and ordinances alone;

> commitment to human rights presupposes an awareness of responsibility and obligations for which both the human head and the human heart must be addressed at the same time;

> law has no permanent existence without ethics, so there will be *no new world order without a world ethic.*

## 5. Contribution of Religions

A former communiqué of the InterAction Council bears the title *In Search of Global Ethical Standards* (1996). It openly addresses the negative role which the religions have often played, and still play, in the world: 'The world is also afflicted by religious extremism and violence preached and practised in the name of religion' (InterAction Council 1996: 2). But the positive role of the religions is also noted: 'Religious institutions still command the loyalty of hundreds of millions of people' (InterAction Council 1996: 2), and do so despite all secularisation and consumerism. 'The world's religions constitute one of the great traditions of wisdom for humankind. This repository of wisdom, ancient in its origins, has never been needed more' (InterAction Council 1996: 9). The minimal criteria which make it possible to live together at all are important; without ethics and self-restraint humankind would revert to the jungle. 'In a world of unprecedented change humankind has a desperate need of an ethical base on which to stand' (InterAction Council 1996: 8).

Now follow some statements on ethics and politics: 'Ethics should precede politics and the law, because political action is concerned with values and choice. Ethics, therefore, must inform and inspire our political leadership' (InterAction Council 1996: 9). To respond to the epoch-making change which is coming about, our institutions need a re-dedication to ethical norms: 'We can find the sources of such a re-dedication in the world's religious and ethical traditions. They have the spiritual resources to give an ethical lead to the solution of our ethnic, national, social, economic and religious tensions. The world's religions have different doctrines but they all advocate a common ethic of basic standards. What unites the world's faiths is far greater than what divides them' (InterAction Council 1996: 10).

This declaration defines much more precisely the core of a global ethic which can also be found in the other declarations. The InterAction Council achieves this precision by taking up the Declaration Toward a Global Ethic passed by the Parliament of the World's Religions which I had the honour and burden to prepare (Küng and Kuschel 1993b): 'We are therefore grateful that the Parliament of the World's Religions, which assembled in Chicago in 1993, proclaimed a Declaration toward a Global Ethic which we support in principle' (InterAction Council 1996: 11).

The Declaration Toward a Global Ethic, of course, does not aim to invent a new morality and then impose it on the various religions from outside (and even from the 'West'). It simply aims to make known what religions in West and East, North and South already hold in common but is so often obscured by numerous 'dogmatic' disputes and intolerable self-opinionatedness. In short, this Declaration seeks to emphasise the minimal ethic which is absolutely necessary for human survival. It is not directed against anyone, but invites all, believers and also non-believers, to adopt this ethic and live in accordance with it. In the words of the Declaration:

Through personal experience and our planet's history we have learned:

> that a better global order cannot be created or enforced by laws, prescriptions, and conventions alone;

> that the realisation of peace, justice, and the protection of earth depends on the insight and readiness of men and women to act justly;

> that action in favour of rights and freedoms presumes a consciousness of responsibility and duty, and that therefore both the minds and hearts of women and men must be addressed;

> that rights without morality cannot long endure, and that *there will be no better global order without a global ethic.*

And then the following two fundamental demands are developed:

1. 'Every human being (white or coloured, man or woman, rich or poor) must be treated humanely.'

2. 'What you do not wish done to yourself, so not do to others!' Or in positive terms: 'What you wish done to yourself, do to others!' (found already in the Sayings of Confucius and practically in every great religious tradition on Earth).

On this basis four irrevocable directives are developed. All religions agree on the following commitments:

1. Commitment to a culture of non-violence and respect for life: 'You shall not kill'! Or in positive terms: 'Have respect for life'!

2. Commitment to a culture of solidarity and a just economic order: 'You shall not steal'! Or in positive terms: 'Deal honestly and fairly'!

3. Commitment to a culture of tolerance and a life of truthfulness: 'You shall not lie'! Or in positive terms: 'Speak and act truthfully'!

4. Commitment to a culture of equal rights and partnership between men and women: 'You shall not commit sexual immorality'! Or in positive terms: 'Respect and love one another'!

According to the Parliament of Religions we should commit ourselves to a common global ethic, to better mutual understanding, as well as to socially beneficial, peace-fostering and Earth-friendly ways of life. This is the only efficient way to a universal civilisation. As far as the religions are concerned, this means: in view of a universal civilisation their prime task must be *making peace with one another*. That must be done with every means available today, including the media, and at every level:

clearing up misunderstandings;

working through traumatic memories;

dissolving hostile stereotypes;

working through guilt complexes, both socially and individually;

demolishing hatred and destructiveness;

reflecting on things that are held in common;

taking concrete initiatives for reconciliation.

The change of consciousness needed here is a task for the new century, the 'world century'. And it is for the young generation to realise decisively the sketch for the future presented here. As the famous French writer Victor Hugo says, the future has many names:

> For the weak it is the unattainable.
> For the fearful it is the unknown.
> For the bold it is the opportunity.

---

## QUESTIONS

1. What for Küng are the core values of a global ethic?
2. Why can't a global ethic be based on human rights alone?
3. What for Küng is the role of religion in promoting a global ethic?
4. Küng does not mention global citizenship. Is this significant?
5. Is a 'universal civilisation' desirable?

---

## NOTES

1. For discussion of Samuel Huntington's thesis of a clash of civilisations, see H. Küng (1995) ch. C.V, 9: 'Tasks for an analysis of postmodernity: A war of civilisations?'; H. Küng (1997) chapter A.V, 1, 'A clash between the civilisations – or peace?'
2. See Küng (1991). For a bibliography on a global ethic, see Hans Küng and Karl-Josef Kuschel (1998: 493–511), and the homepage of the Global Ethic Foundation website.
3. Huber (1955/56: 305f. and 328f.). Professor Dieter Senghaas recently drew my attention to this important article by Max Huber in which, happily, the term 'global ethic' (*Weltethos*) already appears (329). It (still) seemed impossible to Huber to get beyond the multiplicity, variety and contrast in the existing religions and ideologies and to bring them together in a 'global ethic'; in his view a 'global legal organisation' could be achieved more easily than a global ethic. Huber also points out: 'Law can be broken like iron when it is not itself ethic. But ethic is like a diamond' (329). To this it may be replied, from a present-day perspective: while diamonds may differ in size, form and brilliance, they have similar internal structures. Today we know that, despite all the differences between the religions, there are basic common factors, particularly in their ethics, and thus it has proved possible to arrive at a global ethic.

# 11. GLOBAL ETHICS AND GLOBAL CITIZENSHIP

## Nigel Dower

### INTRODUCTION

In this chapter we look at one central element of the idea of global citizenship which almost anyone would agree on, whether they favoured it or rejected it, and whatever else they would or would not build into the idea of global citizenship. When someone says of himself 'I am a global citizen', he is making some kind of moral claim about the nature and scope of our moral obligations. That is, he accepts that he has obligations in principle towards people in any part of the world; for instance, help alleviate poverty, work for international peace, support organisations trying to stop human rights violations, or play one's part in reducing global warming. And if someone says, of people in general and not merely of herself, that 'we are global citizens', she means to say that people generally have these kinds of obligations, whether or not they are currently aware of them or accept them. Thus Piet Hein, a Danish poet, once said at an international conference 'We are global citizens with tribal souls' precisely to make the point that we have global responsibility but most of us most of the time do not have an appropriate consciousness or identity to match this (quoted in Barnaby 1988: 186).

Perhaps for many people who favour global citizenship there is little more being claimed than just this, that we have moral responsibilities in principle towards anyone in the world, and that in some sense we belong morally to one world community of human beings (and, for many thinkers, of non-humans as well), whatever the divisions of nation-states and bounded social communities that in practice divide us. The Stoics, whose philosophy or way of life was very influential over several centuries in the ancient Graeco-Roman world, very much stressed this idea of 'cosmo-polites' – being a 'polites' (citizen) of the 'cosmos' (universe or world) – and stressed the contrast between the accident of birth in any particular political community and the common attribute of humanity (and, for them, rationality) (Heater 1996).

## 1. EXAMPLES OF GLOBAL CITIZENSHIP ACTION

Here are some examples of actions which are done by people, many of whom would describe themselves as 'world citizens'. Currently there is a campaign in the UK called Trident Ploughshares. Its members wish the UK to get rid of Trident nuclear submarines and they are engaged in actions at naval bases which, though non-violent against people, are acts of civil disobedience and aimed at symbolically damaging nuclear submarines. Second, Greenpeace, the environmental organisation committed to taking strong action to stop what its members see as environmentally damaging activities, has, for instance, confronted whaling boats to try and stop whaling. Third, in the USA there has been a movement called the Sanctuary movement in which members of churches hide, contrary to the law, economic refugees illegally entering the USA from Latin America in churches.

These are all actions taken by people because they believe they ought to take strong action, contrary to law, to promote what they see as important causes which are global in nature – a more peaceful world, protecting the whales on a global scale, addressing the poverty of people in the South. They are acting as global citizens.

Now many readers will be thinking about these examples: 'I'm not at all sure I approve of that kind of action; if global citizenship involved an ethical component, that is not ethical'. This does not mean, though, that they are not *acting as world citizens*, since they are acting on principles which are based on an ethic and which they *take* to be correct. But it does raise an important issue we need to make explicit. Consider the following examples.

In July 1996 the World Court delivered a legal opinion on the legality of nuclear weapons in international law to the effect that, with one qualification, possessing nuclear weapons is illegal! But the point to be made here is that this opinion would not have been sought by the UN unless many thousands of ordinary people acting as citizens of the world had signed what were called 'declarations of public conscience', which put pressure on the UN to request an opinion. Second, apart from a large number of *private* actions people perform for the global environment, like cutting down on $CO_2$ emissions or recycling waste, many publicly protest at things they oppose by boycotts, like boycotting an oil company (as with Shell at the time of the Brent Spar incident). Third, the Jubilee 2000 movement mobilised hundreds of thousands of people to take action to pressurise governments to offer debt relief to many Third World countries.

These actions will no doubt appeal to a lot more people but not everyone. It is quite possible for someone to be passionately concerned about world peace but believe that the problem is not the existence of nuclear powers, rather it is the distrust between nations, and that it is much more important to work for international understanding. There are those who believe that if poverty is to be reduced and environmental protection achieved, what is important is the stimulus of economic development and good governance throughout the world, not protests or acts of symbolic self-sacrifice.

People working in these many different ways are all, I suggest, world citizens in so far as they have a conception of what is good for the world and they act on a sense of obligation to do something about it and to encourage others to do so as well. It is worth noting that the differences between the actions indicated above are really of two kinds. Although they are all based broadly on the premise that peace, environmental protection and the reduction of poverty are good things, they differ over the means adopted. The difference between the first group and the second group resides at least partly in whether certain means, like civil disobedience, are ethically *acceptable*. The difference between the second and third groups resides more in different views about what kinds of action are *effective* in achieving the desired changes.

There is a third kind of difference between different people each acting as world citizens, and this is more profound, since it has to do with different values or goals being pursued. Two examples will illustrate. For much of the second half of the twentieth century the world was locked in a struggle between communism and liberal democracy but there is no doubt that many of those on both sides pursuing their respective agendas against each other passionately believed that their values were right and needed to be adopted by everyone in the world (as was the case with the Crusades). Another type of conflict, which is of great importance in the modern world, is the conflict between fundamentalism and pluralism. By fundamentalism I mean here a commitment to a highly specific set of beliefs, usually religious but sometimes political, which one is committed to spreading to the rest of the world but which the rest of the world does not accept, and by pluralism I mean an approach according to which we should (within limits) accept, even welcome, diversity of cultures/beliefs/worldviews in different parts of the world, and seek to live at peace with others whilst ensuring that all have the necessary preconditions for successfully pursuing their different ways of living.

In the first case, two mutually incompatible ideologies were in conflict. In the second case, we have conflict between a certain kind of dogmatic idealism and a 'live and let live' accommodation which is based on a much more modest or limited claim about what is universally valuable for all human beings.

## 2. IMPLICATIONS FOR GLOBAL ETHICS

The above discussion of examples brings out two important points. First, anyone who sees herself as a global citizen will have some set of moral values – beliefs about what values are important in the world and what we ought to do to promote them. Second, there is a great amount of variation in the ethical views which people hold, about which values are important, what kinds of action are effective, what kinds of means are morally acceptable.

Does this mean that we cannot, after all, give an account of what global ethics underlie global citizenship? Yes and no. We certainly cannot offer an account which everyone will agree on. On the other hand, this does not mean that rational enquiry is ruled out. Whether or not we think there are 'moral' truths, we can still give our *reasons* why we think certain values are important anywhere and why we and others ought to do something about promoting them.

We should no more expect world citizens to agree on what to do or aim for than we expect ordinary citizens of a nation-state to agree on such matters. But the parallel here is instructive. First, citizens may differ about many things, and be opposed to one another on some matters, but if they are acting as citizens, they have at least some values which they share (or at least think they share with one another). Second, we need to accept that in the phrase 'world citizen' the word 'citizen' needs to say something more significant than merely standing for 'moral agent'. Whatever this institutional 'extra' is, my concern here is with the *component* of ethical commitment to some kind of global ethic.

What, then, are the elements of this global or 'cosmopolitan' ethic which underpin world or global citizenship? (I shall use 'world' and 'global' interchangeably.) We first note some core elements; and then indicate in more detail some of the great variety of positions which have been briefly indicated above and which could each constitute a different global ethic, both in respect to the theories people hold and in respect to the general norms and values promoted by them.

## 3. THE COMMON CORE

### 3(i) Global scope of responsibility

We do not merely have duties to act in accordance with the moral rules we accept; we also have a broader responsibility to promote certain values which we think to be important. Thus if I am committed to non-violence, I do not merely (try to) act non-violently, I seek to promote peace and non-violence. If I affirm human rights, I do not merely respect other rights, I may work for an organisation which defends others' rights. The key element here is the idea of active support for the community one belongs to – in this case, the global community.

### 3(ii) Attitude towards one's society/nation-state

Anyone who accepts a global ethic accepts that, in an ultimate sense, one's loyalty is to this global ethic and to the moral community it affirms. What this means in practice will depend a lot on the particular values and beliefs of individuals. Cosmopolitanism certainly does not require rejection of the values and duties of local communities or the importance of national identity. On the other hand, it has two kinds of consequence: the balance of one's duties and responsibilities towards one's local community and state and those towards the world will make some difference to what one does, and might on occasion for some bring one into conflict with what one's own state or its laws expects, as we saw in some examples above. At the very least, if one puts time, effort and money into some global cause, like alleviating world poverty, then that may well mean less time, effort and money for socially good deeds nearer to home.

One's attitude towards the assessment of one's nation's foreign policy will be significantly different from that of someone without this perspective. At the very least one will be much less likely to endorse foreign policy decisions on the grounds that they serve the 'national interest', and one will be more inclined to see the assessment of a country's relations with other countries in terms of the wider 'global good' which one's ethical theory supports.

Most global citizens would accept a further feature of their ethical thinking, outlined below.

### 3(iii) All human beings have an equal moral status.

This claim has two components: universal values and equal moral consideration. That is, whatever the important elements of human well-being are (and there may be some disagreement about what these are), these elements belong to all human beings: for example, nutrition, health, shelter, security, autonomy and so on are universally valued in any community. Others have duties to give equal consideration to these elements of well-being, and basic moral rules of societies are the essential precondition for their maintenance.

For many supporting global ethics, this fundamental moral status is expressed in terms of a claim about human *rights* – rights, that is, which we possess in virtue of our humanity (and which do not depend upon variable conventions or laws of particular communities). Corresponding to rights are duties in others to respect and support these rights.

It is because of these goods and the duty in others to respect and promote them, that a global citizen accepts her responsibility to help promote those goods (at a distance, where appropriate) and recognises that her responsibility is an extension of those basic rules of social existence. Thus, whatever moral rules are accepted as part of a social ethic, rules to do with truth-telling, non-killing or -stealing, fair treatment, kindness and so on, apply in one's dealings with any human beings. This is sometimes called the principle of 'universali-sability'. Thus, if it is wrong to deceive others, it is wrong to deceive a foreigner in my country and equally wrong for me to deceive someone in another country with whom I engage in a financial transaction. If I have obligations to help people who suffer, then, if opportunities arise for effective action, I would be somehow morally partial if I always favoured helping those in front of me or in my own country and never responded to human need in other parts of the world.

As I indicated above, this claim about the universal values, that is, universal elements of human well-being and common moral rules, is not one that would necessarily be accepted by all those accepting global citizenship. Part of the difficulty here turns on the use of the language of 'universality', which can provoke a rather negative reaction, particularly amongst those who have been influenced by postmodernism (the thesis that there is no universal discourse, since meaning, rationality and value are socially constructed), communitar-ianism (the thesis that moral values are embedded in social traditions) or relativism (the thesis that moral values vary from culture to culture).

Two reasons for this negative response are that the term 'universal' suggests, first, some set of fairly precisely stated values which may belong to a particular society but which do not belong to other societies; and second, a set of values which have been determined to be *objectively* true by a process of abstract theorising or a priori thinking. As such, it may be rejected on the grounds that any ethic so stated is one that is to be imposed on the rest of the world and is thus a kind of proselytising or cultural imperialism; this accusation has often been made about the kinds of values which have come out of Europe – both earlier Christianity and later the Enlightenment (in-cluding the idea of human rights itself). It may also be rejected on the grounds that the discourse of universal values presupposes a false view about how we come to have values. Values emerge through convention, traditions, con-sensus, negotiation within and between societies, and are not timeless truths discovered by reason.

It is of course true that, especially in the past, many who accepted a universal ethic did see it as highly specific and based on reason. But equally, the idea of values being universal *need not be* so understood. The values which are accepted as universal may only be those which form a common core accepted in any society – basic elements of human well-being, core rules for social existence and so on. Furthermore, the values which are genuinely universal, along with global responsibilities, may well come to be accepted by the convergence of interests and processes of negotiation.

A global ethic, then, may be seen not so much as something to be discovered by ethical reflection on first principles, but as something to be constructed or created by agreement, negotiation and dialogue. Under the conditions of the modern world, with its common problems and threats, a set of common shared principles and norms need to be worked out for the mutual advantage of all peoples. In many ways this can be seen as reflecting a form of communitarianism which sees the development of a global community as precisely what is happening in the modern world (see, for example, Thompson 1992). At a more practical level we can see the Parliament of the World's Religions and Hans Küng's Global Ethics Foundation as engaged in the project of fashioning a 'global ethic' as a code which has force because it has been widely accepted (Küng and Kuschel 1993b).

Perhaps, then, hesitation about seeing what I indicated under 3(iii) as part of the definition of the global ethic element of global citizenship is based on a misunderstanding of 'universality'. My task here has not been to assess the plausibility of these ways of thinking of ethics but rather to indicate why I think that, even if one adopts them, one can still think in terms of universal values. But it remains, whatever I suggest, a sensitive issue amongst those who discuss the nature or possibility of a world ethic. At any rate, it is difficult for anyone who says he is a world citizen not to accept at least that certain things *matter* in other parts of the world, and in mattering *matter to him*, and that this is the basis for being committed to action for the sake of what matters.

## 4. VARIETIES OF GLOBAL ETHICS

There are great differences between global ethics, both in terms of the theories underlying them and in terms of the values which are promoted. Many of the differences in theory will emerge depending on whether someone adopts an essentially religious or theological understanding of human beings and the world or adopts some kind of secular account. There will, of course, be differences *between* religious beliefs as well as difference between different secular theories. A few of the latter approaches are briefly discussed below.

### 4(i) Consequentialism/Utilitarianism

Utilitarianism is the best known of the consequentialist theories. Consequentialism is the view that the rightness of action is determined by consequences. In its classical form, as expounded by Bentham and Mill, it was understood in terms of the maximisation of happiness. Happiness itself was understood hedonistically as pleasure. There are many variations, and later theories understand the good to be promoted in other ways. But at the heart of the theory is the promotion of the best balance of good over bad. One of the most attractive features of Utilitarianism is its global reach. 'Everybody to count for one, nobody for more than one' (Bentham quoted in Mill 1962: ch. 5). Theoretically, the theory sees all human beings as in principle equally relevant or 'morally considerable' for ethical decision-making. What is crucial is whether one's action may affect the well-being of any other human beings (or, more generally, sentient beings), however distant in space or time. Membership of one's community or state is not the determining factor. Utility is no respecter of borders. Bentham himself was very interested in this dimension and his advocacy of international law was based on his belief – surely, in general, correct – that its strengthening would lead to greater human happiness. A good example of this approach is Peter Singer's application of Utilitarian reasoning to the alleviation of world poverty: 'If it is in our power to prevent something very bad happening without thereby sacrificing anything of comparable moral importance, we ought to do it' (Singer 1979: ch. 8).

### 4(ii) Kantianism

The label 'Kantian' is often used as a way of describing a general approach inspired by the writing of the great eighteenth-century German philosopher Immanuel Kant. The fundamental feature of this approach is the idea of all human beings standing in an ethical relationship to one another on the basis of their being fellow rational beings or 'persons'. As rational beings we are required to act on certain principles (not based on consequences) in relation to fellow human beings.

Kant saw moral duties as the demands of our 'practical reason' – that is, as 'categorical' demands or 'imperatives'. A categorical demand is contrasted with 'hypothetical' imperatives because whereas the latter are based on desire and on what reason requires us to do to get what we *desire*, the former as a demand of duty is simply something we are rationally required to do, whether we want to do it or not. He formulated this categorical imperative in several ways, including:

> Formula of universal law (universalisability): act on that maxim which you can will to be universal law.

> Formula of ends: so act that you always treat humanity, whether in yourself or in other persons, as an end and not merely as a means. (Kant 1949: 88 and 96).

We can illustrate this if we consider the case of a lying promise, and more generally coercive and deceitful behaviour. To act on the maxim of making a lying promise to get out of some difficulty is to act on a maxim which cannot be universalised (since communication would be unintelligible) and is therefore contrary to practical reason and wrong. Likewise, if one makes a lying promise to someone, one fails to treat her as a rational pursuer of ends (because to respect her would be to give her a *true* not a *false* picture of the world) but rather to treat her merely as means to one's own ends. The point here is that any human being as a rational agent is the object of respect/concern, and what is universalised is behaviour to be performed by any rational being. The framework is clearly global in conception. Indeed Kant's vision was one of a global ethical order or what he called a 'kingdom of ends'.

Kant also developed an impressive account of the normative basis of international relations (Kant 1949; Kant 1970; Dower 1998). His views were progressive and challenged any 'realist' interpretations of international relations. Other recent writers in the Kantian tradition like Onora O'Neill see Kant's theory giving rise to a radical critique of state practices, and as underpinning a more radical demand for social justice (O'Neill 1989: ch. 7–8). She makes much of the principles of non-deception and non-coercion, which apply as much to the actions of corporate agents such as nation-states or business companies, and also of what she calls the principle of 'material justice' – that we are morally required to come to the aid of those whose material need undermines the development of their rational autonomy.

## 4(iii) Human Rights

If all human beings have certain rights in virtue of their human nature (and rights are not all socially constituted or formed), then this universal framework provides a firm basis for cosmopolitan obligations to respect and further them. There are various theories which ground these rights (notably, but not only, natural law/rights theories).

A human right is a right attributed to a human being as a human being; and a right asserted to exist on the basis of a moral theory or moral reasoning. Feinberg states: 'I shall define "human rights" to be generically moral rights of a fundamentally important kind held equally by all human beings unconditionally and unalterably' (Feinberg 1973: 85). Thus a human right is contrasted to a legal or conventional right which exists in virtue of the laws and conventions of a given society. People have conventional rights as members of a legal community, not as human beings. Even an international declaration like the United Nations' *Universal Declaration of Human Rights* (1948) neither establishes the existence of human rights nor limits what are, ethically, human rights. For instance, a right to conscientious refusal to join the army may be a human right before it is encoded in international law. (Of course, the presence of a right in international law contributes towards its being part of a world ethic qua global social reality.)

A human right exists by virtue of a universal moral theory which postulates the whole world as one moral sphere or community. As Vincent says: 'it is at the level at which what is appealed to is not any kind of positive law, but what ought by some rational calculation to prevail' that the justification of human rights is sought (Vincent 1986: 11). Amongst the approaches are theories such as the natural rights tradition, global contract theory and a rational construction of morality theory such as Gewirth's (Gewirth 1978). A theory of human rights is therefore opposed to any form of cultural relativism which denies universally applicable values.

We should note a distinction here between human rights as (part of) a theory held by a thinker or his 'source' story about the nature of global ethics, and as something established by consensus (of many people throughout the world, though not necessarily all) and supported by diverse ethical theories. Thus many ethical theories can support the existence of internationally agreed rights in instruments such as the *Universal Declaration of Human Rights*.

What kind of cosmopolitan theory we get from the assertion of human rights will depend upon a number of factors but most notably, at the level of theory, upon what rights are asserted and what the nature and extent are of the correlative duties. Traditionally a distinction has been drawn between negative rights (liberty rights, rights of action) and positive rights (socio-economic rights of recipience). Broadly negative rights are rights to be free from certain kinds of interference or harm, and positive rights are rights to receive some benefit if one has not got it. The duties corresponding to these are duties to refrain from certain kinds of action (not to restrict someone's liberty, not to steal, not to attack other persons) and duties to engage in certain kinds of positive action (help or intervention) respectively. As O'Neill points out, it makes a big difference to the kind of global ethic one has whether one stresses liberty rights or one stresses 'welfare' rights (O'Neill 1993). If one stress the latter then the duties of others across the world to provide the conditions for welfare could be potentially enormous.

### 4(iv) Comment on these theories

All the above theories share two characteristics: first, that they are generally presented as *theoretical* in the sense that they appeal to first principles which are worked out or accepted by a theorist and do not depend upon what is accepted by others; second, they are essentially human-centred, in that it is human well-being which is of central, if not exclusive, concern (for many Utilitarians, the extension to higher animals as bearers of sentience is made). Third, they are in explicit form *secular*, making no explicit reference to religious assumptions.

Whilst it is true that these theories have tended to be put forward as 'objective' theories, there is no necessity that the *content* of them has to be justified in this way. Utility and respect for persons could well be seen as values which are consensual or negotiated by agreements, and as I have already indicated, human rights are often thought of as a public discourse, support for which could come from a variety of theoretical starting points. Whilst these theories are secular in content, they are not anti-religious, and indeed religious premises may well support the acceptance of one or other of these normative approaches. This is not to deny that religious ethics may also be quite distinct from these.

Environmental concerns can, of course, be built on the basis of the above theories, and would as such be anthropocentric in form – that is, based on human interests. However, many forms of environmental ethics extend the boundaries of what is called the 'morally considerable' to include non-human life, whether sentient or not, and to include not just the well-being of individual living things but the value of species, ecosystems or the 'biotic community'. Thus famously Aldo Leopold advocated the following principle: 'A thing is right when it tends to promote the integrity, stability and beauty of the biotic community. It is wrong if it tends otherwise' (Leopold 1949). Environmental ethics then constitute a very rich mine of ethical approaches which are global in form, and which this brief discussion hardly does justice to.

## 5. WHAT GLOBAL NORMS?

Even if global citizens disagree about their theories, they may still agree on what global goals are worth promoting. A Christian and a humanist may both campaign for the right not to be tortured; Marxists and liberals may both campaign for debt relief; a Kantian and a biocentric environmentalist may still have common cause to preserve an area of natural beauty. On the other hand, whatever theories people espouse, there may be significant differences in practical goals even if one's theories are similar (because everyone has a different factual understanding of the world). Thus two people could have very different views about the ethics of aid, if one thought aid generally worked and the other that it did not. Some real differences between global ethics as sets of important norms are set out below.

### 5(i) Fundamentalism

First there are fundamentalisms of various kinds, religious and political: adherents may have clearly defined sets of values which they seek to impose on the rest of the world. Here there is a danger of various kind of conflicts, including wars. Often the suspicion of global ethics (and hence global citizenship as part of it) is that there is a danger that someone who is committed to it will be guilty of intolerance and cultural imperialism, as noted earlier.

### 5(ii) Libertarianism

One modern reaction to the above has been to advocate a rather different kind of morality in which liberty is stressed, particularly economic liberty underpinning, for instance, the global free market, but also the importance of liberty for individuals and cultural groups to choose their own 'conceptions of the good' or ways of life. This model has become in the modern world the dominant model and arguably suffers from two defects. First, in practice, if not in theory, it tends to promote a Western conception of the good life and is therefore insufficiently sensitive to cultural differences; second, it hardly puts enough emphasis upon the idea of responsibility for responding to suffering and conditions generally which undermine human well-being. This suggests a third model which I believe is emerging as a more attractive middle position between the other two.

### 5(iii) Multicultural responsibility or solidarist-pluralism

This is the idea of there being a responsibility to promote the conditions of human flourishing and basic rights but at the same time there also being a responsibility to respect diversity of belief and practice within and between societies. This is the idea of a multicultural world based on *solidarity* between people for creating the conditions for flourishing within it. If this is the right ethical framework, then arguably global citizenship at its best will be the commitment to working for such a world (Dower 1998).

---

QUESTIONS

1. 'We are global citizens with tribal souls.' Do you accept this or reject this?
2. Are rights or duties more important to your conception of being a global citizen?
3. Which values would be important in a global ethic that you would support?
4. Is it important that a global ethic is expressed though publicly agreed documents like the *Declaration Toward a Global Ethic* (Parliament of the World's Religions 1993)?

---

# 12. GLOBAL JUSTICE, GLOBAL INSTITUTIONS AND GLOBAL CITIZENSHIP

## Christien van den Anker

### INTRODUCTION

A debate on global justice, global institutions and global citizenship is especially relevant at the present moment. The context of the end of the Cold War, the contested process of economic, political and social-cultural globalisation and changing relationships between citizens and their governments within nation-states provide a background to the present debate. For some time optimism has been expressed about the growing sense of global responsibility that is shown by both the international community and by global civil society. Examples often mentioned are the increased willingness of states to contribute to international intervention and punishment in cases of human rights violations and international regime-building to cope with global environmental change. Some view these developments as indicators of a form of global citizenship developing, whereas others see them merely as an illustration of the need to develop stronger global institutions.

Political theory and especially theories of justice are needed to develop moral perspectives and just policies in response to a changing world, yet the changes in the world today pose new challenges to theories, too. Therefore, this chapter reflects on the accounts of global citizenship implied by recent theories of global distributive justice and puts forward an analysis of the present state of global citizenship and some normative arguments regarding global citizenship as required by cosmopolitan principles of global justice.

The chapter is structured in the following way. The first section outlines the main theories of global justice coming out of the Rawlsian debate on distributive justice. In the second section the institutional implications of these theories of global justice are discussed and in the third section they are linked to a discussion of conceptions of global citizenship. In conclusion it is suggested that although we are not global citizens institutionally yet, we are global citizens in a moral sense and therefore we have an obligation to build global institutions that are effective in implementing the duties created by global principles of distributive justice. Those institutions should be accountable and based on democratic participation. This conception therefore differs from a traditional notion of citizenship linked to the government of a nation-state in at least two important respects. First, in the context of a nation-state citizenship is based on legal rights and duties instead of on moral norms only; and second, solidarity is mainly focused on fellow citizens of one state instead of humanity at large.

## COSMOPOLITAN VIEWS OF GLOBAL JUSTICE

Recent debates on distributive justice have their origin in the publication of John Rawls' *A Theory of Justice* in 1972. The scope of justice in this debate was one nation-state. The boundaries of the nation-state were implicitly considered to be the boundaries of principles of distributive justice. The debate focused on the content of the principles as defended by Rawls and on the method of deriving those principles as the right ones for a Western democratic society (Kukathas and Petit 1990; Daniels 1974; Barry 1973).

The Rawlsian framework for a theory of justice proposed to use a hypothetical 'Original Position', where the principles of justice for the basic institutions of society were chosen under circumstances of rough equality and risk aversion. The people in the Original Position were assumed to be under a veil of ignorance, which hid their knowledge of their social status in life from them. According to Rawls, people would choose a principle of equal liberty with all positions open to all and, second, a principle that would distribute benefits and burdens equally to all, unless inequalities could be justified on the grounds that they were to the advantage of the worst off in society. Implicitly, Rawls relied on a theory of trickle down of wealth, in the sense that he foresees that inequalities will be justified on those grounds. Talented people need incentives to remain economically active in society and it would be to the advantage of the worst off, according to him, to provide those incentives. Egalitarians have criticised this position, arguing that wealth may not trickle down automatically and incentives could be given in ways other than monetary rewards (Baker 1987). Further criticisms ranged from external critics disagreeing with an abstract derivation of principles of justice unrelated to the specific traditions of a particular community to internal critics arguing for variations in the specification of the Original Position (Mulhall and Swift 1992; Kukathas and Petit 1990).

Some of the critics of Rawls' theory of justice noted that the method used by Rawls was useful and his principles were valid but that the scope of justice as limited to one nation-state was too restrictive. Especially in the light of concerns over increasing global poverty and inequality, a theory with a wider scope was required. Beitz, Pogge and Barry developed theories of justice with a global scope, partly developing and extending Rawlsian ideas, partly as a criticism of Rawls (Beitz 1979; 1983; 1999; Pogge 1989; 1992; 1998; Barry 1995).

In the context of this chapter it will not be possible to analyse the wide variety of recent theories of global justice in detail. As Charles Beitz has noted: 'International liberalism is at an early stage compared with the more familiar liberalism of the territorial state. But [. . .] there is evidence of progress in both the richness and the diversity of recent liberal thought about the distributional aspects of international relations' (Beitz 1999: 292). In addition, there are now many publications on global justice from other backgrounds than liberalism, too (for example, Lensu 2000).

In his *A Theory of Justice*, Rawls commented on the issue of international justice and stated that what was needed was a second original position of representatives of states to choose principles of international justice (Rawls 1972). However, this method was criticised by two authors who were to set the terms of debate for a long time to come. Beitz and Pogge each developed their own theories of international justice based on a Rawlsian framework but altered to such an extent that the principles of justice defended were quite different to Rawls'.

Beitz originally based his theory on the growing interdependence in the world economy (Beitz 1979). The form this global interaction has taken led, according to Beitz, to a strong argument for global duties of redistribution. He argued that since nation-states are no longer self-contained (as Rawls assumed in his theory) justice becomes a global matter and cannot be coherently theorised within models of one society.

> . . . [I]f evidence of global economic and political interdependence shows the existence of a global scheme of social co-operation, we should not view national boundaries as having fundamental moral significance. Since boundaries are not co-extensive with the scope of social co-operation, they do not make the limits of social obligations. Thus, the parties to the Original Position cannot be assumed to know that they are members of a particular national society, choosing principles of justice for that society. The veil of ignorance must extend to all matters of national citizenship. (Beitz 1985: 298)

In addition to matters of national citizenship being part of the veil of ignorance, Beitz also argued that the distribution of natural resources between states is arbitrary from a moral point of view. Therefore Beitz concluded that these are two good reasons why the Rawlsian principles should apply globally.

Critics have pointed out that global interdependence cannot be the basis for principles of global justice. There are two arguments here: one of a methodological nature and one empirical (van den Anker 1999). The methodological argument holds that principles of justice are universal in both time and space and cannot therefore be dependent on the empirical fact of globalisation or growing interdependence. This is sometimes argued by strictly Kantian positions. The empirical argument holds that, despite growing interdependence, there is also growing fragmentation and increasing reliance upon particularistic points of view that lead to conflict. For example, Brown argues that a sense of obligation towards people across borders is not 'something that can be expected to emerge simply as a result of individuals and peoples coming to have more contact with one another, because such contact need not generate the essentially moral consciousness of common identity that is required' (Brown 1995a: 94). Although this empirical argument can be answered by arguing that if the necessary moral motivation is not present yet, the fact of interdependence could still justify moral obligations, Beitz has revised his argument and relies in his later work on a notion of human equality to justify principles of global justice (Beitz 1983).

Pogge arrives at similar conclusions to Beitz but his theory is different in important respects (Pogge 1989; 1994; 1998). He gives an interpretation of the Rawlsian framework whereby he argues that Rawls would be committed to a global scope of justice if he took his own starting point of taking people to be free and equal moral beings seriously. Pogge therefore holds that justice is owed across borders and he would defend that position even if we lived in a world of isolated nation-states. In Pogge's view a global Original Position would arrive at a principle for the compensation of having a lesser share of natural resources than other countries. Yet we live in an interdependent world and this fact makes it even clearer, according to Pogge, that justice ought to be approached globally. The global Original Position would make the position of the globally worst off a central concern.

Barry argues for a theory of justice as impartiality with a global scope (Barry 1989; 1995). The main argument is that, given the motivation of all people to justify their behaviour to others, agreement can be reached on principles of justice by looking for those principles that cannot be reasonably rejected by others. This theory has the advantage that there is no need for a complicated argument specifying the Original Position. It also moves beyond the Rawlsian assumption that justice becomes an issue only in situations where people cooperate for mutual advantage. Therefore, in Barry's theory the existence of a global system of cooperation does not have to be shown for principles of global justice to be valid.

An important criticism of cosmopolitan theories of justice is put forward by the position of liberal-nationalism. This position holds that the duties generated by global principles of justice cannot be realised without jeopardising the obligations people have towards their fellow citizens within a nation-state (Miller 1995; Tamir 1993). Since the ties with fellow nationals are very important to people, they argue, people ought to be allowed to prioritise them over helping others outside the nation-state. In addition, the kind of solidarity present in a national scheme of redistribution is simply not available on a global scale, according to Miller. Although the balance between duties on different levels is an important issue to be the focus of further research, the immediate answer to the nationalist objection to cosmopolitan theories of justice is that moral motivation may need to be developed. But the lack of this motivation cannot in itself be an argument against the justice of the principles proposed (Freeman 1994).

## INSTITUTIONAL IMPLICATIONS OF THEORIES OF GLOBAL JUSTICE

Theories of global justice vary with respect to their position on global political and economic institutions. Some cosmopolitans argue for some form of world government or supranational institutions instead of the present system of sovereign nation-states. However, other cosmopolitan theories focus on the principles underlying institutional arrangements rather than institutions themselves. This moral cosmopolitanism does not necessarily adhere to some form of political cosmopolitanism (Pogge 1992: 49).

A second important general point regarding cosmopolitan theories of justice and political institutions is that a theory of justice does not necessarily link up with one specific form of institution. There is room for a plurality of institutional forms within the scope of the principles of justice as defined. This means that rather than prescribing institutional arrangements, theories of justice can be used to restrict the range of institutional set-ups that are considered to be just (Follesdal 2000a).

Institutions can be understood in several ways. Some people would define institutions as all rules and social practices present in a social system. Although this can be useful in other contexts, in this chapter institutions are defined as those bodies that can enforce rules. This means that a national government is taken to be an institution, as well as subnational institutions like the church or a school system and supranational institutions like the United Nations or the World Bank and the International Monetary Fund (IMF). However, the social practice of greeting one's neighbours is not included nor the social practice of providing development aid. In the context of global justice it is important to make a sharp distinction between the enforcement of principles of justice by institutions and the encouragement of social practices such as giving to charities and other matters in the domain of personal morality. Even when recognising the importance of a flourishing civil society and an active attitude of citizens, justice must be backed up by a set of political and economic institutions with the power to enforce. However, enforcement need not be based on violence or the threat of violence; there is an important role to be played in the enforcement of international law by social norms, diplomacy, public pressure or trade sanctions, for example. This is analogue to the enforcement of national laws as only partially based on the state's monopoly of violence and to a larger extent on the socialisation of people into the law-abiding behaviour they generally show in a democracy.

Institutional prescriptions vary from one cosmopolitan theory to another. According to Rawls' *The Law of Peoples*, international law should not go beyond the existing arrangements protecting sovereignty and a strong principle of non-intervention (Rawls 1993a; 2000). Others defend some form of global taxation, generating resources to be redistributed to poor people (not necessarily via their national governments). Beitz, for example, defends a global difference principle and a natural resources fund. Pogge argues for a global resources dividend and Barry would ideally like to see global progressive taxation and reform of the United Nations. In order to implement any of these proposals, some institutions of global governance need to be created that would have the responsibility for the taxation and redistribution on a global scale.

Some theorists have proposed to establish a cosmopolitan democracy. One of the most well-known advocates of such a project is David Held. His argument is based on the idea that in the present global order there is increasingly less symmetry between the effects of a policy and the people included in the forum of decision-making. In other words, decisions by one jurisdiction increasingly influence people outside that jurisdiction. In order to restore the symmetry between the decision-makers and those affected by the decisions, Held argues for several changes to the present system of political decision-making. He calls, for instance, for a new Charter of Rights and Obligations, a Global Parliament with limited revenue-raising capacity and an interconnected global legal system, including an international criminal court (Held 1995a: 279).

Other recent proposals for global democracy and global governance have been put forward in the context of the United Nations. The United Nations Development Programme (UNDP) in its 1999 *Human Development Report* argues for several long-term proposals, such as a stronger and more coherent United Nations including a two-chamber general assembly to allow for civil society representation, a global central bank, a World Trade Organisation with a mandate extending to global competition policy with anti-trust provisions and a code of conduct for multinational corporations, a world environmental agency, a world investment trust with redistributive functions and an international criminal court with a broader mandate for human rights (UNDP 1999).

It could be argued that cosmopolitan democracy is needed to implement principles of global justice. To make the proposals of Pogge, Beitz and Barry feasible, it is clear that the present institutions will not suffice. More importantly, these proposals show that there is an urgent need to rethink global institutions beyond the traditional terms of debate on global government. Falk's world orders project is relevant in this respect but more generally the increasingly interdisciplinary debate between international relations, international law and political theory is promising (Falk 1987).

One of the dilemmas in the proposals for cosmopolitan democracy is the place of sovereignty. On the one side, current international law is built on sovereign states making agreements voluntarily. On the other side, a global government would impose rules even if they were decided upon democratically. In the middle, for fear of authoritarianism, global governance is commonly preferred over global government. The task of the advocates of cosmopolitan democracy is to show how their proposals avoid the possible lack of accountability of global government and the lack of adequate provision of binding norms and enforcement mechanisms of the current system.

International law creates binding norms through treaties or through customary law. Since non-binding declarations of rights may take a long time to become part of customary law and the content of customary law is contested between international lawyers, in order to create global justice global institutions of governance may need to have more authority than in the present system. For example, the United Nations' *Universal Declaration of Human Rights* of 1948 contains only a few rights that are widely considered to be binding and cannot be derogated from under any circumstances: the right to life, the prohibition of slavery, the prohibition of torture and the prohibition of retroactive legislation. Other rights that cannot be derogated from but are not binding are freedom of religion and the right to be a person under the law. Rights that can be derogated from but are binding under customary law are the right to be presumed innocent and the prohibition of arbitrary detention (van den Anker 1990: 57). This list of rights is too short from the perspective of global justice and it does not include any of the social rights protected under international law. Moreover, international law in its present form suffers from lack of enforcement mechanisms. These problems would need to be overcome by a new system of global governance based on principles of global justice.

Kaldor has suggested that horizontal institutions would overcome the above dilemma. Horizontal institutions have a degree of sovereignty so they can interfere with the behaviour of nation-states. Kaldor envisages horizontal institutions as based on democratic principles and not relying on some external threat for legitimacy. This means that (i) their field of competence needs to be defined; (ii) as many decisions as possible are taken by the smallest political unit (subsidiarity); and (iii) they have to be open and accountable to public opinion. In order to implement this, those new institutions need to have enabling mechanisms that essentially provide the conditions through which local institutions can solve problems. In addition, a horizontal network of non-governmental organisations should be developed that can engage with international institutions (Kaldor 1998). In the context of global institutions, a similar case could be made.

Finally, the debate on global institutions implementing principles of justice could look into suggestions of non-territorial citizenship. This would have significant effects on migration and the status of refugees and asylum-seekers, as well as on people who are presently stateless.

## GLOBAL CITIZENSHIP: LEGAL RIGHTS OR MORAL DUTIES?

Citizenship is traditionally understood as membership of a nation-state. Although citizenship existed in the ancient Greek city-states, who already debated notions of cosmopolitan citizenship, women and slaves were excluded. Historically, modern notions of equal citizenship have their origin in the process of building sovereign nation-states. Initially, the emphasis of citizenship was on the struggle for formal rights such as the right to be a subject under the law (important for the right to ownership and access to adjudication in conflict) and the right to political participation. Again women, poorer men and slaves were excluded for a long time and had their rights recognised much later than tax-paying men. Later still, in the period of industrialisation, claims for social rights were made. Collective struggle resulted in the right to union organisation and a social minimum guaranteed by the state. This whole process has led to our main identification of citizenship with the context of the state, rather than with units on other levels of politics. It also resulted in the identification of citizenship with legal rights. At present this conceptualisation of citizenship can still be observed in debates over citizenship rights for immigrants. Citizenship is linked with obtaining the nationality of the country of residence and sharing full and equal rights with the 'original' citizens.

More recently the duties linked with citizenship have been a focus of debate. For immigrants this requires some level of integration and for 'traditional' citizens it requires active participation in the moral and political culture of society.

In recent debates on citizenship this conceptualisation of citizenship as a set of national rights and duties has been challenged in several ways. Linklater, for example, has identified a new characteristic of citizenship in recent times. Although traditionally the struggle for rights and justice took place mainly within national boundaries, increasingly there are 'global citizens' as part of a global civil society fighting for justice independent of the boundaries between states (Linklater 1992). Human rights organisations are an obvious example. Others have challenged the national conception of citizenship by pointing at the development of supranational identities such as the European one. One could conceive of a European citizenship whereas there is (as yet) no European central government (Lehning and Weale 1997). This illustrates that the possibility of a global citizenship is not as far-fetched as it was once regarded to be, since there is no necessary link between the defence of a global government and global citizenship anymore.

So how could we conceptualise global citizenship in the present? At this moment in time there is no global government but there are global institutions that together generate a set of regimes of global governance. Examples are the human rights regimes in the United Nations and the Council of Europe. The way in which citizens globally interact with those institutions (for example, through non-governmental organisations (NGOs) with consultative status) could be seen as a form of global citizenship. There are many different NGOs that are working towards justice globally and lobby the IMF, the World Bank, the United Nations and the World Trade Organisation, amongst others. Some have argued that this global concern of an increasing number of people is a form of global citizenship. The major demonstrations in Seattle and Geneva to protest unfettered economic globalisation can also be seen as an expression of a sense of global citizenship.

However, there are conceptions of global citizenship that broaden the notion of citizenship so far that we may not recognise any of the central elements of the traditional conceptions of citizenship at all. For example, it is sometimes argued that the development of a sense of justice that includes people across national borders in the present institutional set-up is already a meaningful form of global citizenship (Dower 2000). This means that institutional change is not required for global citizenship to become relevant. Although such a sense of responsibility across borders may be conducive to developing notions of global citizenship, the meaning of citizenship is stretched too far if these sentiments and the actions they motivate are seen as indications of global citizenship existing. Such a broad notion of citizenship confuses the debate. Citizenship is related to political institutions if it adds anything to the duties fellow humans feel and act upon towards one another. We can then distinguish clearly between global ethics as based on common humanity and global citizenship as requiring some form of shared political institutions and governance.

How does global citizenship relate to global distributive justice? There is a link between citizenship, democracy and social justice on the national level (Held 1991). The state has been portrayed as the most powerful actor to tame the forces of private capitalism. Yet people also need protection from the state violating their human rights. Citizenship combines both elements. It relies on democratic participation and equal formal rights as well as on a notion of social justice. Once social justice comes in, we move beyond the model of liberal citizenship as formal equal rights towards the role of the state as redistributor. There is a parallel development internationally, with civil and political rights being accepted more readily as human rights than economic, social and cultural rights. However, at present the latter category of rights has an official equal standing to the former and in practice social rights are more emphasised internationally. Claims for global justice are phrased in terms of both political freedom and social protection.

Interestingly, the struggle for global citizenship has not started with claims for democratic participation, although the human rights doctrine places stronger emphasis on liberty than on equality. Democratic participation is often still seen as an issue on the level of nation-states, although recent protests have emphasised the undemocratic nature of decision-making in international organisations and in the international community as a whole.

What kind of political institutions are required for a complete account of global citizenship? A new model of global citizenship would not require the existence of a global state but of a global community that provides protection against the overwhelming power of the nation-state to its own citizens and the power of multinational corporations over people's lives. A model of global citizenship involving protection by global institutions implementing global principles of justice can be seen in parallel to the national model: protection from the state in the form of universal human rights and protection from full-blown liberal market capitalism by a scheme of redistribution worldwide. Then the global community could also play a role as the 'redistributor' of resources. It alone is said to be powerful enough to tame global capital. In such a model people would be global citizens with rights and duties parallel to rights of citizenship as we know them from the national cases.

Finally, it is sometimes objected that global governance does not exist in relevant forms for global citizenship to become meaningful. However, in the tradition of moral and political theory concerned with issues of justice, it is not necessary to have the right type of institutions yet, since they can be an aim to work towards. Questions of political feasibility and of motivation need to be resolved but the construction of a viable theory of justice which can be used in conceptualising these changes is very useful in itself and necessary for the first stage. New institutions need to be imagined before people can be attracted to them by a political strategy.

## CONCLUSION

The main argument in this chapter aimed to show that theories of global justice make a case for global institutions of a democratic nature which would create a form of global citizenship. At this moment in time this form of global citizenship does not exist yet, although there is a large and increasing group of people who already take their role as future global citizens seriously in their actions to influence global institutions and multinational companies. This fight for justice through non-governmental organisations, however, cannot substitute a full global citizenship where individual people have rights and duties globally. These would include rights to democratic participation in global decision-making and duties to contribute resources to a fund for global redistribution. This does not necessarily mean that the way forward is to create a global government. As this chapter has shown, global governance can be a valuable alternative, although accountability can only be achieved through active participation of all and not through non-representative non-governmental organisations. The risk of non-governmental organisations as representatives of global citizens is that existing power structures are reflected in their membership. There must be participation by and accountability to the people with least power in global decision-making. This needs an institutional safeguard that is the democratic participation of all.

One objection to this way of imagining a fully inclusive global citizenship might be that it relies on the model of national citizenship too much. It still links citizenship to a state-like institution on a global scale. However, this is not necessarily the case. Interesting proposals have been made for thinking about citizenship in non-territorial ways. Democratic representation may take place on the basis of non-territorial constitutions. However, the detailed development of such a proposal falls outside the scope of this chapter. Another innovation that would be interesting to follow up is the idea that democratic representation does not necessarily mean copying the current system of party representation. A new model of leadership and accountability could take care of some of the problems of scale of a global democracy. Unfortunately, the development of such an innovative approach also falls outside the scope of this chapter.

Therefore, global citizenship should mean that people show their sense of justice and responsibility to care for all other human beings anywhere in the world; but it also has a component of accountability of global decision-making and a component of duties to contribute to global redistribution.

---

## QUESTIONS

1. Do you think that justice is a concept that should apply globally?
2. Does justice depend on equal citizenship rights nationally? And globally?
3. Would you find a theory of justice more attractive if it concentrated on duties or on rights?
4. Is your conception of citizenship more focused on duties or on rights?
5. Does global citizenship depend on global institutions, such as a global government?
6. What do you think motivates people to feel a duty towards people who are not their fellow citizens? Would global citizenship motivate more people to feel a duty beyond their fellow nationals?
7. Are you active yourself in changing the world? If so, what motivates you? If not at all, then why not?
8. Do you feel you are a global citizen?

---

# 13. GLOBAL CITIZENSHIP AND COMMON VALUES

## Sabina Alkire

### INTRODUCTION

Imagine that you are told tomorrow an exchange student is coming to your house to live in the room next to yours for three weeks. The purpose of her visit is not to learn English – let's presume that her native language is English. Rather, she is coming to learn about British culture. She has never left her country before. You have not visited her country either – in fact, if we're perfectly honest about the matter, you are not quite sure where it is. It's not America or Australia but is apparently some remote island that escaped being colonised because it was in dangerous waters. You have no clue why they speak English but presume there must be a shipwreck and love story involved somewhere along the way.

Now what do you do to prepare for her? What thoughts and questions flit through your mind? Perhaps you go to buy in some food for her first dinner and wonder vaguely what she likes to eat, if any foods are forbidden by her religion – if she has a religion. Your grandmother telephones and tells you to put a lock on your door. You tell her not to be ridiculous, then put the phone down, have a cup of tea and go buy the lock. Your housemates wonder if she will be pretty and if she can dance and if she will help you all to do the garden next week. There is a formal dinner for your cricket team next week and you sign her down as your guest – then wonder uneasily whether she has brought along a dress and realise you have no clue what she might be wearing. There are *so many* uncertainties – about what she is like, about her habits and her prejudices. You don't know what you might have let yourself in for!

Clearly there are terribly many strong questions about your new arrival. You know that there will be differences between your cultures but you do not know how deep they will be. Or do you?

This chapter will study the problem of common values in society. It will ask what evidence there is that common values exist at all. It will discuss what values, if any, could be 'universal' and what does that mean when we are also weak-willed people who fail to live up even to our own values. And it will discuss how different groups of people could suggest, modify and reflect on a proposed set of 'core values' for global citizenship. The focus will be on foundational issues rather than on proposing particular core values.

## 1. WHAT WE HAVE IN COMMON: EMPIRICAL EVIDENCE

What evidence exists that there may be universal values? Some 'evidence' you might pick up by reflecting on your interaction with the exchange student. For example, suppose that she asks you, the morning of her second day, why people grasp hands with her when they see her. She says that she finds this intimidating and is baffled as to what on earth it means. You explain that a handshake is a form of greeting. She asks why you need to do this. That takes a bit more thought – her question reminds you vaguely of your two-year-old nephew. Finally you say that people shake hands as a sign of recognition. It's not friendship yet – but it (usually) expresses a kind of human warmth and acknowledgement of another person that is a sort of dilute kind of friendship. Your answer sounds awkward and self-conscious. But when you explain these reasons, she breathes a sigh of relief and says she understands.

Now if the above example is plausible, you have stumbled across some evidence for universal values, which is that the mere intelligibility of other cultures – the ability of one person or group to explain itself to another – could not happen if your values were so different that when you mentioned the concept 'friendship' you got a blank stare. Rather, she *already* understood friendship or sociability – from her own experience or from some other person or source. And so when you gave friendship as a reason for shaking hands, although she might think it was an odd way of going about expressing oneself, she would understand your explanation and so begin to enlarge her understanding of British culture.

However, this example is rather narrow. There are a number of more systematic inquiries into universal values and a few are quite large. For example, consider one of the biggest empirical tests of universal values, that has been done to date, which is the work of Shalom Schwartz.

Shalom Schwartz, a professor of psychology in Jerusalem, has proposed and revised a 'theory of the universal content and structure of human values' based on empirical cross-cultural research. This theory covers 'the substantive content' of values; the 'comprehensiveness' of the values; whether the values have an equivalent meaning across groups of people; and whether there is a meaningful and identifiable structure of relations among different values internationally.

Schwartz defines universal values as 'desirable transsituational goals, varying in importance, that serve as guiding principles in the life of a person or other social entity. Implicit in this definition of values as goals is that (i) they serve the interests of some social entity, (ii) they can motivate action, giving it direction and emotional intensity, (iii) they function as standards for judging and justifying action, and (iv) they are acquired both through socialisation to dominant group values and through the unique learning experiences of individuals' (Schwartz 1994: 21).[1] There is much more to Schwartz's theory, of course. But what is of interest to us is his evidence. First, how did he collect it?

If Schwartz came to this class today to test your universal values, you would be handed a sheet of paper with a list of 56 potential values.[2] Each value is described by a couple of phrases. First, you would be asked to read through the list and choose which value is most important to you, and which is least. You would assign the number 7 to the most important; 1 to the least. Then you would go through all of the 56 items and rate how each value fares 'as a guiding principle in my life' on a scale from minus 1 to 7.[3]

Schwartz has done this test in different countries (in all inhabited continents), regions, religions and language groups. Altogether he has done about 200 surveys in 64 countries involving well over 60,000 respondents.[4] In some country tests, Shalom went to university campuses and had students fill out his questionnaire. But his data also includes 13 near-representative[5] national samples and eight samples using adolescents. Schwartz then analyses people's responses to see whether or not people do have significant values in the same different areas and what these areas are.

Schwartz suggests that the data identify the following comprehensive[6] set of universal values:

---

- **Power** (social status and prestige, control or dominance over people and resources)
- **Achievement** (personal success through demonstrating competence according to social standards)
- **Hedonism** (pleasure and sensuous gratification for oneself)
- **Stimulation** (excitement, novelty and challenge in life)
- **Self-direction** (independent thought and action – choosing, creating, exploring)
- **Universalism** (understanding, appreciation, tolerance and protection for the welfare of all people and for nature)
- **Benevolence** (preservation and enhancement of the welfare of people with whom one is in frequent personal contact)
- **Tradition** (respect for, commitment to and acceptance of the customs and ideas that traditional culture or religion provide)
- **Conformity** (restraint of actions, inclinations and impulses likely to upset or harm others and violate social expectations or norms)
- **Security** (safety, harmony and stability of society, of relationships and of self)

---

Box 13.1    Shalom Schwartz: Universal Human Values

Schwartz asserts, in defence of this list, that '[i]t is possible to classify virtually all the items found in lists of specific values from different cultures . . . into one of these ten motivational types of values'(Schwartz 1994: 23). Now this is important. Notice that he is not saying that each person or each culture *has* all of these values, or that they are all of the same importance. But he is saying that the values that anyone holds as 'guiding principles of their life' will *all* be understandable in relation to one or another of these categories. In other words, you could explain them all to your exchange student because even if she herself was a heedless soul and unconcerned, at present, about security, she would know or could imagine others who were concerned about it.

## 2. WHAT WE HAVE IN COMMON: A PHILOSOPHICAL PROPOSITION

Schwartz does seem to have found out some interesting things about the dimensions of human values. But where does that get us? We cannot simply cite the above list and say that these 'are' global values, or the values of global citizenship. Read it again – what would it mean if you signed up to these values? Well, it's not clear. They are too general, there is a lot of room for interpretation. And principles could conflict – for example, how would you reconcile values of 'conformity' and 'stimulation' when you are deciding?

One way of getting around this would be to divide up the process of identifying 'core values' of global citizenship into two stages. The first would be to identify the dimensions of value which are, it can be argued, 'universal'. The second would be to reflect on what particular 'core values' should reflect global citizenship.

Let us consider the first issue using a professor of jurisprudence at Oxford, John Finnis, who has worked in the Aristotelian conception of natural law. Finnis proposes that the particular ways we express values may not be universal (telling the truth, directing our own lives) and certainly are not of the same status in different cultures. But he proposes that the substratum of core values *is* universal. How do we identify this substratum? Finnis suggests it is founded on practical reason – the reason that people use in deciding what to do. Go back to the handshake example. Remember what happened? Your exchange student asked you why you and others shook hands. You tried to answer her but the answer didn't mean much. So you went deeper and tried to get at the most basic reason you could give as to why handshakes matter. It may have sounded lame to your own ears but the best you could do was to mention friendship and affiliation. And your guest finally understood. Why did she understand? Finnis would suggest that she, too, has recognised that friendship is a good reason to act.

Furthermore, Finnis suggests that if your exchange student were to keep asking you these questions as you went about your daily life, as taxing as that might be to your patience, you would eventually start to repeat yourself. You would realise that all of your actions could relate to a rather small set of reasons for action and that your exchange student might understand these reasons.

It might be worth pointing out one philosophical aspect before we continue, which is that what is really new and significant about Finnis' theory is that these reasons are identified by reflection on one's own experience and planning – in other words, by practical reason. Finnis thinks that we cannot use cross-cultural anthropological and psychological studies to infer what is or is not universal. Rather, we can use this data only as 'an assemblage of reminders of the range of possibly worthwhile activities and orientations open to one' (Finnis 1980: 81, 81–5, 97). Knowledge of the general dimensions of human flourishing remains, epistemologically, a recognition of the reasons that actually engage practical reason.

Now what does he think these 'dimensions' of value, or reasons for action, are? Finnis has, over many years, suggested and refined a substantive set of these dimensions.

---

**Life itself:** its maintenance and transmission – health, and safety.

**Knowledge** and **Aesthetic Experience:** Human persons can know reality and appreciate beauty and whatever intensely engages their capacities to know and to feel.

Some degree of excellence in **Work** and **Play:** human persons can transform the natural world by using realities, beginning with their own bodily selves, to express meanings and serve purposes. Such meaning-giving and value-creation can be realised in diverse degrees.

**Friendship:** various forms of harmony between and among individuals and groups of persons – living at peace with others, neighbourliness, friendship.

**Self-integration:** within individuals and their personal lives, similar goods can be realised. For feelings can conflict among themselves and be at odds with one's judgements and choices. The harmony opposed to such inner disturbance is inner peace.

**Self-expression,** or **Practical Reasonableness:** one's choices can conflict with one's judgements and one's behaviour can fail to express one's inner self. The corresponding good is harmony among one's judgements, choices and performances – peace of conscience and consistency be-tween one's self and its expression.

**Transcendence:** most persons experience tension with the wider reaches of reality. Attempts to gain or improve harmony with some more-than-human source of meaning and value take many forms, depending on people's worldviews. Thus, another category . . . is peace with God, or the gods, or some non-theistic but more-than-human source of meaning and value.

---

Box 13.2 John Finnis: Basic Reasons for Action

First, please note that Finnis (who has revised his list more than once) wrote even at the outset that there is 'no magic number' of basic reasons and there is 'no need for the reader to accept the present list, just as it stands, still less its nomenclature (which simply gestures towards categories of human purpose that are each, though unified, nevertheless multi-faceted)'. He claims the list is analytically useful[7] and contains 'all the basic purposes of human action' (Finnis 1980: 92).

In recognising most basic reasons for the actions of individuals and communities, one is recognising reasons which are, in James Griffin's words, 'worth wanting' (Griffin 1996: 28) that is, *good*. But they are good in a particular not-yet-virtuous way, and because *so much* rests on this distinction I will quote in full the passage where Finnis explains this relationship between the dimension (*knowledge* in this example – any would do) and its *goodness* or *value*:[8]

> A number of common misunderstandings threaten to short-circuit our understanding of practical reason and its relationship to morality, just at this point. So we should bracket out these misunderstandings one by one. . . (i) To think of knowledge as a value is not to think that every true proposition is equally worth knowing, that every form of learning is equally valuable, that every subject-matter is equally worth investigating. Except for some exceptional purpose, it is more worthwhile to know whether the contentions in this book are true or false than to know how many milligrams of printer's ink are used in a copy of it. (ii) To think of knowledge as a basic form of good is not to think that knowledge, for example, of the truth about these contentions, would be equally valuable for every person. (iii) Nor is it to think that such knowledge, or indeed any particular item of knowledge, has any priority of value even for the reader or writer at the moment; perhaps the reader would be better off busying himself [or herself] with something else, even for the rest of his life . . . (iv) Just as 'knowledge is good' does not mean that knowledge is to be pursued by everybody, at all times, in all circumstances, so too it does not mean that knowledge is the only general form of good or the supreme form of good. (v) To think of knowledge as a value is not, as such, to think of it as a 'moral value'; 'truth is a good' is not, here, to be understood as a moral proposition, and 'knowledge is to be pursued' is not to be understood, here, as stating a moral obligation, requirement, prescription. . . In our reflective analysis of practical reasonableness, morality comes later. (vi) At the same time, finally, it is to be recalled that the knowledge we here have in mind as a value is the knowledge that one can call an *intrinsic* good, i.e. that is considered to be desirable for its own sake and not merely as something sought after under some such description as 'what will enable me to impress my audience' or 'what will confirm my instinctive beliefs' or 'what will contribute to my survival'. In sum (vii) to say that such knowledge is a value is simply to say that reference to the pursuit of knowledge makes intelligible

(though not necessarily reasonable-all-things-considered [nor moral]) any particular instance of human activity and commitment involved in such pursuit. (Finnis 1980: 61)

Finnis suggests that these dimensions are *non-moral*, which means that one can analytically identify the intelligible 'ends' of most immoral actions with reference to these same dimensions. A robber may obtain money by mugging as a means to buy paintings so he can enjoy aesthetic appreciation, or as a means to lots of entertaining so he can enjoy food and friendship; a terrorist may plant a bomb in order to express his solidarity with his home community. Finnis also claims the dimensions are per se nota or self-evident (anyone who has the necessary experience and openness will understand the value just by knowing the meaning of its terms).[9] He further characterises these as *incommensurable*, by which he means that all of the desirable qualities of one are not present in the other, and there is no common measuring scale between them, and *irreducible* (the list cannot be made any shorter).

These dimensions are understood by Finnis as never permanently 'achieved' once and for all.

Another key characteristic of the dimensions is that they are *non-hierarchical,* which means that at one time *any* of these dimensions can be the most important, and others may be legitimately sidelined. They cannot be arranged in any permanent hierarchy either for an individual or for a community. On the day of a significant performance a singer may not eat very much, nor see friends, nor read the newspapers, nor go to the market because he is preparing himself to sing with all the resonance and beauty he can.

So basically the 'dimensions of value' give us a palette of primary colours of values. The idea is that any value in any culture – whether it seems to you to be 'moral' or 'immoral' – could be described by looking at the basic dimensions of value to which it pertains. Of course this loses a lot – like describing the colour of a magenta foxglove as 'a combination of red and blue with more red than blue'. But it is certainly helpful in finding a general or 'vague' description that is going to help persons with different values or ways of expressing them to communicate their reasons for acting or holding certain values.

## 3. PRINCIPLES AND PROCEDURES

What if you wished to act consistently, without contradicting yourself, and to make every action you took, valuable? In this case we can start to talk about morality or ethics. Finnis writes that the first principle of morality is that: 'in voluntarily acting for human goods and avoiding what is opposed to them, one ought to choose and otherwise will those and only those possibilities whose willing is compatible with a will toward integral human fulfilment'

(Grisez et al. 1987: 128).[10] Integral human fulfilment refers to the fulfilment of all persons and their communities across time in all dimensions of their well-being or flourishing.

It may be worth spending a moment considering how this 'first principle' arises. One of the dimensions Finnis identifies is sociability, the relational good which people often pursue in friendship and social interactions even with strangers. Now if your housemate Adam is interested in pursuing his own good, then one way he may choose to do so is to cook a nice meal for himself, or learn to excel in hang-gliding. Another way to pursue his own good, perhaps, is to cultivate a friendship with your exchange student.[11] However, when he considers friendship, the understanding of possible human ends immediately becomes more complex. This is because friendship involves him in considerations not only of his own good but also of the exchange student's. And her 'good' might also be understood with reference to any of the various reasons for action, including *her* friendship or sociability with yet more people. And so, bit by bit, everyone else's good comes into the picture until you must be concerned for integral human fulfilment even in order to act rationally in pursuit of your own flourishing.

The final piece of the puzzle comes from applying this principle to different situations that happen in the space of a human life. Finnis suggests that many of the moral principles philosophers have proposed are particular ways of applying this principle. For example, in *The Fundamentals of Ethics* (1983: 75) Finnis suggests nine principles that the one master moral principle may give rise to:

1. have a harmonious set of orientations, purposes and commitments;
2. do not leave out of account, or arbitrarily discount or exaggerate, any of the basic human goods;
3. do not leave out of account, or arbitrarily discount or exaggerate, the goodness of others' participation in human goods;
4. do not attribute to any particular project the overriding and unconditional significance which only a basic human good and a general commitment can claim;
5. pursue one's general commitments with creativity and do not abandon them lightly;
6. do not waste your opportunities by using needlessly inefficient methods, and do not overlook the foreseeable bad consequences of your choices;
7. do not choose directly against any basic human good;
8. foster the common good of your communities;
9. do not act contrary to your conscience.

These principles are interesting because they represent a different *kind* of value which will come into an agreed set of core values. These principles are criteria by which any plan of action is to be examined and judged – efficiency, justice, respect for human rights and so on.

## 4. VALUES AND RELATIVE WEIGHTS

We are now in a position to discuss how different groups of people could suggest, modify and reflect on a proposed set of 'core values' for global citizenship. We argued in part 1 of this chapter that there was some empirical evidence for universal values but that it did not go so far as to suggest that people actually did all value 'truth-telling' and so on; it merely established that Schwartz could categorise cross-cultural values into his ten dimensions. Part 2 suggested that what *is* universal are not the actual values people hold but rather the simplest kinds of different reasons for action that people have. Part 3 suggested that the principles of morality (which can include things such as being efficient, being sustainable, acting with integrity, fostering the common good) are general ways in which the one principle of morality may be individuated into plural principles.

How does this part relate to the task at hand, which is to construct a set of common core values around which global citizenship may gather?

I will argue that this is *all* we can agree on as constituting 'universal values'. By universal, I do not mean that everyone *does* agree with me that any one of the many beautiful examples of human flourishing can be understood with reference to the dimensions (of life, knowledge, meaningful work, friendship, harmony with the environment, practical reasonableness, self-integration, harmony with the greater-than-human source of meaning and value). Nor do I mean that everyone *does* agree that any immoral action can be recognised by considering whether it violates any of the principles of practical reasonableness. But I do mean – perhaps ambitiously – that everyone *could* agree to this and that their agreement would be based on their own experience or practical knowledge of these dimensions, not on a Western education or an imbalance of power and knowledge. Of course, a Buddhist monk might recognise that his conception of flourishing can be articulated with reference to these dimensions and principles but that also does mean that he will *explicitly* use these in his own decisions. For him, the moral life may be only about following his master.

I have said that these goods and principles alone constitute 'universal values'. By 'value' there are many things I do not mean.[12] I do not mean 'ethical'. Because as was mentioned before, most classes of immoral actions can also be understood with reference to these universal values – and in fact reflecting on the relationship between an immoral action and these goods helps you to understand why a bank robber does what she does; why a corrupt bureaucrat does what he does. By value I also do not mean 'an exhaustive list of everything that is valuable under the sun'. In fact, far from it – I mean the primary colours of *any* values. And by having red and blue and yellow on your palette, you cannot predict what colours will be developed at all. But I do mean that the value of any valuable human action or project can be recognised, and sketched quite precisely, by reference to these universal values.

What is the use of this account of common values to the project of global citizenship? I will close with two thoughts – one about the dimensions or goods and the other about the principles.

The first is that the dimensions can work to help us keep our eyes open to the possible diversity of valuable human beings and doings. For example, in my college town there is a very popular restaurant called the Mongolian Wok. If you go into this restaurant, you are given a plate and pointed towards a long bar of raw foodstuffs and sauces. You fill your plate with these, take it around to a very large wok where a man cooks your plate of goodies into a meal. You could go back sixty different times and make sixty different meals with different selections from the same ingredients. Now what if you took your exchange student to the MW and she asked what was the best combination? Well, you could probably point out what could go wrong – if the food were undercooked or burned. You could also probably point out some foods that you thought were particularly delicious and some combinations that the restaurant itself suggested as useful. And you could warn her against the undesirability of a meal made only of bean sprouts. But you could not say that there was exactly one best meal. In this way, our account of universal values can act as a guard also against those who wish to absolutise their values and say that there is a best way of being a global citizen, or of being a human being. The conception of universal values is a very useful tool for appreciating the diversity of valid, truly human cultural forms.

My second reflection is that the principles are helpful to rule out immoral options, or at least to draw our attention to the morally ambiguous (or immoral) characteristics of alternative plans of action. To see this, take a possible action that you want to do – perhaps take your exchange student to London for a weekend. Try to formulate your plan clearly. Then 'test' it by looking at each of Finnis' principles mentioned earlier and asking how they apply. It takes a couple of tries to learn to apply the principles. But when you do, they form a pretty good way of thinking through decisions.

Using principles to rule out immoral options might seem to be a rather negative and depressing task. But I argue that this is as far as we can go. The principles cannot normally dictate what should be done. Because normally there will be more than one option that is fully moral. Or else all options violate some principle or another and the decision-maker has to judge which to do anyway. There is a huge arena left over, after we have applied universal values, for exercising free choice, self-determination and creativity *even if* we have ruled out the more undesirable options. Universal values identify immorality. But the moral, the truly human sets of action, the 'right' thing to do, is underdetermined. It requires free choice.

So having and agreeing on universal values is helpful, I argue, in ruling out some options that are clearly immoral, drawing our attention to the possible moral ambiguity of different options, and articulating to others how we understand the value of what we are doing. The final, and most important use of the values, is to keep all of the diversity of possibly valuable human ends and procedures in view. The last helps us to avoid narrowing our action to parochial concerns or national interests. It helps us to avoid absolutising – it is one thing to walk away from the Mongolian Wok with a bowl full of what we feel at the moment is the very most delicious meal imaginable. It is another thing to order the Mongolian Wok never to serve any other meals at all. This would be particularly reassuring to your exchange student, who thinks that black beans and chives are the very most delicious Mongolian Wok treat. But more generally, this last aspect might be particularly useful to our under-standing of global citizenship, which should involve both an acceptance of the diversity of valuable human ends and a willingness to make one's actions harmonise with such values anywhere.

---

## QUESTIONS

All of the points in this chapter might be illustrated by an imaginary discussion with your exchange student. Imagine that you both sit down one afternoon, one week before her departure, and decide to try to generate a set of common values that each of you will follow towards others.

1. How will your core values relate to human flourishing? Refer to Finnis' list of dimensions of human development. Which will you focus on? Which will you exclude? Why?
2. What principles of practical reasonableness will you draw on in forming core values? Which will you exclude? Why?
3. How specific will your values be? Will they be 'principles for action' that are always valid? Will they be goals that can be accomplished in one year? Will they be priorities for attention and action that you both will periodically revise?
4. What procedure will you both use to decide upon the core values? How will you resolve disagreements if they come up?

---

### NOTES

1. See also Schwartz and Bilsky 1987; 1990; Schwartz 1992.
2. Schwartz compiled his list of 56 values from previous work in cross-cultural psychology, (such as Rokeach 1973; Braithwaite and Law 1985; Chinese Culture Connection 1987; Hofstede 1980; Levy and Guttman 1974; Munro 1985), and the 'examination of texts on comparative religion and from consultations with Muslim and Druze Scholars' (Schwartz 1992: 17).

---

3. 7: of supreme importance. 6: very important. 5, 4: unlabelled. 3: important. 2,1: unlabelled. 0: not important. -1: opposed to my values.

4. Schwartz 1994 summarises progress until that date. His work also cross-references other values theories and research. The 64 countries include 2 African, 2 North American, 4 Latin American, 8 Asian, 2 South Asian, 8 East European, 1 Middle Eastern, 14 European, 2 Mediterranean, Australia and New Zealand.

5. Near-representative samples represent subgroups in proportions similar to their population proportions and cover the full range of ages, gender, occupations and educational levels. But near-representative samples do *not* employ rigorous sampling techniques. The 13 countries include 'Australia – a near-representative sample of Adelaide adults (n=199); Chile – a representative national sample (n=304); China – a near-representative sample of Shanghai factory workers (n=208); East Germany – a near-representative sample of Chemnitz adults (n=295); Finland – two representative national samples averaged (n=3120); France – a representative national sample (n=2339); Israel – a near-representative sample of Jerusalem adults (n=170); Italy – a representative national sample (n=210); Japan – a representative sample of Osaka adults (n=207); the Netherlands – a representative national sample of employed males (n=240); Russia – a representative sample of Moscow adults (n=189); South Africa – a representative sample of employed whites in Midrand (n=249); West Germany – a near-representative sample of adults from several states (n=213).' Quoted from Schwartz, Personal Communication, 19 May 1999.

6. For an explanation of the test of comprehensiveness see Schwartz 1992: 37.

7. In this way we can analytically unravel even very 'peculiar' conventions, norms, institutions and orders of preference, such as the aristocratic code of honour that demanded direct attacks on life in duelling. (Finnis 1980: 91)

8. See also Finnis et al., 1987: 126f.; Finnis 1998: 103–31.

9. Self-evidence is used in a very particular philosophical sense which 'entails neither (a) that [the dimension] is formulated reflectively or at all explicitly by those who are guided by it, nor (b) that when it is so formulated by somebody his formulation will invariably be found to be accurate or acceptably refined and sufficiently qualified, nor (c) that it is arrived at, even only implicitly, without experience of the field to which it relates.' (Finnis 1980: 68). See the instructive exchange between George and Perry: (George 1989; 1990; Perry 1989).

10. Finnis (1997) inserts 'and other persons, sofar as satisfying their needs is dependent on one's choosing and willing, have a right that one choose and will'.

11. It is not necessary for him actually to pursue friendship in order to be flourishing – he may be a flourishing hermit instead, of course. But ideally a hermit could, on Finnis' account, recognise the intelligibility of other people's valuing and pursuing friendship.

12. See also earlier quote from Finnis on what the value of knowledge is not.

# SECTION 4

# SPECIFIC AREAS: ENVIRONMENT, ECONOMIC GLOBALISATION, TECHNOLOGY, IMMIGRATION AND PEACE

# SECTION INTRODUCTION

## Nigel Dower

In this section of the reader the authors all focus on some particular area of global concern – environmental problems, economic globalisation, technology and peace. The main question is: what attitudes will global citizens take in relation to these areas of concern? All the authors in this section assume a global citizenship perspective, in the sense that they take for granted what has elsewhere been called the ethical component of being a global citizen. Some of the chapters – by Attfield, Smyth and Blackmore, and Dower – also have things to say about the idea of global citizenship, including its links with citizenship and with global civil society, about its institutional embodiment and about the ideal of a global citizen, and thus continue the discussions of the other sections. (Conversely, many of the earlier chapters of course contain discussion of particular issues as illustration of general themes. Section boundaries are not exact.)

In this section introduction we first outline the main ideas of each of the chapters and then make some general remarks by way of comparison and overview.

### Outline of Authors

Robin Attfield's piece 'Global Citizenship and the Global Environment' focuses on the global environment and usefully combines an examination of environmental problems with analysis of the idea of global citizenship which links his discussion with themes in section 1. Having identified the global nature of environmental problems, his first strategy is to emphasise the need to accept global obligation/responsibility (as part of what global citizenship is about) in relation to our *shared* environment which is under threat in so many ways. He therefore rejects both the argument that the global environment is merely an abstraction, since we all relate to local and particular environments, and the argument arising from certain forms of communitarianism that our obligations arise from particular communities with shared traditions and so global obligations are either non-existent/ marginal or contingent on whatever particular communities happen to share as values. He also invites the reader to extend her ethical concern beyond concern for humans to include the good of non-humans (animals and plants) as part of a wider biotic 'community of interdependence'. This wider community broadly corresponds with what he sees as the moral community of all beings who are moral 'patients' in the sense of having a moral status (without being agents). These two senses of community are contrasted with the human community of responsible moral agents who have responsibilities towards moral patients, that is, non-human life as well. The latter community of moral agents constitutes the domain of global citizenship. However, without the development of 'global civil society', especially the development of non-governmental organisations (NGOs), global citizens would not find the bases for adequate expression of their concerns.

John Smyth and Chris Blackmore also tackle the problem of the environment but do so from a somewhat different perspective from that of Attfield. They adopt what is called the 'systems' approach. This gets away from the dominant linear 'cause–effect' thinking which tends to see the effects of particular actions (the trees) and fails to attend to the whole system of interaction (the shape of the wood). Examples of interaction are given, including that of the global water system which, whilst renewable, is finite on the planet and is now shared by 6 billion people as opposed to 2 billion in 1900. Since some of these systems are essentially global, the approach of global citizenship is essential if we are to make the right choices (whether our concern is for the planet or for all the people who live on it). Systems are not the same as environments, they are rather 'a combination of internal elements and processes which together form a whole that has a purpose': the system has a boundary and what lies outside the boundary is its environment. We all think and live in many different systems, some local, some global. The extent to which people can think on global systems levels is a function of how open the various local systems are. We need an 'inner' globalisation of mental outlook. The authors usefully give an example of the mindset of a global citizen as indicated by the profile given in a recent Oxfam publication. The authors also note that attempts to implement Agenda 21 – the programme of action agreed at the Rio Earth Summit in 1992 – are often limited because a wide enough systems approach is not adopted. One advantage of the systems approach is that we will recognise more readily the limits the physical environment sets for us. (Whilst it is not clear that one has to adopt a systems approach in order to see the wider picture and to see the limits set by the environment, there is no doubt that this approach highlights the need for a comprehensive approach to global problems.)

In his chapter 'Economic Globalisation and Global Citizenship', David Newlands sets out to examine the process of economic globalisation, particularly in the last fifty years. He traces the process of trade liberalisation, the impact of the World Bank and the International Monetary Fund (IMF) and the growing role of transnational corporations which invest and trade across the world. He is at pains to bring out that, whilst there are immense benefits coming from this process of economic development, there are also significant costs in terms of the widening gap between rich and poor countries, and in terms of the effects of economic globalisation generally and the imposition of 'conditionalities' for loans (from the IMF and World Bank in particular), on the life conditions of the very poor. He relates this to global citizenship in three ways. First, he notes that extreme poverty deprives poor people of the capacity to be effective citizens participating in the social and political affairs of their society. In effect, their human rights as global citizens are undermined, as are their rights – often thwarted – to emigrate to other countries in search of better work (c. f. Ottonelli's chapter). Second, a global citizenship perspective will seek a middle position between economic disintegration and complete liberalisation, in the form of much needed regulation of the global economy to protect poor people and so on. Third, active global citizenship will express itself in various forms of activism like working for Jubilee 2000 to get Third World debt reduced and the activism at Seattle in December 1999 over the plans of the World Trade Organisation to further trade liberalisation.

Sytse Strijbos' paper on 'Citizenship in our Globalising World of Technology' continues the theme of globalisation but from a somewhat different angle. He asks us to consider carefully the role of technology in shaping our globalised world, and whilst he recognises the constraints which this imposes, he reminds us that there are also possibilities for the exercise of citizenship responsibility at the global level. It is important to recognise the pervasive nature of modern technology and see that technology is not so much the material objects – tools, gadgets, machines – but is a *system*, a form of organisation of human activity linked to a mindset. The aeroplane, for instance, functions as part of a complex system of organised transportation, of regulation by air traffic control and so on. Moreover, the effect of this system has been to create an ethical vacuum. First, we have not adapted our notion of ethical responsibility enough to the ways our patterns of activity have large-scale cumulative effects, as with the emissions of $CO_2$. Second, our political and social institutions, based on the assumption of democratic liberalism, are inadequate to the task. Third, a source of our problems is the reliance on science to provide new 'facts' to solve our problems, which displaces ethics. At root this is a spiritual challenge. Luckily we are not wholly determined by this system and the challenge is to find adequate ethical values which are the values of global citizenship. The real possibility for change is reflected in the development of global civil society as an aspect of a globalised world, where 'civil society' is seen as the third force alongside governments and the market.

With Valeria Ottonelli's chapter 'Immigration – What Does Global Justice Require?' we have a change of subject matter and a change of style to something in the domain of political philosophy. She provides a forthright defence of an open immigration policy, or at least one that is much more open than what is currently practised by most Western countries. She is careful to distinguish between the right of naturalisation – that is, the right to become a citizen of a political community – and a right of immigration to enter a country to live and work there (a right not restricted to political refugees or asylum-seekers). The right to the latter should in principle be extended to all human beings as required by the principle of impartiality, whereas the right to the former may be restricted by the principle of self-determination (PSD). The latter allows members of a political community to restrict membership in a way which is consistent with the impartiality requirement of global justice (and so could be accepted by global citizens). On the other hand, the principle of political justice (PPJ) requires that if people come to a country then they should be accorded citizen rights. The tension between PSD and PPJ can be resolved not by banning immigration but by recognising that for practical but impartial reasons, because of the structural limits of a society (for example, how much change it can bear), a society could allow two classes of residents, citizens and non-citizens, the latter not enjoying full social and political rights. Although this 'solution' could be acceptable even to global citizens, in practice there is very little evidence for the need to deny alien residents citizen rights and every reason to suppose that 'while contributing to the removal of the economic and political causes of immigration, global citizens should take action to bring their countries to adopt the most liberal immigration policy they can afford'. (The argument is robust and complex but repays careful study, since our attitude towards immigrants (and, as a subclass, asylum-seekers) is a very good litmus test of how far we are cosmopolitan in attitude.)

Nigel Dower argues in the chapter 'Peace and Global Citizenship' that the commitment to peace is – or at least ought to be regarded as – central to the concerns of global citizens, since peace is in normal circumstances the precondition of almost all other human goods, as well as the effective promotion of aid, environmental protection and the protection of human rights. He illustrates the dimension of global responsibility as a commitment to peace (as a goal to be achieved by everyone in the world) through parallels with domestic citizenship and the variety of ways citizens promote order and peace within a society (for example, respect of diversity within a multicultural society). Whilst not all global citizens will agree on exactly what is to be pursued or about the best or acceptable ways of promoting it – a point about varieties of ethical position consistent with global citizenship which he stressed in Chapter 11 on global ethics – Dower argues that certain approaches to international relations and what determines foreign policy concerning peace, war and armaments are ruled out for those who accept that they are global citizens. For instance, 'realist' views that foreign policy is determined by national interests or 'internationalist' thinking that sees it as a matter of states' diplomacy and negotiation without significant roles for individuals in shaping approaches to peace or developing a 'culture of peace' are ruled out. Amongst various factors important to developing the latter culture of peace at the global level is the willingness amongst adherents of different belief systems (religious or political) to accept or respect these differences where agreement can be reached over agreed practical values.

## COMMENTARY

In the light of the above survey we can see a number of themes and issues emerging.

1. We can identify at least three aspects of being a global citizen *in the moral sense* (a claim about global values and responsibilities) which are generally being either assumed or asserted.

First, a global citizen is a bearer of rights or at least the locus of values to be respected and promoted by others: global citizenship is about our equal moral status, which should be acknowledged wherever we live. As a passive citizenship claim, it may not seem very strong but it is significant nevertheless. This is most clearly brought out by Newlands in the right to escape the evils of poverty and achieve the enjoyment of social and political rights; likewise Ottonelli's piece essentially asserts the rights of individual global citizens to emigrate in search of work and a better life elsewhere.

Second, being a global citizen is being someone who is committed to some view, based on one's ethical theory, about what ought to happen in the world or what would be good for the world in terms of what others generally – including governments and economic bodies – should do. All authors have views about what should be done to protect the environment, promote development or aid, maintain peace, make technology responsive to human ends, pursue liberal immigration policies.

Third, A global citizen is someone who accepts (or ought to accept) an obligation to do things herself to advance global goals in some way. This is the active citizenship side of global citizenship. Again all the authors assert this, at least at the end as the corollary of the general ethical analysis which precedes it, saying in effect 'given that this is what ought to happen in the world, a global citizen should work to help make this possible'. Attfield, Dower and Smyth and Blackmore make more of this than the others do, and in the latter case there is an interesting reference to the Oxfam catalogue of the competencies of an ideal global citizen!

2. Each of the chapters includes some discussion of what may be called impediments to global citizenship or to the realisation of the global principles which are advocated by global citizens. For instance, the technological system

is seen by Strijbos as a system that, though it can be modified for human benefit by adequate moral and spiritual values, does powerfully constrain the way we think and act. Thinking within 'closed' systems, Smyth and Blackmore suggest, makes the global perspective difficult to achieve; and we need to recognise that, in terms of the pursuit of human values, the planet does constitute a definite limit or constraint. False theories of ethics, Attfield suggests, such as a narrow-minded communitarianism which sees obligations primarily located within established societies, may impede the acceptance of the right global approach. Powerful globalising tendencies in the economy, Newlands argues, make attempts to reform or regulate the global economy for the benefit of the poor a difficult task. Certain theories of international relations, Dower suggests, such as the view that national interests ought to dominate foreign policy, are inconsistent with the approach of the global citizen and to the extent that they are accepted impede the realisation of global values.

3. The authors generally assume that the values underlying global citizenship are to be accepted and that these values are uncontroversially what their own theories assume or advocate. Smyth and Blackmore take it for granted (reasonably enough) that adopting a global 'systems' approach is essential to our grasping adequately what needs to be done to meet the universal needs of humans sustainably. The challenge they address is mainly about how to get people to accept the relevant worldview; the values are assumed. Strijbos, apart from regretting the ethical vacuum created by modern technology, sees the need to fill the vacuum with global responsibility for example, recognising how one's acts cumulatively form part of serious environmental impacts; but the ethical principles are not developed. Newlands, whilst seeing the advantages of trade liberalisation for general economic prosperity, is concerned with the failure of the poor to realise their economic, social and political rights as a result of the world economy, not with defending a theory of rights. Ottonelli advocates the principle of political justice as a principle of global justice which creates a presumption in favour of liberal immigration policies while accepting that other theories might be accepted as well by global citizens as providing a basis for the same conclusion, but on her view anyone accepting a global citizenship view would advocate some form of liberal immigration policy. Attfield, having dealt with objections to a global perspective as such, takes it as self-evident that we should be committed to protecting our common environment; what he thinks may be a matter of debate is whether our reasons for such protection are essentially human-based or should be extended to include biocentric considerations. Dower makes a point of noting that there may be very different views about the legitimacy or efficacy of various types of action one might take to promote peace but more or less assumes that anyone who is a world citizen will be keen to promote peace in the world as a universal value (not just because it suits his or her country).

It is no criticism that these chapters do not contain longer arguments in defence of their ethical positions: such developments belong to other domains or levels of inquiry. But it is worth noting that, of course, none of these positions is free from controversy – either controversy over whether the values or principles advocated are to be accepted, or controversy over the justification of the values, even if there is acceptance and shared agreement about the values themselves. With regard to the latter, as Dower stresses, it is important to minimise such controversy if there is convergence on the values to be acted on. Certainly if the agreed values are global values, there could be global citizens with different theories but sharing common commitments. With regard to the former, we need to ask whether disputes about these values would only arise between global citizens and others who were not global citizens, or also between different groups of global citizens. This leads to the last issue.

4. There is a general assumption that the ethical positions adopted are those that global citizens would generally accept. How far is this right?

On the one hand, it seems reasonable to suppose that anyone at all concerned with creating a better world wants a world in which people have environments which are healthy, resource-full in sustainable ways (and aesthetically pleasing); in which economic conditions are such that everyone has the necessities of life and indeed sufficient means to be able to fulfil themselves and participate fully in the life of their society; in which people can live in peace both in terms of their social order and basic security of one's person and property, and in terms of freedom from external attack and threat thereof; in which both technology and legal and political institutions serve rather than thwart these humanistic ends; and in which, given that these values are things which are values for all human beings equally (often defined as human rights equally held by all), the existence of nation-states and of borders should not be seen as impediments to ways in which these other values can be effectively achieved for all (through either effective aid programmes or through appropriate immigration policies). This is a world that a global citizen not only wants and believes that governments and other bodies ought to be committed to promoting but also one in which a global citizen accepts responsibility to play his or her part in helping to create. All this seems to constitute the minimum bedrock of a global ethic acceptable to those embracing or advocating global citizenship.

On the other hand, whilst it is true that all the authors in this reader who are not sceptical about global citizenship accept this 'package', it is by no means clear that *any* thinker thinking within a global citizenship framework would accept this as it stands. There are really two issues.

4(i) Even if this package is accepted as a minimum baseline, what else might be advocated by a global citizen? That is, what further objectives might be added which bring one thinker into conflict with another (even if they are both global citizens)? What is problematic about the package is not what it says but what it leaves out. For instance, someone who was a deep ecologist might think that the failure to add concern for non-human life or for the planet to the list of humanistic goals was a serious defect. (Attfield does not push this, though his gentle advocacy of biocentrism should alert us to this issue.) Someone who was an ardent adherent to some particular religious or political ideology – fundamentalist Christianity, secular humanism, communism, liberal individualism – might see the promotion of these beliefs as quite as important as the basic preconditions of human well-being. Finally, as a more concrete illustration of the latter point, someone who believed in the sanctity of human life ruling out abortion would take a very different view of population policies from someone who took a strongly feminist line on the right of women to choose.

4(ii) Would all global citizens necessarily accept the package indicated above anyway? It is not obvious that they would. For instance, even if we accept an ideal view of a better world in which peace, prosperity and protection of the environment were accessible to all, someone might suppose that no obligations exist for governments or individuals to promote these things elsewhere in the world. This might stem from an acceptance of the universal value of liberty, especially economic liberty, as having priority; or from a view about the desirable division of the world into separate political communities within which by and large human well-being is pursued more effectively if countries or people do not interfere in one another's affairs. These views do not commend themselves generally to the authors in this reader; nor probably will they to most readers. Yet we cannot rule out the possibility that some who call themselves global citizens will accept them. They may be, from one's own point of view, less than satisfactory or misguided global citizens. But if their thought is inspired by a global ethic and they describe themselves as global citizens, who are we to say that they are not global citizens?

# 14. GLOBAL CITIZENSHIP AND THE GLOBAL ENVIRONMENT

## Robin Attfield

### INTRODUCTION

Environmental responsibilities form the most obvious focus of concern for global citizens, as well as the territory where global obligations most clearly arise. However great the need may be for global citizenship in matters of development, peace, human rights and democracy, the importance of universal obligations and of concerted action grounded on such obligations is apparently least deniable with regard to our shared but vulnerable planet, with its global problems of climate change, pollution and the imperilled condition of renewable resources and of the global commons. If these responsibilities are ignored, then succeeding generations will suffer, as will the fellow species with which we share the planetary biosphere. (Some further aspects of the concept of global citizenship will be discussed below.)

Yet these apparently clear-cut responsibilities of global citizens are the implicit targets of several kinds of criticism, criticisms which need to be tackled if belief in global citizenship is to be defensibly held in environmental contexts. Some of the criticisms are specific to environmental issues, as when it is suggested that the global environment is nothing more than an abstraction from the environments of actual individual experience. Other objections are common to global citizenship across the whole of its potential range of application and concern whether there are universal obligations of the kind suggested, as opposed to obligations arising out of communities or relationships, the extent of which is restricted to those ties of relationship or community of which the subject of responsibilities is conscious; for on such a communitarian basis the scope of responsibilities could not be unrestricted and those distanced from us either in space or in time might well be no concern of ours. There again, criticisms are liable to be directed at ethical theories that recognise environmental responsibilities not only as international (transcending national boundaries), and as intergenerational (transcending the sequence of the generations) but also as interspecific (transcending boundaries between species). Problems arise here sometimes from adherents of human-centred ethics, who are liable to reject such wider responsibilities, and sometimes, paradoxically, from those who regard all species as warranting equal concern regardless of their diverse capacities, sensitivities and forms of life, who are liable to protest if creatures of any sort are prioritised over others. Concern for the animal kingdom also raises the question of whether global citizenship can itself be restricted to humanity.

If the criticisms and objections can be overcome, further issues arise of the nature and extent of global citizenship, and of its relationship to more immediate or more local loyalties. Believing that the criticisms and objections are not insuperable, I have written in other places about these issues, most substantially in *The Ethics of the Global Environment*, and have developed there a platform of positions relating to responsibilities and desirable policies on some of the more detailed issues, such as principles concerning sustainable development, not least in matters of sharing fresh water, of preserving forests and fish stocks, and of population policies, principles of biodiversity preservation and of intergenerational equity (Attfield 1999: 207–22). Since time and space will prevent me discussing most of these issues here, I will perforce be referring from time to time to what is argued there; it will also be more appropriate here to relate the understanding of global citizenship that I defend to civil society and to its counterpart at the global level, global civil society. For whereas civil society is frequently what makes the exercise of local citizenship a serious possibility, global civil society is plausibly indispensable for global citizenship, global environmental citizenship included. Indeed, in the absence of global civil society the future of the global environment would be even more at risk than current problems show it to be.

## 1. THE GLOBAL ENVIRONMENT NOT AN ABSTRACTION

It is sometimes suggested that the global environment is an abstraction from the environments of individual experience and that it is a matter of concern for rootless intellectuals only. Our environments are the territorial roots or familiar fields of concern of each of us, it is said; concern for anything broader can only arise if we first experience and love our own environment in this sense. This is partly a conceptual claim; environments are necessarily relational, it is claimed, and attempts to conceptualise an international or a global environment ignore this at their peril.

Now there is no need to reject the relational sense of 'environment' as an intelligible sense. Nevertheless, I follow Nigel Dower (1994) and Holmes

Rolston (1995) when they point out that this sense of 'environment' pre-supposes the existence of a shared environment in the distinct sense of what environs all people, and maybe all living creatures, and in all generations at that. For if nothing thus environs us, then there could be no environments in the relational sense. We are each born into a shared environment but for which we could not exist; only later do we form attachments to local scenes and neighbourhoods (and only then if we are fortunate enough to find ourselves somewhere moderately congenial). Further, the environment (in the shared sense, as opposed to the relational sense) extends to all the inhabitable and visitable tracts of the planet, including the entirety of its surface, its seas and its atmosphere; for wherever we go, we encounter an environment continuous with the one where our travels began.

The shared environment can be regarded as a causal system, including ecosystems, weather and climate, a system that makes relational environments possible, thus forming a fit object of study, as in environmental science. But an encompassing system has further properties liable to generate attitudes distinct from those relating to impartial study. It can also generate respect of the kind often felt by mariners for the oceans and for mountains by mountaineers; and, in contrast with familiar environments, this respect can be focused on the otherness (and sometimes the wildness) of the natural environment and on its indifference with regard to ourselves. The experience of otherness, however, is premised on the natural environment being there to be discovered and thus being independent of ourselves, and also on it having existed prior to our births; for if it were understood to be our creation, as some constructivists regard it, then its otherness would at best be a derivative otherness and it could scarcely be regarded seriously as other at all.

Hence the shared environment is far from an abstraction; and in view of its importance and vulnerability, it is also a fit object of concern, both for those already concerned to protect a particular local environment and for those who lack this concern, whether through beginning life in unfavourable settings, or through mobility and frequent travel, or because their concerns (religious concerns included) focus on humans in other places or times (and thus on their environment), or on the environment that is shared by themselves and the people they are concerned about. Concern for the global environment is not concern for an abstraction, is not confined either to intellectuals or to the rootless, and is fortunately spreading as people discover that our own future and that of all life on Earth depends on it.

## 2. UNRESTRICTED VERSUS RESTRICTED APPROACHES TO ETHICS

Even if it is granted that the global environment is not an abstraction, it is possible to claim that universal obligations, applying alike and without restriction to individuals and bodies with the ability to make a difference to the global environment, are themselves an abstraction. This view, it might be held, abstracts from the concrete material and social situations of agents who in large measure owe their identity to these settings. Hence generalisations about their responsibilities are likely to gloss over important differentiating factors and to be worthless.

This particular criticism is easily tackled. For where agents are differentiated by material circumstances that are relevant to their powers to act, then their responsibilities will be different; at the same time, those who in different places have similar wealth, power and knowledge could still have similar responsibilities, at least in theory, and plausibly have similar responsibilities in reality where they also have like opportunities. They may have other responsibilities, arising from commitments to those around them, which will sometimes complicate the issue of what they ought to do, all things considered, but the existence of extra responsibilities need not and does not obliterate that of universal responsibilities.

However, the more radical criticism is sometimes made that, since all responsibilities arise out of relationships and communities, there need be no obligations that all agents have in common and, if there are some, that is because the moralities of most communities happen to overlap. Essentially the extent of an agent's responsibilities and the range of agents to which they apply depends on the expectations of the communities to which each belongs.

This claim, however, is itself at least equally subject to charges of abstraction. It assumes that community boundaries are clear enough for the expectations of communities to be identified, both by observers and by the individual agent, and it also assumes that most agents belong to just one community each. It assumes that moral obligations do not apply to relations between communities, except where one or another community happens to believe otherwise. Besides these implausible assumptions, it further assumes that if obligations arise within communities, in the senses of originating in community settings and being learned by each generation in such settings, then the scope of such obligations must be limited to the community in question, plus any extensions of scope that it recognises. But this is equally implausible and has led a variety of people for well over two thousand years to suggest that if there is any one community with this kind of status, it is the global community of humanity. Otherwise we are all committed to discriminating between insiders and outsiders, between neighbours and strangers, and in such a way that the latter would often receive no consideration at all. But where there are no relevant differences between Samaritans and Jews, or between compatriots and aliens, this kind of discrimination is surely indefensible. Issues also arise about whether morality stops short at the boundaries of humanity; to some of those issues I will be returning.

Communitarianism is, however, much in evidence in the contemporary world and its relevance to global citizenship has to be taken seriously. To confine this discussion to environmental aspects of global citizenship, communitarians are free to act for the good of humanity as a whole and not just that of their community, for the good of future generations and not just that of their own generation, and even for the good of fellow species, both of their own locality and of others, but only if they regard this as in the interests of their community of first allegiance, or alternatively if this community happens at present to value acting in these ways. But if considerations of communal interest and communal values are opposed to such action and related policies, then consistent communitarians would have to disown any obligations beyond their own community or generation, plus whatever species they may happen to value. Hence any communitarian commitment to global citizenship is a happenstance, contingent on shifts either of interests or of values, and liable to wax and wane with such fluctuations.

This can, of course, prove a comfortable position, as responsibilities are restricted and are less likely to seem overwhelming. But it could also prove disastrous. Thus if the values of any community incline them to produce and emit CFCs, let alone justify this practice, and loyal members of that community act accordingly, then most living creatures everywhere on earth will be liable to skin cancer through disruption of the protective ozone layer. Self-interest is far from certain to prevent this, since libertarians were recently maintaining that prohibition is wrong on the grounds that everyone is free to avoid this danger by wearing protective clothing, although environmentalists were able to reply that this scarcely applies to wildlife (Attfield 1999: 177–8). Numerous other examples will come to mind of cases where a pursuit of local values could prove globally fatal.

If, by contrast, we have to take into account the good of all people who can be affected by action, including future people to the extent that they would foreseeably be affected, and members of other species too, then it is much less likely that our beliefs will direct us towards generating disasters and much more likely that foresight will be used to anticipate and prevent them. So there could well be benefits from the widespread adoption of a universalist ethic and recognition of the kind of obligations that global citizens have. But there are such benefits only because there are good reasons for such recognition. If the well-being of one individual counts as a ground of obligation, so does that of others (both close and distant, present and future) and indeed of all the others. It is difficult to resist the belief that the likely benefits of widespread recognition of this derive from its being true.

### 3. THE RELEVANCE OR IRRELEVANCE OF SPECIES BOUNDARIES

It is sometimes suggested that it is unnecessary and undesirable to appeal to the good of non-humans in matters affecting the environment, since appeal to the interests of future human generations as well as of the present generation yields all the right policies anyway. A fuller discussion of this, the so-called convergence hypothesis, can be found in *The Ethics of the Global Environment* (Attfield 1999: 155–73), in the chapter on global justice (See also

Norton 1991: 216). Here it may reasonably be pointed out that appeals to human interests alone are unlikely adequately to support the preservation of those species, at present the large majority, that have not yet been discovered and hence of whose value and merits current agents are unaware.

Now most people recognise these days that cruelty to individual animals is wrong in itself and that the same applies to neglect of the animals in our care. But those who grant this have already abandoned anthropocentrism, the belief that none but human interests count and that only humans have moral standing. The moral standing of living creatures does not mean that they all count equally for all purposes, or that cows and sheep, for example, should be given voting rights. What it does mean is that genuine interests matter, such as the interest of sentient animals in not being subjected to avoidable suffering at human hands.

Rejection of anthropocentrism does not involve the view that all species warrant equal concern, since the species do not all have like interests or the same range of interests or capacities. Non-humans cannot be given votes because of their lack of powers of self-determination and, at least in most cases, their lack of language. The suggestion of some 'deep ecologists' that we have equal obligations with regard to all species probably helps account for the reversion of some people (in reaction to this) to anthropocentrism, as if there were no positions in between these extremist camps. For opponents of anthropocentrism are free to recognise that moral agency and moral respon- sibility qualify most humans for distinctive recognition and respect by virtue of their powers of self-determination and all that goes with these powers.

This debate also has a bearing on the question of whether non-human creatures should be regarded as global citizens. When Aldo Leopold suggested that humanity should cease to be a conqueror of the land community (roughly, nature) and become a plain member and citizen of it (Leopold 1953: 204) he probably envisaged other species as fellow citizens in the community of life on the planet. But for this sense of community, membership simply involves interdependence in the cycles of nature. It does not involve being a responsible agent. A quite different sense of community is in use when 'community' is used to refer to the network of relations of responsible agents, the sense used, for example, in discussion of communities as sources of obligations in part 2 above. This, I suggest, is also the sense of community relevant to global citizens and global citizenship. For example, the community which jointly shoulders the task of caring for the natural environment is a community of responsible agents (that is, people who are responsible to some degree but not without qualification).

There is, however, a third sense of community, the set of moral patients or beings that responsible agents should take into account. This is a kind of moral community and its recognition means that there is no need to exclude non-humans from the moral community in all senses, even though they are all (or nearly all) excluded from my second sense of community. It may be worth adding that my belief is that the moral community in the third sense is roughly coextensive with the membership of the planetary community in the first sense (Earth's biological community), although the community of moral patients much more obviously includes future creatures than talk of the biological community of Earth's creatures usually does.

I conclude at this point that the boundaries of moral concern, including the concern of global citizens, do not and should not exclude non-human interests, even though global citizenship is almost entirely confined to human beings. Respect for non-human creatures need not erode concern for fellow humans, with their distinctive characteristic capacities.

## 4. Global Citizenship and Global Civil Society

Civil society, in the most usual sense, comprises a loose network of associations independent of the state (Walzer 1995b: 1). Associations such as trade unions, churches, NGOs, political parties and societies for neighbourhoods, hobbies or sports are common examples. 'Civil society' has also been used quite differently to refer to the market (O'Neill 1993: 177) and this helps explain the critique of the later Marx of civil society as exploitative (Wilkins 1996: 102–3). Indeed where civil society, broadly conceived, involves systemic evils such as racial discrimination, class or caste distinction and the oppression of women, this is a reasonable verdict. But a completely different verdict is in place, as John O'Neill remarks, where 'civil society' primarily refers to voluntary associations and networks (O'Neill 1993: 177–8); indeed the presence of these in a country is often thought to be necessary for the maintenance of democracy there (Walzer 1995a: 170; see also Attfield 1999: 191–208).

Civil society is thus frequently held to be what makes the exercise of local citizenship a serious possibility; and in the same way global civil society is plausibly indispensable for global citizenship, global environmental citizenship included. Global civil society comprises international voluntary associations and their members, whether they regard their role as tackling global problems or not. In this sense, international civil society partly comprises committed international non-governmental bodies like Greenpeace and Amnesty International, or like the International Red Cross, Médecins sans Frontières and the International Campaign to Ban Land Mines.

However, it also includes such non-governmental international bodies as the World Council of Churches, the Roman Catholic Church and other worldwide religious bodies, or again the International Soccer Federation (Crocker 1998: 39), for bodies can contribute to global civil society without embracing among their aims specific global objectives such as the preservation of the global environment. International peace groups, federations of trade unions and networks of organisations of indigenous people, minorities and ethnic groups (such as the Environmental Justice Movement) should not be forgotten.

But global civil society also comprises individual citizens and pressure groups, and the networks in which they participate, including those harbouring concerns for environments other than their own, such as the Antarctic or the Amazon Basin (or indeed for the global environment). Fortunately, as Janna Thompson points out, people do develop such concerns and without this the prospects for the global environment might well be slender (Thompson, unpublished: 10). Campaigning focuses not only on international conferences (such as Kyoto) and organisations (like the IMF) but also on transnational corporations, as when the World Development Movement recently persuaded Del Monte to allow independent trade unions in its banana plantations in Central America, and as in WDM's lobbying of other large banana companies to do likewise and to curtail the aerial spraying of bananas, the environment and plantation workers alike with herbicides and pesticides.

Campaigning NGOs cannot be assumed to be flawless, sometimes oppose each other and are sometimes open to significant criticism, as over the failure of the feminist lobby at the Cairo Population Conference to stress the structural requirements of development. But more often they work together, as recently in the Real World Alliance in Britain (Jacobs 1996), and they probably represent the best hope of kindling willing compliance with what the Commission on Global Governance sensibly claims to be vital to good global governance, a global civic ethic (Commission on Global Governance 1995: 335) with a scope including respect for human rights and concern to preserve the global environment and its more significant components.

Without global civil society, the prospects for the global environment would be grim; for countries would not regard their international dealings as subject to scrutiny, and nor would transnational corporations. At the same time, campaigners would be obliged either to act alone or to operate within the limits of national pressure groups or parties. A sense of international identity might be achievable through individual international contacts but for most people would be extremely difficult to attain. The existence of global civil society changes all these matters, partly through introducing scrutiny of international activities and partly through facilitating concerted international action by scattered campaigners, plus the possibility of a sense of international identity on their part. Participants in such campaigns could reasonably regard themselves as global citizens.

This would not be the case if global citizenship required loyalty to an already established international regime on the analogy of national citizenship, often accompanied as it is by loyalty to a nation-state. Nor would global citizenship be as depicted here if it involved working towards the abolition of sovereign states in favour of world government. But this is in no way involved. Indeed, many internationalists are sceptics where world government is concerned, and of course none owes loyalty to a world sovereign as no such sovereign exists. Nevertheless those concerned with solving or mitigating global problems, and thus with improving global governance, whether through cooperation between sovereign states or through international bodies in which a small measure of sovereignty is vested, can reasonably claim to be global citizens on this basis. If the phrase 'global citizen' were somehow unavailable to describe people of this kind – possibly through restrictions on its use of the kind just mentioned – then another name would have to be invented for the kind of globally-oriented citizenship in which these people partake.

The notion of citizenship is not, in any case, confined to membership of sovereign states or Leopold could not have described the role of humanity in the biosphere as that of 'plain citizen'. Citizens can be understood as such through membership of a community bound together by characteristics other than relation to an independent political structure, as with citizens of a city which forms just a small part of a sovereign state. Nor does the community to which citizens belong have to be restricted to a human collective; citizens of cities or countrysides can be proud of and concerned for their parks, woodlands, landscapes and mountains, as much as they are of their museums, galleries and cultural achievements. Communities, as has been seen, can have overlapping boundaries and, fortunately, admit of dual and sometimes multiple loyalties.

Global civil society itself sometimes comprises the community of which global citizens are members. But more importantly it points beyond itself to the community of humanity and to the community of Earth's inhabitants, albeit in a slightly different sense, the first of the three senses of 'community' mentioned previously, a sense that could be called 'the interdependence sense'. It also points to obligations with regard to this community, obligations held by the community of humanity, or rather by those of its members with the ability to make relevant differences. Thus members of the community of humanity can have obligations with regard to the community of Earth in the interdependence sense, even though membership of the latter does not of itself involve obligations at all. (I say 'with regard to' rather than 'owing to' so as to cover the possibility that these obligations may not correspond to rights and that their beneficiaries may not in all cases yet exist, being people or creatures of the future, or be yet known to exist, being members of the millions of species so far undiscovered.) Meanwhile individuals can be members of both of these communities; and, granted the possibility of plural citizenship, their being so in no way detracts from their membership of the city, region or country of their birth or adoption. Thus we can analogise from familiar cases of citizenship to unfamiliar kinds without the latter destroying or invalidating the former.

The global environment, meanwhile, is undergoing unparalleled stress, as is betokened by the multiple problems of pollution (including global warming and destruction of the ozone layer), soil erosion, desertification, deforestation, overfishing, loss of species, habitats and ecosystems, and generally overstress of renewable resources. I cannot discuss policies, local or global, for tackling these problems here. But they are most unlikely to be tackled at all unless they are confronted at the global level as well as local, regional and national levels. Forms of global governance are predictably indispensable for tackling them. If so, it is equally predictable that global citizens are going to be indispensable, both to advocate the introduction of forms and institutions of global govern-ance, to mould their aims, objectives and policies, and to monitor their performance. They would have slender prospects of effectiveness in the complete absence of global civil society but fortunately the rudiments of this exist already. Beginning from these beginnings, global citizens are urgently needed in many global realms. The realm of the global environment has been argued to be one of special urgency and importance. It would be surprising if this ceases to be the case at any stage of the millennium that has just begun.

---

## QUESTIONS

1. Give three examples of global environmental problems. What makes them *global* problems? (See further Attfield 1999: ch.1)
2. Granted that the principle of keeping promises is one example of a universal ethical principle, name any two others. Need principles be recognised by everyone before they can be held to apply to everyone?
3. Are non-human animals like whales and dolphins members of the moral community in any of the normal or recognisable senses of that phrase?
4. Give three examples of organisations or bodies comprising examples of civil society in your own country. Do the organisations you have chosen make a positive contribution to the development or mainten-ance of democracy?
5. Give two examples not mentioned above of organisations or bodies comprising examples of global civil society. Are the organisations or bodies you have chosen likely to contribute, either directly or indir-ectly, to the solution of global environmental problems?

# 15. LIVING WITH THE BIG PICTURE: A SYSTEMS APPROACH TO CITIZENSHIP OF A COMPLEX PLANET

## Chris Blackmore and John Smyth

The idea of global citizenship may conjure up many images but it would be difficult to dissociate it from *both* people *and* the planet Earth. However, reconciling the different priorities that people attach to issues of human society and welfare with the qualities and constraints of our physical and biological environment is easier said than done. In our experience there has been a tendency among those who focus on global issues to polarise between human and non-human dimensions, often with little recognition and understanding that the two ends of the spectrum are now interdependent (Smyth, 1995). Against this background, becoming a citizen of the globe, with the inference that individuals take responsibility for the effects of their actions, seems an immensely challenging goal. Human behaviour is much less governed than that of other inhabitants of the Earth by patterns laid down by natural selection and adjusted by fine-tuning to their particular environment during a relatively standardised process of development. Humans have capacities to adapt the environment to their own perception of needs. Skills are required to be able to understand how 'the wood' as well as 'the trees' is faring, to understand the interrelationships and to know whether, when and how to intervene, or to stop intervening.

As humans we have many choices to make about how we live in the world. Our decisions and actions are underpinned by what we know, believe and value and we are influenced by events taking place around us at many different levels. Few would dispute that most of our activities affect others and our environment, both in and beyond the immediate locations in which we live. Many of us recognise, for instance, that there are effects associated with our use of natural resources or disposal of wastes. But the nature of these effects, what we can do about them and whether or not they matter, are questions that are harder to understand and to judge. In order to address them there is often a need to get away from reductionism and linear 'cause and effect' thinking which, although very useful, tend to prevail in our society and are often used inappropriately. More 'systems thinking' is needed to make sense of the complexity we experience in the world. How we can use systems thinking to act in ways that take account of both human and non-human factors of global citizenship is the main topic of this chapter.

## INTERCONNECTIONS

There are many interconnections between ourselves and our environmental systems. These were crystallised by the World Conservation Strategy (IUCN et al. 1980) into the maintenance of life-support systems, the maintenance of biodiversity and the sustainable use of renewable natural resources. The first of these recognises the whole biosphere as a unitary system (Spaceship Earth), the second comprises the intricate machinery needed to keep it operational through conditions which change in both short and long term, and the third gives sound advice to its human occupants on how to survive as dependent parts of it, introducing the concept of sustainable development. Our continuing existence as global citizens depends on each of these.

It would be naïve to suggest that, in our attempts to achieve global citizenship, we can do more than learn our way to achieving more sustainable relationships with other parts of what we experience as a highly complex planet. Water, for example, is one of the components of our environment on the supply of which we are wholly dependent. This issue has now reached the top of many international agendas, including those of the UN Commission on Sustainable Development which meets annually in New York to review progress on the action plan (Agenda 21) to which governments signed up in Rio de Janeiro in 1992 (Quarrie 1992).

Water is essential to life. It is a renewable resource at a global level because it has a natural cycle and can be re-used for different purposes but supplies of freshwater are finite. At the beginning of the eighteenth century there were less than a billion people in the world sharing less than a million cubic kilometres of fresh water. In 1900 there were about 2 billion people sharing the same amount. Now there are more than 6 billion people and the fresh water supply has remained constant (Topfer 1998).

At regional or local levels in many parts of the world fresh water is a scarce resource imposing constraints on human action and threatening both life-support and biodiversity. This scarcity may be due to drought conditions or because it has been degraded through pollution or salinisation. Many large cities around the world are dependent on ground water and increased demand has led to declining water levels and quality in urban aquifers. How and how much water is used by people in one area may affect how and whether it may be used elsewhere. There is competition for fresh water at different levels, ranging from international to local, and managing its supply and use has become a complex process. The late Sir Geoffrey Vickers, in 1966, described the following situation:

> For many millennia the River Thames has earned its name as a continuing entity. It is in fact the way in which water from a stable catchment area finds its way to the sea. It expresses the relationships, changing but continuous, between rainfall, contours and porosity of the area, vegetation and a host of other physical variables.
>
> Throughout this time until very recently its valley provided a habitat for many species, including men, who long ago learned to live above its floodmarks and to cultivate its alluvial soil. Then we began to incorporate this river, once an independent variable, into our own man-made socio-technical system. We controlled its floods with barrages and dykes. We adapted it for transportation. We distributed its water. We used it as a sewer. Our demands rose and began to conflict with each other, making necessary, for example, the control of pollution. Now these demands have begun to conflict in total with the volume of the river. We plan to supplement it by pumping out deep reservoirs. Soon, unless some other solution appears, we shall be supplementing its flow by pumping desalted water from the sea. By then the Thames as an independent physical system, part of the given environment, will have virtually disappeared within a human socio-technical system, dependent on new physical constructions, new institutions, and a new attitude to the use of water and the regulation of the whole water cycle. (Vickers 1966: 76–7)

Such a scenario could also be described in many other natural resource contexts that are associated with global citizenship. Resources such as air, water and land can be used in many ways and their use optimised but they remain relatively fixed in terms of their capacity. Their quality for the purpose of supporting life can either be sustained or degraded. Managing such resources, where there are multiple stakeholders and interconnections among social, economic and environmental factors, requires an approach that goes beyond analysis of individual components of the relevant systems, be they people, physical resources or both. It is necessary to consider whole systems in the context of larger wholes and to understand the interrelationships and the systemic effects of different courses of action. It is our view that systems approaches offer a great deal to help develop understanding of complex situations and how to act within them as global citizens in a way that takes account not just of human elements but of the non-human elements on which we depend.

## TAKING A SYSTEMS APPROACH

By taking a systems approach we mean using systems thinking, which in this case means systemic (a property of the whole) rather than systematic (linear step-by-step) thinking to inform action. We shall say more about what we mean by systems thinking later in this chapter but in brief it can be captured by considering an entity or situation within the context of a larger whole. In our example of fresh water, using systems thinking in our decision-making may mean becoming more aware of the context of household water supply and the effects of using and disposing of water (not just at a local level but also much further afield). In turn, this may lead to some modification of our use of fresh water to take account of our environment and the needs of others. This action is consistent with ideas of global citizenship, particularly those of being aware of the wider world and taking action to make the world more equitable whilst taking responsibility for our own actions.

There is no guarantee that people who have a good understanding of their system of interest within the context of a larger whole will act on that understanding, or if they do, how they will act. Many factors affect our decisions and actions, including values, beliefs and personal circumstances. However, we suggest that learning to take a systems approach can help people, who wish to do so, to learn to become global citizens in terms of harmonising their behaviour with these many factors. In this context, taking a systems approach involves thinking in terms of being part of a system rather than a separate entity; appreciating a range of different perspectives and motivations as well as one's own and understanding relevant interconnections. Our perspectives on the world are partial and we cannot understand the whole unless we take multiple perspectives into account. Yet there seems to be limited recognition of this among humankind and many do not appear to recognise that we are only a part of a global system of life-support processes sustained by biodiverse machinery.

## WHAT DO WE MEAN BY 'SYSTEM'?

We have already used the word 'system' several times and now want to make clear what we mean. 'System' is a part of general everyday language and like so many other words relating to global citizenship, such as environment, development and sustainability, it is used in a range of different ways. We use it in this chapter in a specific sense. By a system we mean a whole entity that has a boundary. Outside the boundary is the system's environment. The system and its environment are always structurally coupled so the system's environment and the system interact. The system may have subsystems or may be a subsystem of a larger system. The use of the term system to denote a whole, where the properties of the whole differ from those of its parts, goes back many years and systems theory has come from a synthesis of ideas from many different disciplines. We use the word system in the sense that it is a combination of interconnected elements and processes, which together form a whole that has a purpose. These elements and processes are affected by being within the system and the system would be affected by removing them from the system. This definition is similar to those used in several Open University courses (Open University 1984; 1991; 1997) and by a range of systems authors (Checkland 1984; Ison 1993; Capra 1996; Clayton and Radcliffe 1996).

It also seems worth noting that there are different ontological (nature of reality) assumptions that underpin different epistemological (how it is we know) perspectives regarding systems. Some believe systems exist in the so-called real world and that a system's purpose also exists and is not necessarily attributed by an observer. Others believe that systems do not exist out in the world but are always constructs in people's minds, with the system's purpose attributed by one or more observers in conformity with a particular world-view. Yet others fall somewhere between the two. We do not claim ontological and epistemological neutrality in outlining this range of beliefs. We both fall between the two extremes in our own beliefs and have found the idea of systems as constructs very useful in our own practice, which has clearly influenced how we have presented our arguments in this chapter. However, we do claim that whatever the belief – whether it is that systems and their purposes are 'out there', in the mind or between the two – it is possible to recognise that different people will identify different boundaries between what lies inside and outside their systems of interest. They may also see different relationships between them because of their different worldviews and the different purposes they have in mind in defining these systems. In the context of global citizenship it is also arguable that there is sufficient commonality in human experience for agreements to be reached among groups of people about the purposes of systems and where their boundaries lie.

In considering unique environmental and planetary systems at a global level, such as those that encompass the oceans, the atmosphere or the whole water cycle, questions of existence and purpose seem rather different questions from those faced when considering much more localised human activity systems, such as those that focus on, say, agriculture at a local level. However, human activity has had its effects on the most remote parts of our planet and perceptions of oceans and atmosphere as systems are still held only by humans, so it is possible to consider even unique whole planetary systems as human activity systems with different perceptions of boundaries, at least in part. In order to draw human and non-human factors together it is important not to think of them as just parts of separate systems but as different parts of a whole.

Take an example closer to home to consider the question of identifying different boundaries and purposes. Aberdeen University may be thought of as a system, with its faculties as subsystems. It may also be thought of as a subsystem of a system of Scottish universities. Even in this example, it is possible to see that different people would place different boundaries around any one of these systems and subsystems. The purpose of Aberdeen University may be expressed in many different ways, for instance as a system to enable its students and staff to achieve a specific range of learning outcomes, which may be underpinned by the worldview that includes valuing those particular learning outcomes. Alternatively, it may be thought of as a system to provide employment in the Aberdeen area, which may be underpinned by a different worldview. In each case it is possible to identify different elements and processes as part of that system and different relationships between them.

## What and Whose Systems are Relevant to Global Citizenship?

At a global level it is arguably beyond the capacity of humankind to reconstruct whole systems, at least in physical terms, except in details. Major changes in how we live our lives took place in the late twentieth century. They resulted in gross alterations to the properties of the Earth's surface, contamination of air, water and land by irregular and complex deliveries of unwanted products of our activity (waste), and overexploitation of its natural resources for food, fuel and raw materials. So how do we reconcile certain types of human activity with the limits of the Earth's capacities to sustain life? How can we ensure that systemic effects of our actions be recognised in our planning processes? Will the gain of one group be the loss of another or can we learn our way to 'win-win' situations?

Norman Uphoff, an academic and development practitioner from Cornell University, is among those who has commented on the need to consider open and closed systems, particularly to recognise positive-sum (win-win) rather than zero-sum (win-lose) or negative-sum (lose-lose) dynamics (Uphoff 1995; 1996). Systems may be considered open or closed in terms of matter, energy or information (Boulding 1971). A closed system is one that is closed to inputs from and outputs to its environment. The metaphor 'Spaceship Earth' came largely from thinking of Earth as a closed system dependent on its own resources. The idea of closed and open systems seems very relevant to global citizenship. Whether we perceive systems at levels below the global level as open or closed seems likely to determine our actions.

In one of his papers Uphoff concluded that 'However limiting physical resources may be, our minds are more constricting and they are where we should look for solutions to our various resource scarcities and constraints' (Uphoff 1995).

Others have written in similar vein, for instance Ervin Laszlo, who discussed the links between the outer and inner dimensions of globalisation.

> We need to take into consideration another dimension of the globalisation process: the 'inner' rather than the 'outer' dimension. The outer dimension . . . is the evolutionary system-building process heading toward a globe-spanning and globally interdependent socio-economic

and ecologic system. The inner dimension, on the other hand, is the human dimension: it consists of the way people perceive the globalisation process and the way they and their societies internalise it in their culture. The inner dimension decides whether the outer dimension is oriented to move along humane and sustainable pathways, or whether it leads to mounting crises, and ultimately disaster. (Laszlo 1999)

These comments are also a reminder that different perceptions are products of interactions between external and internal environments and that people will make different selections and interpretations in relation to their environment which will affect what systems they perceive to be relevant to a situation.

There are many examples to show that how we think about and structure what we experience in the world can determine our actions. Taking an example from our own practice, if we drew boundaries around our 'environmental education' system to include only formal-sector education we would perceive stakeholders to be a particular group of people. However, an environmental education system that included non-formal education would include others in the educational community from a wide range of non-governmental organisations. Similarly, if we adopted a narrow meaning of environment that was biased towards either non-human or human elements we might also identify different stakeholders from an environmental education system that adopted a broader definition. These boundaries would be significant if, say, we wanted to involve stakeholders in developing educational policy to help address an issue such as transport.

Another example may be how Oxfam appears to see global citizenship. One of their summary documents includes the following:

### The Global Citizen

Oxfam sees the Global Citizen as someone who:
- is aware of the wider world and has a sense of their own role as a world citizen;
- respects and values diversity;
- is willing to act to make the world a more equitable and sustainable place;
- takes responsibility for their actions. (Oxfam 1998: 2)

### The Key Elements for Responsible Global Citizenship

Knowledge and understanding
- Social justice and equity
- Diversity

- Globalisation and interdependence
- Sustainable development
- Peace and conflict

Skills
- Critical thinking
- Ability to argue effectively
- Ability to challenge injustice and inequalities
- Respect for people and things
- Co-operation and conflict resolution

Values and attitudes
- Sense of identity and self-esteem
- Empathy
- Commitment to social justice and equity
- Value and respect for diversity
- Concern for the environment and commitment to sustainable development
- Belief that people can make a difference (Oxfam 1998: 3)

The intended curriculum clearly covers a broad range of knowledge and understanding, skills, values and attitudes that are highly relevant to the discussion on global citizenship. The detail given in the teachers' and education guide from which the above extracts have been taken gives a much fuller picture. But judging the way in which global citizenship is being considered just from these lists alone, it seems to us that some of the non-human factors are implicit rather than explicit. It would be interesting to hear what systems those who have developed and used these lists would consider relevant and whether different boundaries would be drawn by those using them if some of the non-human factors, on which human activities depend, were made a little more explicit.

Working out what systems are relevant in problem situations, where people are seeking to take purposeful action, has been one of the focuses of soft systems methodology (SSM) which was designed and developed by Peter Checkland through a long-standing action research programme at Lancaster University. One of Checkland's reflections on selecting relevant systems is that 'No human activity system is intrinsically relevant to any problem situation, the choice is always subjective. We have to make some choices, see where the logical implications of those choices take us, and so learn our way to truly "relevant systems"' (Checkland and Scholes 1990). SSM includes describing systems of interest in terms of the mnemonic 'CATWOE':

| | |
|---|---|
| Customers | the victims or beneficiaries of T |
| Actors | those who would do T |
| Transformation process | the conversion of input to output |
| 'Weltanschauung' | the worldview that makes this T meaningful in context |
| Owners | those who could stop T |
| Environmental constraints | elements outside the system which it takes as given. |

(Checkland and Scholes 1990: 35)

A human activity system can, as a result, be given a series of different definitions depending on what is perceived as its purpose (that is, the transformation process that is central to it), its underpinning worldview, what is constraining it and who is involved. One example could be a system to reclaim glass bottles for recycling, which could be described much more specifically through a 'root definition' as

A local authority-owned and staffed system to enable members of the public to return glass bottles they have used so that they can be reprocessed rather than going to landfill.

C = members of the public
A = local authority and members of the public
T = used and dispersed glass bottles to collected glass bottles for recycling
W = it is more desirable for glass bottles to be reclaimed and recycled than for them to go to landfill
O = local authority
E = technical feasibility of recycling, market for reclaimed glass

This is a simple example but CATWOE can be used in much more complex situations as a way of making more apparent what is going on, why and who is involved. Even with this example some of our assumptions become apparent. Use of CATWOE is only one part of SSM and there is not the space here to go into the detail or give examples of how it works in practice. The process of drawing out the details of transformation, worldview, who is involved and so on, may be considered systematic but it is part of a methodology that can be used systemically. Many people have used SSM, and other systems methods and methodologies, to gain insights into their systems of interest and what actions may be appropriate. By using simple examples in this chapter we are not trying to suggest that systems approaches provide quick and easy solutions to problems in complex multistakeholder situations. Nor are we suggesting that they should necessarily replace other approaches. We are saying that systems methods and methodologies provide ways of taking multiple partial views of a whole system, recognising underlying assumptions and worldviews and working out what and whose systems are relevant to a situation. As such, systems approaches have been found to be useful not just for understanding situations but in helping in negotiation processes and in resolution of issues.

One example of working out what systems are relevant in the context of global citizenship comes from Agenda 21, which has been taken up by many people who are trying to operate as citizens at different levels; local, national and global. The Commission on Sustainable Development (CSD) has responsibility for following up Agenda 21's many recommendations at an international level. The decision-making processes of the CSD have evolved since 1992. There have been many negotiations and much drafting and re-drafting of documents in this international arena. In general, the approach has not appeared to be systemic. More systems thinking among participants would probably have been useful. Attention has been given to cross-cutting issues, participation of representatives of many different stakeholder groups and initiatives such as the Committee of the Whole (COW). But in breaking down Agenda 21 to its constituent parts in attempts to implement and monitor, some vital links have either not been made or not sustained. Among them are links between educators and carers for the environment and those within governments among different departments with responsibilities for environmental sustainability, economic development and social justice. It is therefore perhaps not surprising that many of Agenda 21's issues still remain unaddressed and the holistic vision of Rio seems once again to have become fragmented and arguably less of a threat to established ways of doing things (Harvey 1995; Smyth et al. 1997; Blackmore and Smyth 1998).

## SYSTEM LEVELS AND EMERGENT PROPERTIES IN RELATION TO GLOBAL CITIZENSHIP

Norman Uphoff's insights into systems came from many years of working in agriculture in developing countries. He is one practitioner who has focused not just on elements of systems but on trying to gain understanding of the relationships between them. In a paper describing insights into systems from his work on irrigation, Uphoff wrote:

> Anyone who works in and on irrigation systems comes to appreciate the interconnectedness of physical and social systems (which are really subsystems), with irrigation itself becoming understood as a socio-technical enterprise (Uphoff 1986: 3–11). The physical aspects of irrigation need to be disaggregated into a number of subsystems – soils, crops, water (hydraulic), structures (engineering) – and likewise the social and organisational elements – administrative systems, households,

farm enterprises. And all irrigation systems exist within larger ecosystems and are affected by factors like rainfall, topography, and competing water uses. Systems thinking should come naturally to engineers, administrators, social scientists and others who deal with irrigation, because of the manifold connectedness of components. But despite use of the word 'system' as a descriptive term, there is little explicit consideration of the implications of the nestedness and interaction of subsystems and systems. (Uphoff 1996: 1–2)

Figure 1 is a systems map we have drawn of the irrigation system described by Uphoff.

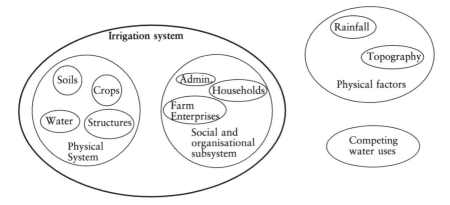

Figure 15.1 systems map of the irrigation system

The concept of system levels seems central to global citizenship, where individuals who may become global citizens also operate at a range of other levels. It is an important one to consider because systems often possess emergent properties that their subsystems do not. One classic example of emergent properties is that of the wetness of water when the gases hydrogen and oxygen combine. The emergent properties of a system are unpredictable and cannot be understood just by analysing the parts of the system. The idea of emergent properties extends into many situations and they are sometimes discussed as environmental surprises (for example, by Myers 1997 and Kates and Clark 1996). Ozone depletion, for instance, can be considered a surprise at a system level that allows relatively inert chlorofluorocarbons to be released from refrigerators and break down into simpler substances in the upper atmosphere during the polar winter, which then destroy ozone when the sun returns in spring. (Though ozone depletion could also be thought of quite differently, depending on what systems are being considered, by whom and for what purpose.) Another example from our own experience was when the subsystems of environmental and development educationalists in the UK got together to prepare and later follow up educational objectives of the Rio Earth

Summit as the Education for Sustainability Forum. Environmental and development educationalists focus on many of the same issues of people and their environment, albeit with different emphases. While there may be as much variation within these subsystems as between them, because of different interests and understandings of environment or development, it seems to us that a system that includes them both and allows them to interact shows quite different properties from its subsystems.

It will not be possible to predict what properties may emerge at different system levels in different people's global citizenship systems. But it may help to think systemically and to recognise different system levels to work out how to facilitate interaction and to realise that these systems will not simply be a sum of their parts. The interdependence of humankind and its environment means that global citizenship cannot be achieved through concentrating on human factors alone. It is essential that political, economic, social, biological and physical dimensions be seen as parts of one system so that we recognise the effects of our actions. While we have scope to construct and reconstruct many systems, both physically and conceptually, and to be creative, efficient and ethical in our endeavours, there are limits to what we as humans can use, pollute and control. We believe that a systems approach to global citizenship has much to offer both to help us in working out our future actions for global citizenship and in recognising where these limits lie.

---

### QUESTIONS

1. Why do the authors seem to think that more systems thinking is needed to make sense of the complexity people experience in the world?
2. Draw a systems map (of the type shown in Figure 1 in this chapter) of one of your global citizenship systems of interest. Be sure to label the diagram clearly showing the boundaries of your system and its sub-systems and what lies in its environment.
3. Say why you think your system of interest is relevant to global citizenship.
4. The authors state that they think the idea of system levels is central to global citizenship. Why do they appear to think this? Do you agree?
5. Can you identify any emergent properties at different levels in your system of interest?

---

# 16. ECONOMIC GLOBALISATION AND GLOBAL CITIZENSHIP

## David Newlands

### INTRODUCTION

The last fifty years have witnessed a process of economic globalisation which has led to the rapid growth of world production and trade but at the expense of enormous inequality between and within countries. This has important implications for the nature and prospects of global citizenship. Many of the world's people do not have command over sufficient resources to satisfy their basic material needs. In addition to the obvious effects on health and life expectancy and the inability to maintain a minimum standard of living, it is increasingly recognised that poverty curtails participation in social and political affairs. Citizenship is not just a political or legal process. It also relates to the quality of involvement in the affairs of the community. In this sense, the poor are not equal citizens. Indeed, one writer has argued that 'Properly understood, a poor citizen is a contradiction in terms' (Vincent 1991: 205).

This paper discusses the economic aspects of globalisation. The concept of economic globalisation and the principal processes by which it takes place are considered first. There is then a separate discussion of the experience of globalisation in less developed countries. The consequences of economic globalisation for global citizenship are analysed next. Finally, some of the issues and options for the future are discussed.

### 1. ECONOMIC GLOBALISATION

The globalisation of trade and finance has been under way for decades, if not centuries, depending on how it is defined. The major institutions of the

Western international economic order were created after 1945. They have presided over a dramatic reduction in the barriers to free international trade and a corresponding expansion in the extent of world trade. Controls over the movement of finance have also been reduced and there has been an explosion in the volume of international capital flows. The figures are mind-blowing. Trillions (thousands of millions) of dollars are moved between countries every day, some to finance productive investment, most to exploit minuscule differences in interest rates or shifts in exchange rates.

Transnational corporations have been a major vehicle of the expansion of both trade and finance. In the last ten years, the abandonment of central planning by formerly communist countries has led to the further expansion of the scope of the capitalist world order based on relatively free international trade and capital movements.

After 1945, government policy decisions led to the liberalisation of trade. Increasing trade between countries then brought closer financial relationships in its train and pressure to liberalise capital flows. The liberalisation of trade and international financial movements was also due to a shift in opinion as to the appropriate role of government in the economy. Support for government intervention has fallen, with a consensus emerging in developed countries that, at the very least, a prominent role should be given to market forces.

Among the principal vehicles of the globalisation of trade and finance are the General Agreement on Tariffs and Trade (GATT), which was superseded by the World Trade Organisation (WTO) in 1995, the International Monetary Fund (IMF) and the World Bank. The GATT provided a framework for the reduction of trade barriers and management of multilateral trade agreements. There were eight Rounds in which GATT members negotiated mutual reductions in trade barriers, from the Geneva Round in 1947 to the Uruguay Round in 1994. The WTO also seeks to settle disputes between members.

The objective of the IMF is to provide a financial framework conducive to the expansion of international trade. It provides loans to countries experiencing balance-of-payments problems. However, over the years it has applied stringent conditions to loans and these have proved very controversial. This has been particularly the case in less developed countries but developed countries have been affected as well. The UK Labour government had to agree to cuts in public spending as part of a loan package from the IMF in 1976.

The World Bank aims to promote economic development by providing loans on favourable terms to finance investment projects where private capital is not forthcoming. However, it too has been accused of pursuing an agenda of market-oriented structural adjustment policies to the neglect of the alleviation of poverty. More generally, it has been argued that the World Bank and the IMF reflect the interests of Western developed countries because of the way in which they are funded and organised. While they are both owned collectively by over 180 member countries, the voting strength of each country depends on its contribution which is in turn proportional to its economic size. Richer countries make larger contributions and are rewarded with greater power over the policies of the IMF and the World Bank.

In parallel with these institutions of the Western international economic order, the growth of transnational corporations has been a key development in the expansion of international trade and capital movements.

This is the principal evidence of economic globalisation over the last half-century or more. However, doubts have been expressed as to the extent of globalisation and even of its existence. While there has been a considerable reduction in the obstacles to the free movement of goods and of capital, this has not been true of labour. The reasons for this are discussed below.

The grounds for questioning the whole idea of globalisation arise because of the continued existence, and even entrenchment, of regional economic blocs. For example, the processes of economic integration have gone furthest in Western Europe, with the expansion and strengthening of the European Union (EU) since its formation in 1957. However, in many ways the EU can be seen as a regional economic empire no different from those empires that have existed throughout all human history. Over the last forty years membership of the EU has grown and, in a number of faltering steps, of which the launch of the Euro is the latest, the degree of integration of the member economies has increased. At the same time, though, as the EU has brought down barriers to the free movement of goods and finance within its boundaries, it has maintained barriers between itself and the rest of the world. Further economic empires exist in North America, centred on the US, and in Asia, centred on Japan.

## 2. The Experience of Globalisation in Less Developed Countries

The relationship between trade and development has been the subject of fierce controversy. In the 1950s and 1960s, in particular, there was considerable 'trade pessimism'. Many less developed countries (LDCs) raised trade barriers and sought to industrialise behind them. Since the 1960s there has been a widespread shift towards 'trade optimism'. To some extent there was a greater appreciation of the economic arguments as to why exports should be encouraged. However, in general, 'changing attitudes towards trade policies in LDCs were driven by observation rather than by any intellectual argument' (Pomfret 1997: 104). Most attempts to industrialise behind trade barriers were unsuccessful. In addition, there was the example of such countries as Taiwan and South Korea which appeared to prosper in global markets. Both adopted policies to encourage exports around 1960, with dramatic results.

Others remain sceptical. It has been argued that exporters of primary products face declining prices for their products. Transnational corporations exert monopolistic control over international product and technology markets. Many also contend that the very success of the East Asian countries has provoked developed countries to try to close the door on LDCs coming behind South Korea or Taiwan. Despite a general trend towards reduced protectionism, developed countries still impose tariff and non-tariff barriers on the exports of LDCs. A further source of doubt has been the recent experiences of Asian economies, including crashes in the stock markets of several countries, which provide graphic illustrations of the risks, as well as potential gains, from participation in international trade and financial markets.

Most of all, critics of the global economic order argue that it disproportionately benefits rich countries. A number of East Asian economies have succeeded in catching up on developed countries over the last thirty or forty years but they are very much the exception. For example, between 1985 and 1995 income per capita in developed countries rose by 1.9 per cent per annum. In Latin America and the Caribbean, it rose by just 0.3 per cent per annum, while in Africa income per capita *fell* by 1.1 per cent per annum. As a result the (already large) income gap between rich and poor has increased dramatically. In 1960 the income levels of the richest 20 per cent of the world's population were 30 times those of the poorest 20 per cent. By 1991 this ratio had increased to 61 to 1 (Todaro, 2000).

In addition to trade, the other principal aspect of globalisation in LDCs is the option to borrow on world financial markets. The theory of commercial borrowing is that LDCs can use such funds to finance a development strategy which remains under national control, something which may not be true if there is heavy reliance on foreign direct investment by transnational companies. If borrowed funds are invested in profitable projects, repayment need not pose a problem. However, borrowing has led many LDCs to severe problems of debt repayment. In absolute terms, debt is greatest in Latin America but, relative to export revenues or national income, the position of many low-income African countries is much worse.

The IMF and many Western banks and governments have argued that less developed countries should tackle their debt problems by reducing imports and increasing exports. The IMF in particular has sought to impose devaluation and deflation. This has led to increasing poverty, cuts in public services and increasing unemployment. Often, this has been self-defeating, since it merely strengthens the vicious circle by which the diversion of funds to service debts reduces the prospects of extrication from further borrowing. On the other hand, there has been some recent softening of the IMF position.

Various groups have been affected by the debt crisis. Western banks have been unable to fully recover their loans and have had to make provision for bad debts. However, Western governments have increasingly come under pressure to ease the banks' problems. Not least, in most developed countries, banks receive tax relief on provision for bad debts. The ruling groups in less developed countries have also managed to escape many of the consequences of excessive borrowing despite their responsibility for a large part of the debts. It is these ruling groups which have pursued wildly ambitious industrialisation strategies and other prestige projects such as international airports or new capital cities. It is they who have spent vast sums of money on arms. And it is they who have secretly and illegally transferred borrowed capital abroad. It has been the poor who have borne the brunt of price increases on basic foodstuffs, cuts in employment and wages, and reduced spending on health, education and nutrition programmes which are the various ways in which the debt crisis manifests itself in practice.

## 3. THE CONSEQUENCES OF ECONOMIC GLOBALISATION FOR GLOBAL CITIZENSHIP

The arguments underlying the liberalisation of trade and capital movements are that they increase economic efficiency and the rate of economic growth. Higher exports and inflows of foreign capital increase the resources available for investment. An emphasis on exports helps concentrate investment in the most efficient sectors of the economy, those in which the country concerned can compete internationally. Participation in a global economy increases access to advanced technology and the other sources of economic dynamism. Firms are forced to be efficient and productive if they are to survive. People benefit from being able to buy goods and services at the lowest prices and from higher real incomes.

At the same time, liberalisation imposes costs, often very considerable ones. Those businesses which cannot compete in international markets contract or fold and those who work in them become unemployed. Pressure to keep costs down and profits up may mean that all sorts of shortcuts are taken with severe consequences for the natural environment and the health, safety, working conditions and wages of employees. Even if overall benefits exceed costs, the experience of free trade may not be positive at the level of individual countries or regions or industries.

Most countries, rich and poor, are keen to attract transnational investment. It is seen as a source of capital but also as providing access to new technology and scarce managerial and other skills. There is a well-developed critique of this position in which it is argued that transnational corporations often employ inappropriate technologies, establish few local economic linkages, create relatively little direct employment and extract excessive profits. Transnational corporations have been seen as one of the principal vehicles of the spread of Western capitalism in less developed countries and, more recently, in former communist countries.

These developments can be viewed as the triumph of capitalism in which peoples across the world acknowledge that the global capitalist system is the most efficient means of delivering increased output and income and thus higher material standards of living. 'Its guiding image is that the world is becoming unified around a common business elite' (Falk 1994: 134–5). The price to be paid is the acceptance that there will inevitably be economic instability and enormous economic inequality. This, in turn, means an acceptance, if only implicit, that there will be constraints on some citizens' ability to fully participate in social and political affairs.

There is nothing new about the idea of poverty and economic insecurity limiting citizens' social and political involvement. However, economic globalisation has resulted in a severe mismatch between the scope of capitalist economic forces and the effectiveness of institutions, such as welfare state systems, which seek to mitigate the consequences of such forces. Thus there has been a 'progressive divergence between political and economic boundaries. The nation-states to which governments address their economic policies often deviate from the economic areas in which global market forces operate' (Guitian 1999: 27). Others go further and argue that globalisation has created 'a world in which states are "losing control"' (Delanty 2000: 86).

The widespread belief that substantial net economic benefits follow from free trade and free capital movements has led to trade and financial movements being encouraged. However, while the same type of economic arguments might suggest that net economic benefits arise from international movements of labour, such movements of people are not encouraged. Indeed, the *Universal Declaration of Human Rights* includes the right to leave but not the right to enter a country. Reflecting the origin of the *Universal Declaration of Human Rights* in the Cold War era, the statement of the right to leave a country was directed primarily at dissidents in communist countries.

The economic reasons for the opposition to free international movement of people are not difficult to identify. Migrants from low-wage to high-wage countries typically benefit from an increase in income. People in countries which migrants leave typically benefit since some of the downward pressure of labour supply on wage levels is relieved. However, people in countries to which people migrate will find that the same downward pressure of labour supply on wage levels is increased. Thus loosening restrictions on immigration will generally lead to lower wages.

The consequence is that countries may admit migrants if they have trouble filling the type of low-status, badly paid jobs that nationals will not consider. Alternatively, if the migrants are wealthy they may gain entry. For example, many countries would only admit people leaving Hong Kong on its return to China if they brought minimum (often large) amounts of money with them. Many economic migrants are not granted citizenship and are not eligible to receive welfare benefits. Few countries consider escape from poverty and unemployment to be a consideration for the admission of refugees. There has nevertheless been a significant increase in economic migration, much of it illegal. Restrictions on legal immigration thus preclude access to formal citizenship and increase the social exclusion of ethnic minorities.

## 4. ISSUES AND OPTIONS

What of the future? One possibility, albeit a remote one, is a reversal of the process of economic integration which has taken place over the last fifty years. 'Disintegration' has happened before. It happened in the 1930s when there were several rounds of competitive devaluations of the major currencies as countries sought to steal a march on each other. These beggar-my-neighbour policies then exacerbated the economic problems of the Great Depression leading to a dramatic reduction in the volume of world trade. Trade in manufactured goods fell by 31 per cent between 1926–30 and 1931–3 and trade in primary products fell by 47 per cent over the same period.

While a general reversal of the process of integration is very unlikely, some countries nevertheless choose to withdraw from the global capitalist system. However, their number is small and falling. The price of isolation from the globalisation of trade and finance, in terms of economic backwardness, appears to be unacceptably high.

At the opposite end of the spectrum of possible options, countries could entrust themselves to the free market. However, no countries seem prepared to abandon themselves to the roller-coaster of global capitalism. A major reason is that even those countries with well-organised economic systems, productive and competitive firms, and effective government policies, cannot insulate themselves from the mistakes of others.

There is an intermediate option, in which global citizenship is interpreted as a concern with the better management of the global economic order. In this view of the future, the constraints on national economic decision-making that a global system imposes are recognised and accepted, however grudgingly, and effort is devoted to the design of a framework to regulate international trade and finance more effectively. The controversy lies with the degree and instruments of management and with distributional issues such as which countries and peoples reap the benefits of intervention and which bear the costs.

There have been various suggestions as to the components of a reformed international framework for the management of trade and finance. Some have argued for the creation of new international institutions, notably a world central bank which would replace the IMF and World Bank. This would aim to promote global financial stability and to act as a lender of last resort to national financial institutions.

Even if the IMF and World Bank survive, there are growing calls for them to be radically reformed. For example, it has been argued that 'the IMF needs to function more as a development institution and less as an international policeman for the developed world and its international banks. It should exhibit greater flexibility in its conditionality requirements and focus more on reviving growth in debt-laden countries and less on imposing a fixed menu of stabilisation measures' (Todaro 2000: 715). Some progress has been made in this direction in recent years.

New global taxes have been advocated. The American economist James Tobin has argued for a tax on international currency transactions. Others have argued for a carbon tax. Such taxes might achieve global objectives: a reduction in financial speculation and instability in the case of the Tobin tax and a reduction in pollution and the depletion of non-renewable energy sources in the case of the carbon tax. Simultaneously, they might also raise additional resources to aid those who have not shared in the benefits of globalisation.

Attitudes to aid, including debt relief, are often viewed as the litmus test of the viability of creating a global economic community. Prompted by the Jubilee 2000 coalition, some debt relief programmes for the world's poorest countries have been introduced. Moreover, there has been serious discussion of how to avoid the damaging side-effects of aid. The problem is that many studies of past aid (including debt relief) programmes suggest that aid does little to alleviate poverty or improve the economic performance of recipients. Indeed, there are arguments that aid impedes development. There are numerous examples of aid being used to support ineffective or corrupt governments. It may encourage irresponsible financial policies. The benefits of aid may be appropriated by richer groups. Aid may weaken economic incentives. Designing more effective aid programmes, however, will not be easy.

The slow pace of construction of new international economic institutions to manage international trade, capital and labour movements has meant that the gap between the effects of global capitalist forces and efforts to regulate such forces has increased rather than decreased.

This has given impetus to another interpretation of global citizenship as transnational activism. The type of action represented by the Jubilee 2000 coalition has been pursued by other groups on issues such as 'fair trade' and a huge range of environmental campaigns. One of the most prominent networks is called 50 Years Is Enough. Linking citizens' groups in the US, Eastern Europe and the Third World, it was formed on the fiftieth anniversary of the foundation of the IMF and the World Bank and is pressing for changes to the statutes and policies of these two bodies to, amongst other things, reduce the relative voting strength of rich countries, involve civil society in less developed countries more in the design and implementation of development programmes, and police the operations of transnational corporations more effectively.

Transnational activism could also be extended to include 'anti-capitalist' demonstrations, such as that seen at the meeting of the WTO in Seattle in 2000. Some will resent the association of such demonstrations, and their attendant violence, with the growth of global citizenship but it could be argued that they represent one of the best examples of the development of a global political identity and community.

QUESTIONS

1. In economic terms, is 'globalisation' just a new name for the growth of world trade?
2. Why has the explosion in world trade and capital movements not been accompanied by a corresponding growth in international movements of labour?
3. Should less developed countries become more integrated in the global economy? Do they have any effective choice in the matter?
4. What sort of global institutions should be established so as to better manage the international economy?
5. What opportunities exist within a global capitalist economy for the exercise of active global citizenship?
6. What forms do, or could, active global citizenship take?

# 17. CITIZENSHIP IN OUR GLOBALISING WORLD OF TECHNOLOGY

## Sytse Strijbos

### INTRODUCTION

Technology normally calls to mind all the machines and technical appliances we surround ourselves with and use for a wide range of purposes. We turn on the television to find out what is going on in the world – locally and far away. We push our shopping cart filled with groceries to the cashier who, to the tune of little beeps, reads the barcodes on the items we have placed on the conveyor belt. With the mouse on our computer we click on 'print' and the article we have just completed rolls from our printer. With a pile of paper in our hands we stroll to the photocopier and run off a number of copies. We pick up the telephone to have a moment's contact with someone nearby or far away. With the click of a button we send our e-mails via the Internet and download the information we want to have. We step into a car, train or aeroplane to go to work or on vacation. In every facet of life, technology helps us to achieve our everyday objectives.

This description of our wonderful world of technology could be called naïve – not in the pejorative sense of the term, to be sure, but in the sense of what comes directly to mind from our everyday experience. Copernicus notwithstanding, we still say the sun comes up in the morning and goes down at night, for example. And this depiction has lost none of its meaningfulness for our everyday lives. Yet to understand certain phenomena we do have to know that the sun does not orbit the earth and that it forms the fixed centre point of the solar system.

Now something of the same sort, it seems to me, applies to the way we speak about technology. Thus in order to gain a good grasp of the significance of technology for global citizenship, I shall first endeavour to move away from the naïve depiction of technology expressed above and to penetrate instead into 'the real world of technology' that underlies our everyday experience.

## THE SYSTEMS CHARACTER OF TECHNOLOGY

Striking in the description of technology with which we started is the emphasis on material artefacts. It is a depiction focused on appliances, instruments and machines. Directly connected with this emphasis is a second characteristic of the naïve conception of technology. We use the apparatuses at our disposal to perform certain operations. We do things with them. Technology considered at the level of the artefact concerns the acts of individuals. The world of technology is portrayed as a collection of separate things that an individual can utilise at will in order to achieve a certain goal. Just as we use a hammer to drive a nail into the wall or a rake and shovel to trim the garden in our spare time, so also, according to the naïve conception of technology, do we send an e-mail by computer and drive to work by car. The auto and the computer are nothing more than objects of human use.

It should not be surprising that the naïve conception of technology, which refers to the individually acting person and to everyday experience, originally permeated the philosophy of technology. Ernst Kapp (1808–96), who may be regarded as one of the first philosophers of technology and the person who first used the term philosophy of technology, defended in his *Grundlinien einer Philosophie der Technik* (1877) the model of technology as the projection of human organs. To Kapp there is an intrinsic connection between the organs of the human body and the technological tools that people have produced in history. In his tools, man constantly produces himself. Thus the hand is the natural instrument that is continued in the diversity of hand tools bequeathed to us by primitive cultures. 'The bent finger becomes a hook, the hollow of the hand a bowl; in the sword, spear, oar, shovel, rake, plough and spade one observes sundry positions of arm, hand, and fingers, the adaptation of which to hunting, fishing, gardening, and field tools is readily apparent' (Kapp 1877: 45). Continuing in this vein with examples from our own age, one could say that the crane is a projection of the human arm and the bulldozer of the human hand.

In the meantime, many who have thought deeply about technology have abandoned this naïve view of technology. Ursula Franklin, an emeritus professor of physics at the University of Toronto, published a fascinating book about 'the real world of technology'. In it she discusses the various models that underlie our ideas and our discussions about technology. 'Technology', according to Franklin (1990: 12), 'is not the sum of the artefacts, of the wheels and the gears, of the rails and electronic transmitters. Technology is a *system*. It entails far more than its individual material components. Technology involves organisation, procedures, symbols, new words, equations, and, most of all, a mindset.' In depicting technology as a system, Franklin represents a widely shared view. The systems thinker and biologist von Bertalanffy observed, for example, that the very development of technology led to a different approach to technology in terms not of independent machines, as was long customary, but in terms of systems. The auto, train and aeroplane, for example, depend for their use on an infrastructure or system. The auto presupposes a road network with a complex system of rules for its use, prescriptions for maintenance, financial regulations and the like. On both the user's and the designer's side the systems character of technology makes itself felt. One makes use of the car, train or aeroplane together with others, and in so doing participates in a collective traffic system. And viewed from the design side, one can say with von Bertalanffy (1968: 2) that 'air or even automobile traffic is not just a matter of the number of vehicles in operation, but is a system to be planned or arranged'.

The systems character of technology accordingly means recognising the connections between material artefacts. The traffic system as a technological system is composed of a great variety of components. Thinking about technology in terms of systems also means seeing that such systems function through the participation of many different agents. The 'real world of technology' that underlies the many material artefacts surrounding us in our habitat is composed of countless systems. Technology is not a gadget or apparatus that stands separated from us as an external object but is 'the house' in which we all dwell today. Technology determines the public space of our existence. If we utilise technology by driving our car to work, for example, we participate in one of the systems within which modern society happens. Technology is not only, and not even primarily, a matter of individual actions but of collective forms of action in which modern, so-called 'technological society' takes shape (Ellul 1964; 1980).

## TECHNOLOGY, THE ETHICAL VACUUM AND THE CHALLENGE TO CITIZENSHIP

The Copernican-like insight that technology does not consist of a multiplicity of independent things in our environment but that, on the contrary, technology itself forms our environment, has important implications. The development in technology from artefact to the shared house in which we all dwell has totally altered our social order, not only relations between individuals and within social connections and groups but also relations between nations and individuals, between nations in international intercourse and between all of us and our natural surroundings. This still rather new situation confronts us with new questions at the level of ethics and politics, questions concerning our moral and political responsibility in a world of technology (Strijbos 1998b).

One of my favourite texts for introducing students of information theory to a course in the philosophy and ethics of technology is an essay by Langdon Winner (1990) in which the writer criticises the 'case studies' approach that is so often used in teaching ethics to aspiring professional technicians. In the endeavour to relate the lessons in ethics to actual practice in the most telling way possible, he asserts, precisely that which is most important is lost to view. To illustrate his thesis Winner (1990: 53) uses the following example of a case: 'You are an engineer working for a defence contractor helping to assemble the latest version of the cruise missile. One day you discover that the paint used on the shell of the missile is emitting toxic fumes that may be dangerous to people working in the assembly plant. The project is behind schedule and your boss has made it clear that it must be completed within deadline. Should you blow the whistle on the toxic fumes or keep silent thereby avoiding risk to your own job and career?'

Now, one of the difficulties with paper casuistry is, of course, that a concrete situation must always be described in terms of a selection of the facts. The moral problem is therefore always already identified, implicitly or explicitly, in the description of the case. And since students are confronted with such a description in an academic context, they probably miss of necessity what is perhaps most important for their moral forming, namely, the recognition of moral problems in concrete practical situations they themselves are involved in. Yet this is not the objection to argumentation in ethical education that Winner has in mind. His concern is not that the identification of the moral problem requires a selection of the facts as these are presented in a case study. The heart of his critique is that the technician's practical situation is separated from the broader social cultural context. The moral problem is thereby narrowed to one of individual ethics. 'Should you blow the whistle?' That is the question with which the student is ultimately confronted. The societal objectives to which technicians contribute with their work are left out of consideration. All attention is focused on problem situations that appear within contexts which are themselves withdrawn from critical review, such as the building of thermonuclear weapons in the case above.

Ethical education of this sort, Winner (1990: 54) observes correctly, tends to legitimate and reinforce the status quo. Students learn to cope with moral dilemmas in their professional activities and gain insight into questions at the level of individual ethics but are not made conscious of the political and societal dimensions of the responsibility of the technical expert. Technology and politics remain separated domains for them.

While I do not question the usefulness or the need for programmes in ethics in the university curriculum, their possibilities should not be overestimated (Strijbos 1998a). One may indeed hope that educational efforts will contribute to a clear consciousness in the technical professions of a broader societal responsibility. Yet even the best instruction cannot eliminate the signalised gap between technology and ethics. Winner (1995) seems quite well aware of this. He does not hesitate to speak of a vacuum in ethics when it comes to important choices in our society involving the application and development of new technologies. A similar note is struck by Jonas (1984). This philosopher of technology, while seeking to articulate a new ethics for our technological times, adopts the term 'ethical vacuum'. In line with both these thinkers, I would now like to say three things about this matter.

In the first place, the ethical vacuum in question has an intellectual background. The development of technology and the Copernican revolution in the conception of technology that goes with it – from artefact to system – makes mandatory the formation of new ethical theories as well. Technology, according to Jonas, has confronted us with entirely new dimensions of human power and a qualitative change in the realm of human action. Modern technology considered as the environment in which we live means a strong interweaving of individual human actions that can amplify one another. It is not the individual agent or the individual act but the aggregate, the collective subject, that is characteristic of various processes in the era of technology. The emission of $CO_2$ into the environment by traffic, households and industry, resulting in the greenhouse effect, is a familiar example. In traditional situations an action and its effects could be identified with a fair degree of certainty but that is ever less possible given the interweaving of factors to which we have just alluded. Thus one of the problems we face is to stimulate ethical theory formation for a field of collective human action (cf. Strijbos 1998a: 278–9).

The ethical vacuum has in the second place a social or political component. Namely, one of the consequences of the interdependencies that mark our technological environment is that it is difficult, if not impossible, to identify the agents, be they persons or organisations, that have the authority to take the necessary decisions. In our capitalistic liberal-democratic complex with its free-market economy, clearly defined social channels and institutions for identifying important moral issues and dealing with them effectively simply do not exist. 'Typically, what happens in such cases', according to Winner, 'is that, as time passes, a mixture of corporate plans, market choices, interest group activities, lawsuits, and government legislation takes shape to produce jerry-built policies' (Winner 1995: 65).

Jonas (1984: 147) too wrestles with this problem and even weighs at the theoretical level the pros and cons of an absolute civil authority led by a well-informed elite. It is silly to accuse him, as has at times been done, of championing a global eco-dictatorship. Such a criticism simply evades an unresolved and apparently inherent problem of our current social-political order, namely, that of how democratic citizenship and the responsible shaping of our technological society can be made to rhyme. Is it possible to cultivate in our liberal democracies a form of citizenship that can steer and, on a world scale, provide guidance to the current processes of the technicisation and globalisation of society? Here we already touch upon a question to which we must return. First, however, an observation about a third and (to my mind) most fundamental aspect of the ethical vacuum.

It is true that the moral impotence affecting our societies has something to do with intellectual shortcomings and with the absence of the political structures necessary for guiding our technological world along paths that are good. Yet the solution we seek cannot be found solely in the latest discoveries from the laboratories of today's 'ethical engineers' or in the implementation of improved democratic procedures for consultation and decision-making. For the concurrence of our being adrift, on the one hand, and of the enormous planetary dynamics of technology, on the other hand, is not just an accidental and highly unfortunate coincidence. 'For the very same movement', to speak with Jonas, 'which put us in possession of the powers that have to be regulated by norms – the movement of modern knowledge called science – has by a necessary complementarity eroded the foundations from which norms could be derived; it has destroyed the very idea of norm as such' (Jonas 1984: 22).

The fact that our technological world has come to lack a moral compass is at bottom a spiritual and religious matter having, as it were, metaphysical roots. 'First it was nature that was neutralised with respect to value, then man himself. Now we shiver in the nakedness of a nihilism in which near-omnipotence is paired with near-emptiness, greatest capacity with knowing least for which ends to use it' (Jonas 1984: 23). This assessment of our situation does not lead Jonas to the claim of his mentor Heidegger (1977) that only a god can save us now. Religion and an appeal to God do not relieve ethics of its proper task. Nonetheless, Jonas expressly seeks a metaphysical anchor for the new ethics with the 'heuristic of fear' as its most important rule.

It is tempting to see here more broadly the relation between religion and ethics, particularly because 'fear' interpreted as the 'fear of the Lord' is also a key notion in the biblical tradition. Resisting this temptation, I return to the subject at hand in order to say about the idea of citizenship: is technology beyond control by human agency in the emerging world system or does globalisation offer new possibilities to the citizen who is consciously participating in the global technological society?

## RESPONSIBLE CITIZENS IN A GLOBALISING WORLD

Thinking globally has been much in vogue in recent years, at least in the industrialised countries of the world. In that context 'globalisation' is a magical word. Although it is not always clear precisely what the term means, it is in any case a matter under constant and animated discussion in scientific circles, particularly amongst economists and sociologists, and amongst leading figures in industry and politics. Telling for the importance of the subject is the fact that in my country, the Netherlands, one of the most prominent political figures since the Second World War, Ruud Lubbers, following his departure from the political arena as prime minister of the Netherlands accepted an appointment as a professor of economic globalisation.

Striking in the stream of publications about the phenomenon of globalisation is the strong emphasis on economics that one finds in them. There are allusions to a world economy, to the globalisation of the market and the growth of multinational companies, and to the role of competition. Certainly the role of technology is acknowledged but to my mind that role is still insufficiently understood inasmuch as it is still the naïve conception of technology that comes through in most of the thinking. In his monumental study Manuel Castells adopts the revolution in information technology as his 'entry point in analysing the complexity of new economy, society, and culture in the making' (Castells 1996: 5). This methodological choice, which he emphatically justifies, does not mean that in his view new social forms and processes are purely a consequence of technological change. The writer rejects technological determinism but also its reverse – that is, the conception that society does not follow but rather that it determines technological development. Technological determinism places us before a false dilemma, according to Castells, 'since technology *is* society, and society cannot be understood or represented without its technological tools' (Castells 1996: 5). Technology and society cannot simply be juxtaposed as independent entities. Now although I agree with this – our 'technological tools' are indeed a part of society, and society avails itself of these 'technological tools' – I want to emphasise here again that technology can no longer be understood as a collection of human 'tools'. Society has become a system, a world in which we live within which 'technological tools' have been interwoven and within which they fulfil their function.

What is today called globalisation is in fact nothing other than some more or less fundamental structural changes that are going on in a world technological system that has existed for some time. Technology considered as humanity's habitat is by nature unimpeded by national boundaries. That is also true of the effects of technology on the natural environment. 'Global warming', for example, manifests the reverse side of the 'global technical system.' The boundary-exceeding technological infrastructures of communications, traffic and transport have been transformed in recent decades by information and computer technology into gargantuan 'megamachines', to borrow a term from a fascinating study of globalisation by the Group of Lisbon (1995: 4), led by Riccardo Petrella, head of the Forecasting and Assessment in Science and Technology (FAST) programme at the Commission of the European Union in Brussels and professor at the Catholic University of Louvain: 'Air traffic is constantly being integrated by increasingly sophisticated computer monitoring and control systems; aeroplanes themselves are being transformed into flying terminals of a global computer system. A megamachine is growing.' In the same development that has required pilots to yield control of their aircraft to a megamachine that embraces the entire globe, national authorities lose control of their airlines and skies. A development similar to the one in air traffic may be observed in automobile traffic.

There too there is a development in the direction of a 'global transportation machine' controlled in large measure by the large auto manufacturers and oil companies.

Against the background of these developments in the technological system, the phenomenon of globalisation takes shape. In the environment of mega-technological structures, there would seem to be little or no future for democratic control and steersmanship (Mander 1996: 358). Globalisation and the progressive technicisation of our habitat through its translation into information and computerisation are coherent processes in what would appear to be an unstoppable movement over which we have lost every possibility of social-political control. 'New technologies make the boundaries ever more permeable,' observes Lubbers (1998: 17). 'That is globalisation.' However, that has led to vitiation of national policies geared to particular territories. While a national regime may have the power, with a view to the quality of society, to restrict the economy and its interaction with technological innovation in some measure, the market will prevail in the end. That is why our politicians sigh with ever greater frequency and intensity: we can do nothing, for if we raise taxes our firms will relocate across the border. The technological order of modern society begins, more and more, to exhibit totalitarian features.

It is tempting to conclude that, with the globalisation of society, the political dimension tends to shrivel away into insignificance. Democratic citizenship cannot enter or penetrate the world technological order, which seems to obey only the rules of its own dynamics. However, there is something to do for responsible citizens facing the trends in a globalising world of technology. In the view of the Group of Lisbon the current situation demands for a new type of global governance. In particular a need exists for the development of a new generation of social contracts on a global scale. Societies today are confronted with the same problem as nineteenth- and early twentieth-century societies. The difference lies in the scale of the problem. As a promoter and guarantor of the public interest, the state intervened and bridled the excesses of competitive capitalism on a national scale. Today we have to find policies on a global scale. The most important goal in the era of globalisation does not relate to higher competitiveness in global economic wars but should be concerned with identifying solutions to satisfy the material and immaterial needs of the world's population.

It is precisely in this context that the idea of the civil society is gaining renewed importance and comes to the fore in the political debate. In the debate the term 'civil society' has multiple meanings, however (Cohen and Arato 1992; Walzer 1995b). In the approach of the Group of Lisbon the civil society is pictured as a middle ground differing from both state and market. Traditionally the nation-state protects the public good. In the market, which is regulated by competition, private producers and consumers exchange goods and services. In the civil society private individuals and groups freely join together inspired by common ideals. They include a wide range of movements and organisations such as Greenpeace, Amnesty International, the Red Cross and many other examples. Now that the power of traditional politics has been vitiated to the point that it can offer little resistance to the preponderance of the technological-economic complex, we are witnessing the rise of countless organised social groups and institutions desiring to reassert fundamental human values at various levels, local, national and planetary. Through processes of globalisation and technicisation, people are also ever better connected with one another worldwide. The same forces that power the world technological system onward seem to awaken new forms of global citizenship in a global civil society. The Group of Lisbon (1995: 14) puts it this way: 'Despite the importance of global imagery and the infrastructure of information and communications technologies, they are not the primary forces in the making of the global world. [. . .] The primary creators of the global world are people, their value systems, and the means they employ to achieve their goals.'

---

QUESTIONS

1. Give some examples of technological artefacts you are acquainted with in your environment. How do these artefacts constitute the 'world of technology' or the technological systems in which you live?
2. Take the traffic system as an example of a technological system underlying our society. Which actors are involved in its use and maintenance, how are these actors related to each other and what are, in your view, the ethical responsibilities of the different actors?
3. Reflect on computer and information technology as a technology of globalisation. Do you discern positive possibilities for promoting global citizenship?

---

# 18. IMMIGRATION: WHAT DOES GLOBAL JUSTICE REQUIRE?

## Valeria Ottonelli

In most countries the access to the territory of the state is limited by immigration laws. Those who enter and live on the territory without the permission of the state's authorities are labelled 'illegal aliens'. Coercion can be used against them in order to expel them from the country. Trying to avoid such a fate, most illegal aliens undergo all the pains and risks which are associated with the condition of being an 'outlaw'.

The denial of legal personality to illegal aliens and the use of coercion against them in order to restrict their freedom of movement are grounded on the right of states to limit immigration. Such a right, which is clearly assumed by all the so-called First World countries in their foreign policy, is implicitly recognised by the *Universal Declaration of Human Rights*, where no mention is made of the freedom of movement into a country from another country.

In the following pages I will consider the legitimacy of restrictions on immigration from the perspective of global justice – that is, from the perspective a global citizen should adopt. As we will see, this will imply some limitations on the kinds of arguments which can be employed in defending such policies. Before illustrating the meaning of these limitations, let me spend a few words on the definition of 'freedom of immigration' I am assuming here.

### LEGAL IMMIGRANTS, CITIZENS, REFUGEES

By 'freedom of immigration' to a foreign country I mean the freedom to live and work within its borders, being subject only to the same restrictions to personal freedom that apply to the rest of the resident population.

Freedom of *immigration* must be distinguished from the right to *naturalisation*. Naturalisation is the acquisition of citizenship – that is, of full membership within the political community and of the rights and duties which are attached to it. The rights enjoyed by citizens usually extend much further than the mere freedom to live and work within the borders of the country. They include the right to benefit from the welfare system, the right to public health care (where it exists), the right to public education and, in sum, all those rights which in the classical distinction by T. H. Marshall are called 'social rights', as well as the rights of participation in political decision-making, those known as 'political rights' (Marshall 1973). Granting the freedom to immigrate does not necessarily entail granting social and political rights, that is, full membership in the political community. The question of whether free immigration should be allowed, then, should be kept separate from the question of whether citizenship and the rights attached to it should be extended to foreigners who desire it.

If justifying freedom of immigration implies less than arguing for the right to naturalisation, it implies more than arguing for the right to admission claimed by refugees. Such a right can be recognised at least by anyone who acknowledges the duty to rescue necessitous strangers who are in danger. But freedom of immigration and the correlative duty to allow it are much broader in scope: they concern anybody who decides to move to a foreign country for any reason whatsoever. Since moving to a foreign country implies enormous costs and losses, people have generally very serious reasons for doing so. But not all immigrants are refugees and an argument for free immigration does not imply that immigrants must be in extreme need.[1]

Given this definition, asking whether restrictions on freedom of immigration are legitimate amounts to asking whether states are justified in denying non-citizens the right to move to their territory and the right to work within their borders.

## STATE PARTIALITY AND THE GLOBAL PERSPECTIVE

What does it mean to ask this question from a global perspective? It means to impose some limitations on the kinds of arguments that can be offered for and against free immigration. One of the central features of the understanding of justice from the perspective of a global citizen is the requirement to give equal consideration to each one's rights, interests and well-being independently of nationality, religion, ethnicity, or any other distinction within the universal category of 'humanity'. We can call this the requirement of impartiality.[2] When we assess alternative immigration policies from a global perspective, we ask whether they can be justified from such an impartial standpoint.

Now at first sight it might seem that, once we adopt the requirement of impartiality, the choice between different immigration policies is easily made in favour of open borders. Anti-immigration policies are by definition about the state being 'partial' as to the distribution of the right to move freely and work within its territory.[3] But we should be careful in drawing this conclusion for it is grounded on an interpretation of the requirement of impartiality that is too demanding, and, what is more important, fundamentally misleading. Such interpretation implies that from the perspective of global ethics we must judge that no kind of differential treatment is *ever* justified and that *all* our actions should be inspired by an impartial consideration of the interest of all human beings.

The interpretation in question makes the commitment to global responsibilities unattractive to most of us. We all have special bonds to particular people: the members of our family, our friends, the people we have promised to help, the people we have associated with for trade or other purposes and so on. Having these bonds involves having special obligations towards the people we are bound to and having special obligations entails that, when considering what course of action to adopt, we should give special consideration to the interests and well-being of the people in question. This is a form of partiality. But we value these special bonds and obligations and our capability to establish them. If the commitment to global responsibilities required us to give up our capability to enter special relations with other people or make contractual agreements with them, we might well think that this would be too high a price to pay to become a global citizen.

Second, and most importantly, this strict interpretation of the requirement of impartiality would miss a fundamental point about the nature and the justification of the special bonds in question. For it is false that they cannot be justified from an impartial perspective. Having the ability to establish or entertain those bonds is a good that is valuable to every human being. Other things being equal, a world in which people can establish special relationships with friends and relatives or enter agreements and contracts with other people is a world that everybody would prefer to one where entertaining such special obligations were impossible. So even though the existence of such practices constitutes a ground for partial treatment, in so far as they confer rights on certain people but not on others, at a more fundamental level they can be justified by impartial considerations: they constitute a good that furthers the interest and the well-being of *every* human being and therefore the right to create or fulfil such special obligations can be equally recognised to every human being with equal strength and for exactly the same reasons.

It might be argued that the partial treatment the state reserves for its citizens can be grounded on impartial assumptions in a similar way. This is, in fact, the strategy many advocates of restrictions on immigration have adopted. They have claimed that the partial treatment the state reserves for its members can be grounded on either of two universal rights that should be recognised in relation to all human beings: the right of association and the right to belong to a community. Freedom of association can ground the state's partiality towards its members if we see it as a free cooperative enterprise, where by 'cooperation' we mean not only economic cooperation for the production of wealth, but all the forms of regulated social interaction which give shape to the institutions of a society. In the same way, if we understand the state as a 'community' – that is, as a group of people who are bound together by a common history and a common understanding of the basis for social co-existence – then we can ground its partiality towards citizens as a consequence of the exercise of the right to belong to a community.

As Michael Walzer has pointed out, if we understand the state as a community or as an association (Walzer 1983: 35–42),[4] the requirement of impartiality is misplaced not only because it is in the nature of the bonds in question to be partial but also because the very goods which are partially distributed constitute a product of such entities, so that if people were not allowed to be partial in the sense specified the very goods that are at stake would not exist.[5] Not only wealth and social rights but peaceful coexistence and economic relations are not 'natural goods'; rather they are the product of the cooperative effort of people bound together by special obligations. For these reasons it would be wrong to treat the issue of the distribution of the rights attached to citizenship as if it concerned a mere problem of unequal distribution of natural goods.

According to this perspective, freedom of association and freedom to belong to a community do not only justify the state's partial treatment towards its citizens, they also imply the right to decide who the citizens are. This is another kind of partiality; not all human beings are eligible to receive the partial treatment that the state reserves for its members. Also this sort of partiality is essential to the rights in question: my freedom to associate with other people through contractual agreements would not be such if I did not have the right to decide with whom and for what purposes I want to associate. The same holds for the right to belong to a community: it would be pointless if anybody could decide to enter it. The criteria for membership are chosen by the existing members of associations and culturally inherited by the existing members of communities. We can call this the principle of self-determination of political communities (PSD).

Even though global citizens share a strong commitment to impartiality, and in considering political issues they accord equal consideration to the interests and needs of all human beings, being a global citizen is not incompatible with valuing the special bonds and relationships that may make our social life richer and fuller. This means that, in so far as PSD does not conflict with the basic principles of global justice, a global citizen does not have to but can accept it as a principle for the distribution of the relevant rights.

## IMMIGRATION AND THE LAND

All this means that as global citizens we cannot reject anti-immigration policies on the sole ground that they are not impartial between citizens and non-citizens, since there are forms of partiality which can be justified also from a global perspective. On the other hand, this truth is not sufficient either to establish that anti-immigration policies are always justified. If the state's partiality towards its citizens is justified by the value of the bonds which are established and created by the existence of the political community, anti-immigration laws are justified only in so far as immigration can be proven to be conflicting with the existence of such bonds or undermining of them.

A simple argument that has been advanced in this direction is the following: the particular kinds of communities and associations that states are need to have a territorial basis. If we want to recognise such communities' right to exist, then we must recognise their right of control over a certain territory. This means that we must allow them the right to exclude non-members from that territory (Walzer 1983: 44).

Is this a binding argument? Its first assumption is controversial, since territoriality is not a necessary condition for a political community to exist. But it is true that the modern state is a particular kind of political community that must necessarily have (and that many political communities do, in fact, have) a territorial basis. Even in these cases, though, the conclusion that non-members should be denied access to the territory does not follow. In this argument two different meanings of 'control' are confused. The first meaning refers to the right of a community to rule over a certain territory. In modern times such a right has been recognised to the state as one of its main prerogatives and we can imagine that in many cases such a right is necessary for a political community to exist as a specific form of social organisation.[6] Granting a political community such a right does not mean, of course, recognising it has the right to use coercion in order to enforce any system of rules, including cruel and oppressive ones. But justice can be administered in many different forms and legal systems can vary greatly in content and shape from place to place, depending on the prevailing culture and history of the country and the material conditions existing at a given time. Allowing political communities the right to enforce their rules over a certain territory can be essential to their continued existence; it implies that, once a political community has established its rule over a certain territory, nobody can try to enforce a rival system of rules over the same area. This implies, then, that immigrants should accept to subject themselves to the rules already existing in the host society.

But this must be distinguished from a different interpretation of the idea that a political community must have 'control' over a certain territory. In this second sense 'control' is interpreted as meaning 'exclusive enjoyment'. Now even if we concede that 'control' in the first sense explained might be vital to the existence of a political community, there is no ground for also claiming that the exclusive enjoyment of the land is to be considered as essential to it. Nor is the enjoyment of the land among the products of social cooperation, which means that we can't argue for the right of exclusive control by the members of a community on the same ground as for the right to distribute membership and the social rights attached to it.

Some libertarians have tried to argue for the right of exclusive enjoyment by appealing to the natural right to hold property: if we ascribe such a right to the members of a community then we must recognise the right of the community as a whole to own – and then to enjoy exclusively – the portion of land which is constituted by the sum of its citizens' properties.[7]

Besides the controversial nature of the libertarian assumptions about property rights, this argument cannot hold. If all the territory of the state were a common or collective property of its citizens then there would not be any private property within the state. If only the public areas were considered as common property of its citizens, then it should be possible for immigrants to access them at least in so far as this would be instrumental to the enjoyment of the rights that they could legitimately acquire by buying, renting or simply lawfully occupying some private property within the territory (Carens 1987; Hudson 1984; 1986).

In conclusion, arguments against free immigration cannot be grounded on the state's right of exclusive enjoyment over its territory, since such a right cannot be derived from the rights of association and of membership in a community that we have considered as the foundation of the state's partiality toward its members.

Furthermore, arguing this way seems to miss the point of the discussion about immigration. For immigration is not about the enjoyment of land and immigrants do not move to a foreign country in order to exploit its natural resources. They are not colonisers.[8] Focusing on land overlooks the social dimension of immigration: immigrants do not only move to a different land, but also to a different society, and this is the real source of all troubles.

## IMMIGRATION AND MEMBERSHIP

A more complex argument against open borders,[9] which takes into account the social dimension of immigration, can be put as follows.

A fundamental principle of justice (let's call it the principle of political justice, PPJ) requires that whoever is permanently subject to the laws of a country should have a voice in their making and that whoever takes part in the economy of a country should also participate in the social benefits deriving from the economic cooperation. This principle is intended to prevent differential treatment among the members of the same society – that is, the existence within the society of a class of people who, while sharing the same burdens as the rest of the population, do not share the same benefits arising from the social cooperation. Such a political arrangement could plausibly be considered exploitative and unfair.

Allowing foreigners to establish themselves on the national territory, the argument continues, means allowing them to subject themselves permanently to the laws of the country and to take part in the local economy. This amounts to allowing them to become beneficiaries of the social and political rights which are granted by the principle of political justice. Granting these rights, though, means no less than granting them *citizenship* – that is, full membership in the political community. Such a result clearly conflicts with the principle that communities have a right to shape their membership (PSD).

So even though the right to free immigration does not in itself violate the right of self-determination of political communities, as a matter of fact, through the operation of the principle of political justice, the conflict is inevitable; and if we recognise the right to immigrate we cannot but deny the right of the political community to determine membership. If we want to preserve the latter, conversely, we need to suppress the right to immigration.

About this argument two points need to be made. First of all, much of its plausibility comes from the appeal to the principle of political justice; but such an appeal, in this context, is misleading. The argument assumes that establishing oneself on the national land and becoming a beneficiary of the principle of political justice are one and the same thing. This is the reason why the argument assumes that by banning immigration to the national land one prevents foreigners from becoming beneficiaries of PPJ. But at a closer inspection we find that this is implausible. PPJ applies to anybody who contributes to the national economy and is subject to the laws of the land, independently of where the people involved are located. There is no reason, for example, why someone who is employed by an Italian factory in Hong Kong or Thailand should not fall under the scope of PPJ, as applied to the Italian society, as much as someone who is employed in a factory in Italy. If we want to prevent the principle from being applicable to foreigners, we should not limit ourselves to banning immigration but should ban any form of social and economic cooperation with foreigners.

A similar line of reasoning also holds for political rights. The principle of political justice far from implying any ban on immigration, would require all the people who are concerned by the immigration laws of a country – that is, all foreigners – to have a say in their making. It is plausible to assume that this would not result in the kind of heavy restrictions on freedom of movement which are enforced in the present world.

At a closer look, then, we realise that PPJ does not play any role in the argument considered. What is implicitly assumed in the argument, rather, is a completely different principle, that is the principle of territoriality (PT), which states that whoever lives on the national land should be conferred social and political rights. PT, as far the argument we are considering is concerned, makes PPJ completely irrelevant. Only if we assume PT as a principle for the distribution of membership it is plausible to argue that the presence of non-authorised foreigners on the national territory leads to conflict with PSD.

Once we have clarified the argument in this way, though, it looks much weaker. PT is a much less appealing principle than PPJ and looks much more difficult to justify, not only from the global perspective we are assuming but even from communitarian perspectives. Why should entitlement to social and political rights be conditional upon the crossing of a border, independently of one's relation with the community who is established on the territory?

For the sake of the argument, though, let's assume that we can accept PT as a valid criterion for the conferral of political and social rights, and let's address the central issue of this discussion. PT conflicts with PSD and it is evident that the conflict would never arise in practice if no foreigner ever crossed the national borders; is this a sufficient reason for the adoption of anti-immigration policies?

Clearly, it is not. To realise it, it is sufficient to ask where PT comes from. If we answer that it is a principle of justice which holds independently of any political decision then PSD does not hold: it is false that membership is *entirely* a matter of choice or of cultural tradition. If we answer that PT is chosen by the political community itself then it falls under PSD but it becomes clear that all the troubles come from the fact that the community chooses conflicting membership criteria: a principle of territoriality on one hand and traditional, cultural or economic criteria on the other. No matter how we want to rank these criteria, one thing is clear: we should make up our mind. We cannot write on our borders 'whoever enters this land will enjoy full social and political rights' and then use coercion against whoever tries to enter, since we feel in our heart that only the members of our ethnic group or our economic partners are entitled to full membership within our community.

## IMMIGRATION AND EXPLOITATION

The preceding arguments have been grounded on the conceptual distinction between the freedom of immigration (that is, the right to move to a foreign country and live there) and the right to naturalisation (that is, the right to enjoy full membership in the political community and all the benefits attached to it). The argument did not take sides on the issue of whether all immigrants should be naturalised. Of course, those who think that political communities should enjoy an absolute right to determine their membership will deny that all immigrants should be received as members. This implies that, at least in principle, they must recognise the right of a community to keep on its territory resident workers without granting them the social and political rights that are recognised in relation to the citizens. They cannot ban immigration on the ground that this kind of partiality is unfair and exploitative, since it is implied by PSD itself.

Presumably, a global citizen will not adopt this view and will think instead that each country should follow the mandate of PPJ, extending all the rights and benefits attached to membership *at least* to all its resident workers. For PPJ is a basic political principle that, forbidding any unfair distribution of the burdens and benefits of social cooperation, responds to the requirement of impartiality. We should note here that PPJ does not deny that we can be partial as a consequence of having established special relationships with other people (in other words, it does not deny PSD); what it requires is that, when we do establish such special relations, like when we have someone work for us, or we impose our laws on someone else, we treat all the people involved by the same standards.

However, there is an impartial argument for restricting membership that is binding even for those who accept PPJ. As a matter of fact, there might be structural limits to how many people can resort to the institutional tools which the state sets up in order to secure the enjoyment of social and political rights. Since depriving of them those who are already members would be more traumatic than denying them to those who are not, this latter seems to be the only possible policy to be followed. If we allow free immigration in these circumstances we will necessarily have on the same territory and within the same society two classes of people who, while sharing the same duties and the same burdens, will not enjoy the same rights. Should not global citizens, who accept the principle of political justice, believe that immigration should be restricted at least in these cases in order to prevent a situation that, according to such a principle, should be seen as exploitative and unfair?

On this topic various points need to be made. First of all, it is very likely that our projections about the impossibility of extending membership to all the actual alien residents, and the a fortiori impossibility to extend it to all those who would become residents if free immigration were allowed, are not grounded on sufficient empirical evidence. Actually, it has been proven that, far from putting any real strain on the welfare system, in many countries the presence of immigrant workers has contributed greatly towards relieving precarious financial conditions (Trebilock 1995).

In the same way, there is no evidence of the fact that the extension of political rights to resident aliens would put the democratic system in danger. In truth, the few experiments that have been tried in some European countries do not reveal any evidence of a destabilising impact on the democratic system. Even if immigrants had a tendency to opt for destabilising political choices, this would not be sufficient for them to constitute a serious danger for the democratic regime of the receiving countries. For even though it is true that in many Western countries the proportion of the population represented by resident aliens would be large enough to influence the political outcomes, we must remember that in a developed democracy not only numbers count; what is really important, in many cases, is political organisation. As a matter of necessity newcomers are not politically organised and it is plausible to expect that it would take them a long time before they could organise.[10]

Finally, the projections about the numbers of people who would immigrate to First World countries if they adopted a policy of free immigration are mainly based on statistics about population growth and trends in the economies of Third World countries.[11] There is no doubt that these can be among the major factors of emigration. But no precise correlation has been established yet between these numbers and the flow of immigration to First World countries and no precise forecast can be established about the development of the situation in ten or twenty years. To all this we should add that it is misleading to assume that the trends of population growth and economic development are determined independently of what the rest of the world will do in order to make them follow a more beneficial course.

The second point that needs to be made concerns the assumption that citizenship must be an all-or-nothing issue. In truth, when problems of scarcity and overcrowding arise there is no reason why social and political rights should be denied or granted as a whole package. It is very likely that different institutions (health care system, school, welfare and so on) will have different levels of saturation, which can be fluctuating and changing. This means that, where the exclusion from membership depends on structural limits of the sort considered here, there is no need to imagine that a two-class society will form. Rather, the result would be a multi-layered and complex structure of rights which would not create the kind of social stigmatisation which is accompanied by the division of society in the two separated classes of the citizens and the resident aliens.

A third point concerns the legitimacy of what appears to be a paternalistic restriction of the immigrants' freedom of choice. Some authors have argued that closing borders in order to prevent people from being exploited is unjustified, since it denies the principle that people are the best judges of their own interest.[12] In truth, even though there are grounds for believing that usually the immigrants' choice to move to a different country is rational and informed,[13] this is not a valid reply. Sometimes preventing people from being exploited, even when by doing so they improve their situation, is a justifiable means for putting them in a stronger bargaining position, providing them with an alternative that is both non-exploitative and subjectively preferred. This could be the case with immigrants. By accepting unfair terms of cooperation the immigrants might improve their personal condition at the cost of worsening the general condition of the international working class or of their nationals back in their home countries; this might have them end up with a worse result than what they would achieve if the bargaining position of foreign workers as a class were strengthened by bans on immigration.[14]

This argument, though, does not apply to the case we are considering. By definition it is impossible to avoid exploitation by granting citizenship to everybody, so that strengthening the immigrants' bargaining position would not improve their condition in this respect. As far as the effects on the bargaining position of the labour class as a whole are concerned, it must be noted that for the bans on immigration to be effective as an antidote to the exploitation of cheap foreign labour they must be combined with bans on the exportation of capital and trade, and with bans on the importation of manufactured products from less developed countries. Both policies seem to be unlikely to be adopted and might have adverse effects in some other respect.[15]

Finally, if the argument for closed borders is grounded on the concern for the exploitative nature of a 'two-track' society, where different classes of people are differently entitled to the enjoyment of social and political rights, we should recall that closing the borders to immigrants necessarily implies creating a 'two-track' society where the lowest class of residents, the illegal aliens, are exposed to the most demeaning forms of exploitation and abuse. If the army is efficient enough, the number of the exploited might be lower than in the first case but the forms of exploitation will be much worse. Banning immigration is not an efficient way to reduce exploitation.

## CONCLUSION

Restricted membership in a political community, and the special rights attached to it, can be considered as an instance of partiality that, in so far as it does not conflict with the requirements of global justice, can be legitimated also from a global perspective and can be justified also by a global citizen. We have considered two main impartial arguments for justifying it. On one hand, one can appeal to the right people have to establish special relations with other people of their choice. On the other hand, one can appeal to the fact that there are structural limits to the extension of the rights which are attached to citizenship, so that if political communities must exist at all they must necessarily be limited in size and scope. Both these impartial arguments for the limitation of membership in a political community do not constitute sufficient grounds for restricting immigration. In truth, the anti-immigration arguments which appeal to the existence of a conflict between the right of self-determination of political communities and the principle of political justice only show that, for global citizens, who must accept PPJ, the idea of the state as a private club or as a traditional community is substantially unacceptable.[16]

People can have very different reasons for leaving their countries but it is well-known that economic imbalances and disparities are among the main causes of emigration. Global citizens should give their support to redistributive activities and all the forms of international cooperation that are meant to improve the living conditions in the poorest countries of the world. While contributing to the removal of the economic and political causes of immigration, global citizens should take action to bring their countries to adopt the most liberal immigration policy they can afford.

## QUESTIONS

1. If all the members of the world population could decide together upon an ideal system of immigration laws, to be adopted by all the countries of the world, which system of rules do you think they would choose?
2. Do you think global justice would require the richer political communities to contribute to the removal of one of the main causes of immigration, that is economic disparity between the world's countries? Do you think that, if they did, that would entitle them to ban immigration to their lands?
3. Do the arguments against immigration which are the most popular in your country fulfil the requirement of impartiality?
4. Is the principle of political justice compatible with the requirements of global justice? Is it mandated by them?
5. Is there anything you can do to improve conditions for immigrants in your own country? Do you think a global citizen has the duty to contribute to such improvements?

## NOTES

1. Of course, it is true that many immigrants move to a different country because they are in need. But not all of them are in desperate conditions, even when in the new country they accept living standards that to our eyes look desperate. Grounding an argument for free immigration on the assumption that immigrants must be people in serious need would produce at least four undesirable consequences: (i) it would narrow the number of eligible people; (ii) it would create endless discussions about what 'need' means; (iii) it would endorse the stereotypical picture of the immigrant as a seriously destitute and resourceless human being, that is, someone who can be seen only as a burden for the host society; and (iv) it would fail to recognise the existential and psychological complexity of human beings – including those who are born in 'Third World' countries – and of their reasons for taking such dramatic decisions.
2. For a specific account of the requirement of impartiality and of its role within the notion of global justice see N. Dower's 'Global Ethics and Global Citizenship' in Chapter 11 of this reader, and especially points 3(i) and 3(ii) about the common core of global ethics.
3. Many writers, in fact, have argued against anti-immigration policies by appealing to the requirements of impartial justice. For a very clear example of such a strategy cf. Ackerman 1980: 88–95. For useful discussions of the issue, cf. Beitz 1983; Shue 1983; King 1993.
4. Cf. also Coleman and Harding 1995; Finnis 1992. The two views of the state do not usually go together. The view of the state as an association established through a more or less explicit contract among individuals is typical of the classical liberal tradition and is usually supported today by libertarian writers. The view of the state as a community is typical of communitarian writers, who sometimes reinterpret in this way the republican tradition. In Walzer's argument the two views of the state are combined; I will follow such an approach, since for the purpose of my argument they are essentially interchangeable, grounding in a similar way the partiality of the state on impartial moral assumptions.

5. There are serious doubts to be advanced about the accuracy of such a description of how the social goods enjoyed by First World countries are produced. Besides the fact that it could be reasonably argued that many of them are the product of exploitative activities, it would be extremely arduous to claim that the production of such goods does not require the cooperation of foreigners. But challenging these arguments for the state's partiality on empirical grounds is not my present purpose.

6. What I have particularly in mind are small communities that would be endangered by the presence of foreigners who were following and enforcing a different system of social rules.

7. On illegal immigration as trespassing cf. Joppke 1999: 44.

8. For this important distinction see Kymlicka 1995: 15.

9. Walzer 1983: 52–63 argues along these lines.

10. Against the idea that immigrants constitute a threat for the stability of Western Democracies cf. Kymlicka 1996.

11. Two other grounds for building projections about immigration flows are the number of work visa applications from source countries and the trend that emigration has displayed in countries where emigration to a wealthier country is possible, like Puerto Rico. In both cases, though, it is very difficult to assess the relevance of the concurring factors and of the specificity of the situation, and generalisations appear to be quite arbitrary. For a survey of studies of immigration flows to highly developed countries since 1945 cf. Castles and Miller 1993: 65–97.

12. Hudson 1986 argues in this sense, also pointing out that the immigrants' choice to undergo exploitation in a foreign country represents a Pareto improvement.

13. This does not necessarily mean that moving to a foreign country always improves a person's life conditions. Some immigrants undergo a period of work in a foreign country in order to collect the financial means that will allow them to start a better life in their homeland. Some undergo an initial worsening of their life conditions because they reasonably hope to improve them later. Some are just granting a better life for their relatives back in their country. All these reasons are rational but do not imply an immediate improvement of the life conditions of the immigrant workers.

14. This is actually the main point of some Marxist views of the issue. Importing cheap work from poor countries is a means by which Western capitalism can procrastinate its own inevitable collapse. If such a solution were impossible, the end of capitalism and the improvement of the working classes which would follow would come sooner (cf. Brown 1992a).

15. On these aspects of globalisation in trade and finance, see David Newlands' paper 'Economic Globalisation and Global Citizenship' in Chapter 16 of this reader.

16. On this point cf. Hampton 1995.

# 19. GLOBAL CITIZENSHIP AND PEACE

## Nigel Dower

### INTRODUCTION

If in the 1960s someone asked what being a global citizen was all about the chances are that the answer would have been 'getting involved in the campaign to ban the bomb'; working to alleviate poverty in the third world might have been mentioned but protecting the environment – possibly the area most people would think of first nowadays – would not have been thought of. Since 1989 and the end of the Cold War, the threat of nuclear annihilation has receded in popular consciousness (though it has certainly not gone away). Although there are a few still active in the 'peace movement', most people – even amongst those who think of themselves as world citizens – would not focus on peace issues. What I hope to show in this chapter is that campaigning to get rid of nuclear weapons (though in my opinion still an important goal) is only a small part of what *promoting* peace is all about and that working for the conditions of peace remains – and should be seen to remain – an important area of concern for anyone who takes the global point of view. There are many ways we either contribute or fail to contribute towards the promotion of peace – ways we may not always recognise as such or see as manifestations of global citizenship.

### 1. WHY PEACE IS IMPORTANT

There is something paradoxical about peace and global citizenship. If global citizenship involves the active exercise of responsibility by individual global citizens, it is not immediately obvious to most people what individuals ought to do (except in times of war when people are called up). War and peace are so much in the domain of international relations conducted by the representatives of states that the contribution of individuals seems marginal or intangible. By contrast, with concerns like the environment, aid and human rights it is relatively easy to identify things that engaged world citizens might do – like recycling waste, sending money to charities or engaging in a letter campaign.

And yet there is a sense in which peace is fundamental compared with aid, human rights and the environment because peace is the precondition of other goods, and the duty to promote peace is correspondingly fundamental. This may not initially be obvious, since in another sense peace is not more fundamental. From the point of view of an individual, having enough food/shelter/clothing (subsistence), having a basically sound environment (resource-full and healthy), and having a basic liberty to give effect to one's choices may be equally important as personal security (freedom from attack on one's person and property), since all are preconditions of whatever kind of life one wants to lead – whatever 'conception of the good' one may pursue (to use the terminology in John Rawls' seminal work *A Theory of Justice* (Rawls 1972)). But in so far as humans can *cooperate* to create and maintain the conditions under which these goods are achieved for individuals, there has to be a set of relationships which constitute the conditions of peace between individuals. In conditions of war and conflict aid cannot be effectively delivered; the protection of human rights is undermined; efforts to protect the environment are largely thwarted (especially in war, where the environment is one of the first casualties). In other words, the capacity for human beings to support one another in the provision of these basic goods depends crucially on certain conditions of communication, cooperation and the absence of arbitrary thwarting of interests.

It is interesting to note that Hobbes insisted that the primary law of our nature *(lex naturalis)* was to seek peace as a condition in which there was not merely no 'battle' or period of active warfare but a period of time in which there was no disposition to go to battle (or war, as we would say (Hobbes 1991)). He believed that this could only be achieved within political communities under a strong rule of law from the sovereign but thought that international relations were inherently warlike. Although Hobbes was right to see peace as more than merely the absence of overt conflict and to recognise that it was important for us to achieve peace in this sense if we can, he was unduly pessimistic about the need for coercion to achieve domestic peace within nations and about his assessment of international relations. Indeed, even on his terms people cannot really live at peace in a state if there is always the possibility and sometimes the actuality of conflict between their state and other states. Kant recognised this and argued that if real, 'perpetual' peace is to be achieved it requires a transformation of international relations so that not only is there peace within states but permanent peace between them: for this, various 'articles of peace' would need to be agreed in a federation of states (Kant 1970). Both saw that peace, to the extent that it was achievable, was of the utmost importance as the social precondition for the achievement of the well-being of individuals.

Despite the fact, then, that working for peace does not seem to be the first thing that people think of when thinking of global citizenship (and it is striking that relatively little attention has been paid to this dimension in recent literature), there is a case for its centrality in discussions of global citizenship. We can first indicate this by looking at ordinary citizenship and membership of a political community, both because the parallel with ordinary citizenship is instructive and because a focus on this helps to dispel the idea that the issues of war and peace are simply remote from individuals. Since peace is a crucial feature of social life, the issues of war and conflict/violence (a second contrast to peace) are of immediate importance to us all.

## 2. PARALLEL WITH ORDINARY CITIZENSHIP

First of all, we in fact generally recognise a duty, both morally and legally, to uphold peace/order. This is done through a variety of activities. Unless our only motive for obeying the law is fear of punishment, we assert the value of peace by obeying the law and encouraging the same in others. This does not mean we have to be uncritical of laws, especially if some laws are in fact divisive and reinforcing of inequality and civil disobedience – breaking the law conscientiously for moral or religious reasons in order to change the law is perfectly consistent with the spirit of this position, if conducted under certain clearly defined conditions (Rawls 1972: ch. 55–9; Singer 1993: ch. 11). Second, and more generally, there are various ways of promoting the conditions of peace. If, as I remarked above, some laws are themselves socially divisive or violate the rights of social groups (where violation is itself a form of violence) then working to change them through political processes is in a sense working for peace (though it may not be described in those terms). Third, an important aspect of promoting peace is respecting cultural diversity and upholding the values underpinning a multicultural society in modern pluralistic societies; this shows itself particularly in attitudes of mutual acceptance between different religious groups. Fourth, working in private capacities or through bodies such as citizens' advice bureaux or racial equality councils to uphold people's legal rights is an important aspect of upholding the framework of rights. This, whatever other values it protects, helps to maintain the conditions of peace. Finally, and most generally, the use by oneself and the encouragement in others of dialogue/negotiation/consensus-building as a way of reaching agreements or resolving conflicts is a basic manifestation of a commitment to peace and to creating the 'culture of peace'. (This perception was, for instance, reflected in the fact that the year 2000 was declared the UN International Year for the Culture of Peace.)

The attitudes and practice indicated here are not merely important for the maintenance of the conditions of peace within societies. They are linked to similar attitudes and practices in relation to the rest of the world. They are linked both in the sense that they already indicate a range of attitudes and practices to be replicated at a global level and in the sense that if they are well-established within a society they already form the basis for the extension to the global level. How, then, does all this translate into the global level?

### 3. PEACE AT THE GLOBAL LEVEL

Global citizenship expresses itself through a wide variety of activities: (i) the private activities of individuals (who do what they do because they consider themselves members of a world community or as promoting global causes): for instance, developing and maintaining personal links (like penfriends in other countries, keeping in contact with people one meets from abroad) or encouraging the development of appropriate global citizenship values and attitudes in other people *in one's own society* through cosmopolitan education (Nussbaum 1996); (ii) involvement in non-governmental organisations (NGOs) (which themselves engage in many kinds of activities like political lobbying, education, fostering cultural exchanges, civil disobedience): working for interfaith dialogue and the development of a global ethic of mutual tolerance such as the *Declaration Toward a Global Ethic* of the Parliament of the World's Religions (Küng and Kuschel 1993), working within peace organisations such as the Fellowship of Reconciliation or within organisations devoted to promoting conceptions of development and environmental responsibility which are seen as conducive to peace; (iii) political lobbying, joining political parties with a view to advancing international peace agendas.

This is a brief indication of the *forms* which the expression global citizenship can take, which are discussed more fully in other parts of this reader. The examples given, however, illustrate a number of general points about the ways global citizenship can be expressed. Activities like keeping up with a penfriend from abroad illustrate a feature of many appropriate actions and while the development of such links throughout the world is generally conducive to peace it is hardly the *reason* why people do what they do: contributing to peace may be a by-product of other activities. Working towards an agreed global ethic or for adequate conceptions of development and environmental responsibility are not as such focused on peace but on other global goals which constitute the conditions of peace: peace is the goal but under various guises. Working for interfaith dialogue in one's own community also illustrates another important feature of a goal like peace: global peace is in large measure (though not entirely) constituted by local peace or rather many local peaces. Finally, it is worth remarking that only one of the above activities actually works through the *concept* of global citizenship – namely the promotion of cosmopolitan education in schools. All the activities may be done by people who think of themselves as world citizens but most do not make it their explicit goal.

In the remainder of this chapter I will examine one key area to do with peace, namely foreign policy, and indicate some background conditions which are relevant to the pursuit of peace.

## 4. FOREIGN POLICY

There are at least three dimensions to foreign policy relevant to peace and the possible involvement of citizens in promoting it: first, the country's armaments policy; second, its particular responses to particular conflicts; and third, the general tenor of its foreign policy in terms of promoting or undermining the conditions of peace.

Thus (i) a global citizen might work for nuclear disarmament by political campaigning, going on demonstrations and vigils, or engaging in civil disobedience as with the current Trident Ploughshares initiative. The latter involves peace activists who seek to draw attention to the wrongness of a defence policy based on Trident nuclear submarines by illegally entering submarine bases. (ii) A person might be opposed to a particular military conflict as many were in the UK over the war in the Gulf in 1991 or Kosovo in 1999 and take various forms of action in response. (iii) Again, someone might work against the prevailing tendency to 'demonise' the enemy, in time of war (or during the Cold War) or the tendency to polarise the world into friends and enemies, for instance seeing Islam as the enemy, as the notorious Huntington thesis had it (Huntington 1996), rather than recognising that Islamic countries and cultures should not be tarred with the brush of our perception of militant Islam. Another example of a general approach would be if someone who thought that North–South inequalities or the dynamics of greed underlying modern materialist development were among the background causes of conflict were to campaign for changes of attitude in foreign policy (and in public attitudes more generally) *partly* for the sake of peace – though, of course, for many other reasons as well.

I do not expect all others to accept that these forms of action are necessarily right or appropriate. The examples are chosen deliberately to make the point: what someone does as a global citizen may not be regarded as right by others. (i) Others may not approve of using the *means* of civil disobedience in stopping the Trident submarine programme or may disagree with the *end/ goal* of nuclear disarmament on the grounds that such peace as can be achieved in the world requires some (responsible) nuclear states. (ii) Others may think that the Gulf War and its mode of operation was justified as contributing to the containment of dictatorships and the development of peace conditions in the long run. (iii) A different reading of the geopolitical facts of the Middle East might see the Islamic threat as inevitable and therefore needing to be confronted and not avoided in a soft liberal pluralist compromise. North–South inequalities may not as such be seen as a cause for conflict (though extreme poverty might need to be tackled) and economic growth may be seen as the engine of prosperity which is in turn the condition of peace.

The point is that if a person acts with a concern for peace in the world as a whole, and operates through a variety of institutions with a view to influencing things, then she acts as a global citizen with a commitment to peace.

Whilst obviously, from any particular point of view, certain forms of action will be better than others – both in terms of appropriate means and in terms of the kinds of goals pursued (linked to different conceptions of peace) – the general claim can I think be made that it is better overall if more people are actively concerned about peace at a global level (whatever their views) than if fewer people are.

In this context global citizenship is doubly normative. First, it is normative in that what people advocate in the name of global citizenship will be a particular set of prescriptions based on their values and their reading of the world and what will be effective in it. Second, it is normative in that there are arguments for saying that it is a good thing that people think that they are global citizens and for encouraging others to think so as well, whatever their views. 'Whatever their views' needs qualification, since there will be limits on what global citizens would regard as reasonable views to be encouraged in other global citizens if we regard the spread of global citizenship thinking to be important. The limits will vary from person to person, depending on one's own global values. Thus most global citizens would not welcome someone who advocated neo-Nazi views or a disregard for human poverty in the name of some extreme ecological worldview (such as 'ecofascism'), even if they did advocate them as global values; though even here a culture which *allows* the expression of such views is more likely to encourage the critical development of global perspectives which are progressive than one in which they are suppressed. Again, a member of a 'pro-life' organisation is unlikely to welcome what a member of the International Planned Parenthood Federation does and vice versa, even if members of each think of themselves as global citizens.

We can, however, despite this fluidity of what is or is not endorse by global citizens, indicate broadly what approaches to war and peace are *inconsistent* with *any* global citizenship approach. First, someone who advocated a 'realist' view of international relations or foreign policy would regard 'ethics' as irrelevant to such considerations: foreign policy is shaped by strategic interests and although peace as the absence of war may often be preferable from the point of view of national interests, war may sometimes be seen as expedient and 'the continuation of politics by other means' (Clausewitz). Since global ethics are irrelevant, global citizenship is too. Second, on the 'internationalist' view, even if one thinks that moral norms do (and should) determine the behaviour of states, the role of individuals is largely irrelevant to such matters, since the 'morality of states' operates at the level of agreements amongst states. The pursuit of peace is a matter for state-level negotiation and diplomacy, not something for citizens to get involved in. Third, whatever theories one might have about international relations, one might have a general pessimism about human nature as selfish and about the fragility of the human condition which renders working for peace as a 'global goal' a futile exercise. Global citizenship requires a degree of optimism about the possibility of progress which may simply be denied.

## 5. BACKGROUND CONDITIONS FOR THE
## MORE EFFECTIVE REALISATION OF PRIMARY ACTIVITIES

Here I am thinking of a range of activities which, if engaged in, will make one a more effective global citizen because one will be informed by adequate information about the world, will have properly worked-out values, an adequate conception of peace and appropriate attitudes. Amongst these, I should mention briefly the following:

### 5(i) Interest in the rest of the world

This is the recognition of the importance of being globally educated (including proper knowledge of the United Nations). Whatever else is necessary, like appropriate attitudes and moral commitments, one needs to know the *facts* about the world – knowledge of other cultures, the realities of aid, the role of transnational companies, the causes of conflict and so on. As Nussbaum remarks, it is not enough to know about the world in an abstract way: detailed knowledge of other cultures is important, both because the knowledge is practically important and because in knowing how other people live one can understand oneself better – what is essential to being human and what is accidental or contingently true of one's being American, British or Indian (Nussbaum 1996).

### 5(ii) Thinking about the nature of ethics at a global level

Although, of course, some would dispute this way of thinking about ethics, it seems to be important that one explicitly acknowledges the *global* dimension to ethics. In this way it becomes clear that one's interest in peace is properly ethical, that it is based on a concern for the value of peace for anyone in the world, not just for oneself or one's own country. If one took the latter view, one's interest in the conditions of peace would turn out to be largely, if not wholly, prudential or self-interested. One idea I find attractive is that of R. M. Hare who once argued that an ethical theory based on the primacy of individual human interests could avoid the dangers of nationalism (putting the interests of people in one's own nation first) and fanaticism (setting up abstract ideals as more important than the interests of people) (Hare 1972). If, as I have argued in Chapter 11 of this reader, a global ethic stresses the importance of a common core of values, the equal status of all human beings and the idea of global responsibility, then it underscores the point that if local peace is valuable to people in particular places, local peace anywhere is equally important to others and therefore global peace is an object of endeavour. Not all global ethics, however, will have the same emphases; as I note elsewhere, a global ethic with a dogmatic proselytising agenda might well not be a good basis for the promotion of peace.

### 5(iii) Interest in the conditions of peace and conceptions of peace

Peace is not a simple concept (Curle 1981; MacQuarrie 1973). Unless we settle for a very superficial idea of peace as the 'absence of war', we need to understand the inner dynamics of peace and war/violence. One suggestion I have found useful is that of Iredell Jenkins who argued that amongst the conditions of peace is the development of divided loyalties (Jenkins 1973). Suppose people have different loyalties, for example to their country but also to other groups such as their church, their professional community, sporting fraternity, members of international NGOs (or even, I would add, loyalty as global citizens to the global community itself). Suppose also that the membership of these groups which these loyalties involve do not coincide. One is less likely to go to war in response to one of one's loyalties if this means fighting members of other groups one has loyalty to.

Those like MacQuarrie and Curle who advocate a more positive conception of peace (as opposed to a 'negative' conception as the absence of war or violence) wish to stress the links with the idea of wholeness and harmony (suggested, for instance, by the word 'shalom') (MacQuarrie 1973) and with moral values which are integral to peace in a richer sense. Peace is not something which just happens; it is sustained by positive actions themselves informed by moral values. In particular the idea of justice is stressed, since a peace which is maintained in the face of continuing injustice is not a real peace and is not in the long run sustainable (Curle 1981).

Whilst, of course, very different views can be held about what peace means and what the conditions are for peace, it is reasonable to suppose that peace is more likely to be achieved the more people are willing to give thought to its nature and causes.

### 5(iv) Understanding the bases of multiculturalism

This is linked to all three dimensions above – knowledge of the world, global values and an understanding of peace itself – but is worth singling out because of its importance and controversial character. Hans Küng once argued: 'there will be no peace in the world without peace among the religions; there will be no peace among the religions without dialogue between them' (Küng 1991; Chapter 10 in this reader). Differences in religious faith are not, of course, the only source of conflict between different cultural groups but they are a powerful potential source of conflict and illustrate the challenge raised. The challenge is to see how to get those within different cultural groups to engage in dialogue rather than confrontation and to recognise that common values such as peace are better served this way than otherwise.

One aspect of this is the recognition that whilst it is reasonable to seek a common core of mutually acceptable values, it is not reasonable to expect those with different worldviews – religious or philosophical – to accept one's own worldview. Thus we may seek a common global ethic as a set of shared values whilst accepting a diversity of global ethics as theories or 'source stories' (Dower 1998).

However, matters are complicated by the fact that this way of putting the challenge may itself be challenged. Why should the presumption be that peace is more important than the promotion of one's values or beliefs or, more to the point, more important than opposing the values and beliefs of other groups that one believes to be seriously in error? An important issue is raised here, both of general significance and of relevance to our understanding of global citizenship and peace. Clearly a middle way needs to be found between confronting all beliefs and practices which are at all different from our own and tolerating everything. Few people will try and accommodate those who preach racism, strident nationalism or fanaticism. It is a matter – a difficult matter – of determining where to draw the line between mutual acceptance of diversity and the need, in terms of one's moral values and religious beliefs, to confront what lies beyond the pale of the reasonable. On the other hand, it seems clear that most of what counts as cultural differences should fall within the realm of accommodation and mutual acceptance. The need for this is important at the global level, both for its own sake and also, as Nussbaum has argued, because it provides the proper universal basis for grounding multi-culturalism within a pluralist society as well (Nussbaum 1996).

## CONCLUSION

Global citizenship cannot involve an unqualified commitment to peace. Peace may always be a long-term goal, even if war and conflict occur in the short term. As Augustine said, we wage war for the sake of peace, we do not have peace in order to go to war (Augustine 1947: bk xix ch. xii). But peace may not always be the right means in all circumstances. Though Sidney Bailey once said 'peace is process not (merely) an end' (Bailey 1996), there may be circumstances in which the right processes in interacting with others are not fully peaceful but confrontational. (Whether armed confrontation is ever justified is a matter of dispute.) Nevertheless the presumption is, if my analysis is right, that the way of peace is to be preferred in most circumstances and that being a global citizen involves accepting that presumption and acting on it in the various ways which I have outlined above.

---

### QUESTIONS

1. How would you define peace? Why is peace important?
2. Is concern for peace a significant part of being a global citizen?
3. If one is committed to peace, what are the most important things to do?
4. Why are some global ethics conducive to peace and others not conducive to peace?

---

# CONCLUSION

It will be apparent from the chapters in this book that there are few definite answers concerning global citizenship. Contributors disagree whether we are global citizens and indeed about what is meant by being a global citizen. When someone claims that we are global citizens she may have in mind one or more of several strands: first, that we have significant obligations to play our part in creating a better world; second, that we are as a matter of fact global citizens in virtue of various facts about the modern world like the legal fact that we have internationally instituted human rights and the causal fact that our actions do have global impacts for which we are responsible; third, that as a matter of fact many people, by their choices, are global citizens by virtue of their involvement or participation in a variety of activities (such as working through NGOs with global concerns); fourth, that although the institutions in the world do not really reflect this as yet, being a global citizen is about being committed to the development of appropriate institutions at a global level, either forms of global governance and global democracy that fall short of world government or world government itself.

None of these senses is such that it is right and the others are wrong. They each represent a reasonable strand of a remarkably complicated idea. In the first two senses it makes more sense to say that we are *all* global citizens, whether we recognise it or not. In the second two senses, it makes more sense to say that some by their own choices and self-conception are global citizens, whereas others are not. But it remains true that for those who advocate global citizenship, whatever combination of the strands they stress, there runs though it a view that it is a good thing, that people who do not think of themselves as global citizens ought to think of themselves in this way, and that there are things that ought to be done by individuals to help create a better world than we have now.

It is this common moral energy associated with the conception which gives rise to much, though not all, of the opposition to the idea. For all four senses, there are others who will question the claims that we are global citizens. The root moral commitment to some form of cosmopolitanism may be disputed; the facts about the world at present in relation to human rights or causal impacts do not, it may be said, amount to a coherent notion of citizenship; those who commit themselves to NGOs and so on may well be worthy and responsible moral agents but there are not, despite their own self-identities, really citizens at all; and it is not clear that strengthening global institutions to make citizenship coherent at that level is necessarily a good thing at all.

If we accept that global citizenship generally presupposes some form of global ethics, we need to recognise that there is great variation in the way this is understood. Not all will agree on what the content of a global ethic should be. Should a conception of justice based on redistribution be stressed or one that stresses the fundamental liberty of individuals? Should tolerance and respect for diversity be an important element or not? Would an ethic of caring be more appropriate? Should respect for nature be seen as an important addition to our ethical norms? Nor is there agreement about the justification for this global ethic. Is an ethic a timeless truth of some kind, equally accessible to the ancient Stoics and modern thinkers? If so, what ethic should it be? A God-given natural law? Kantianism? Utilitarianism? If not, does a global ethic depend for its existence upon peculiarly modern conditions – the circumstances of shared worldwide problems on the one hand or areas of agreement and convergence on the other?

If ethics are not to be hopelessly abstract, we need to see the exercise of global citizenship in the context of the real world, of what is happening in the world, and of the forces and processes at work which constrain and shape the real possibilities for choice. What are, for instance, the constraints and opportunities posed by modern technology or by the development of the global economy? How far do the attitudes of electorates shape the options of governments in respect to immigration policy, foreign aid or effective mea-sures to protect the environment? Almost all will agree that globalisation in its many facets has altered the global landscape but how, in what ways and with what consequences are questions to be answered in different ways. Almost all agree that the position of the nation-state has undergone major changes – the old paradigms of the international order of states is simply inadequate to the facts of the world today – but what the consequences are for individuals within them is again a matter of dispute.

Let us suppose that, for a variety of reasons, more and more people come to see themselves as global citizens. Will it make much difference? How much difference depends on many factors – just what the values and norms are that are accepted, and what strength of global responsibility is accepted for what individuals should do. Despite all these variations, it seems clear that an important shift of perspective would take place and that the more people accepted the global citizenship perspective, the more they would be reinforced in that perspective by a sense of solidarity.

The parallel with ordinary citizenship is instructive in this regard. Civil society is strengthened the more members of a political community take their citizenship responsibility seriously and enter public deliberation about the public good; that they have different views about the public good is neither here nor there. It is the perspective or attitude of civil responsibility that is important. Likewise with global citizenship: even if different global values are promoted, the very fact of participation in public deliberation and activities for the global common good is what is important. This global perspective is not at odds with ordinary civic responsibility at all; indeed, they generally complement each other and share a common opposition to what is really inimical to our maintaining what is good about the world and opposing what is bad – namely selfishness and indifference.

# BIBLIOGRAPHY

Books, Articles and Websites Referred to in the Text

Ackerman, Bruce (1980), *Social Justice in the Liberal State,* New Haven: Yale University Press.

Alkire, Sabina and Rufus Black (1997), 'A Practical Reasoning Theory of Development Ethics: Furthering the Capabilities Approach', *Journal of International Development*, vol. 9, no. 2.

Allen, Beverley (1996), *Rape Warfare: The Hidden Genocide in Bosnia-Herzogovina and Croatia*, Minneapolis: University of Minnesota Press.

Almond, Brenda (1990), 'Alasdair MacIntyre: The Virtue of Tradition', *Journal of Applied Philosophy*, vol. 7, no. 1.

Archibugi, Daniele and David Held (eds) (1995), *Cosmopolitan Democracy*, Cambridge: Polity Press.

Ashworth, Georgina (1999), 'The Silencing of Women' in Tim Dunne and Nicholas J. Wheeler (eds), *Human Rights in Global Politics*, Cambridge, Cambridge University Press.

Attfield, Robin (1998), 'Environmental Ethics and Intergenerational Equity', *Inquiry*, vol. 41.

Attfield, Robin (1999), *The Ethics of the Global Environment*, Edinburgh: Edinburgh University Press.

Augustine [c. 412] (1947), *City of God*, London: Dent.

Baier, Kurt (1989), 'Justice and the Aims of Political Philosophy', *Ethics,* vol. 99.

Bailey, S. (1996), *Peace is a Process*, London: Quaker Home Service.

Baker, J. (1987), *Arguing for Equality*, London: Verso.

Barber, Benjamin (1998), *A Place for Us: How to Make Society Civil and Democracy Strong*, New York: Hill and Wang.

Barkan, Elazar (2000), *The Guilt of Nations: Restitution and Negotiating Historic Injustices*, New York: Norton.

Barnaby, Frank (ed.) (1988), *Gaia Peace Atlas*, London: Pan Books.

Barry, Brian (1973), *The Liberal Theory of Justice: A Critical Examination of the Principal Doctrines in* A Theory of Justice *by John Rawls*, Oxford: Clarendon Press.

Barry, Brian (1989), *Theories of Justice: A Treatise on Social Justice Volume I*, Hemel Hempstead: Harvester Wheatsheaf.

Barry, Brian (1991), 'Is Democracy Special?', in Brian Barry, *Democracy and Power: Essays in Political Theory*, Oxford: Oxford University Press.

Barry, Brian (1995), *Justice as Impartiality: A Treatise on Social Justice Volume II*, Oxford: Clarendon.

Basu, Amrita (1995), 'Introduction' in Amrita Basu (ed), *The Challenge of Local Feminisms: Women's Movements in Global Perspective*, Boulder, CO: Westview Press.

Beck, Ulrich (1999), *World Risk Society*, Cambridge: Polity.

Becker, Lawrence C. (1996), 'Trust as Noncognitive Security about Motives', *Ethics*, vol. 107, no.1.

Beetham, David (1998), 'Human Rights as a Model for Cosmopolitan Democracy', in Daniele Archibugi, David Held and Martin Köhler (eds), *Re-imagining Political Community: Studies in Cosmopolitan Democracy*, Cambridge: Polity Press.

Beitz, Charles R. (1979), *Political Theory and International Relations*, Princeton: Princeton University Press.

Beitz, Charles R. (1983), 'Cosmopolitan Ideals and National Sentiment', *Journal of Philosophy*, vol. 80, no. 10.

Beitz, Charles R. (1985), 'Justice and International Relations', in Charles R. Beitz, Marshall Cohen, Thomas Scanlon and A. John Simmons (eds), *International Ethics: A Philosophy and Public Affairs Reader*, Princeton: Princeton University Press.

Beitz, Charles R. (1999), 'International Liberalism and Distributive Justice: A Survey of Recent Thought', *World Politics*, vol. 51, no. 2.

Bellamy, Richard and R. J. Barry Jones (2000), 'Globalization and democracy – an afterword', in Barry Holden (ed.), *Global Democracy: Key Debates*, London: Routledge, pp. 202–16.

Benhabib, Seyla (1992), *Situating the Self: Gender, Postmodernism and Community in Contemporary Ethics*, Cambridge: Polity.

Bentham, quoted in Mill [1861] (1962), *Utilitarianism*, in M. Warnock (ed.), *Utilitarianism*, London: Fontana.

Bertalanffy, Ludwig von (1968), *General System Theory: Foundations, Development, Application*, Harmondsworth: Penguin Books.

258

Bertrand, M. (1985), *Some Reflections on the Reform of the UN*, Joint Inspection Unit Report, JIU/REP/85/9, Geneva: UN.

Blackmore, Christine and John Smyth (1998), *Systemic Approaches to Learning in the Context of Agenda 21*, Australia and New Zealand Systems Society Conference Proceedings, October.

Booth, Ken (1991), 'Security and Emancipation', *Review of International Studies,* vol. 17, no. 4.

Booth, Ken (1995), 'Human Wrongs and International Relations', *International Affairs,* vol. 71, no. 1.

Boulding, Kenneth (1971), 'The Economics of the Coming Spaceship Earth', in Kenneth Boulding, *Collected Papers*, Boulder, CO: Associated University Press, vol. 2.

Boutros-Ghali, Boutros (2000), 'An Agenda for Democratization: Democratization at the International Level', in Barry Holden (ed.), *Global Democracy: Key Debates*, London: Routledge.

Bradley, F. H. (1876), *Ethical Studies*, Oxford: Oxford University Press.

Braithwaite, V. A. and H. G. Law (1985), 'Structure of Human Values: Testing the Adequacy of the Rokeach Value Survey', *Journal of Personality and Social Psychology,* vol. 49, no. 1.

Braybrooke, David (1987), *Meeting Needs,* Princeton: Princeton University Press.

Brody, Reed and Michael Ratner (2000), *The Pinochet Papers: The Case of Augusto Pinochet in Spain and Britain,* The Hague: Kluwer Law International.

Brown, Chris (1992a), 'Marxism and Transnational Migration', in Brian Barry and Robert E. Goodin (eds), *Free Movement*, New York: Harvester Wheatsheaf.

Brown, Chris (1992b), *International Relations Theory: New Normative Approaches*, Hemel Hempstead: Harvester Wheatsheaf.

Brown, Chris (1995a), 'International Political Theory and the Idea of World Community', in Ken Booth and Steve Smith (eds), *International Relations Theory Today*, Cambridge: Polity Press.

Brown, Chris (1995b), 'International Theory and International Society: The Viability of "The Middle Way"', *Review of International Studies,* vol. 21, no. 2.

Bubeck, Diemut (1998), 'Ethic of Care and Feminist Ethics', *Women's Philosophy Review*, vol. 18 (Spring).

Bull, Hedley (1977), *The Anarchical Society: A Study of Order in World Politics,* Basingstoke: Macmillan.

Bull, Hedley (1979), 'Human Rights and World Politics', in R. Pettman (ed.), *Moral Claims in World Politics*, London: Croom-Helm.

Buruma, Ian (2001), 'The Japanese Malaise', *New York Review of Books,* vol. 48, no. 11.

Calhoun, Craig (1996), 'Identity Politics and the Post-Communist Societies', in *Identity Formation, Citizenship and Statebuilding in the Former Communist Countries of Eastern Europe*, ARENA Working Paper no. 20/96.

Capra, F. (1996), *The Web of Life – A New Synthesis of Mind and Matter,* London: HarperCollins.

Carens, J. H. (1987), 'Aliens and Citizens: The Case for Open Borders', *The Review of Politics,* vol. 49, no. 2.

Castells, Manuel (1996), *The Rise of the Network Society* (vol. 1 of *The Information Age: Economy, Society and Culture*), Cambridge: Polity Press.

Castells, Manuel (1997), *The Power of Identity* (vol. 2 of *The Information Age: Economy, Society and Culture*), Cambridge: Polity Press.

Castells, Manuel (1998), *The End of the Millennium* (vol.3 of *The Information Age: Economy, Society and Culture*), Cambridge: Polity Press.

Castles, Stephen and Mark J. Miller (1993), *The Age of Migration: International Population Movements in the Modern World,* Basingstoke: Macmillan.

Cerny, Philip G. (2000), 'Restructuring the Political Arena: Globalization and the Paradoxes of the Competition State', in Randall Germain (ed.), *Globalization and Its Critics: Perspectives from Political Economy,* Basingstoke: Macmillan.

Checkel, Jeffrey (1999), 'Social Construction and Integration', *Journal of European Public Policy,* vol. 6, no. 4.

Checkel, Jeffrey and Andrew Moravcsik (2001), 'A constructivist research program in EU studies?', *European Union Politics,* vol. 2, no. 2.

Checkland, Peter B. (1984), *Systems Thinking, Systems Practice,* Chichester: Wiley.

Checkland, Peter B. and Jim Scholes (1990), *Soft Systems Methodology in Action,* Chichester: Wiley.

Chinese Culture Connection (1987), 'Chinese Values and the Search for Culture-Free Dimensions of Culture,' *Journal of Cross-Cultural Psychology,* vol. 18.

Clarke, Paul Barry (1994), *Citizenship,* London: Pluto.

Clayton, A. M. H. and N. J. Radcliffe (1996), *Sustainability – A Systems Approach,* London: Earthscan.

Closa, Carlos (1992), 'The Concept of Citizenship in the Treaty on European Union', *Common Market Law Review,* vol. 29.

Cohen, Jean L. and Andrew Arato (1992), *Civil Society and Political Theory,* Cambridge, MA: MIT Press.

Coleman, J. and S. K. Harding (1995), 'Citizenship, Justice and Political Borders', in W. F. Schwartz (ed.), *Justice in Immigration,* Cambridge: Cambridge University Press.

Coleman, James (1990), *Foundations of Social Theory,* Cambridge MA: Harvard University Press.

Commission on Global Governance (1995), *Our Global Neighbourhood,* Oxford: Oxford University Press.

Cooper, David E. (1992), 'The Idea of Environment', in David E. Cooper and Joy A. Palmer (eds), *The Environment in Question,* London: Routledge.

Crawford, James (1994), *Democracy in International Law,* Cambridge: Cambridge University Press.

Crocker, David A. (1998), *Transitional Justice and International Civil Society*, Working Paper #13, University Park, MD: The National Commission on Civic Renewal.

Curle, Adam (1981), *True Justice*, London: Quaker Home Service.

Daniels, N. (ed.) (1974), *Reading Rawls*, New York: Basic Books.

Danspeckgruber, Wolfgang with Arthur Watts (1997), *Self-Determination and Self-Administration: A Sourcebook*, Boulder, CO: Lynne Reiner.

Delanty, Gerard (2000), *Citizenship in a Global Age: Society, Culture, Politics*, Buckingham: Open University Press.

Della Porta, Donnatella, Hanspeter Kriesi and Dieter Rucht (eds) (1999), *Social Movements in a Globalizing World*, Basingstoke: Macmillan.

Development Assistance Committee (1996), *Annual Report*, Paris: OECD.

Dower, Nigel (1994), 'The Idea of the Environment', in Robin Attfield and A. Belsey (eds), *Philosophy and the Natural Environment*, Cambridge: Cambridge University Press.

Dower, Nigel (1998), *World Ethics – the New Agenda*, Edinburgh: Edinburgh University Press.

Dower, Nigel (2000), 'The Idea of Global Citizenship – A Sympathetic Assessment', *Global Society*, vol. 14, no. 4.

Dunne, Tim and Nicholas J. Wheeler (1998), 'Constructivism and International Legitimacy: Good International Citizenship and Post-Westphalian Statecraft', Paper to Third ECPR/ISA Pan-European Conference on International Relations, Vienna, September.

Dunne, Tim and Nicholas J. Wheeler (eds) (1999), *Human Rights in Global Politics*, Cambridge: Cambridge University Press.

Egeberg, Morten (1999), 'Transcending Intergovernmentalism? Identity and Role Perceptions of National Officials in EU Decision-Making', *Journal of European Public Policy*, vol. 6, no. 3.

Egeberg, Morten and Jarle Trondal (1999), 'Differentiated Integration in Europe: The Case of the EEA Country Norway', *Journal of Common Market Studies*, vol. 37, no. 1.

Ellul, Jacques (1964), *The Technological Society*, New York: Vintage Books.

Ellul, Jacques (1980), *The Technological System*, New York: The Continuum Publishing Corporation.

Elshtain, Jean Bethke (1987), *Women and War*, Brighton: Harvester Press.

Enloe, Cynthia (1983), *Does Khaki Become You? The Militarisation of Women's Lives*, London: Pluto Press.

Falk, Richard (1987), *The Promise of World Order: Essays in Normative International Relations*, Philadelphia: Temple University Press.

Falk, Richard (1994), 'The Making of Global Citizenship', in Bart Van Steenbergen (ed.), *The Condition of Citizenship*, London: Sage.

Falk, Richard (1995), *On Humane Governance: Toward a New Global Politics*, Cambridge: Polity Press.

Falk, Richard (2001), *Religion and Humane Global Governance*, New York: Palgrave.

Feinberg, Joel (1973), *Social Philosophy*, Englewood Hills, NJ: Prentice-Hall.

Finnis, John (1980), *Natural Law and Natural Rights*, Oxford: Clarendon Press.

Finnis, John (1983), *The Fundamentals of Ethics*, Oxford: Oxford University Press.

Finnis, John (1992), 'Commentary on Dummet and Weithman', in Brian Barry and Robert E. Goodin (eds), *Free Movement*, New York: Harvester Wheatsheaf.

Finnis, John (1994), 'Liberalism and Natural Law Theory', *Mercer Law Review*, vol. 45.

Finnis, John (1997), 'Commensuration and Public Reason' in Ruth Chang (ed.), *Incommensurability, Incomparability and Practical Reason*, Cambridge MA: Harvard University Press.

Finnis, John (1998), *Aquinas: Moral, Political, and Legal Theory*, Oxford: Oxford University Press.

Finnis, John, J. Boyle and G. Grisez (1987), *Nuclear Deterrence, Morality, and Realism*, Oxford: Oxford University Press.

Follesdal, Andreas (1997a), 'Citizenship and Political Rights in the European Union: Consensus and Questions', in Reiner Bauböck and Josef Melchior (eds), *Grundrechte in der Europäischen Union*, Wien: Institut für Höhere Studien.

Follesdal, Andreas (1997b), 'Do Welfare Obligations End at the Boundaries of the Nation State?', in Peter Koslowski and Andreas Follesdal (eds), *Restructuring the Welfare State: Theory and Reform of Social Policy*, Berlin: Springer.

Follesdal, Andreas (1998), 'Subsidiarity', *Journal of Political Philosophy*, vol. 6, no. 2.

Follesdal, Andreas (2000a), 'Justice: International and European', in *Global Society*, vol. 14, no. 4.

Follesdal, Andreas (2000b), 'The Future Soul of Europe: Nationalism or Just Patriotism? On David Miller's Defence of Nationality', *Journal of Peace Research*, vol. 37, no. 4.

Follesdal, Andreas (2001), 'Union Citizenship: Unpacking the Beast of Burden', *Law and Philosophy*, vol. 20, no. 3.

Fox, Gregory H. and Brad R. Roth (eds) (2000), *Democratic Governance and International Law*, Cambridge: Cambridge University Press.

Franck, Thomas M. (1992), 'The Emerging Right to Democratic Governance', *American Journal of International Law*, vol. 86, no. 1.

Franklin, U. (1990), *The Real World of Technology*, Montreal: CBC Enterprises.

Freeman, M. (1994), 'Nation-State and Cosmopolis', *Journal of Applied Philosophy*, vol. 11, no. 1.

Frost, Mervyn (1998), *Ethics in International Relations: A Constitutive Theory*, Cambridge: Cambridge University Press.

Galtung, Johan (2000), 'Alternative models for global democracy', in Barry Holden (ed.), *Global Democracy: Key Debates*, London: Routledge.

George, Robert P. (1989), 'Human Flourishing as a Criterion of Morality: A Critique of Perry's Naturalism', *Tulane Law Review,* vol. 63.

George, Robert P. (1990), 'Self-Evident Practical Principles and Rationally Motivated Action: A Reply to Michael Perry', *Tulane Law Review*, vol. 64.

George, Robert P. (1993), *Making Men Moral*, Oxford: Clarendon Press.

Gewirth, Alan (1978), *Reason and Morality,* Chicago: Chicago University Press.

Giddens, Anthony (1990), *The Consequences of Modernity*, Cambridge: Polity Press.

Giddens, Anthony (1995), *Beyond Left and Right: The Future of Radical Politics*, Stanford: Stanford University Press.

Gilligan, Carol (1982), *In a Different Voice: Psychological Theory and Women's Development*, Cambridge, MA: Havard University Press.

Goodin, Robert E. (1988), *Reasons for Welfare: The Political Theory of the Welfare State*, Princeton: Princeton University Press.

Griffin, James (1996), *Value Judgement: Improving our Ethical Beliefs*, Oxford: Clarendon Press.

Grimm, Dieter (1995), 'Does Europe Need a Constitution?', *European Law Journal*, vol. 1, no. 3.

Grisez, G., J. Boyle and J. Finnis (1987), 'Practical Principles, Moral Truth and Ultimate Ends', *American Journal of Jurisprudence*, vol. 32, no. 1.

Group of Lisbon (1995), *Limits of Competition*, Cambridge, MA: MIT Press.

Grubb, M. et al (2000), *The Kyoto Protocol*, London: Royal Institute of International Affairs.

Guitian, M. (1999), 'Economic Policy Implications of Global Financial Flows', *Finance and Development,* vol. 36, no. 1.

Habermas, Jürgen (1992), 'Citizenship and National Identity: Some Reflections on the Future of Europe', *Praxis International,* vol. 12, no. 1.

Habermas, Jürgen [1995] (1998), 'Does Europe Need a Constitution? Remarks on Dieter Grimm' in Jürgen Habermas, Ciaran Cronin and Pablo de Grieff (eds), *The Inclusion of the Other: Studies in Political Theory*. Cambridge, MA: MIT Press.

Hampton, J. (1995), 'Immigration, Identity and Justice', in W. F. Schwartz (ed.), *Justice in Immigration*, Cambridge: Cambridge University Press.

Hardin, Russell (1996), 'Trustworthiness', *Ethics*, vol. 107, no. 1.

Hare, R. M. (1972), 'Peace', in R. M. Hare, *Applications of Moral Philosophy*, Basingstoke: Macmillan.

Harris, Adrienne and Ynestra King (eds) (1989) *Rocking the Ship of State: Toward a Feminist Peace Politics*, Boulder, CO: Westview Press.

Harvey, T. (1995), 'An Education 21 Programme: Orienting Environmental

Education Towards Sustainable Development and Capacity Building for Rio', *The Environmentalist*, vol. 15.

Heater, Derek (1996), *World Citizenship and Government: Cosmopolitan Ideas in the History of Western Political Thought*, Basingstoke: Macmillan.

Heidegger, Martin (1977), 'Only a God Can Save Us Now' (Martin Heidegger interviewed in *Der Spiegel*, trans. D. Schendler), *Graduate Philosophy Journal*, vol. 6, no. 1.

Held, David (1991), 'Between State and Civil Society: Citizenship', in Geoff Andrews (ed.) *Citizenship*, London: Lawrence and Wishart.

Held, David (1995a), *Democracy and the Global Order: From the Modern State to Cosmopolitan Governance*, Cambridge: Polity Press.

Held, David (1995b), 'Introduction', in Daniele Archibugi and David Held (eds), *Cosmopolitan Democracy*, Cambridge: Polity Press.

Held, David (1996), *Models of Democracy* (second edition), Cambridge: Polity Press.

Held, David (1998), 'Democracy and Globalization', in Daniele Archibugi, David Held and Martin Köhler (eds), *Re-Imagining Political Community: Studies in Cosmopolitan Democracy*, Cambridge: Polity Press.

Held, David (2000), 'The Changing Contours of Political Community: Rethinking Democracy in the Context of Globalization', in Barry Holden (ed.), *Global Democracy: Key Debates*, London: Routledge.

Held, David, Anthony McGrew, David Goldblatt and Jonathon Perraton (1999), *Global Transformations: Politics, Economics and Culture*, Cambridge: Polity Press.

Held, Virginia (1993), *Feminist Morality: Transforming Culture, Society and Politics*, Chicago: University of Chicago Press.

Hirst, Paul (2001), 'Beyond the Local and the Global: Democracy in the Twenty-First Century', in Roland Axtmann (ed.), *Balancing Democracy*, London: Continuum International Publishers.

Hirst, Paul and Grahame Thompson (1996), *Globalization in Question*, Cambridge: Polity Press.

Hirst, Paul and Grahame Thompson (1999), *Globalization in Question* (second edition), Cambridge: Polity Press.

Hobbes, Thomas [1651] (1991), *Leviathan*, Cambridge: Cambridge University Press.

Hofstede, G. (1980), *Culture's Consequences: International Differences in Work-Related Values*, Beverly Hills, CA: Sage Press.

Holden, Barry (ed.) (2000), *Global Democracy: Key Debates*, London: Routledge.

Huber, Max, (1955/56), 'Prolegomena und Probleme eines internationalen Ethos', *Die Friedens-Warte*, vol. 53, no. 4.

Hudson, J. C. (1984), 'The Ethics of Immigration Restriction', *Social Theory and Practice*, vol. 10, no. 2.

Hudson, J. C. (1986), 'The Philosophy of Immigration', *The Journal of Libertarian Studies*, vol. viii, no. 1.

Huntington, Samuel P. (1996), *The Clash of Civilizations and the Remaking of World Order*, New York: Simon & Schuster.

Hutchings, Kimberely (1994), 'Borderline Ethics', *Paradigms: Kent Journal of International Relations*, vol. 8, no. 1.

Hutchings, Kimberley and Roland Dannreuther (eds) (1999), *Cosmopolitan Citizenship*, Basingstoke: Macmillan.

Imber, Mark, (1994), *Environment, Security and UN Reform*, Basingstoke: Macmillan.

Independent International Commission on Kosovo (2000), *The Kosovo Report: Conflict, Response, Lessons Learned*, Oxford: Oxford University Press.

Inglehart, R. (1970), 'Cognitive Mobilisation and European Identity', *Comparative Politics*, vol. 3, no. 1.

InterAction Council (1996), *In Search of Global Ethical Standards*, available at: http://www.asiawide.or.jp/iac

InterAction Council (1997), *A Universal Declaration of Human Responsibilities*, Tokyo.

International Union for the Conservation of Nature (IUCN), the Worldwide Fund for Nature (WWF) and the United Nations Environment Programme (UNEP) (1980), *The World Conservation Strategy*, Gland, Switzerland: IUCN.

Ison, Ray L. (1993), 'Soft systems: a non-computer view of decision support', in J. W. Stuth and B. G. Lyons (eds), *Decision Support Systems for the Management of Grazing Lands: Emerging Issues*, UNESCO-Man and the Biosphere Book Series, vol. 11, Carnforth, UK: Parthenon Publishing.

Jackson, Robert (1969), *A Study of the Capacity of the UN Development System*, UNDP/5, vol. 1, Geneva: UN.

Jackson, Robert H. (1990), *Quasi-States: Sovereignty International Relations and the Third World*, Cambridge: Cambridge University Press.

Jacobs, Michael (1996), *The Politics of the Real World*, London: Earthscan.

Jacobson, D. (1996), *Rights Across Borders: Immigration and the Decline of Citizenship*, Baltimore and London: Johns Hopkins University Press.

Jenkins, I. (1973), 'The Conditions of Peace', *Monist*, vol. 57.

Joerges, Christian, Yves Mény and J. H. H. Weiler (eds) (2000), *What Kind of Constitution for What Kind of Polity? Responses to Joschka Fischer*, Badia Fiesolana: European University Institute, available at: http://www.iue.it/RSC/symposium/

Jonas, Hans (1984), *The Imperative of Responsibility: In Search of an Ethics for the Technological Age*, Chicago: University of Chicago Press.

Jones, R. J. Barry (2000), *The World Turned Upside Down? Globalization and the Future of the State*, Manchester: Manchester University Press.

Joppke, Christian (1999), *Immigration and the Nation State: The United States, Germany and Great Britain*, Oxford: Oxford University Press.

Joy, Bill (2000), 'Why the Future Doesn't Need Us', *WIRED*, vol. 8, no. 4.

Judt, Tony (1996), *A Grand Illusion: An Essay on Europe*, London: Penguin.

Kaldor, Mary (1998), 'Reconceptualising Organised Violence', in Daniele Archibugi, David Held and Martin Köhler (eds), *Re-imagining Political Community: Studies in Cosmopolitan Democracy*, Cambridge: Polity Press.

Kant, Immanuel [1785] (1949), *The Groundwork of the Metaphysic of Morals*, in H. Paton (ed.), *The Moral Law*, London: Hutcheson.

Kant, Immanuel [1795] (1970), *Perpetual Peace*, in H. Reiss (ed.), *Kant's Political Writings*, Cambridge: Cambridge University Press.

Kates, R. W. and W. C. Clark (1996), 'Environmental Surprise: Expecting the Unexpected', *Environment*, vol. 38, no. 2.

Kapp, Ernst (1877), *Grundlinien einer Philosophie der Technik Zur Enstehungsgeschichte der Culture aus Neuen Gesichtspunkten*, Dusseldorf: Braunschweig.

King, T. (1993), 'Immigration from Developing Countries: Some Philosophical Issues', *Ethics*, vol. 93.

Kukathas, Chandran and Philip Petit (1990), *Rawls: A Theory of Justice and its Critics*, Cambridge: Polity Press.

Küng, Hans (1987), *Christianity and the World Religions: Paths of Dialogue with Islam, Hinduism, and Buddhism*, New York: Doubleday.

Küng, Hans (1991), *Global Responsibility – In Search of a New World Ethic*, London: SCM Press.

Küng, Hans (1992), *Judaism: The Religious Situation of Our Time*, London: SCM Press.

Küng, Hans (1995), *Christianity: Its Essence and History*, London: SCM Press.

Küng, Hans (ed.) (1996), *Yes to a Global Ethic*, London: SCM Press.

Küng, Hans (1997), *A Global Ethic for Global Politics and Economics*, London: SCM Press.

Küng, Hans (1998), *A Global Ethic for Global Politics and Economics*, London: SCM Press.

Küng, Hans with J. van Ess, H. V. Stietencron and H. Berchert (1987), *Christianity and the World Religions – Paths of Dialogue with Islam, Hinduism and Buddhism*, New York: Doubleday; (1993) London: SCM Press.

Küng, Hans with J. Ching (1989), *Christianity and Chinese Relgions*, New York: Doubleday.

Küng, Hans and Helmut Schmidt (eds) (1993a), *A Global Ethic and Global Responsibilities: Two Declarations*, London: SCM Press.

Küng, Hans and Karl-Josef Kuschel (1993b), *A Global Ethic – The Declaration of the Parliament of the World's Religions*, London: SCM Press.

Küng, Hans and Karl-Josef Kuschel (eds) (1993c), *Weltfrieden durch Religionfrieden: Antworten aus den Weltreligionen*, Munchen: Piper Verlag.

Küng, Hans and Karl-Josef Kuschel (eds) (1998), *Wissenschaft und Weltethos*, Munchen: Piper Verlag.

Kütting, Gabriela (2000), *Environment, Society and International Relations: Towards More Effective International Environmental Agreements,* London: Routledge.

Kymlicka, Will (1995), *Multicultural Citizenship,* Oxford: Oxford University Press.

Kymlicka, Will (1996), 'Social Unity in a Liberal State', *Social Philosophy and Policy,* vol. 13, no. 1.

Kymlicka, Will (1998), 'Is Federalism a Viable Alternative to Secession?', in Percy B. Lehning (ed.), *Theories of Secession,* London: Routledge.

La Torre, Massimo, (1998), 'Constitution, Citizenship, and the European Union', in Massimo La Torre (ed.), *European Citizenship: An Institutional Challenge,* The Hague: Kluwer Law International.

Lam, Maivan Clêch (2000), *At the Edge of the State,* Ardsley, NY: Transnational Publishers.

Laszlo, Ervin (1999), 'Globalization: The Outer and the Inner Dimensions', *World Futures,* vol. 53.

Lehning, P. B. and A. Weale (eds) (1997), *Citizenship, Democracy and Justice in the New Europe,* London: Routledge.

Lemco, Jonathan (1991), *Political Stability in Federal Governments,* New York: Praeger.

Lensu, M. and J. Fritz (eds) (2000), *Value Pluralism, Normative Theory and International Relations,* Basingstoke: Macmillan.

Leopold, Aldo (1949), *A Sand County Almanac and Sketches Here and There,* Oxford: Oxford University Press.

Leopold, Aldo (1953), *Round River,* New York: Oxford University Press.

Levy, S. and L. Guttman (1974), *Values and Attitudes of Israeli High School Youth,* Jerusalem: Israeli Institute of Applied Social Research.

Lifton, Robert Jay (1999), *Destroying the World to Save It: Aum Shinrikyo, Apocalyptic Violence and the New Global Terrorism,* New York: Henry Holt.

Lijphart, Arend (1977), *Democracy in Plural Societies: A Comparative Exploration,* New Haven: Yale University Press.

Lind, Michael (1994), 'In Defense of Liberal Nationalism', *Foreign Affairs,* vol. 73, no. 3.

Linklater, Andrew (1992), 'What is a Good International Citizen?', in Paul Keal (ed.), *Ethics and Foreign Policy,* London: Allen & Unwin.

Linklater, Andrew (1996), 'Citizenship and Sovereignty in the Post-Westphalian State', *European Journal of International Relations,* vol. 2, no. 1.

Linklater, Andrew (1998a), 'Cosmopolitan Citizenship', *Citizenship Studies,* vol. 2, no. 1.

Linklater, Andrew (1998b), *The Transformation of Political Community: Ethical Foundations of the Post-Westphalian Era,* Cambridge: Polity Press.

Linklater, Andrew (1998c), 'Citizenship and Sovereignty in the Post-Westphalian European State', in Daniele Archibugi, David Held and Martin

Köhler (eds), *Re-Imagining Political Community: Studies in Cosmopolitan Democracy,* Cambridge: Polity.

Linklater, Andrew (1999a), 'Cosmopolitan Citizenship', in Kimberley Hutchings and Roland Dannreuther (eds), *Cosmopolitan Citizenship,* Basingstoke: Macmillan.

Linklater, Andrew (1999b), 'The Evolving Spheres of International Justice', *International Affairs,* vol. 5, no. 3.

Locke, John [1690] (1963), *Two Treatises of Government,* New York: New American Library, Mentor.

Loury, Glen (1987), 'Why Should We Care About Group Inequality?', *Social Philosophy and Policy,* vol. 5, no. 2.

Lubbers, Ruud (1998), 'De geschiedenis van de mensheid begint nu pas echt', (Ruud Lubbers, former prime minister of the Netherlands, interviewed by Daan Govers and Rene Gude), *Filosofie Magazine,* vol. 7, no. 2.

MacCormick, Neil (1996), 'Liberalism, Nationalism, and the Post-Sovereign State', *Political Studies,* vol. 44, Special Issue.

MacCormick, Neil (1997), 'Democracy, Subsidiarity, and Citizenship in the "European Commonwealth"', *Law and Philosophy,* vol. 16, no. 4.

Macmurray, John (1957), *Persons in Relation,* London: Faber & Faber.

MacQuarrie, John (1973), *The Concept of Peace,* New York: Harper & Row.

Mander, Jerry (1996), 'Technologies of Globalisation', in Jerry Mander and Edward Goldsmith (eds), *The Case Against the Global Economy: And for a Turn Toward the Local,* San Francisco: Sierra Book Clubs.

Mann, Michael (1986), *The Sources of Social Power,* Cambridge: Cambridge University Press, vol. 1.

March, James G. and Herbert A. Simon [1958] (1993), *Organizations,* (second edition), Oxford: Blackwell.

Marchand, M. H. and J. L. Parpart (eds) (1995), *Feminism, Postmodernism, Development,* London: Routledge.

Marks, Susan (2000), *The Riddle of All Constitutions: International Law, Democracy and the Critique of Ideology,* Oxford: Oxford University Press.

Marshall, T. H. (1973), *Class, Citizenship and Social Development,* Westport, CN: Greenwood Press.

Mason, Andrew (1999), 'Political Community, Liberal-Nationalism, and the Ethics of Assimilation', *Ethics,* vol. 109, no. 2.

McGrew, Anthony G. (1992), 'Conceptualizing Global Politics', in Anthony G. McGrew and Paul G. Lewis (eds), *Global Politics: Globalization and the Nation State,* Cambridge: Polity.

Melvern, Linda (1995), *The Ultimate Crime: Who Betrayed the UN and Why?,* London: Alison-Busby.

Miller, David (1997), *On Nationality,* Oxford: Oxford University Press.

Miller, David (1999), 'Bounded citizenship', in Kimberley Hutchings and Roland Dannreuther (eds), *Cosmopolitan Citizenship,* Basingstoke: Macmillan.

Mingst, Karen and Margaret Karns (2000), *The United Nations in a Post-Cold War Era*, Boulder, CO: Westview.

Mohanty, C. T., A. Russo and L. Torres (eds) (1991), *Third World Women and the Politics of Feminism*, Bloomington: Indiana University Press.

Mulhall, Stephen and Adam Swift (eds) (1992), *Liberals and Communitarians*, Oxford: Blackwell.

Munro, D. (1985), 'A Free-Format Values Inventory: Explorations with Zimbabwean Student Teachers', *South African Journal of Psychology*, vol. 15.

Murphy, Craig N. (1994), *International Organization and International Change*, Cambridge: Cambridge University Press.

Myers, N. (1997), 'The Scientific Enterprise', *The Environmentalist*, vol. 17.

Nicholson, Linda (ed) (1990), *Feminism/Postmodernism*, London: Routledge.

Nierop, Tom (1994), *Systems and Regions in Global Politics*, London: John Wiley.

Norton, Bryan (1991), *Toward Unity Among Environmentalists*, Oxford: Oxford University Press.

Nozick, Robert (1974), *Anarchy, State and Utopia*, Oxford: Basil Blackwell.

Nussbaum, Martha (1996), 'Cosmopolitanism and Patriotism', in Joshua Cohen (ed.), *For Love of Country, Debating the Limits of Patriotism*, Boston: Beacon Books.

Nussbaum, Martha (2000), 'In Defense of Universal Values' in Martha Nussbaum, *Women and Human Development: The Capabilities Approach*, Cambridge: Cambridge University Press.

Ohmae, Kenichi (1990), *The Borderless World*, London: Collins.

Olsen, Johan P. (2000), 'How, Then, Does One Get There?'in Christian Joerges, Yves Mény and J. H. H. Weiler (eds), *What Kind of Constitution for What Kind of Polity? Responses to Joschka Fischer*, Badia Fiesolana: European University Institute available at: http://www.jeanmonnetprogram.org/papers/00/00f0901.html

O'Neill, John (1993), *Ecology, Policy and Politics: Well-Being and the Natural World*, London: Routledge.

O'Neill, Onora (1973), 'International Justice: Distribution', in L. C. Becker and C. B. Becker (eds), *Encyclopaedia of Ethics*, Chicago: St James Press.

O'Neill, Onora (1989), *Faces of Hunger*, London: Allen & Unwin.

Open University (1984), T301 *Complexity Management and Change: Applying a Systems Approach*, Milton Keynes: Open University Press.

Open University (1991), T247 *Working with Systems*, Milton Keynes: Open University Press.

Open University (1997), T860 *Environmental Decision Making: A Systems Approach*, Milton Keynes: Open University Press.

Overseas Development Institute (1996), *New Sources of Finance for Development, Briefing Paper 1*, London: Overseas Development Institute.

Oxfam (1998), *A Curriculum for Global Citizenship: A Guide for Teachers and Education Workers*, London: Oxfam.

Parliament of the World's Religions (1993), *Declaration Toward a Global Ethic*, Chicago: Parliament of the World's Religions.

Perry, Michael (1989), 'A Brief Comment', *Tulane Law Review,* vol. 63.

Peterson, V. Spike (1990), 'Whose Rights? A Critique of the "Givens" in Human Rights Discourse', *Alternatives*, vol. 15, no. 2.

Pettman, Jan Jindy (1996), *Worlding Women: A Feminist International Politics*, London: Routledge.

Pines, B. Y. (1984), *A World Without the UN*, Washington, DC: Heritage Foundation.

Pogge, Thomas W. (1989), *Realizing Rawls*, London and Ithaca: Cornell University Press.

Pogge, Thomas W. (1992), 'Cosmopolitanism and Sovereignty', *Ethics*, vol. 103.

Pogge, Thomas W. (1998), 'A Global Resources Dividend', in David A. Crocker and Toby Linden (eds), *Ethics of Consumption: The Good Life, Justice and Global Stewardship,* Lanham: Rowman & Littlefield.

Pomfret, Richard (1997), *Development Economics*, Hemel Hempstead: Prentice Hall.

Preuss, Ulrich K. (1995), 'Problems of a Concept of European Citizenship', *European Law Journal,* vol. 1, no. 3.

Preuss, Ulrich K, (1996), 'Two Challenges to European Citizenship', in Richard Bellamy and Dario Castiglione (eds), *Constitutionalism in Transformation: European and Theoretical Perspectives*, Oxford: Blackwell.

Putnam, Robert D. (1993), *Making Democracy Work: Civic Traditions in Modern Italy*, Princeton: Princeton University Press.

Putnam, Robert D. (1995), 'Tuning in, Tuning Out: The Strange Disappearance of Social Capital in America', *Political Science & Politics,* vol. 28, no. 4.

Quarrie, Joyce (ed.) (1992), *Earth Summit, 1992: The United Nations Conference on Environment and Development, Agenda 21,* London: The Regency Press.

Rawls, John (1972), *A Theory of Justice*, Oxford: Clarendon Press.

Rawls, John (1980), 'Kantian Constructivism in Moral Theory', *Journal of Philosophy*, vol. 77, no. 9.

Rawls, John (1993a), 'The Law of Peoples', in Susan Hurley and Stephen Shute (eds), *On Human Rights: The Oxford Amnesty Lectures 1993*, New York: Basic Books.

Rawls, John (1993b), *Political Liberalism*, New York: Columbia University Press.

Rawls, John (1999 & 2000), *The Law of Peoples*, Cambridge, MA: Harvard University Press.

Resnick, P. (1998), 'Global Democracy: Ideals and Reality', in Roland Axtmann (ed.), *Globalisation and Europe*, London: Pinter.

Righter, Rosemary (1995), *Utopia Lost*, New York: The Twentieth Century Fund Press.

Robinson, Fiona (1999), *Globalizing Care: Ethics, Feminist Theory and International Relations*, Boulder, CO: Westview Press.

Rohde, David (1997), *A Safe Area*, London: Simon & Schuster.

Rokeach, Milton (1973), *The Nature of Human Values*, New York: Free Press.

Rolston, Holmes, III (1995), 'Does Aesthetic Appreciation of Landscape Need to be Science-based?', *British Journal of Aesthetics,* vol. 35, no. 4.

Rosenau, James N. (1997), *Along the Domestic-Foreign Frontier: Exploring Governance in a Turbulent World*, Cambridge: Cambridge University Press.

Rosenau, James N. (1998), 'Governance and Democracy in a Globalizing World', in Daniele Archibugi, David Held and Martin Köhler (eds), *Re-imagining Political Community: Studies in Cosmopolitan Democracy*, Cambridge: Polity Press.

Rousseau, Jean-Jacques [1762] (1978), *On the Social Contract*, New York: St Martin's Press.

Ruddick, Sara (1990), *Maternal Thinking: Towards a Politics of Peace*, London: The Women's Press.

Ruddick, Sara (1993), 'Notes Toward a Feminist Peace Politics', in Miriam Cooke and Angela Woolacott (eds), Gendering War Talk, Princeton: Princeton University Press.

Scharpf, Fritz W. (1997), 'Economic Integration, Democracy and the Welfare State', *Journal of European Public Policy*, vol. 4, no. 1.

Schwartz, Shalom H. (1992), 'Universals in the Content and Structure of Values: Theoretical Advances and Empirical Tests in 20 Countries', *Advances in Experimental Social Psychology,* vol. 25.

Schwartz, Shalom H. (1994), 'Are There Universal Aspects in the Structure and Contents of Human Values?', *Journal of Social Issues,* vol. 50, no. 4.

Schwartz, Shalom H. and Wolfgang Bilsky (1987), 'Toward a Universal Psychological Structure of Human Values', *Journal of Personality and Social Psychology,* vol. 53, no. 3.

Schwartz, Shalom H. and Wolfgang Bilsky (1990), 'Toward a Theory of the Universal Content and Structure of Values: Extensions and Cross-Cultural Replications', *Journal of Personality and Social Psychology,* vol. 58, no. 5.

Shaw, Jo (1997), 'European Citizenship: The IGC and Beyond', *European Integration Online Papers,* vol. 1, no. 3, available at: http://eiop.or.at/eiop/texte/1997–003a.htm

Shaw Martin (2000), *Theory of the Global State: Globality and the Unfinished Revolution*, Cambridge: Cambridge University Press.

Shue, Henry (1983), 'The Burdens of Justice', *The Journal of Philosophy*, vol. LXXX, no. 10.

Singer, Peter (1979), *Practical Ethics*, Cambridge: Cambridge University Press.

Singer, Peter (1985), 'Famine, Affluence and Morality', in Charles R. Beitz, Marshall Cohen, Thomas Scanlon and A. John Simmons (eds), *International Ethics,* Princeton: Princeton University Press.

Singer, Peter (1993), *Practical Ethics*, (second edition), Cambridge: Cambridge University Press.

Smith, J. et al. (eds) (1997), *Transnational Social Movements and Global Politics: Solidarity Beyond the State*, Syracuse: Syracuse University Press.

Smyth, John (1995), 'Environment and Education: a View of a Changing Scene', *Environmental Education Research*, vol. 1, no. 1.

Smyth, John, Christine Blackmore and T. Harvey (1997), 'Education for Sustainability at the United Nations: Making Progress?', *The Environmentalist*, vol. 17, no. 3.

Steans, Jill (1998), *Gender and International Relations: An Introduction*, Cambridge: Polity Press.

Stinchcombe, Arthur L. (1986), 'Reason and Rationality', *Sociological Theory*, vol. 4, Fall.

Streeck, Wolfgang (1996), 'Neo-Voluntarism: A New European Social Policy Regime?', in Gary Marks, Fritz W. Scharpf, Philippe Schmitter and Wolfgang Streeck (eds), *Governance in the European Union*, London: Sage.

Strijbos, Sytse (1998a), 'Science and the University in a "Cultureless Time": The Need and Possibilities for Ethics', *World Futures*, vol. 51.

Strijbos, Sytse (1998b), 'Ethics and the Systemic Character of Technology', *Techne: Electronic Journal for the Society for Philosophy and Technology*, vol. 3, no. 4.

Tamir, Yael (1993), *Liberal Nationalism*, Princeton: Princeton University Press.

Taylor, Michael (1969), 'Proof of a Theorem on Majority Rule', *Behavioral Science*, vol. 14, no. 3.

Thompson, Janna (1992), *Justice and World Order: A Philosophical Enquiry*, London: Routledge.

Thompson, Janna, 'Toward a Green World Order' (unpublished)

Todaro, Michael P. (2000), *Economic Development*, (seventh edition), Harlow: Addison Wesley, Longman.

Topfer, K. (1998), 'Editorial', *Our Planet*, vol. 9, no. 4.

Toynbee, Arnold (1970), *A Study of History*, Oxford: Oxford University Press.

Treaty on European Union (1992), available at:
www.europa.eu.int/eur-lex.en.treaties.index1999.html

Trondal, Jarle (2000), 'Multiple Institutional Embeddedness in Europe: The Case of Danish, Norwegian, and Swedish Government Officials', *Scandinavian Political Studies*, vol. 23, no. 4.

UNA-USA (2000), *A Global Agenda: Issues Before the 55th General Assembly of the United Nations*, New York: United Nations Association of the USA.

UNDP (1999), *Human Development Report 1999*, New York/Oxford: Oxford University Press.

United Nations (1945), *Charter of the United Nations*, available at:
www.un.org/abontun/charter/index.html

United Nations (1948), *Universal Declaration of Human Rights*, available at:
www.un.org/overview/rights.html

Uphoff, Norman (1986), *Improving International Irrigation Management with Farmer Participation: Getting the Process Right*, Boulder, CO: Westview.

Uphoff, Norman (1995), 'Why NGOs are not a Third Sector: a Sectoral Analysis with Some Thoughts on Accountability, Sustainability and Evaluation', in M. Edwards and D. Hulme (eds), *Non-Government Organisations – Performance and Accountability Beyond the Magic Bullet*, London: Earthscan Publications Ltd.

Uphoff, Norman (1996), 'Understanding the World as a Heterogeneous Whole: Insights into Systems from Work on Irrigation', *Systems Research*, vol. 13, no. 1.

van den Anker, Christien (1990), *Welfare Rights: Too Costly an Ideal? A Confrontation Between International Law and Political Theory*, MA dissertation, University of Amsterdam (in Dutch).

van den Anker, Christien (1999), 'Global Ethics and the Moral Implications of Globalisation', in Martin Shaw (ed.), *Politics and Globalisation: Ethics, Knowledge and Agency*, London: Routledge.

Vickers, Geoffrey (1966), *Value Systems and Social Process*, London: Tavistock Publications.

Vickers, Jeanne (1993), *Women and War*, London: Zed Books.

Vincent, David (1991), *Poor Citizens: The State and the Poor in Twentieth Century Britain*, London: Longman.

Vincent, R. J. (1986), *Human Rights and International Relations*, Cambridge: Cambridge University Press.

Walker, R. B. J. (1988), *One World, Many Worlds: Struggles for a Just World Peace*, Boulder, CO: Lynne Reiner Publishers.

Walzer, Michael (1983), *Spheres of Justice*, New York: Basic Books.

Walzer, Michael (1985), 'The Rights of Political Communities', in Charles R. Beitz, Marshall Cohen, Thomas Scanlon and A. John Simmons (eds), *International Ethics*, Princeton: Princeton University Press.

Walzer, Michael (1995a), 'The Civil Society Argument', in Ronald Beiner (ed.), *Theorizing Citizenship*, Albany, NY: State University of New York Press.

Walzer, Michael (1995b), 'Introduction', in Michael Walzer (ed.), *Toward a Global Civil Society*, Providence, RI: Berghahn.

Walzer, Michael (ed.) (1995c), *Toward a Global Civil Society*, Providence, RI: Berghahn.

Warren, Karen J. and Duane L. Cady (eds) (1994), *Hypatia Special Issue: Feminism and Peace*, vol. 9, no. 2.

Weiler, J. H. H. (1991), 'The Transformation of Europe', *Yale Law Review*, vol. 100, no. 1.

Weiler, J. H. H. (1995), 'Does Europe Need a Constitution: Reflections on Demos and Telos in the German Maastricht Deccision', *European Law Journal*, vol. 1, no. 3.

Wessels, Wolfgang (1999), 'Comitology as a Research Subject: A New Legitimacy Mix?', in Christian Joerges and Ellen Vos (eds), *EU Committees: Social Regulation, Law and Politics*, Oxford: Hart.

Wheeler, Nicholas J. (2000), *Saving Strangers: Humanitarian Intervention in International Society*, Oxford: Oxford University Press.

Wheeler, Nicholas J. and Tim Dunne (1998), 'Good International Citizenship: A Third Way for British Foreign Policy', *International Affairs*, vol. 74, no. 4.

Wiener, Antje (1997), *European Citizenship Practice – Building Institutions of a Non-State*, Boulder, CO: Westview Press.

Wilkins, Barry (1996), 'Civil Society', in Michael Payne (ed.), *A Dictionary of Cultural and Critical Theory*, Oxford: Blackwell.

Williams, Abiodun (2000), *Preventing War: The UN and Macedonia*, Oxford: Rowman & Littlefield.

Williams, John (1999), 'The Ethics of Borders and the Borders of Ethics: International Society and Rights and Duties of Special Beneficence', *Global Society*, vol. 13, no. 4.

Winner, Langdon (1990), 'Engineering Ethics and Political Imagination', in P. T. Durbin (ed.), *Broad and Narrow Interpretations of Philosophy of Technology*, Dordrecht: Kluwer Academic Publishers.

Winner, Langdon (1995), 'Citizen Virtues in a Technological Order', in A. Feenberg and A. Hannay (eds), *Technology and the Politics of Knowledge*, Bloomington: Indiana University Press.

World Commission on Culture and Development (1995), *Our Creative Diversity*, Paris: UNESCO.

World Commission on Global Governance (1995), *Our Global Neighbourhood*, Oxford: Oxford University Press.

Zolo, Danilo (1997), *Cosmopolis: Prospects for World Government*, Cambridge: Polity Press.

## FURTHER BOOKS AND ARTICLES OF GENERAL INTEREST

Abraham, John (1991), *Food and Development: The Political Economy of Hunger and the Modern Diet*, London: Kogan Page.

Albrow, Martin (1996), *The Global Age: State and Society beyond Modernity*, Cambridge: Polity Press.

Albrow, Martin and Elizabeth King (eds) (1990), *Globalization, Knowledge and Society*, London: Sage.

Andreopoulos, George J. and Richard Pierre Claude (eds) (1997), *Human Rights Education for the Twenty-First Century*, Philadelphia: University of Pennsylvania Press.

Appadurai, Arjun (1996), *Modernity at Large: Cultural Dimensions of Globalization*, Minneapolis: University of Minnesota Press.

Archibugi, Daniele, David Held and Manfred Köhler (eds) (1998), *Re-imagining Political Community: Studies in Cosmopolitan Democracy*, Cambridge: Polity Press.

Athanasiou, Tom (1996), *Slow Reckoning: The Ecology of a Divided Planet*, London: Secker & Warburg.

Baker, Dean, Gerald Epstein and Robert Pollin (eds) (1998), *Globalization and Progressive Economic Policy*, Cambridge: Cambridge University Press.

Barker, Chris (1997), *Global Television: An Introduction*, Oxford: Blackwell.

Barker, Chris (1999), *Television, Globalization and Cultural Identities*, Milton Keynes: Open University Press.

Barnet, Richard J. and John Cavanagh (1994), *Global Dreams: Imperial Corporations and the New World Order*, New York: Touchstone/Simon & Schuster.

Bauman, Zygmunt (1998), *Globalization: The Human Consequences*, Cambridge: Polity Press.

Beck, Ulrich (1995), *Ecological Politics in an Age of Risk*, Cambridge: Polity Press.

Benedick, Richard E. (1991), *Ozone Diplomacy: New Directions in Safeguarding the Planet*, Cambridge, MA: Harvard University Press.

Benthall, Jonathan (1993), *Disasters, Relief and the Media*, London: I. B. Tauris.

Boli, John and George M. Thomas (eds) (1999), *Constructing World Culture: International Nongovernmental Organizations since 1875*, Stanford, CA: Stanford University Press.

Boulding, Elise (1988), *Building a Global Civic Culture*, Syracuse: Syracuse University Press.

Braithwaite, John (1984), *Corporate Crime in the Pharmaceutical Industry*, London: Routledge.

Brandt, Willy (1980), *North-South: A Programme for Survival*, London: Pan and Cambridge, MA: MIT Press.

Brecher Jeremy, John Brown Childs and Jill Cutler (eds) (1993), *Global Visions: Beyond the New World Order*, Boston: South End Press.

Brundtland, Gro Harlem (1987), *Our Common Future*, Oxford: Oxford University Press.

Burbach, Roger and Patricia Flynn (1980), *Agribusiness in the Americas*, New York: Monthly Review Press.

Burbach, Roger, Orlando Nunez and Boris Kagarlitsky (1997), *Globalization and its Discontents: The Rise of Postmodern Socialisms*, London: Pluto.

Callicott, J. Baird and Fernando J. R. Da Rocha (eds) (1996), *Earth Summit Ethics: Toward a Reconstructive Postmodern Philosophy of Environmental Education*, Albany: State University of New York Press.

Castles, Stephen and Alastair Davidson (2000), *Citizenship and Migration: Globalization and the Politics of Belonging*, Basingstoke: Macmillan.

Caufield, Catherine (1996), *Masters of Illusion: The World Bank and the Poverty of Nations*, New York: Henry Holt and Basingstoke: Macmillan and London: Pan.

Cheah, Pheng and Bruce Robbins (eds) (1998), *Cosmopolitics: Thinking and Feeling beyond the Nation*, Minneapolis: University of Minnesota Press.

Childers, Erskine B. (1996), 'Whose whispers are in the gallery?', in George

Gerbner, Erskine B. Childers, H. Mowd and H. Schiller (eds), *Invisible Crises: What Conglomerate Control of Media Means for America and the World*, Boulder, CO: Westview.

Cohen, Stanley (2000), *States of Denial: Knowing about Atrocities and Suffering*, Cambridge: Polity Press.

Coleman, Simon (2000), *The Globalisation of Charismatic Christianity: Spreading the Gospel of Prosperity*, Cambridge: Cambridge University Press.

Cosgrove, Denis (1994), 'Contested Global Visions: One-World, Whole-Earth and the Apollo space photographs', *Annals of the Association of American Geographers*, vol. 84, no. 2.

Crosby, Barbara C. (1999), *Leadership for Global Citizenship: Building Transnational Community*, London: Sage.

Davies, Peter (ed.) (1988), *Human Rights*, London: Routledge

De Freitas, Geoffrey (1998), 'Immigration, Inequality and Policy Alternatives', in Dean Baker, Gerald Epstein and Robert Pollin (eds), *Globalization and Progressive Economic Policy*, Cambridge: Cambridge University Press.

Deibert, Ronald J. (1997), *Parchment, Printing and Hypermedia: Communication in World Order Transformation*, New York: Columbia University Press.

Dixon, C. J., D. W. Drakakis-Smith and H. D. Watts (eds) (1986), *Multinational Corporations and the Third World*, London: Croom-Helm.

Dodds, Felix and Tom Bigg (1995), *Three Years Since the Rio Summit*. UNED-UK.

Dower, Nigel (1996), 'Europe and the Globalisation of Ethics', in Paul Dukes (ed.) *Frontiers of European Culture*, Lampeter/Lewston, NY: Edwin Mellen Press.

Dower, Nigel (1998), 'Human Rights, Global Ethics and Globalisation', in Roland Axtmann (ed.), *Globalization and Europe*, London: Pinter.

Eade, John (1997), *Living the Global City: Globalization as a Local Process*, London: Routledge.

Fabian, Johannes (1983), *Time and the Other: How Anthropology Makes its Object*, New York: Columbia University Press.

Falk, Richard (1993), 'The Making of Global Citizenship', in Jeremy Brecher, John Brown Childs & Jill Cutler (eds), *Global Visions: Beyond the New World Order*, Boston: South End Press, pp. 39–50.

Falk, Richard (2000), 'Global Civil Society and the Democratic Prospect', in Barry Holden (ed.), *Global Democracy: Key Debates*, London: Routledge.

Farmer, Paul (1999), *Infections and Inequalities: The Modern Plagues*, Berkeley: University of California Press.

Featherstone, Mike (ed.) (1990), *Global Culture: Nationalism, Globalization and Modernity*, London: Sage.

Featherstone, Mike, S. Lash and R. Robertson (eds) (1995), *Global Modernities*, London: Sage.

Frank, André Gunder and Barry K. Gills (eds) (1993), *The World System: Five Hundred Years or Five Thousand?*, London: Routledge.

Freeman, Christopher and Luc Soete (1997), *The Economics of Industrial Innovation* (third edition), London: Pinter.

Fröbel, Folker (1980), *The New International Division of Labour*, Cambridge: Cambridge University Press.

Gabriel, Yiannis and Tim Lang (1995), *The Unmanageable Consumer: Contemporary Consumption and its Fragmentations*, London: Sage.

Garrett, Laurie (1994), *The Coming Plague: Newly Emerging Diseases in a World out of Balance*, Harmondsworth: Penguin.

George, Susan (1988), *A Fate Worse than Debt*, Harmondsworth: Penguin.

George, Susan and Fabrizio Sabelli (1994), *Faith and Credit: The World Bank's Secular Empire*, Boulder, CO: Westview.

Germain, Randall D. (2000), 'Globalization in Historical Perspective', in Randall D. Germain (ed.), *Globalization and its Critics: Perspectives from Political Economy*, Basingstoke: Macmillan.

Glyn, Andrew (1998), 'Internal and External Constraints on Egalitarian Policies', in Dean Baker, Gerald Epstein and Robert Pollin (eds), *Globalization and Progressive Economic Policy*, Cambridge: Cambridge University Press.

Goldman, Robert and Stephen Papson (1998), *Nike Culture: The Sign of the Swoosh*, London: Sage.

Goodstein, Eban (1998), 'Malthus Redux? Globalization and the Environment', in Dean Baker, Gerald Epstein and Robert Pollin (eds), *Globalization and Progressive Economic Policy*, Cambridge: Cambridge University Press.

Greenwood, Justin and Henry Jacek (eds) (2000), *Organized Business and the New Global Order*, Basingstoke: Macmillan.

Hamelink, Cees (1994), *The Politics of World Communication*, London: Sage.

Hamelink, Cees (1995), *World Communication: Disempowerment and Self-Empowerment*, London: Zed Books.

Hannertz, Ulf, (1990), 'Cosmopolitans and Locals in World Culture' *Theory, Culture and Society*, vol. 7.

Harvey, David (1989), *The Condition of Postmodernity: An Enquiry into the Origins of Cultural Change*, Oxford: Blackwell.

Held, David, Anthony McGrew, David Goldblatt and Jonathon Perraton (1999), *Global Transformations: Politics, Economics and Culture*, Cambridge: Polity Press.

Hertzman, Clyde (1996), 'What's Been Said and What's Been Hid: Population Health, Global Consumption and the Role of National Health Data Systems', in David Blane, Eric Brunner and Richard G. Wilkinson (eds), *Health and Social Organization*, London: Routledge.

Hewitt de Alcantara, Cynthia (ed.) (1996), *Social Futures, Global Visions*, Oxford: Blackwell.

Hewitt, Patricia (1996), 'Social Justice in the Global Community?', in Martin Bulmer and Anthony M. Rees (eds) *Citizenship Today*, London: UCL Press.

Hills, Jim (1996), 'The Silent War: Debt and Africa', in George Gerbner, Hamid Mowlana and Herbert I. Schiller (eds), *Invisible Crises: What Conglomerate*

*Control of Media Means for America and the World*, Boulder, CO: West-view.

Hoogvelt, Ankie (2001), *Globalisation and the Postcolonial World* (second edition), Basingstoke: Palgrave.

Hough, Peter (1998), *The Global Politics of Pesticides: Forging Consensus from Conflicting Interests*, London: Earthscan.

Hurrell, Andrew and Benedict Kingsbury (eds) (1992), *The International Politics of the Environment: Actors, Interests and Institutions*, Oxford: Oxford University Press.

Hurrell, Andrew and Ngaire Woods (1999), *Inequality, Globalization and World Politics*, Oxford: Oxford University Press.

International Coalition for Development Action (1997), *Behind the Swoosh: The Struggle of Indonesians Making Nike shoes*, Uppsala: Global Publications Foundation/ICDA.

Ives, Jane (1985), *Transnational Corporations and Environmental Control Issues: The Export of Hazard*, London: Routledge.

Jackson, Ben (1994), *Poverty and the Planet: A Question of Survival*, Harmondsworth: Penguin.

Jones, Charles (1999), *Global Justice: Defending Cosmopolitanism*, Oxford: Oxford University Press.

Jones, Tara (1988), *Corporate Killing: Bhopals Will Happen*, London: Free Association Books.

Keck, Margaret E. and Kathryn Sikkink (1998), *Activists Beyond Borders: Advocacy Networks in International Politics*, Ithaca: Cornell University Press.

Kiely, Ray and Phil Marfleet (eds) (1998), *Globalisation and the Third World*, London: Routledge.

King, Anthony D. (ed.) (1991), *Culture, Globalization and the World-System*, Minneapolis: University of Minnesota Press.

Korey, William (1998), *NGOs and the* Universal Declaration of Human Rights: 'A Curious Grapevine', Basingstoke: Macmillan.

Krippendorf, Jost [German edition 1984] (1987), *The Holiday Makers: Understanding the Impact of Leisure and Travel*, London: Heinemann.

Laïdi, Zaki [1994] (1998), *A World Without Meaning: The Crisis of Meaning in International Politics*, London: Routledge.

Lanfant Marie-Françoise, John B. Alcock and Edward M. Bruner (eds) (1995), *International Tourism: Identity and Change*, London: Sage.

Lipschutz, Ronnie D. and Judith Mayer (1996), *Global Civil Society and Global Environmental Governance*, Albany: State University of New York Press.

MacGregor, Brent (1997), *Live, Direct and Biased? Making the News in the Satellite Age*, London: Edward Arnold.

McGrew, Anthony G. (1992), 'Conceptualizing Global Politics', in Anthony G. McGrew and Paul G. Lewis (eds), *Global Politics: Globalization and the Nation State*, Cambridge: Polity.

McGrew, Tony (1992), 'A Global Society?', in Stuart Hall, David Held and Tony McGrew (eds), *Modernity and its Futures*, Milton Keynes: Open University Press (Course D213/4).

Medawar, Charles, and Barbara Freese (1982), *Drug Diplomacy: Decoding the Conduct of a Multinational Pharmaceutical Company and the Failure of a Western Remedy for the Third World*, London: Social Audit.

Melucci, Alberto (1992), 'A Search for Ethics', in *Challenging Codes: Collective Action in the Information Age*, Cambridge: Cambridge University Press.

Meyer, Carrie A. (1999), *The Economics and Politics of NGOs in Latin America*, New York: Praeger.

Michie, Jonathan and John Grieve Smith (eds) (1998), *Globalization, Growth and Governance: Creating an Innovative Economy*, Oxford: Oxford University Press.

Miller, Daniel (1997), 'Consumption and its Consequences', in Hugh Mackay (ed.), *Consumption and Everyday Life*, London: Sage.

Mitchell, John V. (ed.) (1998), *Companies in a World of Conflict: NGOs, Sanctions and Corporate Responsibility*, London: Earthscan.

Mitter, Swasti (1986), *Common Fate, Common Bond: Women in the Global Economy*, London: Pluto Press.

Mol, Arthur P. J. (2000), 'Globalization and the Environment: Between Apocalypse-Blindness and Ecological Modernization', in Gert Spargaren, Arthur P. J. Mol and Frederick H. Buttel (eds), *Environment and Global Modernity*, London: Sage.

Muller, Mike (1982), *The Health of Nations*, London: Faber & Faber.

Norgaard, Richard B. (1994), *Development Betrayed: The End of Progress and a Coevolutionary Revisioning of the Future*, London: Routledge.

O'Neill, Helen B. and J. F. J. Toye (eds) (1998), *A World without Famine? New Approaches to Aid and Development*, Basingstoke: Macmillan.

Pattullo, Polly (1996), *Last Resorts: The Cost of Tourism in the Caribbean*, London: Cassell.

Pearce, Frank and Michael Woodiwiss (eds) (1993), *Global Crime Connections: Dynamics and Control*, Toronto: University of Toronto Press.

Potter, George Ann (2000), *Deeper than Debt: Economic Globalisation and the Poor*, London: Latin America Bureau.

Prendergast, Mark (1993), *For God, Country and Coca Cola: The Unauthorized History of the Great American Soft Drink and the Company that makes it*, London: Phoenix.

Princen, Thomas and Matthias Finger (1994), *Environmental NGOs in World Politics: Linking the Local and the Global*, London: Routledge.

Randall, Neil (1997), *The Soul of the Internet: Net Gods, Netizens and the Wiring of the World*, London: International Thomson Computer Press.

Riddell, Roger (1987), *Foreign Aid Reconsidered*, Baltimore, MD: Johns Hopkins University Press.

Rist, Gilbert (1997) *The History of Development: From Western Origins to Global Faith*, London: Zed Books.

Ritzer, George (1998), *The McDonaldization Thesis: Explorations and Extensions*, London: Sage.

Robbins, Bruce (1999), *Feeling Global: Internationalism in Distress*, New York: New York University Press.

Robertson, Roland (1992), *Globalization: Social Theory and Global Culture*, London: Sage.

Rose, Gillian (1995), 'Place and Identity: A Sense of Place', in Doreen Massey and Pat Jess (eds), *A Place in the World? Places, Cultures and Globalization*, Open University Press (Course D215/4).

Rossi, Philip J. (1994), 'Moral Imagination and the Media: Whose "World" do we see, Whose "World" should it be?', in Philip J. Rossi and Paul A. Soukup (eds), *Mass Media and the Moral Imagination*, Kansas City: Sheed & Ward.

Rotblat, Joseph and Tom Milne (eds) (1997), *World Citizenship: Allegiance to Humanity*, Proceedings of Pugwash Workshop 1994, Basingstoke: Macmillan.

Ryan, Frank (1996), *Virus X: Understanding the Real Threat of the New Pandemic Plagues*, London: HarperCollins.

Sachs, Wolfgang (ed.) (1993), *Global Ecology*, London: Zed Books.

Said, Edward W. (1997), *Covering Islam: How the Media and the Experts Determine how We See the Rest of the World*, (second edition), New York: Vintage Books.

Scott, Alan (ed.) (1997), *The Limits of Globalization*, London: Routledge.

Seitz, John L. (1995), *Global Issues: An Introduction*, Oxford: Blackwell.

Silverman, Milton, M. Lydecker and P. R. Lee (1992), *Bad Medicine: The Prescription Drug Industry in the Third World*, Stanford, CA: Stanford University Press.

Skelton, Tracey and Tim Allen (eds) (1999), *Culture and Global Change*, London: Routledge.

Sklair, Leslie (1995), *Sociology of the Global System*, Baltimore, MD: Johns Hopkins University Press.

Smith, Anthony (1991), *The Age of Behemoths: The Globalization of Mass Media Firms*, New York: Priority.

Smith, N. Craig (1990), *Morality and the Market: Consumer Pressure for Corporate Accountability*, London: Routledge.

Snarr, Michael T. and Neil Snarr (eds) (1998), *Introducing Global Issues*, Boulder, CO: Lynne Rienner.

Sosa, Nicholas M. (1996), 'The Ethics of Dialogue and the Environment', in J. Baird Callicott and Fernando J. R. Da Rocha (eds), *Earth Summit Ethics: Toward a Reconstructive Postmodern Philosophy of Environmental Education*, Albany: State University of New York Press.

Spargaren, Gert, Arthur P. J. Mol and Frederick H. Buttel (eds) (2000), *Environment and Global Modernity*, London: Sage.

Spybey, Tony (1996), *Globalization and World Society*, Cambridge: Polity Press.

Standage, Tom (1998), *The Victorian Internet*, London: Weidenfeld & Nicholson.

Stevenson, Nick (2000), 'Globalization and Cultural Political Economy', in Randall D. Germain (ed.) *Globalization and its Critics: Perspectives from Political Economy*, Basingstoke: Macmillan.

Sutcliffe, Bob (1998), 'Freedom to Move in the Age of Globalization', in Dean Baker, Gerald Epstein and Robert Pollin (eds), *Globalization and Progressive Economic Policy*, Cambridge: Cambridge University Press.

Swift, Adam (1993), *Global Political Ecology*, London: Pluto.

Szerszynski, Bronislaw and Mark Toogood (1999), 'Global Citizenship, the Environment and the Mass Media', in Stuart Allan, Barbara Adam and Cynthia Carter (eds), *Environmental Risks and the Media*, London: Routledge.

Taylor, Philip M. (1997), *Global Communications, International Affairs and the Media since 1945*, London: Routledge.

Tegegn, Melakou (1997), 'Development and Patronage', in Carol Miller, Deborah Eade and Melakou Tegegn (eds), *Development and Patronage*, London: Oxfam.

Thomas, Caroline (1987), *In Search of Security: The Third World and International Relations*, Hemel Hempstead: Harvester Wheatsheaf.

Thomas, Caroline (1992), *The Environment in International Relations*, London: Frank Cass.

Thomas, Caroline (1994), *Rio: Unravelling the Consequences*. London: Royal Institute of International Affairs.

Tomlinson, John (1999), *Globalization and Culture*, Cambridge: Polity Press.

Turkle, Sherry (1995), *Life on the Screen: Identity in the Age of the Internet*, London: Phoenix.

Urry, John (2000), *Sociology beyond Societies: Mobilities for the Twenty-First Century*, London: Routledge.

van Steenbergen, Bart (1994), 'Towards a Global Ecological Citizen', in Bart van Steenbergen (ed.), *The Condition of Citizenship*, London: Sage.

von Laue, Theodore H. (1987), *The World Revolution of Westernization: Twentieth-Century Global Perspectives*, Oxford: Oxford University Press.

Wallerstein, Immanuel (1983), *Historical Capitalism*, London: Verso.

Wallerstein, Immanuel (1983), *Labor in the World Social Structure*, London: Sage.

Wallerstein, Immanuel (1991), *Geopolitics and Geoculture*, Cambridge: Cambridge University Press.

Wapner, Paul K. (1996), *Environmental Activism and World Civic Politics*, Albany: State University of New York Press.

Waterman, Peter (1993) 'Internationalism is Dead! Long Live Global Solidarity?', in Jeremy Brecher, John Brown Childs and Jill Cutler (eds), *Global Visions: Beyond the New World Order*, Boston: South End Press.

Waters, Malcolm (1995), *Globalization*, London: Routledge.

Weiss, Thomas G. and Leon Gordenker (eds) (1995), *NGOs, the UN and Global Governance*, Boulder, CO: Lynne Rienner.

Wells, Phil and Mandy Jetter (1991), *The Global Consumer: Best Buys to Help the Third World*, London: Victor Gollancz.

Wiesner, Merry E. et al. (1997), *Discovering the Global Past*, Boston, MA: Houghton Mifflin.

Willetts, Peter (ed.) (1982), *Pressures in the Global System: The Transnational Relations of Issue-Oriented Non-Governmental Organizations*, London: Pinter.

Winston, Brian (1998), *Media Technology and Society: A History from the Telegraph to the Internet*, London: Routledge.

Woodiwiss, Anthony (1998), *Globalisation, Human Rights and Labour Law in Pacific Asia*, Cambridge: Cambridge University Press.

Yearley, Stephen (1996), *Sociology, Environmentalism, Globalization: Reinventing the Globe*, London: Sage.

## WEBSITES COVERING SOME AREAS OF RELEVANCE TO GLOBAL CITIZENSHIP

### The general theme of global citizenship and global sharing of relevant information

Institute for Global Communications: http://www.igc.org/ (offshoot of Tides Foundation, aimed at sharing Internet resources)

Interaction (American Council for Voluntary International Action): http://www.interaction.org/

*New Internationalist*: http://www.oneworld.org/ni/ (monthly journal aimed at providing information relevant to global citizenship)

One World International Foundation web-guide: http://www.oneworld.org/themes/guides

One World International Foundation: http://www.oneworld.net/themes/topic/index.html (aims to harness the democratic potential of the internet to promote human rights and sustainable development)

Oxfam GB: http://www.oxfam.org.uk/coolplanet/teachers/globciti/globciti.htm (education for global citizenship)

Renaissance Universal: http://www.ru.org/83hutchi.html (education for global citizenship)

Tides Foundation (USA): http://www.tides.org/ (aims to increase and organise resources for social change in the US and elsewhere)

## (b) Development and developing countries' debts

Christian Aid: http://www.christian-aid.org.uk/

Development Group for Alternative Policies (D'GAP): http://www.igc.org/dgap/ (aims at ensuring that the knowledge, priorities and efforts of women and men of the South inform decisions made in the North about their economies and environments)

Drop the Debt: www.dropthedebt.org/

International Cooperation for Development and Solidarity (CIDSE): http://www.cidse.org/ (Brussels-based coalition of 14 Catholic development organisations)

Jubilee 2000 UK: http://www.jubilee2000uk.org/ (former UK campaign for cancellation by the millennium of unrepayable Third World debts on basis of fairness and transparency, since 2000 continued by Jubilee Plus)

Jubilee 2000 campaign USA: http://www.j2000usa.org/ (US counterpart to above)

Jubilee Plus: http://www.jubileeplus.org/ (continuation of debt campaign waged by Jubilee 2000)

Jubilee South: http://www.jubileesouth.net/

Oxfam: http://www.oxfam.org/educationnow/news/press_releases.htm

Results: http://www.action.org/ (a grassroots US citizens' lobby concerned with solutions to world hunger and poverty)

World Development Movement: http://www.wdm.org.uk/presrel/current/debt_conditions.htm

## (c) Environment

Amazon Watch: http://www.amazonwatch.org/

Forests.org, Inc: http://forests.org/links/

Friends of the Earth International: http://www.foei.org/

Greenpeace: http://www.greenpeace.org/

GreenNet: http://www.gn.apc.org/resources/

Institute for Global Communications EcoNet: http://www.igc.org/igc/gt/EcoNet

## (d) Ethical consumerism

Baby Milk Action: http://www.babymilkaction.org

*Big Issue* and *Red Pepper*: http://www.getethical.com/

Ethical Consumer: http://www.ethicalconsumer.org

Ethical trading initiative: http://www.eti.org.uk

GreenNet: http://www.gn.apc.org/resources/

International Federation for Alternative Trade: http://www.ifat.org

One World International Foundation: http://www.oneworld.org/guides/consumerism/index.html

Oxfam: http://www.oxfaminternational.org/programs/fair_trade.htm

Shoppers Guide: http://homepages.ihug.co.nz/~stu/shoppersguide.htm
Traidcraft: http://www. traidcraft.co.uk

## (e) Health and healthcare

Center for Health and Human Rights:
  http://www.hri.ca/partners/fxbcenter/index.htm
Doctors of the World, USA: http://www.doctorsoftheworld.org/
Doctors without Borders (the United States counterpart of MSF):
  http://www.dwb.org/
German Doctors for Developing Countries: http://www.german-doctors.de/
Health Action International: http://www.hai.org/
Healthwrights [Palo Alto, California]: http://www.healthwrights.org/
International Women's Health Coalition: http://www.iwhc.org/
Médécins sans Frontières: http://www.msf.org/msf/history.htm
Medical International Rapid Response: http://www.mirr.org/
Medicus Mundi International: http://www.medicusmundi.org/
Nestlé again: http://www.twnside.org.sg/title/baby.htm
People's Health Assembly (Bangladesh Dec 2000): http://www.pha2000.org/
People's Health Assembly again: http://www-sph.health.latrobe.edu.au/pha
People's Health Assembly again: http://www.twnside.org.sg/title/pha2000.htm
Refugee Relief International: http://www.RefugeeRelief.org/
Third World Network: http://www.twnside.org.sg/heal.htm

## (f) Human rights

Introductory survey: http://www.hrweb/resource.html
Amnesty International: http://www.amnesty.org/ailib/countries/index.html
Fourth World Documentation Project:
  http://www.halcyon.com/FWDP/fwdp.html
Freedom House: http://www.hrweb.org/groups/fh.html
Human Rights Watch:
  http://www.hrw.org/about/about.html   *or*   www.hrw.org/wr2k   (World
  Report): http://www.hrw.org/hrw/advocacy/index.htm
Institute for Global Communications Internet: http://www.igc.org/igc/issues/hr/
International Women's Rights Action Watch: http://www.igc.org/iwraw
Peace Brigades International: http://www.igc.org/pbi/history.html

## (g) Peace and disarmament

Abolition 2000: www.abolition2000.org/
Acronym Institute: http://www.gn.apc.org/acronym
Campaign Against the Arms Trade: http://www.gn.apc.org/caat/
Campaign for Nuclear Disarmament: http://www.cnduk.org/

Global Anti-Nuclear Alliance: http://www.inter.nl.net/
Hague Appeal for Peace Conference: http://www.haguepeace.org/
Institute for Law and Peace: http://i.am.lawpeace/
International Court of Justice Advisory Opinion text:
    www.ddh.nl/org/ialana/index.html
International Fellowship of Reconciliation: http://www.gn.apc.org/ifor/
Nuclear Age Peace Foundation: http://www.napf.org/
Oxford Research Group (on nuclear weapons): www.oxfordresearchgroup.or-
    g.uk/ or www.oxfrg.demon.co.uk
Peace and Goodwill Site: www.pgs.ca
Peace Pledge Union: http://www.gn.apc.org/peacepledge/
Peaceworkers UK: http://www.peaceworkers.fsnet.co.uk
Proposition One: www.prop1.org/
Trident Ploughshares: www.gn.apc.org/tp2000/
War Resisters International: http://www.gn.apc.org/warresisters/
World Court Project UK: www.apc.org/wcp

## (h) Other websites

Global Ethic Foundation (Tübingen):
    http://www.uni-tuebingen.de/stiftung-weltethos (and)
    http://astro.temple.edu/ (global ethics)
Institute for Global Ethics: http://www.globalethics.org/
InterAction Council: http://www.asiawide.or.jp/iac (global ethics)
Internet Center for Corruption Research (Göttingen University):
    www.dwdg.de/~uwvw/icr.htm (combatting corruption)
*New Internationalist*: http://www.oneworld.org/ni/whatsnew.html
Transparency International (USA): www.transparency-usa.org (combatting
    corruption)
Transparency International: www.transparency.de (combatting corruption)
United Nations Association: http://www.una-uk.org/
Wittenberg Center for Global Ethics: http://www.wcge.org/

# INDEX